Behavioral Decision Making

Behavioral Decision Making

Edited by
George Wright
City of London Polytechnic
London, England

PLENUM PRESS • **NEW YORK AND LONDON**

Library of Congress Cataloging in Publication Data

Main entry under title:

Behavioral decision making.

Bibliography: p.
Includes index.
1. Decision-making. I. Wright, George, 1952–   .
BF441.B393   1985   153.8′3   84-26612
ISBN 0-306-41794-4

47,807

©1985 Plenum Press, New York
A Division of Plenum Publishing Corporation
233 Spring Street, New York, N.Y. 10013

Printed in the United States of America

Contributors

Dina Berkeley • Social Psychology Department, London School of Economics and Political Science, London, England

Barbara G. Brown • Department of Atmospheric Sciences, Oregon State University, Corvallis, Oregon

Lawrence C. Currie • Department of Psychology, City of London Polytechnic, London, England

Jack Dowie • Faculty of Social Sciences, The Open University, Milton Keynes England

Hillel J. Einhorn • Director, Center for Decision Research, Graduate School of Business, University of Chicago, Chicago, Illinois

William R. Ferrell • Systems and Industrial Engineering Department, University of Arizona, Tucson, Arizona

Robin M. Hogarth • Center for Decision Research, Graduate School of Business, University of Chicago, Chicago, Illinois

Patrick Humphreys • Decision Analysis Unit, London School of Economics and Political Science, London, England

Daniel Kahneman • Department of Psychology, University of British Columbia, Vancouver, British Columbia, Canada.

Roger King • Department of Behavioural Sciences, Huddersfield Polytechnic, Huddersfield, West Yorkshire, England

A. John Maule • Department of Behavioural Sciences, Huddersfield Polytechnic, Huddersfield, West Yorkshire, England

v

David M. Messick • Department of Psychology, University of California, Santa Barbara, Santa Barbara, California

Allan H. Murphy • Department of Atmospheric Sciences, Oregon State University, Corvallis, Oregon

John W. Payne • Fuqua School of Business, Duke University, Durham, North Carolina

Humphrey V. Swann • Department of Psychology, City of London Polytechnic, London, England

Amos Tversky • Department of Psychology, Stanford University, Stanford, California

David Weeks • Department of Sociology, City of London Polytechnic, London, England

Sam Whimster • Department of Sociology, City of London Polytechnic, London, England

James A. Wise • Department of Architecture, College of Architecture and Urban Planning, University of Washington, Seattle, Washington

Ayleen D. Wisudha • Decision Analysis Unit, London School of Economics and Political Science, London, England

George Wright • Decision Analysis Group, Department of Psychology, City of London Polytechnic, London, England

Preface

This book is not a set of conference proceedings. In fact, it is the book that I wish was available when I started my own postgraduate research on decision making! It consists of a set of 17 chapters; 14 were specially commissioned, and the remaining 3 are selected reprints of journal articles. The book presents an overview of research and theory in behavioral decision making. Disciplines covered include cognitive psychology, social psychology, management science, sociology and political science. Each of the chapters is written by an established authority, in a manner that should make the content easy to understand. The book reveals that individual, small-group, organizational, and political perspectives are necessary to achieve a full understanding of the decision-making process. An additional multidisciplinary emphasis in the book is on ways of improving aspects of decision making.

We assume that you, the reader, have some elementary knowledge of behavioral decision making. If you do not, then I suggest as a first step that you read Wright (1984) or Hogarth (1980). With this grounding, the entire book should become accessible to you.

John W. Payne investigates how individuals make decisions under risk in the first part, Individual Decision Making. He argues that decision making is sensitive to small changes in the decision task and that the decision task is the major determinant of the type of decision taken. Task complexity, time pressure, the way information is displayed, and the type of response required all appear to change information processing and subsequent decision making. Payne evaluates alternative theoretical frameworks for explaining these task and context effects on risky decision making.

Amos Tversky and Daniel Kahneman take a similar task-oriented point of view and argue that the way in which a decision problem is conceptualized or "framed" is often one of several possible representations. They make a comparison with subjective perspectives on the same visual scene. Outcomes of a decision are perceived as positive or negative in relation to a reference point, and the reference point can vary to such an extent that a given outcome may be evaluated as a gain *or* as a loss.

By contrast, George Wright reviews the literature on decisional variance in the psychological and management journals and identifies two distinct lines of research and theory. Decision making is sometimes held to be contingent on changes in the task, but it has also been conceptualized to be the expression of a cognitive style or trait. Wright argues that a methodology taken from personality psychology could be used to resolve the cognitive style/contingent decision-making issue and allow the relative variance contributed by person, situation, and an interaction of these to be evaluated.

A. John Maule takes the viewpoint of a cognitive psychologist and evaluates research that has importance for understanding individual decision making. His primary concern is the identification of processing stages, and he analyzes some problems with the notion of *limited capacity*, a catchall often used to explain why decision makers do not perform normatively.

David M. Messick, in Part II, Small-Group Decision Making, views decision making as a socially interdependent process. He argues that we are sensitive to the outcomes received by others. Another's good fortune can elate or depress us. Envy is relative! He analyzes the consequence of allowing people to have free access to a valuable but scarce resource that grows at a constant but small rate. If individuals extract too much of the resource, it becomes depleted and so is useless to everyone. Should a superordinate authority replace the system of free access?

William R. Ferrell investigates whether quantitative judgements obtained from small groups are "better" than those obtained from individuals. Judgments can be combined behaviorally or mathematically, and he evaluates methods of aggregating individual judgments to produce a group judgment with the aim of increasing judgmental quality.

In Part III, Organizational Decision Making, George Wright bridges this section of the book with the previous sections by evaluating the effect of cultural influences on organizational, small-group, and individual decision making. He pays special attention to research that has compared Japanese and American organizational decision making.

David Weeks and Sam Whimster analyze sociological conceptualizations of organizational decision making and go on to argue that "rational" decision making is necessarily linked to an analysis of power, control, and social context. The individual is often part of a small social grouping within a larger organization, and individual, group, and organizational interests may conflict.

Roger King focuses on "power" and poses the question of whether the exercise of power always involves a conflict of interests. He argues that the supreme exercise of power may involve the powerful defining a situation in such a way that the powerless may not be aware of any conflict. This silent view of power leads to a conclusion that an absence of overt political participation by business in no way denies political influence.

Humphrey V. Swann addresses the question of whether quantitative decision theory is useful to an organization. He poses this question from the point of view of an occupational psychologist involved with personnel selection and payment schemes. Swann pays special attention to the problems of implementing decisions once they have been taken.

In Part IV, Improving Decision Making: The Role of Decision Aids, Ayleen D. Wisudha assesses the role of computerized decision aids within the decision-making process and proposes guidelines for the development of these aids. She addresses the question fo the extent to which a decision aid should contain substantive problem knowledge or should be adaptive to the decision maker's own problem representation.

Patrick Humphreys and Dina Berkeley argue that uncertainty pervades decision making. Uncertainty enters into the way a decision problem is conceptualized and in the extent to which the decision maker has influence over the future as it is modeled in decision analytic representations. The decision maker may also have reservations about quantitative problem representation *once* the acts and events in the representation begin to unfold as reality. Humphreys and Berkeley analyze the potential of decision support systems to aid resolution of all types of uncertainty.

James A. Wise reviews the role of decision aids for design decision making. For an architect, specifying probabilities and utilities may be of little use in hypothesizing a spatial form. However, Wise shows that a complex design, once formulated, can be evaluated by techniques related to multiattributed utility theory.

Hillel J. Einhorn and Robin M. Hogarth in Part V, Judgmental Forecasting, analyze judgmental forecasting and evaluate the relationship between predictions, actions, and outcomes. They emphasize the probabilistic nature of cues to causality and the uncertainties associated with inference. Causal thinking is examined in detail, and Einhorn and Hogarth discuss the implications of their analysis for improving forecasting.

Allan H. Murphy presents the results and analysis of forecasting in a real-world setting—weather forecasting. Weather forecasters make use of objective guidance forecasts, based on numerical statistical procedures, to help them produce subjective forecasts. In some situations, subjective forecasts are an improvement on objective forecasts; sometimes they are not. Murphy discusses the problems of evaluating the precise role of objective forecasts in the subjective forecasting process.

Jack Dowie, in Part VI, Decision Theory: Areas of Future Impact, analyzes the implications of decision theory for the educational process. Should the teacher's values and uncertainties be open for discussion and criticism? Education, Dowie analyzes, is often concerned with teaching the certainties of high-value knowledge. But should we be educated for uncertainty? Dowie examines the usefulness of requiring students to give probabilistic responses to multiple-choice questions and describes the use of multiattributed utility theory in student assessment.

Lawrence C. Currie argues that Kelly's personal construct theory can be applied to aid our understanding of how people make decisions. Currie deals with the applicability of personal construct theory to the perception of danger and decision making in two-person games.

GEORGE WRIGHT

REFERENCES

Hogarth, R. M. (1980). *Judgment and choice.* Chichester: Wiley.
Wright, G. (1984). *Behavioral decision theory.* Beverly Hills: Sage, and Harmondsworth: Penguin.

Contents

Chapter 3

Decisional Variance 43

George Wright

Chapter 4

Cognitive Approaches to Decision Making...................... 61

A. John Maule

PART II SMALL-GROUP DECISION MAKING

Chapter 5

Chapter 6

PART III   ORGANIZATIONAL DECISION MAKING

Chapter 7

Chapter 8

Chapter 9

Chapter 10

Decision Making in Organizations: The Effective Use of Personnel . 207

Humphrey V. Swann

PART IV IMPROVING DECISIONS: THE ROLE OF DECISION AIDS

Chapter 11

Design of Decision-Aiding Systems 235

Ayleen D. Wisudha

Chapter 12

Handling Uncertainty: Levels of Analysis of Decision Problems 257

Patrick Humphreys and Dina Berkeley

PART VI DECISION THEORY: AREAS OF FUTURE IMPACT

Chapter 16

Education and Decision Theory: A Personal View 363

Jack Dowie

Chapter 17

Choice Decision and the Anticipation of Events 379

Lawrence C. Currie

PART I

INDIVIDUAL DECISION MAKING

CHAPTER 1

Psychology of Risky Decisions

John W. Payne

INTRODUCTION

Most definitions of a decision problem include (1) the courses of action or alternatives available to the decision maker; (2) the possible outcomes and values attached to them, conditional on the actions; and (3) the events or contingencies that relate actions to outcomes (Huber, 1980; Tversky & Kahneman, 1981). The evaluation and/or choice among a set of gambles captures all three of the basic informational elements that constitute most decision problems. Consequently, the study of the psychological processes involved in judgments and choices among gambles has been one of the most active areas of decision research (see Einhorn & Hogarth, 1981; Slovic, Fischhoff, & Lichtenstein, 1977). Understanding how individuals make decisions under risk also has direct relevance for improving decisions in business (Libby & Fishburn, 1977) and public policy (Slovic, 1978). Decision analysts and others whose job is to improve decision performance often use responses to simple gambles as inputs to normative models (Keeney & Raiffa, 1976).

The purpose of this chapter is to present a highly selective review of the literature on individual decision making under risk. The perspective is that risky decision making is a highly contingent form of information processing. That is, risky choice is seen as being highly sensitive to variations in the task environment. More specifically, it is argued that the response to a risky decision problem will involve several stages of processing (e.g., editing and evaluation of options, Kahneman & Tversky, 1979) that will each consist of a number of different

John W. Payne • Fuqua School of Business, Duke University, Durham, North Carolina 27706. Preparation of this chapter was supported by a contract from the Engineering Psychology Programs, Office of Naval Research.

processes that are contingent upon task and context variables. Task variables are associated with the general structural characteristics of a decision problem, such as the number of alternatives; context variables are associated with the particular values of the objects in the decision set (Payne, 1982). The chapter concludes with a suggested approach for studying contingent decision behavior under situations of risk.

MODELS OF RISKY CHOICE

The traditional way of describing gambles has been as probability distributions over outcomes, usually money. Choice among gambles could then be viewed as choice among probability distributions (Arrow, 1951). A variety of decision models have therefore concentrated on the moments of the underlying distributions as the determinants of choice among gambles. The most common assumption is that choice is some function of each distribution's central tendency, although other moments such as variance and skewness have also been incorporated into theories of risky choice behavior (cf. Libby & Fishburn, 1977). One issue in decision research, however, has been the extent to which the description of gambles as probability distributions provides an adequate approximation of the cognitive representations actually used by decision makers (Payne, 1973).

The literature in the area of individual decision making under risk is commonly traced back at least as far as Bernoulli (1738). He proposed a descriptive model of risky decision behavior based on the idea that people maximize expected utility in selecting among gambles. The expected utility (EU) of a gamble is given by:

$$EU = \sum_{i=1}^{n} p_i U(x_i)$$

where $U(x_i)$ is the utility of the ith outcome and p_i is the probability of that outcome. A traditional assumption, although not a necessary part of the EU model, is that the utility function will be concave. This means that given a choice between a sure thing of value $x and a gamble with an expected value of $x, the person will select the sure thing. Such behavior has been defined as risk aversion. A preference for the gamble defines risk seeking. The EU model as proposed by Bernoulli is derived from the principle of the mathematical expectation of a probability distribution. That is, the value of the distribution that could be expected to occur over the long run.

Von Neumann and Morgenstern (1947) showed that the idea of EU maximization is also derivable from a small set of axioms or statements about consistencies in risky choice behavior. Consequently, the expected utility model can be applied to unique choice problems as well as those to which a long-run expectation argument might apply. The axiom system proposed by von Neumann and Morgenstern seemed so reasonable and the axioms so appealing that the EU model has come to define rational decision making in the eyes of many people. It is important to recognize that the expected utility model has served both normative and descriptive purposes.

In the last 35 years or so, a number of variations on the basic EU or expectation type of model have been proposed. Edwards (1955), for example, proposed a subjectively expected utility model where a subjective probability function $S(p_i)$ is used along with a utility function to represent risky preferences. An excellent summary of the variants of the EU model is provided by Schoemaker (1982).

There have been numerous tests of the EU model as a description of risky choice behavior. At times EU types of models have been reasonably successful in overall predictions of decisions among gambles (Coombs, Bezembinder, & Goode, 1967). As Schoemaker (1982) has noted, however, "at the individual level EU maximization is more the exception than the rule" (p. 552). Systematic violations of most of the basic axioms of EU theory have been shown in laboratory settings (e.g., Coombs, 1975; Kahneman & Tversky, 1979; Tversky, 1969). Real-world data also seem inconsistent with an expected utility maximization process (Kunreuther, 1976). Schoemaker traces the failure of the EU model as a descriptive theory to its inadequate concern with cognitive limitations.

An alternative to expected utility theory that has recently generated a lot of interest is *prospect theory* (Kahneman & Tversky, 1979). Prospect theory distinguishes between two phases of the risky choice process, editing and evaluation. The initial phase consists of editing the decision problem into a simpler representation in order to make the second phase of evaluation easier for the decision maker. Easier refers to information-processing demands.

Included in the editing phase are such operations as coding, cancellation, combination, and the detection of dominance. Two of the most important operations are *coding* and *cancellation*. Coding refers to the perception by a decision maker of each of the gamble outcomes as being either a gain or a loss, with a gain or loss being defined relative to a reference point or level of aspiration. Expected utility theory in its traditional form assumes that outcomes are perceived in terms of final wealth positions. Cancellation refers to the discarding of components that are common to each of the offered gambles. The idea is that the decision maker will focus on the differences between options as the fundamental basis of choice. This simplification process is related to the elimination-by-aspects heuristic (Tversky, 1972). According to Kahneman and Tversky (1979), for example, the following choice between the gamble that provides a chance to win $200 with probability .2, $100 with probability .5, or lose $50 with probability .3 (denoted as, $200, .2; $100, .5; −$50, .3), and the gamble, $200, .2;

$150, .5; −$100, .3, would first be simplified by cancellation of the common outcome-probability pair, $200, .2, to a choice between $100, .5; −$50, .3 and $150, .5; −$100, .3. Note that the cancellation of common outcome probability pairs is related to the sure-thing principle (Savage, 1954) underlying the subjective expected utility model and the concept of event independence in multiattribute utility theory (von Winderfeldt, 1980). Coding and cancellation, along with other editing operations, contribute to what Tversky and Kahneman (1981) refer to as the *framing of decisions*.

The second phase in prospect theory consists of the evaluation of edited prospects using a generalized expected-utility process. Of special interest in this phase are the properties of the value function and decision weights (partially a function of probabilities) used in evaluation. For simple gambles involving just two nonzero outcomes, one positive (x) and one negative (y), the basic evaluation equation is

$$V(\text{gamble}) = \pi(p)\ v(x) + \pi(q)\ v(y),$$

where (p) and (q) are the probabilities of receiving (x) and (y), respectively; $\pi(\ \ )$ is a decision weight; and $v(\ \ )$ is a value function. Of special interest in this phase are the properties of the value function and decision weights used in evaluation. The value function, for example, is generally concave for gains and convex for losses. The weighting function, for example, is generally subadditive. That is, $\pi(p) + \pi(1-p)$ is generally less than 1.0.

In my opinion, however, the most exciting contribution of prospect theory is the notion of the editing or framing of decisions. As Kahneman and Tversky (1979) have stated, "Many anomalies of preference result from the editing of prospects" (p. 275). More generally, contingent decision behavior is explicitly suggested by prospect theory because it is assumed that the same set of options might be edited in different ways depending on the context in which it appears.

The rest of this chapter will concentrate on recent efforts to reflect information-processing considerations in explaining task and context effects in risky choice behavior.

CONTINGENT PROCESSING IN RISKY CHOICE

A question of great concern in decision research is the extent to which information processing in risky decision making will be invariant across task environments. A lack of invariance would not only complicate the search for a small set of principles that could describe behavior, it would also raise questions about the validity of the judgmental inputs needed to make many decision aids operational (see Hershey, Kunreuther, & Schoemaker, 1982, for examples of biases in the assessment of utility functions). Increasingly, the answer to that question seems to be that risky decision behavior is highly contingent on the demands of the task. To demonstrate that point, a few of the most important task and context effects in risky decision making will be identified. A more complete survey of the research showing the effects of task and context variables on decision behavior is provided in Payne (1982).

Task Complexity

A frequently explored task variable has been the complexity of the decision problem. The hypothesis is that individuals will utilize different choice heuristics as task complexity changes in order to keep the information-processing demands of the situation within the bounds of their cognitive capacity. Task complexity has been manipulated through variations in the number of alternatives in the choice set, the number of dimensions of information (attributes or outcomes) used to define an alternative, and the amount of time available for making a decision.

Several studies involving both risky and nonrisky choices (Olshavsky, 1979; Payne, 1976; Payne & Braunstein, 1978) indicate that choice strategies are sensitive to the number of alternatives. In Payne and Braunstein (1978), for example, individuals were asked to choose among three-outcome gambles in each of 12 sets of gambles. Each gamble in a set involved a probability of winning (PW), an amount to win ($\$W$), a probability of losing (PL), an amount to lose ($\$L$), and a probability of neither a win nor a loss (PZ), such that $PW+PL+PZ=1.0$. Within the 12 sets of gambles, 4 sets contained two gambles, 4 contained four gambles, and 4 contained eight gambles. The results indicated that when faced with two gambles, subjects tended to use compensatory types of decision strategies (as specified, for example, by information-integration theory; see Anderson & Shanteau, 1970). When faced with more complex (multigamble) decision tasks, however, subjects tended to use other choice strategies such as *elimination by aspects* (Tversky, 1972). There is also some evidence (Payne & Braunstein, 1978) that information-acquisition patterns become more attribute based as the number of alternatives increases. That is, information will be acquired on one attribute, for example probability of winning, for several alternatives in a sequence before information on another attribute is acquired. This effect of number of alternatives on information processing, however, does not appear to be as strong as the shift from compensatory to noncompensatory strategies.

The evidence on the effects of number of dimensions of information and time pressures on decisions is less clear than for number of alternatives. There has been speculation that a small increase in the complexity of gambles through increases in the number of outcomes possible, for example, from gambles of the form a, p, with one nonzero outcome, to gambles of the form a, p, b, with two nonzero outcomes, would affect choice behavior (Lindman & Lyons,1978). Kahneman and Tversky (1979) suggested that very complex gambles (multiple outcomes) would be simplified through some sort of editing process, although "the manner in which complex options, e.g., compound propects, are reduced is yet to be investigated" (p. 288). More recently, Payne (1981) found some support for the possibility that a decision maker might respond to complex gambles by treating all outcomes below and above a certain target or reference point as similar and then combining the probabilities associated with outcomes below the target into a composite probability of failure to meet the target, similarly for above-target outcomes. Such a response to complex gambles would be consistent with coding as an editing operation (Kahneman & Tversky, 1979).

Ben Zur and Breznitz (1981) have found that subjects make less risky choices under high time pressure. Furthermore, it appeared that subjects tended to spend more time observing negative information (amount to lose and probability of losing) under conditions of high time pressure. Related findings on the effects of time horizons on decision strategies are reported by Wright (1974) and Wright and Weitz (1977).

To summarize, there is evidence in support of the hypothesis that increases in task complexity will result in changes in the evaluation/choice strategies used to make both risky and nonrisky choices. There is, however, clearly a need for more research on how people respond to highly complex (multioutcome) gambles.

Information Display

The hypothesis that information processing in decision making will be a function of how information about the decision task is displayed has often been suggested (e.g., Tversky, 1969). A study by Aschenbrenner (1978) has shown convincingly that presentation mode can affect preferences among gambles. Subjects were asked to indicate preferences for gambles presented in the form $x, p; y, 1-p$, where one wins amount x with probability p or loses amount y with probability $1-p$, and also to indicate preferences for gambles of the form $y, p, x+y$, where one pays the stake y, in advance, in order to play the game involving a p chance of winning $x+y$ or winning nothing with probability $1-p$. For given values of x, y, and p, both forms of the gamble are equivalent in terms of final outcomes and probabilities. Nonetheless, Aschenbrenner reported that the preference orders obtained under the two presentation modes showed "hardly any relation for the same gambles" (p. 519).

Aschenbrenner (1978) interpreted his results as showing that subjects use the dimensions of gambles "as they are presented to them rather than transform the gambles into final outcomes or calculate subjective moments" (p. 519). Additional support for the idea that people respond to gambles in terms of the stated outcomes and probabilities rather than moments of the underlying probability distributions is provided by studies by Slovic and Lichtenstein (1968) and Payne and Braunstein (1971). These studies utilized duplex gambles, each consisting of independent win-and-lose gambles. Slovic and Lichtenstein (1968) employed parallel gambles such that for each standard two-outcome gamble $(x, p; y, 1-p)$ there was a duplex gamble that displayed the same stated probabilities and payoffs and was equivalent in expected value but differed in variance. Similar responses to standard and duplex gambles were found with both bidding and choice response modes. Payne and Braunstein (1971) utilized specially constructed pairs of duplex gambles that were identical in terms of underlying probability distributions but that displayed different stated probability values. Subjects had significant preferences between such pairs of gambles. Together, the studies by Aschenbrenner (1978), Payne and Braunstein (1971), and Slovic and Lichtenstein (1968) show that it is the probability and outcome information as displayed, not the moments of the underlying probability distributions, that influence preferences among gambles. A similar conclusion can be reached from studies of the direct assessment of the perceived riskiness of options (Coombs & Lehner, 1981; Payne, 1975; Slovic 1967).

Another interesting example of the importance of display format in determining risky preferences is the response of Savage (1954) to the Allais paradox (Allais, 1953). Variations of the paradox are reported in Kahneman and Tversky (1979). The Allais paradox refers to the responses to two hypothetical decision situations, each involving two gambles.

Situation 1	Choice between:
Gamble 1	5 with probability 1
Gamble 2	25 with probability .10
	5 with probability .89
	0 with probability .01

The outcomes are in units of $100,000. Most people prefer Gamble 1 to Gamble 2.

Situation 2	Choose between:
Gamble 3	5 with probability .11
	0 with probability .89
Gamble 4	25 with probability .10
	0 with probability .90

In this case, most people prefer Gamble 4 to Gamble 3. It is easy to show that the preference pattern G1 > G2 and G4 > G3 is inconsistent with expected utility theory. In particular, that pattern of preferences violates the sure-thing principle (Savage, 1954).

Savage admits that at first he exhibited the conventional pattern of preferences. He suggested, however, another way of "looking" at the Allais problem: Imagine that the two sets of paired gambles (G1 & G2; G3 & G4) could be realized by drawing one of a hundred numbered tickets.

		1	2-11	12-100
		\multicolumn{3}{c}{Ticket Number}		
Situation 1	Gamble 1	5	5	5
	Gamble 2	0	25	5
Situation 2	Gamble 3	5	5	0
	Gamble 4	0	25	0

By using the foregoing representation of the problem, Savage states his original preferences are reversed.

> Now, if one of the tickets numbered from 12 through 100 is drawn, it will not matter, in either situation, which gamble I chose. I therefore focus on the possibility that one of the tickets numbered 1 through 11 will be drawn, in which case situations 1 and 2 are exactly parallel. (p. 103)

In other words, by invoking a display that makes clear the opportunity for cancellation, Savage changes his preferences to be consistent with expected utility theory. Such information display and framing effects are stressed by prospect theory (Kahneman & Tversky, 1979).

Much of the research showing information display effects in risky choice seems supportive of the "concreteness" principle proposed by Slovic (1972). Slovic's idea was that in order to reduce cognitive strain a "decision maker tends to use only the information that is explicitly displayed in the stimulus object and will use it only in the form in which it is displayed" (p. 14).

The fact that information display can affect risky decision behavior is clearly established. Such studies have important implications for the design of messages to inform people about risks they face in their daily lives (Slovic, Fischhoff, & Lichtenstein, 1981) and the design of computer-based decision support systems (Keen & Scott-Morton, 1978). An excellent example of a decision aid based on information display considerations is provided by Russo (1977).

Response Modes

Perhaps the most striking example of a task effect in risky decision making is the preference reversal phenomenon (Lichtenstein & Slovic 1971). It has been found that subjects will often indicate a preference for one gamble over a second gamble when a choice procedure is used, but they would indicate a willingness to pay more to play the second gamble when a bidding procedure was used. Choices tended to favor the gamble with the higher probability of winning but with a smaller amount to be won; the higher bids were made for the gambles with the larger amounts to win but with the lower probability of winning. The preference reversal effect has been extensively investigated (Grether & Plott, 1979; Lichtenstein & Slovic, 1973; Pommerehne, Schneider, & Zweifel, 1982; Reilly, 1982).

One explanation of the preference reversal phenomenon is that variations in response mode cause a fundamental change in the way people process information about gambles (Lichtenstein & Slovic, 1971, 1973). In the choice mode, it is suggested, the processing is primarily dimensional (Tversky, 1969). That is, each dimension of one gamble, for example, probabilities of winning, might be compared with the same dimension of the other gamble. In contrast, the bidding response is seen as leading to an alternative-based processing of information called *anchoring and adjustment*. It is suggested that the amount to win often serves as the anchor for a gamble that is basically attractive. Because the adjustment to the anchor is usually insufficient, the gamble with the larger amount to win often is assigned a higher bid.

Another possible component of the inconsistencies between choices and judgmental responses (e.g., bids) may be that choice often includes a justification process (Slovic, Fischhoff, & Lichtenstein, 1982). Slovic *et al.* argue that part of the deliberation prior to choice consists of "finding a concise, coherent set of reasons that justify the selection of one option over the others." Such deliberations are not seen as a major part of a judgmental response.

There have been a number of other studies of response mode effects (Coombs, Donnell, & Kirk, 1978; Hershey, Kunreuther, & Schoemaker, 1982; Rosen & Rosenkoetter, 1976). These studies, along with those cited previously, have serious descriptive and normative implications. On the descriptive side, it is clear that the conclusion reached by Einhorn and Hogarth (1981) is correct. The kinds of evaluation processes associated with a judgment task where the subject assigns a value to each alternative in a set reflecting its subjective worth is often related to choice behavior, but judgment and choice are not equivalent tasks. On the normative side, variations due to response mode raise questions about the validity of the judgments needed to make procedures like decision analysis (Keeney & Raiffa, 1976) operational. Hershey *et al.* (1982), for example, have shown that there is considerable indeterminacy as to the the nature of people's risk-taking attitudes that are contingent on the response method used to construct utility functions. Unfortunately, the basis for the various response mode differences is not yet completely understood. In practical applications of decision theory, the best recommendation is simply to use multiple response modes and seek (hope for) convergent validation (Hershey *et al.*, 1982).

Quality of Option Set

Task complexity, information display, and response mode variables represent task factors (Payne, 1982). An important context factor affecting the information processing involved in risky decisions is the quality or nature of the options available in the choice set. Williams (1966), for example, suggested that people may react differently to "pure-risk" and "speculative-risk" situations. In both there is doubt or uncertainty concerning the outcomes, but in the pure-risk situation there is no chance of gain. The person faces only a loss or the status quo. In the speculative-risk situation there is a chance of a gain.

A series of experiments by Payne, Laughhunn, and Crum (1980, 1981, 1984) have investigated the idea that choice processes would differ depending on whether the outcomes of the gambles were primarily losses or primarily gains. The first set of experiments involved varying the relationship of a pair of gambles to an assumed reference point, target, or aspiration level by adding or subtracting a constant amount from all the outcomes. For example, in one experiment with business managers as subjects (a trend in decision research is the use of other than college students as subjects), a choice was given between the gamble that had a .5 chance of returning $14,000, a .1 chance of returning −$30,000, and a .4 chance of returning −$85,000 (represented as $14, .5; −$30, .1; −$85, .4), denoted G1, and the gamble given by −$20, .3; −$30, .5; −$45, .2, denoted G2. In this case, 67% of the managers chose G1. Such a choice implies risk seeking as traditionally defined. However, when the gambles G1 and G2 were transformed by adding $60,000 to all outcomes to create new gambles G1′ and G2′, represented by $74, .5; $30, .1; −$25, .4 and $40, .3; $30, .5; $15, .2, respectively, approximately 83% of the subjects chose G2′, a result that implies a risk averse attitude. In other words, a translation of outcomes resulted in a reversal of preference within a pair of gambles. The key determinant of the effect of the translation was whether the size of the translation was sufficient to result in one gamble having outcome values either all above or all below a reference point, whereas the other gamble had outcome values that were both above and below the reference point. Note that because additive translations of all outcomes cannot affect the magnitude of any moment computed about the mean of the probability distributions and because the expected values of the gambles are equal, the observed switching of choices provides evidence against the adequacy of any type of mean–moment model of risky choice. Furthermore, Payne *et al.*, also show that the obtained preference orders are inconsistent with an expected utility model that assumes either a uniformly concave (risk averse) or uniformly convex (risk-seeking) utility function.

A model of the effects of aspiration levels or reference points on risky choice is presented in Payne et al. (1980). The heart of the model is the idea that the preference function that is used to choose among gambles is contingent on whether the choice problem is one involving mainly positive outcomes, a mixture of positive and negative outcomes, or mainly negative outcomes. Interestingly, Coombs and Lehner (1981) have traced the failure of moment-based models of the perception of risk to the failure to distinguish between the contributions of good and bad outcomes. Also, Fishburn (1982) has offered an axiomatic treatment of perceived risk that stresses the distinction between gain outcomes and loss outcomes.

As noted earlier, prospect theory (Kahneman & Tversky, 1979; Tversky & Kahneman, 1981) has, as part of the initial phase of editing, an operation called coding that defines an outcome as being either a gain or a loss, and in which choices among gambles involving only gains generally indicates risk aversion and risk seeking is generally observed for gambles involving only losses. It has been shown that even simple changes in the wording of a decision problem can reverse preferences because of the difference in risk attitudes with repect to gains and losses (Tversky & Kahneman, 1981). McNeil, Pauker, Sox, and Tversky (1982) have shown this effect in a task of potentially great applied value. The study involved comparisons between two therapies, surgery and radiology therapy, for the treatment of lung cancer. Three subject populations were used: physicians, ambulatory patients with different chronic medical conditions (none known to have lung cancer), and graduate students. The subjects were presented with the probabilities of survival during treatment for 1 year and for 5 years for each of the two therapies. Survival rates are less for surgery in the short term but greater in the long term. On average, 84% preferred surgery. In contrast, when the probabilities were expressed in terms of dying rather than living, the percentage of subjects preferring surgery was only 56%. The effect was similar for all three groups of subjects. At each time period, the probability of death is, of course, merely one minus the probability of survival. The results of wording changes reported in Tversky and Kahneman (1981) and McNeil et al. (1982) are also additional examples of the effects of information display on risky choices.

The investigation of risk preferences as a function of whether outcomes are gains or losses recently has been extended to choice among multiattribute risky options. The vast majority of research on risky choice has concentrated on options where the possible outcomes were defined on only a single attribute, most frequently a monetary attribute. It has been recognized, however, that many of the most important decision problems involve both risk and multiattribute outcomes (see Bell, Keeney, & Raiffa, 1977).

Payne, Laughhunn, and Crum (1984) asked 128 professional managers to indicate preferences among pairs of risky capital budget proposals differing on two attributes. Of particular interest were the reponses to pairs of gambles that had identical marginal probability distributions on the attributes. Fishburn (1965) and Richard (1975) have used preference between two gambles with identical marginal probability distributions on the attributes to define the concept of a multiattribute or multivariate risk attitude. To illustrate, consider the following two gambles:

	Gamble 1		Gamble 2	
	.5	.5	.5	.5
A_1	x	0	x	0
A_2	0	y	y	0

Under the assumption that preferences are monotone increasing in x and y and where x and y have the same sign, a decision maker who prefers G1 to G2 exhibits pairwise multiattribute risk aversion. On the other hand, a decision maker who prefers G2 to G1 exhibits multiattribute risk seeking. Indifference between G1 and G2 indicates that a decision maker is multiattribute risk neutral. Although multiattribute risk attitudes intuitively seem to suggest behavior akin to classical single-attribute risk attitudes, risk preferences over a single attribute do not imply anything about the multiattribute risk preferences for the joint probability over combinations of the levels of the different attributes. Furthermore, assumptions about multiattribute risk attitudes play a major role in defining appropriate models for multiple-objective decision analysis (Keeney & Raiffa, 1976).

Payne *et al.* (1984) have reported that for multiattribute gambles involving only gains, the most common form of behavior was multiattribute risk aversion. For multiattribute gambles involving only losses, multiattribute risk seeking was observed. This result reinforces the importance of coding and reference points or aspiration levels found in earlier studies of single-attribute risky choice.

Finally, additional empirical support for the role of choice set quality is provided by experiments reported in Payne (1975), Payne and Braunstein (1971), and Ranyard (1976). Those studies suggest that individuals will often make an initial judgment about whether they are faced with an attractive or unattractive set of gambles before deciding on the choice rule to be used.

FRAMEWORKS FOR TASK AND CONTEXT EFFECTS

We have reviewed just some of the evidence supporting the conclusion that decision making under risk is a highly contingent form of information processing. The sensitivity of risky decision behavior to seemingly minor changes in task and context is one of the major results of years of decision research. In Payne (1982), alternative theoretical frameworks for handling task and context effects were examined: (a) cost/benefit principles; (b) perceptual processes; and (c) adaptive production systems. The cost/benefit framework assumes that the selection of a particular decision strategy in a particular task environment is, in part, a function of the strategy ability to produce an accurate response and the strategy demand for mental resources or effort (Beach & Mitchell, 1978; Russo & Dosher, 1980). A view of strategy selection as involving costs and benefits has several appealing aspects. First, such a principle can maintain the assumption of calculated rationality on the part of the decision maker (March, 1978). Second, certain task effects, for example, number of alternatives, seem very consistent with a cost/benefit framework. There is also strong support for the perceptual framework. Much of the work of Kahneman and Tversky (1979; Tversky & Kahneman, 1981) fits within this framework. Perhaps the best example is the effect on risk taking of slight wording changes (gains vs. losses) reported in Tversky and Kahneman (1981) and McNeil *et al.* (1982). It is difficult to see how such wording changes increase either cognitive effort or the desire for accuracy.

The perceptual view as expressed by Kahneman and Tversky differs from the cost/benefit framework as generally expressed in several ways. For example, Tversky and Kahneman (1981) have stated that people "are normally unaware of alternative frames and their potential effects on the relative attractiveness of options" (p. 457). Russo and Dosher (1980), in contrast, see the selection among decision strategies to be a "deliberate" process. The perceptual framework also seems to suggest a more universal response across subjects to task and context variables, similar to perceptual types of illusions.

The third framework for contingent processing in decisions identified by Payne (1982), adaptive production systems, is in some respects more of a modeling language than a conceptual framework. A *production system* (Newell & Simon, 1972) consists of a set of productions, a task environment, and a working memory. The productions specify a set of actions and the conditions under which they occur. These are expressed as a (condition) → (action) pair, and the actions specified in a production are performed (fire) only when the condition side is satisfied by matching the contents of working memory. Working memory is a set of symbols, both those read from the external environment and those deposited by the actions performed by previous productions. The set of productions possessed by an individual can be thought of as being part of long-term memory. Arguments for the value of production systems as a representation of human cognitive processes and further descriptions of production systems have been presented by Newell (1980). Although the production system framework is a modeling language, it does tend to emphasize the role of learning or the prior experiences of the decision maker more than the other two frameworks. An implication is that there may be larger individual variability in response to a particular task environment than is suggested by the perceptual framework.

Researchers working within each of the three frameworks are likely to continue to make important empirical and conceptual contributions to our understanding of risky decision behavior. It is clear, however, that a complete understanding of contingent decision behavior will include concepts drawn from all three frameworks. Risky decision behavior is likely to consist of multiple systems that interact in various ways. That is, the response to a decision problem will involve a mixture of decision processes, for example, coding, cancellation, elimination by aspects, and compensatory trade-offs, that are contingent on the properties of the decision task (see Broadbent, 1977, for a discussion of the idea that human information processing takes place on many levels). An approach to decision research that may aid in our understanding of contingent decision behavior is illustrated next.

A PRODUCTION SYSTEM APPROACH
TO MODELS OF STRATEGY SELECTION IN CHOICE

A major difficulty in examining the cost/benefit framework has been the development of measures defining the costs and benefits associated with various decision strategies. Johnson and Payne (1985) have proposed an approach to investigating effort and error considerations in choice using production system models and computer simulation. Building on earlier work by O. Huber (1980) and Johnson (1979) and the ideas of Newell and Simon (1972), they suggest that decision strategies be decomposed into sets of elementary information processes (EIPs). A decision strategy or rule could then be thought of as a sequence of events, such as reading the values of two alternatives on an attribute, comparing them, and so forth. A general discussion of the use of the EIP concept in the analysis of human information processing has been provided by Chase (1978).

The effort associated with a given strategy in a particular task environment would be measured by the total number of elementary information processes used in a task. Examples of such EIP counts can be found in a number of studies of cognition (e.g., Card, Moran, & Newell, 1980; Carpenter & Just, 1975). Such counts have been shown to be related to other measures of effort such as response latencies.

Accuracy of choice can be defined in many ways. At a general level, quality of choice can be defined by consistencies in preference, for example, transitivity or the avoidance of gross errors such as selecting a dominated alternative. However, more specific criteria have been suggested for risky choice. As noted earlier, for example, the expected utility principle has been suggested as a normative as well as a descriptive model. A special case of the EU principle—maximization of expected value—has been used by Thorngate (1980) to investigate the accuracy of several heuristics. Johnson and Payne (1985) used EV-based criteria along with expected utility and dominance-based measures of accuracy.

Johnson and Payne implemented six decision rules as production systems capable of being simulated on a computer. The six rules differed markedly in the amount of available information that they considered. *A priori*, this was expected to be an important determinant of both the accuracy and the effort resulting from their use.

At one extreme was the *expected value* rule, which is based on complete search of the available information. The *equiprobable* heuristic similarly examines all the alternatives and all outcomes. It, however, ignores one of the two attributes of a gamble's outcomes, probability, implicitly treating all events as equally likely. To choose a lottery, the equiprobable heuristic adds the payoffs for the outcomes of each alternative and chooses the alternative with the highest total. This heuristic is similar to an equal weight model for nonrisky judgments. The *most-likely* heuristic, in contrast, examines only one outcome for each alternative, the outcome with the highest probability of occurrence, and selects the alternative with the largest payoff for this outcome. Thus, this rule searches each event to find the most-likely outcome and examines only that payoff associated with that event. This heuristic is similar to the lexicographic rule. The *maximin* heuristic ignores probabilities entirely and selects the alternative with the largest minimum payoff. This rule is related to the conjunctive rule. Elimination by aspects is a choice rule proposed by Tversky (1972). A version discussed by Thorngate (1980) that attends only to payoff information has been implemented by Johnson and Payne (1985). Each payoff of a gamble is compared to a cutoff equal to the mean payoff. If a payoff is less than the cutoff, the gamble is eliminated from further consideration. The rule terminates when either (a) one alternative remains, or (b) all attributes have been considered, and one must choose randomly from the remaining alternatives. Elimination by aspects ignores probabilties entirely and performs only partial search of the payoff information. Finally, the *random* choice rule served as a baseline, simply choosing an alternative at random with no search.

Johnson and Payne conducted a series of Monte Carlo studies that varied several aspects of the choice environments. The number of risky alternatives and outcomes were varied at levels of 2, 4, and 8. Another aspect was the amount of variance in probabilities within each gamble. Thorngate (1980) has suggested that probability information may be relatively unimportant in making accurate risky choices:

> A wide variety of decision heuristics will usually produce optimal, or close to optimal results and can thus be termed relatively efficient. The...equiprobable heuristic deserves further comment...its high efficiency suggests that "good" choices can very

often be made with scant regard for the subtleties of accurate probability estimation procedures." (pp. 223–224)

However, Thorngate's method for constructing gambles ensured that the variance in the probability distribution would be small relative to the variance in payoffs. Because expected value is the product of these two quantities, it is not surprising that probability information had little impact on the performance of Thorngate's rules. Further, the tendency of his method to produce low variance in probabilities increases exponentially with the number of outcomes. In their simulation, Johnson and Payne implemented another method of probability generation that produced larger variances in the probability distributions. Finally, the presence or absence of dominated alternatives in the choice sets was varied.

The simulations identified choice rules that approximated the accuracy of normative procedures while requiring substantially less effort. The results, however, were highly contingent upon characteristics of the choice environments. In the environment that closely resembled Thorngate's, for example, the equiprobable rule appeared quite accurate. It was also a rule that maintained roughly the same accuracy as the number of outcomes was increased. In contrast, when the variance of the probabilities was increased, the most-likely heuristic became the most accurate, whereas the equiprobable heuristic displayed a marked decrease in accuracy. Furthermore, the most-likely rule was the only one to maintain accuracy as the number of outcomes increased. Thorngate's earlier statement, therefore, was found to be of limited generality. These results are of particular importance in light of the suggestion by Beach (1983) that Thorngate's results justify deemphasizing the importance of probabilities in decision aids.

Another interesting result was the effect of the presence or absence of dominated alternatives. The removal of dominated alternatives reduced the accuracy of some heuristics to almost chance levels.

Johnson and Payne concluded that heuristics could be accurate but that no single heuristic would do well across all contexts. Instead, if decision makers strive to maintain a high level of accuracy with a minimum of effort, they would have to choose among a repertoire of strategies.

The focus of the Johnson and Payne work was on individual decision rules that could be uniquely applied to a decision problem. That is, a single rule would be used to reach a decision. There is evidence, however, that decision makers will employ strategies that combine rules. For example, Payne (1976) reported that subjects faced with choice tasks involving a large number of alternatives would first use an elimination-by-aspects process to eliminate alternatives. When the choice problem was reduced to a smaller set of alternatives, for example, two, decision makers shifted to a more compensatory decision process.

A number of other researchers have suggested on both theoretical and empirical grounds that an early stage in a complex decision process might involve the reduction of alternatives (e.g., Montgomery & Svenson, 1976). The general rationale seems to be that such a procedure provides a way for the decision maker to simplify a complex task.

Consequently, Johnson and Payne examined one such combined rule suggested by previous empirical evidence. This rule used elimination by aspects until only three alternatives remained and then calculated the expected value of the alternatives on their unexamined attributes. This rule showed some improvement over simple elimination by aspects, choosing the alternative with the highest expected value 15% more often. Most importantly, when compared to the other heuristics, this rule showed much slower increases in effort when the number of alternatives increased. Although the equiprobable heuristic showed a fourfold increase in effort as the number of alternatives increased, the equivalent increase for the phased rule was less than twofold. Thus the combined rule has two attractive aspects: (a) it increases the accuracy of the elimination strategy while (b) maintaining relatively low effort in large choice sets. More research on combined decision strategies seems warranted.

In addition to their simulation results, Johnson and Payne (1985) have discussed how future research into risky choice might be facilitated by the use of production system models and computer simulation. (A more general discussion of the advantages and disadvantages of computer simulation of human behavior has been provided by Starbuck, 1983). Johnson and Payne suggested, for example, that the role of task variables in the design of messages about risk or in the design of decision support systems might be aided by the decomposition of strategies into sets of productions that could be studied under various task conditions through computer simulations. Another suggestion was that the neglected question of strategy development in risky decision making might be examined within the production system framework. As Simon (1981) has noted, "What makes production systems especially attractive for modeling is that it is relatively easy to endow them with learning capabilities" (p. 121).

Issues of learning are likely to play an increasingly important role in understanding decision behavior. It is becoming clear, for example, that experts depend to a great extent on much task-specific information to solve problems. Such information is often represented as sets of if–then rules or productions (Duda & Shortliffe, 1983). As the field of behavioral decision theory becomes more interested in expert decision making, adaptive production system models and ideas will become more and more important. Furthermore, learning concepts are likely to be needed to solve many difficult theoretical issues. For example, one difficulty with the idea that people deliberately decide how to choose is a potential infinite regress—one has to decide how to choose to decide how to choose. A more reasonable perspective is that such decisions are not made often but that the relationship between task and context effects and the efficiency of a decision strategy is learned over time. For example, a decision maker may learn over time that a screening phase will substantially reduce effort in large choice sets. This knowledge can exist as part of the conditions that must be met for a production to fire. Klein (1983) also has suggested that a decision maker's use of heuristics might be related to learning about the nature of task environments.

SUMMARY

Understanding the psychology of risky decisions has been the focus of years of research. Such effort reflects the fact that decisions among gambles involve the integration of the two basic judgments of interest to decision researchers–judgments of values and beliefs. A major finding of the years of research has been the great sensitivity of risky decision behavior to seemingly minor changes in task and context. We are just beginning to understand, however, the underlying psychological mechanisms that lead to contingent risk-taking behavior. An approach for increasing our understanding is proposed and illustrated based on the concepts of adaptive production system models and computer simulations.

ACKNOWLEDGMENTS

I wish to thank Bart van Dissel and Chris Puto for their comments.

REFERENCES

Allais, M. (1953). Le comportement de l'homme rationnel devant le risque: Critique des postulats et axiomes de l'école americaine. *Econometrica, 21,* 503-546.

Anderson, N. H., & Shanteau, J. C. (1970). Information integration in risky decision making. *Journal of Experimental Psychology, 84,* 441-451.

Arrow, K. J. (1951). Alternative approaches to the theory of choice in risk-taking situations. *Econometrica, 19,* 404-437.

Aschenbrenner, K. M. (1978). Single-peaked risk preferences and their dependability on the gambles' presentation mode. *Journal of Experimental Psychology: Human Perception and Performance, 4,* 513-520.

Beach, L. R. (1983). Muddling through: A response to Yates and Goldstein. *Organizational Behavior and Human Performance, 31,* 47-53.

Beach, L. R., & Mitchell, T. R. (1978). A contingency model for the selection of decision strategies. *Academy of Management Review, 3,* 439-449.

Bell, D. E., Keeney, R. L., & Raiffa, H. (Eds.). (1977). *Conflicting objectives in decisions.* Chichester, England: Wiley.

Ben Zur, H., & Breznitz, S. J. (1981). The effects of time pressure on risky choice behavior. *Acta Psychologica, 47,* 89-104.

Bernoulli, D. (1738). Specimen theoriae norae de mensura sortis. *Comentarii Academiae Scientiarum Imperiales Petropolitanae, 5,* 175-192. (Translated by L. Sommer in *Econometrica,* 1954, *22,* 23-26)

Broadbent, D. E. (1977). Levels, hierarchies, and the locus of control. *Quarterly Journal of Experimental Psychology, 29*, 181–201.

Card, S. K., Moran, T. P., & Newell, A. (1980). Computer text editing: An information processing analysis of a routine cognitive skill. *Cognitive Psychology, 12*, 32–74.

Carpenter, P. A., & Just, M. A. (1975). Sentence comprehension: A psycholinguistic processing model of verification. *Psychological Review, 82*, 45–73.

Chase, W. (1978). Elementary information processes. In W. K. Estes (Ed.), *Handbook of learning and cognitive processes* (Vol. 5). Hillsdale, NJ: Erlbaum.

Coombs, C. H. (1975). Portfolio theory and the measurement of risk. In M. F. Kaplan & S. Schwartz (Eds.), *Human judgment and decision processes.* New York: Academic Press.

Coombs, C. H., & Lehner, P. E. (1981). Evaluation of two alternative models for a theory of risk: I. Are moments of distributions useful in assessing risk? *Journal of Experimental Psychology: Human Perception and Performance, 7*, 1110–1123.

Coombs, C. H., Bezembinder, T. C., & Goode, F. M. (1967). Testing expectation theories of decision making without measuring utility or subjective probability. *Journal of Mathematical Psychology, 4*, 72–103.

Coombs, C. H., Donnell, M. L., & Kirk, D. B. (1978). An experimental study of risky preferences in lotteries. *Journal of Experimental Psychology: Human Perception and Performance, 4*, 497–512.

Duda, R. O., & Shortliffe, E. H. (1983). Expert systems research. *Science, 220*, 261–268.

Edwards, W. (1955). The prediction of decisions among bets. *Journal of Experimental Psychology, 50*, 201–204.

Einhorn, H. J., & Hogarth, R. M. (1981). Behavioral decision theory: Processes of judgment and choice. *Annual Review of Psychology, 32*, 52–88.

Fishburn, P. C. (1965). Independence in utility theory with whole product sets. *Operations Research, 13*, 28–45.

Fishburn, P. C. (1982). Foundations of risk measurement. II. Effects of gains on risk. *Journal of Mathematical Psychology, 25*, 226–242.

Grether, D. M., & Plott, C. R. (1979). Economic theory of choice and the preference reversal phenomenon. *American Economic Review, 69*, 623–638.

Hershey, J. C., Kunreuther, H. C., & Schoemaker, P. J. H. (1982). Bias in assessment procedures for utility functions. *Management Science, 28*, 936–54.

Huber, G. P. (1980). *Managerial decision making.* Glenview, IL: Scott, Foresman.

Huber, O. (1980). The influence of some task variables on cognitive operations in an information-processing decision model. *Acta Psychologica, 45*, 187–196.

Johnson, E. (1979). *Deciding how to decide: The effort of making a decision.* Unpublished manuscript. University of Chicago.

Johnson, E., & Payne, J. W. (in press). Effort and accuracy in choice. *Management Science.*

Kahneman, D., & Tversky, A. (1979). Prospect theory: An analysis of decisions under risk. *Econometrica, 47*, 263–291.

Keen, P. G. W., & Scott-Morton, M. S. (1978). *Decision support systems: An organizational perspective.* Reading, MA: Addison-Wesley, 1978.

Keeney, R. L., & Raiffa, H. (1976). *Decisions with multiple objectives: Preferences and value tradeoffs.* New York: Wiley.

Klein, N. M. (1983). Utility and decision strategies: A second look at the rational decision maker. *Organizational Behavior and Human Performance, 31*, 1–25.

Kunreuther, H. (1976). Limited knowledge and insurance protection. *Public Policy, 24*, 227–61.

Libby, R., & Fishburn, P. C. (1977). Behavioral models of risk-taking in business decisions: A survey and evaluation. *Journal of Accounting Research, 15*, 272–292.

Lichtenstein, S., & Slovic, P. (1971). Reversals of preference between bids and choices in gambling decisions. *Journal of Experimental Psychology, 89*, 46–55.

Lichtenstein, S., & Slovic, P. (1973). Response-induced reversals of preference in gambling: An extended replication in Las Vegas. *Journal of Experimental Psychology, 101*, 16–20.

Lindman, H. R., & Lyons, J. (1978). Stimulus complexity and choice inconsistency among gambles. *Organizational Behavior and Human Performance, 21*, 146–159.

March, J. G. (1978). Bounded rationality, ambiguity, and the engineering of choice. *The Bell Journal of Economics, 9*, 587–608.

McNeil, B. J., Pauker, S. G., Sox, H. C., & Tversky, A. (1982). On the elicitation of preferences for alternative therapies. *New England Journal of Medicine, 306*, 1259–1262.

Montgomery, H., & Svenson, O. (1976). On decision rules and information processing strategies for choices among multiattribute alternatives. *Scandinavian Journal of Psychology, 17*, 283–291.

Newell, A., Harpy, production systems and human cognition (1980). In R. Cole (Ed.), *Perception and production of fluent speech*. Hillsdale, NJ: Erlbaum.

Newell, A., & Simon, H. A. (1972). *Human problem solving*. Englewood Cliffs, NJ: Prentice-Hall.

Olshavsky, R. W. (1979). Task complexity and contingent processing in decision making: A replication and extension. *Organizational Behavior and Human Performance, 24*, 300–316.

Payne, J. W. (1973). Alternative approaches to decision making under risk: Moments vs. risk dimensions. *Psychological Bulletin, 80*, 439–453.

Payne, J. W. (1975). Relation of perceived risk to preferences among gambles. *Journal of Experimental Psychology: Human Perception and Performance, 104*, 86–94.

Payne, J. W. (1976). Task complexity and contingent processing in decision making: An information search and protocol analysis. *Organizational Behavior and Human Performance, 16*, 366–387.

Payne, J. W. (1981). *Choice among complex gambles*. Unpublished report to Office of Naval Research.

Payne, J. W. (1982). Contingent decision behavior. *Psychological Bulletin, 92*, 382–402.

Payne, J. W., & Braunstein, M. L. (1971). Preferences among gambles with equal underlying distributions. *Journal of Experimental Psychology, 87*, 13–18.

Payne, J. W., & Braunstein, M. L. (1978). Risky choice: An examination of information acquisition behavior. *Memory & Cognition, 5*, 554–561.

Payne, J. W., Laughhunn, D. J., & Crum, R. (1980). Translation of gambles and aspiration level effects in risky choice behavior. *Management Science, 26*, 1039–1060.

Payne, J. W., Laughhunn, D. J., & Crum, R. (1981). Further tests of aspiration level effects in risky choice behavior. *Management Science, 27*, 953–958.

Payne, J. W., Laughhunn, D. J., & Crum, R. (1984). Multiattribute risky choice behavior: The editing of complex prospects. *Management Science, 30*, 1350–1361.

Pommerehne, W. W., Schneider, F., & Zweifel, P. (1982). Economic theory of choice and the preference reversal phenomenon: A reexamination. *American Economic Review, 72*, 569–574.

Ranyard, R. H. (1976). Elimination by aspects as a decision rule for risky choice. *Acta Psychologica, 40*, 299–310.

Reilly, R. J. (1982). Preference reversal: Further evidence and some suggested modifications in experimental design. *American Economic Review, 72*, 576–584.

Richard, S. F. (1975). Multivariate risk aversion, utility independence and separable utility functions. *Management Science, 22*, 12–21.

Rosen, L. D., & Rosenkoetter, P. (1976). An eye fixation analysis of choice and judgment with multiattribute stimuli. *Memory & Cognition, 4*, 747–752.

Russo, J. E. (1977). The value of unit price information. *Journal of Marketing Research, 14*, 193–201.

Russo, J. E., & Dosher, B. A. (1980). *Cognitive effort and strategy selection in binary choice*. Unpublished manuscript, University of Chicago.

Savage, L. J. (1954). *The foundations of statistics*. New York: Wiley.

Schoemaker, P. J. H. (1982). The expected utility model: Its variants, purposes, evidence and limitations. *Journal of Economic Literature, 20,* 529–563.

Simon, H. A. (1981). *The sciences of the artificial* (2nd ed.). Cambridge: Massachusetts Institute of Technology.

Slovic, P. (1967). The relative influence of probabilities and payoffs upon perceived risk. *Psychonomic Science, 9,* 223–224.

Slovic, P. (1972). *From Shakespeare to Simon: Speculation—and some evidence—about man's ability to process information. Oregon Institute Monograph,* 12(12).

Slovic, P. (1978). Judgment, choice and societal risk taking. In K. R. Hammond (Ed.), *Judgment and decision in public policy formation.* Boulder, CO: Westview Press.

Slovic, P., & Lichtenstein, S. (1968). Importance of variance preferences in gambling decisions. *Journal of Experimental Psychology, 78,* 646–654.

Slovic, P., Fischhoff, B., & Lichtenstein, S. (1977). Behvioral decision theory. *Annual Review of Psychology, 28,* 1–39.

Slovic, P., Fischhoff, B., & Lichtenstein, S. (1981). Informing the public about the risks from ionizing radiation. *Health Physics, 41,* 589–598.

Slovic, P., Fischhoff, B., & Lichtenstein, S. (1982). Response mode, framing, and information processing effects in risk assessment. In R. Hogarth (Ed.), *New directions for methodology of social and behavioral science: The framing of questions and the consistency of response.* San Francisco: Jossey-Bass, 1982.

Starbuck, W. H. (1983). Computer simulation of human behavior. *Behavioral Science, 28,* 154–165.

Thorngate, W. (1980). Efficient decision heuristics. *Behavioral Science, 25,* 219–225.

Tversky, A. (1969). Intrasitivity of preferences. *Psychological Review, 76,* 31–48.

Tversky, A. (1972). Elimination by aspects: A theory of choice. *Psychological Review, 79,* 281–299.

Tversky, A., & Kahneman, D. (1981). The framing of decisions and the psychology of choice. *Science, 211,* 453–458.

von Neumann, J., & Morgenstern, O. (1947). *Theory of games and economic behavior* (2nd ed.). Princeton: Princeton University Press.

von Winterfeldt, D. (1980). Additivity and expected utility in risky mutiattribute preferences. *Journal of Mathematical Psychology, 21,* 66–82.

Williams, C. A. (1966). Attitudes toward speculative risks as an indicator of attitudes toward pure risks. *Journal of Risk and Insurance, 33,* 577–586.

Wright, P. (1974). The harassed decision maker: Time pressures, distraction, and the use of evidence. *Journal of Applied Psychology, 59,* 555–561.

Wright, P., & Weitz, B. (1977). Time horizon effects on product evaluation strategies. *Journal of Marketing Research, 14,* 429–443.

CHAPTER 2

The Framing of Decisions and the Psychology of Choice

Amos Tversky and Daniel Kahneman

Explanations and predictions of people's choices, in everyday life as well as in the social sciences, are often founded on the assumption of human rationality. The definition of rationality has been much debated, but there is general agreement that rational choices should satisfy some elementary requirements of consistency and coherence. In this chapter, we describe decision problems in which people systematically violate the requirements of consistency and coherence, and we trace these violations to the psychological principles that govern the perception of decision problems and the evaluation of options.

A decision problem is defined by the acts or options among which one must choose, the possible outcomes or consequences of these acts, and the contingencies or conditional probabilities that relate outcomes to acts. We use the term *decision frame* to refer to the decision maker's conception of the acts, outcomes, and contingencies associated with a particular choice. The frame that a decision maker adopts is controlled partly by the formulation of the problem and partly by the norms, habits, and personal characteristics of the decision maker.

It is often possible to frame a given decision problem in more than one way. Alternative frames for a decision problem may be compared to alternative perspectives on a visual scene. Veridical perception requires that the perceived relative height of two neighboring mountains, say, should not reverse with changes

This material is reprinted with permission from *Science*, 1981, *211*, 453–458. Copyright 1981 by the American Association for the Advancement of Science.

Amos Tversky • Department of Psychology, Stanford University, Stanford, California 94305. **Daniel Kahneman** • Department of Psychology, University of British Columbia, Vancouver, British Columbia V6T 1W5, Canada. This work was supported by the Office of Naval Research under contract N00014-79-C-0077 to Stanford University.

of the vantage point. Similarly, rational choice requires that the preference between options should not reverse with changes of frame. Because of imperfections of human perception and decision, however, changes of perspective often reverse the relative apparent size of objects and the relative desirability of options.

We have obtained systematic reversals of preference by variations in the framing of acts, contingencies, or outcomes. These effects have been observed in a variety of problems and in the choices of different groups of respondents. Here we present selected illustrations of preference reversals, with data obtained from students at Stanford University and at the University of British Columbia who answered brief questionnaires in a classroom setting. The total number of respondents for each problem is denoted by N, and the percentage who chose each option is indicated in parentheses.

Problem 1 ($N=152$). Imagine that the U.S. is preparing for the outbreak of an unusual Asian disease, which is expected to kill 600 people. Two alternative programs to combat the disease have been proposed. Assume that the exact scientific estimate of the consequences of the programs are as follows:

If Program A is adopted, 200 people will be saved (72%).

If Program B is adopted, there is a one-third probability that 600 people will be saved, and two-thirds probability that no people will be saved (28%).

Which of the two programs would you favor?

The majority choice in this problem is risk averse: The prospect of certainly saving 200 lives is more attractive than a risky prospect of equal expected value, that is, a one-in-three chance of saving 600 lives.

A second group of respondents was given the cover story of Problem 1 with a different formulation of the alternative programs, as follows:

Problem 2 ($N=155$). If program C is adopted, 400 people will die (22%).

If Program D is adopted, there is a one-third probability that nobody will die, and two-thirds probability that 600 people will die (78%).

Which of the two programs would you favor?

The majority choice in Problem 2 is risk taking: The certain death of 400 people is less acceptable than the two-in-three chance that 600 will die. The preferences in Problems 1 and 2 illustrate a common pattern: Choices involving gains are often risk averse, and choices involving losses are often risk taking. However, it is easy to see that the two problems are effectively identical. The only difference between them is that the outcomes are described in Problem 1 by the number of lives saved and in Problem 2 by the number of lives lost. The change is accompanied by a pronounced shift from risk aversion to risk taking. We have observed this reversal in several groups of respondents, including university faculty and physicians. Inconsistent responses to Problems 1 and 2 arise from the conjunction of a framing effect with contradictory attitudes toward risks involving gains and losses. We turn now to an analysis of these attitudes.

THE EVALUATION OF PROSPECTS

The major theory of decision making under risk is the expected utility model. This model is based on a set of axioms, for example, transitivity of preferences, which provide criteria for the rationality of choices. The choices of an individual who conforms to the axioms can be described in terms of the utilities of various outcomes for that individual. The utility of a risky prospect is equal to the expected utility of its outcomes, obtained by weighting the utility of each possible outcome by its probability. When faced with a choice, a rational decision maker will prefer the prospect that offers the highest expected utility (Fishburn, 1970; Raiffa, 1968; Savage, 1954; von Neumann & Morgenstern, 1947).

As will be illustrated later, people exhibit patterns of preference that appear incompatible with expected utility theory. We have presented elsewhere (Kahneman & Tversky, 1979) a descriptive model, called *prospect theory*, which modifies expected utility theory so as to accommodate these observations. We distinguish two phases in the choice process: an initial phase in which acts, outcomes, and contingencies are framed, and a subsequent phase of evaluation. (The framing phase includes various editing operations that are applied to simplify prospects; for example, by combining events or outcomes or by discarding negligible components.) For simplicity, we restrict the formal treatment of the theory to choices involving stated numerical probabilities and quantitative outcomes, such as money, time, or number of lives.

Consider a prospect that yields outcome x with probability p, outcome y with probability q, and the status quo with probability $1-p-q$. According to prospect theory, there are values $v(\, . \,)$ associated with outcomes, and decision weights $\pi(.)$ associated with probabilities, such that the overall value of the prospect equals $\pi(p) \, v(x) + \pi(q) \, v(y)$. A slightly different equation should be applied if all outcomes of a prospect are on the same side of the zero point. (Specifically, if $p+q=1$ and either $x>y>0$ or $x<y<0$, the equation is replaced by $v(y)+\pi(p)[v(x)-v(y)]$, so that decision weights are not applied to sure outcomes.)

In prospect theory, outcomes are expressed as positive or negative deviations (gains or losses) from a neutral reference outcome, which is assigned a value of zero. Although subjective values differ among individuals and attributes, we propose that the value function is commonly S-shaped, concave above the reference point and convex below it, as illustrated in Figure 1. For example, the difference in subjective value between gains of $10 and $20 is greater than the subjective difference between gains of $110 and $120. The same relation between value differences holds for the corresponding losses. Another property of the value function is that the response to losses is more extreme than the response to gains. The displeasure associated with losing a sum of money is generally greater than the pleasure associated with winning the same amount, as is reflected in people's reluctance to accept fair bets on a toss of a coin. Several studies of decision (Eraker & Sox, 1981; Fishburn & Kochenberger, 1979; Kahneman & Tversky, 1979; Laughhunn, Payne, & Crum, 1980; Payne, Laughhunn, & Crum, 1980) and judgment (Galanter & Pliner, 1974) have confirmed these properties of the value function. The extension of the proposed value function to multiattribute options, with or without risk, deserves careful analysis. In particular, indifference curves between dimensions of loss may be concave upward, even when the value functions for the separate losses are both convex, because of marked subadditivity between dimensions.

The second major departure of prospect theory from the expected utility model involves the treatment of probabilities. In expected utility theory, the utility of an uncertain outcome is weighted by its probability; in prospect theory, the value of an uncertain outcome is multiplied by a decision weight $\pi(p)$, which is a monotonic function of p but is not a probability. The weighting function π has the following properties. First, impossible events are discarded, that is, $\pi(0)=0$, and the scale is normalized so that $\pi(1)=1$, but the function is not well behaved near the endpoints. Second, for low probabilities $\pi(p)>p$, but $\pi(p)+\pi(1-p)\leq 1$. Thus, low probabilities are overweighted, moderate and high probabilities are underweighted, and the latter effect is more pronounced than the former. Third, $\pi(pq)/\pi(p)<\pi(pqr)/\pi(pr)$ for all $0<p,q,r\leq 1$. That is, for any fixed probability ratio q, the ratio of decision weights is closer to unity when the probabilities are low than when they are high, for example, $\pi(.1)/\pi(.2)>\pi(.4)/\pi(.8)$. A hypothetical weighting function that satisfies these properties is shown in Figure 2. The major qualitative properties of decision weights can be extended to cases in which the probabilities of outcomes are subjectively assessed rather than explicitly given. In these situations, however, decision weights may also be affected by other characteristics of an event, such as ambiguity or vagueness (Ellsberg, 1961; Fellner, 1965).

Prospect theory and the scales illustrated in Figures 1, and 2 should be viewed as an approximate, incomplete, and simplified description of the evaluation of risky prospects. Although the properties of v and π summarize a com-

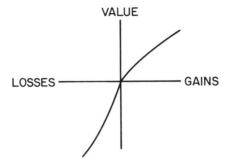

Figure 1. A hypothetical value function.

mon pattern of choice, they are not universal; the preferences of some individuals are not well described by an S-shaped value function and a consistent set of decision weights. The simultaneous measurement of values and decision weights involves serious experimental and statistical difficulties. The scaling of v and π by pair comparisons requires a large number of observations. The procedure of pricing gambles is more convenient for scaling purposes, but it is subject to a severe anchoring bias: The ordering of gambles by their cash equivalents diverges systematically from the preference order observed in direct comparisons (Lichtenstein & Slovic, 1971).

If π and v were linear throughout, the preference order between options would be independent of the framing of acts, outcomes, or contingencies. Because of the characteristic nonlinearities of π and v, however, different frames can lead to different choices. The next three sections describe reversals of preference caused by variations in the framing of acts, contingencies, and outcomes.

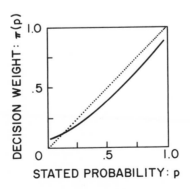

Figure 2. A hypothetical weighting function.

THE FRAMING OF ACTS

Problem 3(N = 150). Imagine that you face the following pair of concurrent decisions. First examine both decisions, then indicate the options you prefer.

Decision 1. Choose between (A) a sure gain of $240 (84%) and (B) a 25% chance to gain $1,000, and a 75% chance to gain nothing (16%).

Decision 2. Choose between (C) a sure loss of $750 (13%) and (D) a 75% chance to lose $1,000, and a 25% chance to lose nothing (87%).

The majority choice in Decision 1 is risk averse: A riskless prospect is preferred to a risky prospect of equal or greater expected value. In contrast, the majority choice in Decision 2 is risk taking: A risky prospect is preferred to a riskless prospect of equal expected value. This pattern of risk aversion in choices involving gains and risk seeking in choices involving losses is attributable to the properties of v and π. Because the value function is S-shaped, the value associated with a gain of $240 is greater than 24% of the value associated with a gain of $1,000, and the (negative) value associated with a loss of $750 is smaller than 75% of the value associated with a loss of $1,000. Thus, the shape of the value function contributes to risk aversion in Decision 1 and to risk seeking in Decision 2. Moreover, the underweighting of moderate and high probabilities contributes to the relative attractiveness of the sure gain in Decision 1 and to the relative aversiveness of the sure loss in Decision 2. The same analysis applies to Problems 1 and 2.

Because Decisions 1 and 2 were presented together, the respondents had in effect to choose one prospect from the set: A and C, B and C, A and D, B and D. The most common pattern (A and D) was chosen by 73% of respondents, whereas the least popular pattern (B and C) was chosen by only 3% of respondents. However, the combination of B and C is definitely superior to the combination A and D, as is readily seen in Problem 4.

Problem 4 (N = 86). Choose between (A and D) a 25% chance to win $240 and a 75% chance to lose $760 (0%) and (B and C) a 25% chance to win $250 and a 75% chance to lose $750 (100%).

When the prospects were combined and the dominance of the second option became obvious, all respondents chose the superior option. The popularity of the inferior option in Problem 3 implies that this problem was framed as a pair of separate choices. The respondents apparently failed to entertain the possibility that the conjunction of two seemingly reasonable choices could lead to an untenable result.

The violations of dominance observed in Problem 3 do not disappear in the presence of monetary incentives. A different group of respondents who answered a modified version of Problem 3, with real payoffs, produced a similar pattern of choices. A new group of respondents ($N=126$) was presented with a modified version of Problem 3, in which the outcomes were reduced by a factor of 50. The participants were informed that the gambles would actually be played by tossing a pair of fair coins and that 1 participant in 10 would be selected at random to play the gambles of his or her choice. To ensure a positive return for the entire set, a third decision, yielding only positive outcomes, was added. These payoff conditions did not alter the pattern of preferences observed in the hypothetical problem: 67% of respondents chose Prospect A, and 86% chose Prospect D. The dominated combination of A and D was chosen by 60% of respondents, and only 6% favored the dominant combination of B and C. Other authors have also reported that violations of the rules of rational choice, originally observed in hypothetical questions, were not eliminated by payoffs (Grether, 1980; Grether & Plott, 1979; Lichtenstein & Slovic, 1973; Lieblich & Lieblich, 1969).

We suspect that many concurrent decisions in the real world are framed independently, and that the preference order would often be reversed if the decisions were combined. The respondents in Problem 3 failed to combine options, although the integration was relatively simple and was encouraged by instructions. (For other demonstrations of a reluctance to integrate concurrent options, see Payne & Braunstein, 1971; Slovic & Lichtenstein, 1968). The complexity of practical problems of concurrent decisions, such as portfolio selection, would prevent people from integrating options without computational aids, even if they were inclined to do so.

THE FRAMING OF CONTINGENCIES

The next trio of problems illustrates the framing of contingencies. Each problem was presented to a different group of respondents. Each group was told that 1 participant in 10, preselected at random, would actually be playing for money. Chance events were realized in the respondents' presence, by drawing a single ball from a bag containing a known proportion of balls of the winning color, and the winners were paid immediately.

Problem 5 ($N=77$). Which of the following options do you prefer: (A) a sure win of $30 (78%) or (B) an 80% chance to win $45 (22%)?

Problem 6 ($N=85$). Consider the following two-stage game. In the first stage, there is a 75% chance to end the game without winning anything, and a 25% chance to move into the second stage. If you reach the second stage, you have a choice between (C) a sure win of $30 (74%) and (D) and 80% chance to win $45 (26%).

Your choice must be made before the game starts, that is, before the outcome of the first stage is known. Please indicate the option you prefer.

Problem 7 (N=81). Which of the following options do you prefer: (E) a 25% chance to win $30 (42%) or (F) a 20% chance to win $45 (58%)?

Let us examine the structure of these problems. First, note that Problems 6 and 7 are identical in terms of probabilities and outcomes, because Prospect C offers a .25 chance to win $30 and Prospect D offers a probability of .25×.80=.20 to win $45. Consistency therefore requires that the same choice be made in Problems 6 and 7. Second, note that Problem 6 differs from Problem 5 only by the introduction of a preliminary stage. If the second stage of the game is reached, then Problem 6 reduces to Problem 5; if the game ends at the first stage, the decision does not affect the outcome. Hence, there seems to be no reason to make a different choice in Problems 5 and 6. By this logical analysis, Problem 6 is equivalent to Problem 7 on the one hand and Problem 5 on the other. The participants, however, responded similarly to Problems 5 and 6 but differently to Problem 7. This pattern of responses exhibits two phenomena of choice—the certainty effect and the pseudocertainty effect.

The contrast between Problems 5 and 7 illustrates a phenomenon discovered by Allais (1953), which we have labeled *the certainty effect:* A reduction of the probability of an outcome by a constant factor has more impact when the outcome was initially certain than when it was merely probable (Allais, 1953; MacCrimmon & Larsson, 1979). Prospect theory attributes this effect to the properties of π. It is easy to verify by applying the equation of prospect theory to Problems 5 and 7, that people for whom the value ratio $v(30)/v(45)$ lies between the weight ratios $\pi(.20)/\pi(.25)$ and $\pi(.80)/\pi(1.0)$ will prefer A to B and F to E, contrary to expected utility theory. Prospect theory does not predict a reversal of preference for every individual in Problems 5 and 7. It only requires that an individual who has no preference between A and B prefer F to E. For group data, the theory predicts the observed directional shift of preference between the two problems.

The first stage of Problem 6 yields the same outcome (no gain) for both acts. Consequently, we propose, people evaluate the options conditionally, as if the second stage had been reached. In this framing, of course, Problem 6 reduces to Problem 5. More generally, we suggest that a decision problem is evaluated conditionally when there is a state in which all acts yield the same outcome, such as failing to reach the second stage of the game in Problem 6, and the stated probabilities of other outcomes are conditional on the nonoccurrence of this state.

The striking discrepancy between the responses to Problems 6 and 7, which are identical in outcomes and probabilities, could be described as a pseudocertainty effect. The prospect yielding $30 is relatively more attractive in Problem 6 than in Problem 7, as if it had the advantage of certainty. The sense of certainty associated with Option C is illusory, however, because the gain is in fact contingent on reaching the second stage of the game.

Another group of respondents ($N=205$) was presented with all three problems, in different orders, without monetary payoffs. The joint frequency distribution of choices in Problems 5, 6, and 7 was as follows: ACE, 22; ACF, 65; ADE, 4; ADF, 20; BCE, 7; BCF, 18; BDE, 17; BDF, 52. These data confirm in a within-subject design the analysis of conditional evaluation proposed in the text. More than 75% of respondents made compatible choices (AC or BD) in Problems 5 and 6, and less than half made compatible choices in Problems 6 and 7 (CE or DF) or 5 and 7 (AE or BF). The elimination of payoffs in these questions reduced risk aversion but did not substantially alter the effects of certainty and pseudocertainty.

We have observed the certainty effect in several sets of problems, with outcomes ranging from vacation trips to the loss of human lives. In the negative domain, certainty exaggerates the aversiveness of losses that are certain relative to losses that are merely probable. In a question dealing with the response to an epidemic, for example, most respondents found a sure loss of 75 lives more aversive than an 80% chance to lose 100 lives but preferred a 10% chance to lose 75 lives to an 8% chance to lose 100 lives, contrary to expected utility theory.

We also obtained the pseudocertainty effect in several studies where the description of the decision problems favored conditional evaluation. Pseudocertainty can be induced either by a sequential formulation, as in Problem 6, or by the introduction of causal contingencies. In another version of the epidemic problem, for instance, respondents were told that risk to life existed only in the event (probability .10) that the disease was carried by a particular virus. Two alternative programs were said to yield a sure loss of 75 lives or an 80% chance to lose 100 lives if the critical virus was involved, and no loss of life in the event (probability .90) that the disease was carried by another virus. In effect, the respondents were asked to choose between a 10% chance of losing 75 lives and an 8% chance of losing 100 lives, but their preferences were the same as when the choice was between a sure loss of 75 lives and an 80% chance of losing 100 lives. A conditional framing was evidently adopted in which the contingency of the noncritical virus was eliminated, giving rise to a pseudocertainty effect. The certainty effect reveals attitudes toward risk that are inconsistent with the axioms of rational choice, whereas the pseudocertainty effect violates the more fundamental requirement that preferences should be independent of problem description.

Many significant decisions concern actions that reduce or eliminate the probability of a hazard, at some cost. The shape of π in the range of low probabilities suggests that a protective action that reduces the probability of a harm from 1% to zero, say, will be valued more highly than an action that reduces the probability of the same harm from 2% to 1%. Indeed, probabilistic insurance, which reduces the probability of loss by half, is judged to be worth less than half the price of regular insurance that eliminates the risk altogether (Kahneman & Tversky, 1979).

It is often possible to frame protective action in either conditional or unconditional form. For example, an insurance policy that covers fire but not flood could be evaluated either as full protection against the specific risk of fire or as a reduction in the overall probability of property loss. The preceding analysis suggests that insurance should appear more attractive when it is presented as the elimination of risk than when it is described as a reduction of risk. As Slovic, Fischhoff, and Lichtenstein have reported, a hypothetical vaccine that reduces the probability of contracting a disease from .20 to .10 is less attractive if it is described as effective in half the cases than if it is presented as fully effective against one of two (exclusive and equiprobable) virus strains that produce identical symptoms. In accord with the present analysis of pseudocertainty, the respondents valued full protection against an identified virus more than probabilistic protection against the disease.

The preceding discussion highlights the sharp contrast between lay responses to the reduction and the elimination of risk. Because no form of protective action can cover all risks to human welfare, all insurance is essentially probabilistic; it reduces but does not eliminate risk. The probabilistic nature of insurance is commonly masked by formulations that emphasize the completeness of protection against identified harms, but the sense of security that such formulations provide is an illusion of conditional framing. It appears that insurance is bought as protection against worry, not only against risk, and that worry can be manipulated by the labeling of outcomes and by the framing of contingencies. It is not easy to determine whether people value the elimination of risk too much or the reduction of risk too little. The contrasting attitudes to the two forms of protective action, however, are difficult to justify on normative grounds. (For further discussion of rationality in protective action, see Kunreuther, 1978.)

THE FRAMING OF OUTCOMES

Outcomes are commonly perceived as positive or negative in relation to a reference outcome that is judged neutral. Variations of the reference point can therefore determine whether a given outcome is evaluated as a gain or as a loss. Because the value function is generally concave for gains, convex for losses, and steeper for losses than for gains, shifts of reference can change the value difference between outcomes and thereby reverse the preference order between options (Eraker & Sox, 1981; Fishburn & Kochenberger, 1979; Laughhunn, Payne, & Crum, 1980; Payne, Laughhunn, & Crum, 1980). Problems 1 and 2 illustrate a preference reversal induced by a shift of reference that transformed gains into losses.

For another example, consider a person who has spent an afternoon at the racetrack, has already lost $140, and is considering a $10 bet on a 15:1 long shot in the last race. This decision can be framed in two ways, which correspond to two natural reference points. If the status quo is the reference point, the outcomes of the bet are framed as a gain of $140 and a loss of $10. However, it may be more natural to view the present state as a loss of $140 for the betting day and accordingly frame the last bet as a chance to return to the reference point or to increase the loss to $150. Prospect theory implies that the latter frame will produce more risk seeking than the former. Hence, people who do not adjust their reference point as they lose are expected to take bets that they would normally find unacceptable. This analysis is supported by the observation that bets on long shots are most popular on the last race of the day (McGlothlin, 1956).

Because the value function is steeper for losses than for gains, a difference between options will loom larger when it is framed as a disadvantage of one option rather than as an advantage of the other option. An interesting example of such an effect in a riskless context has been noted by Thaler (1980). In a debate on a proposal to pass to the consumer some of the costs associated with the processing of credit card purchases, representatives of the credit card industry requested that the price difference be labeled *a cash discount* rather than a *credit card surcharge*. The two labels induce different reference points by implicitly designating as normal reference the higher or the lower of the two prices. Because losses loom larger than gains, consumers are less willing to accept a surcharge than to forego a discount. A similar effect has been observed in experimental studies of insurance: The proportion of respondents who preferred a sure loss to a larger probable loss was significantly greater when the former was called an insurance premium (Fischhoff, Slovic, & Lichtenstein, 1980; Hershey & Schoemaker, 1980).

These observations highlight the lability of reference outcomes, as well as their role in decision making. In the examples discussed so far, the neutral reference point was identified by the labeling of outcomes. A diversity of factors determine the reference outcome in everyday life. The reference outcome is usually a state to which one has adapted; it is sometimes set by social norms and expectations; it sometimes corresponds to a level of aspiration, which may or may not be realistic.

We have dealt so far with elementary outcomes, such as gains or losses in a single attribute. In many situations, however, an action gives rise to a compound outcome, which joins a series of changes in a single attribute, such as a sequence of monetary gains and losses or a set of concurrent changes in several attributes. To describe the framing and evaluation of compound outcomes, we use the notion of a psychological account, defined as an outcome frame that specifies both the set of elementary outcomes that are evaluated jointly and the manner in which they are combined and a reference outcome that is considered neutral or normal. In the account that is set up for the purchase of a car, for example, the cost of the purchase is not treated as a loss nor is the car viewed as a gift. Rather, the transaction as a whole is evaluated as positive, negative, or neutral, depending on such factors as the performance of the car and the price of similar cars in the market. A closely related treatment has been offered by Thaler (1980).

We propose that people generally evaluate acts in terms of a minimal account, which includes only the direct consequences of the act. The minimal account associated with the decision to accept a gamble, for example, includes the money won or lost in that gamble and excludes other assets or the outcome of previous gambles. People commonly adopt minimal accounts because this mode of framing simplifies evaluation and reduces cognitive strain, reflects the intuition that consequences should be causally linked to acts, and matches the properties of hedonic experience, which is more sensitive to desirable and undesirable changes than to steady states.

There are situations, however, in which the outcomes of an act affect the balance in an account that was previously set up by a related act. In these cases, the decision at hand may be evaluated in terms of a more inclusive account, as in the case of the bettor who views the last race in the context of earlier losses. More generally, a sunk-cost effect arises when a decision is referred to an existing account in which the current balance is negative. Because of the nonlinearities of the evaluation process, the minimal account and a more inclusive one often lead to different choices.

Problems 8 and 9 illustrate another class of situations in which an existing account affects a decision:

Problem 8 (N = 183). Imagine that you have decided to see a play where admission is $10 per ticket. As you enter the theater, you discover that you have lost a $10 bill.

Would you still pay $10 for a ticket for the play?
Yes (88%)   No (12%)

Problem 9 (N = 200). Imagine that you have decided to see a play and paid the admission price of $10 per ticket. As you enter the theater, you discover that you have lost the ticket. The seat was not marked, and the ticket cannot be recovered.

Would you pay $10 for another ticket?
Yes (46%)   No (54%)

The marked difference between the responses to Problems 8 and 9 is an effect of psychological accounting. We propose that the purchase of a new ticket in Problem 9 is entered in the account that was set up by the purchase of the original ticket. In terms of this account, the expense required to see the show is $20, a cost that many of our respondents apparently found excessive. In Problem 8, however, the loss of $10 is not linked specifically to the ticket purchase, and its effect on the decision is accordingly slight.

The following problem, based on examples by Savage (1954, p. 103) and Thaler (1980), further illustrates the effect of embedding an option in different accounts. Two versions of this problem were presented to different groups of subjects. One group ($N=93$) was given the values that appear in parentheses, and the other group ($N=88$) was given the values shown in brackets.

Problem 10. Imagine that you are about to purchase a jacket for ($125) [$15], and a calculator for ($15) [$125]. The calculator salesman informs you that the calculator you wish to buy is on sale for ($10) [$120] at the other branch of the store, located 20 minutes drive away. Would you make the trip to the other store?

The responses to the two versions of Problem 10 were markedly different: 68% of the respondents were willing to make an extra trip to save $5 on a $15 calculator; only 29% were willing to exert the same effort when the price of the calculator was $125. Evidently, the respondents do not frame Problem 10 in the minimal account, which involves only a benefit of $5 and a cost of some inconvenience. Instead, they evaluate the potential savings in a more inclusive account, which includes the purchase of the calculator but not the purchase of the jacket. By the curvature of v, a discount of $5 has a greater impact when the price of the calculator is low than when it is high.

A closely related observation has been reported by Pratt, Wise, and Zeckhauser (1979), who found that the variability of the prices at which a given product is sold by different stores is roughly proportional to the mean price of that product. The same pattern was observed for both frequently and infrequently purchased items. Overall, a ratio of 2:1 in the mean price of two products is associated with a ratio of 1.86:1 in the standard deviation of the respective quoted prices. If the effort that consumers exert to save each dollar on a purchase, for instance by a phone call, was independent of price, the dispersion of quoted prices should be about the same for all products. In contrast, the data of Pratt, Wise, and Zeckhauser (1979) are consistent with the hypothesis that consumers hardly exert more effort to save $15 on a $150 purchase than to save $5 on a $50 dollar purchase (Thaler, 1980). Many readers will recognize the temporary devaluation of money that facilitates extra spending and reduces the significance of small discounts in the context of a large expenditure, such as buying a house or a car. This paradoxical variation in the value of money is incompatible with the standard analysis of consumer behavior.

DISCUSSION

In this chapter, we have presented a series of demonstrations in which seemingly inconsequential changes in the formulation of choice problems caused significant shifts of preference. The inconsistencies were traced to the interaction of two sets of factors: variations in the framing of acts, contingencies, and outcomes, and the characteristic nonlinearities of values and decision weights. The demonstrated effects are large and systematic, although by no means universal. They occur when the outcomes concern the loss of human lives as well as in choices about money; they are not restricted to hypothetical questions and are not eliminated by monetary incentives.

Earlier, we compared the dependence of preferences on frames to the dependence of perceptual appearance on perspective. If while traveling in a mountain range you notice that the apparent relative height of mountain peaks varies with your vantage point, you will conclude that some impressions of relative height must be erroneous, even when you have no access to the correct answer. Similarly, one may discover that the relative attractiveness of options varies when the same decision problem is framed in different ways. Such a discovery will normally lead the decision maker to reconsider the original preferences, even when there is no simple way to resolve the inconsistency. The susceptibility to perspective effects is of special concern in the domain of decision making because of the absence of objective standards, such as the true height of mountains.

The metaphor of changing perspective can be applied to other phenomena of choice, in addition to the framing effects with which we have been concerned here (Fischhoff, Slovic, & Lichtenstein, 1980). The problem of self-control is naturally construed in these terms. The story of Ulysses' request to be bound to the mast of the ship in anticipation of the irresistible temptation of the Sirens' call is often used as a paradigm case (Ainslie, 1975; Elster, 1979; Strotz, 1955–1956; Thaler & Shifrin, 1981). In this example of precommitment, and action taken in the present renders inoperative an anticipated future preference. An unusual feature of the problem of intertemporal conflict is that the agent who views a problem from a particular temporal perspective is also aware of the conflicting views that future perspectives will offer. In most other situations, decision makers are not normally aware of the potential effects of different decision frames on their preferences.

The perspective metaphor highlights four aspects of the psychology of choice. Individuals who face a decision problem and have a definite preference, first, might have a different preference in a different framing of the same problem; second, are normally unaware of alternative frames and of their potential effects on the relative attractiveness of options; third, would wish their preferences to be independent of frame; but, fourth, are often uncertain how to resolve detected inconsistencies (Slovic & Tversky, 1974). In some cases (such as Problems 3 and 4 and perhaps Problems 8 and 9) the advantage of one frame becomes evident once the competing frames are compared, but in other cases (Problems 1 and 2 and Problems 6 and 7) it is not obvious which preferences should be abandoned.

These observations do not imply that preference reversals or other errors of choice or judgment are necessarily irrational (Einhorn & Hogarth, 1981; Nisbett & Ross, 1980; Slovic, Fischhoff, & Lichtenstein, 1977; Tversky & Kahneman, 1974). Like other intellectual limitations, discussed by Simon (1955, 1956) under the heading of "bounded rationality," the practice of acting on the most readily available frame can sometimes be justified by reference to the mental effort required to explore alternative frames and avoid potential inconsistencies. However, we propose that the details of the phenomena described in this chapter are better explained by prospect theory and by an analysis of framing than by *ad hoc* appeals to the notion of cost of thinking.

The work described here has been concerned primarily with the descriptive question of how decisions are made, but the psychology of choice is also relevant to the normative question of how decisions ought to be made. In order to avoid the difficult problem of justifying values, the modern theory of rational choice has adopted the coherence of specific preferences as the sole criterion of rationality. This approach enjoins the decision maker to resolve inconsistencies but offers no guidance on how to do so. It implicitly assumes that the decision maker who carefully answers the question "What do I really want?" will eventually achieve coherent preferences. However, the susceptibility of preferences to variations of framing raises doubt about the feasibility and adequacy of the coherence criterion.

Consistency is only one aspect of the lay notion of rational behavior. As noted by March (1978), the common conception of rationality also requires that preferences or utilities for particular outcomes should be predictive of the experiences of satisfaction or displeasure associated with their occurrence. Thus, a man could be judged irrational either because his preferences are contradictory or because his desires and aversions do not reflect his pleasures and pains. The predictive criterion of rationality can be applied to resolve inconsistent preferences and to improve the quality of decisions. A predictive orientation encourages the decision maker to focus on future experience and to ask "What will I feel then?" rather than "What do I want now?" The former question, when answered with care, can be the more useful guide in difficult decisions. In particular, predictive considerations may be applied to select the decision frame that best represents the hedonic experience of outcomes.

Further complexities arise in the normative analysis because the framing of an action sometimes affects the actual experience of its outcomes. For example, framing outcomes in terms of overall wealth or welfare rather than in terms of specific gains and losses may attenuate one's emotional response to an occasional loss. Similarly, the experience of a change for the worse may vary if the change is framed as an uncompensated loss or as a cost incurred to achieve some benefit. The framing of acts and outcomes can also reflect the acceptance or rejection of responsibility for particular consequences, and the deliberate manipulation of framing is commonly used as an instrument of self-control (Ainslie, 1975; Elster, 1979; Strotz, 1955–1956; Thaler & Shifrin, 1981). When framing influences the experience of consequences, the adoption of a decision frame is an ethically significant act.

REFERENCES

Ainslie, G. (1975). Specious reward: A behavioral theory of impulsiveness and impulse control. *Psychological Bulletin, 82*, 463–496.

Allais, M. (1953). Le comportement de l'homme devant le risque: Critique des postulats et axiomes de l'école américaine. *Econometrica, 21*, 504–546.

Einhorn, H. J., & Hogarth, R. M. (1981). Behavioral decision theory: Processes of judgment and choice. *Annual Review of Psychology, 32*, 53–88.

Ellsberg, D. (1961). Risk, ambiguity, and the savage axioms. *Quarterly Journal of Economics, 75*, 643–669.

Elster, J. (1979). *Ulysses and the sirens: Studies in rationality and irrationality.* London: Cambridge University Press.

Eraker, S. A., & Sox, H. C., (1981). Assessment of patients' preferences for therapeutic outcomes. *Medical Decision Making, 1*, 29–39.

Fellner, W. (1965). *Probability and profit: A study of economic behavior along Bayesian lines.* Homewood, IL: Irwin.

Fischhoff, B., Slovic, P., & Lichtenstein S. (1980). Knowing what you want: Measuring labile values. In T. Wallsten (Ed.), *Cognitive processes in choice and decision behavior.* Hillsdale, NJ: Erlbaum.

Fishburn, P. C. (1970). *Utility theory for decision making.* New York: Wiley.

Fishburn, P. C. & Kochenberger, G. A. (1979). Two-piece von Neumann-Morgenstern utility functions. *Decision Sciences, 10*, 503–518.

Galanter, E., & Pliner, P. (1974). Cross-modality matching of money against other continua. In H. R. Moskowitz & B. Scharf (Eds.), *Sensation and Measurement.* Dordrecht: Reidel.

Grether, D. M. (1980). Bayes rule as a descriptive model: The representativeness heuristic. *Quarterly Journal of Economics, 95*, 537–557.

Grether, D. M., & Plott, C. R. (1979.) Economic theory of choice and the preference reversal phenomenon. *American Economic Review, 69*, 623–638.

Hershey, J. C. & Schoemaker, P. J. H. (1980). Risk taking and problem context in the domain of losses: An expected-utility analysis. *Journal of Risk and Insurance, 47*, 111–132.

Kahneman, D., & Tversky, A. (1979). Prospect theory: An analysis of decision under risk. *Econometrica, 47,* 263-291.

Kunreuther, H. (1978). *Disaster insurance protection: Public policy lessons.* New York: Wiley.

Laughhunn, D. J., & Payne, J. W., & Crum, R. (1980). Managerial risk preferences for below-target returns. *Management Science, 26,* 1238-1249.

Lichtenstein, S., & Slovic, P. (1971). Reversals of preference between bids and choices in gambling decisions. *Journal of Experimental Psychology, 98,* 46-55.

Lichtenstein, S., & Slovic, P. (1973). Response-induced reversals of preference in gambling: An extended replication in Las Vegas. *Journal of Experimental Psychology, 101,* 16-20.

Lieblich, I., & Lieblich, A. (1969). Effects of different payoff matrices on arithmetical estimation tasks: An attempt to produce rationality. *Perceptual and Motor Skills, 29,* 467-473.

MacCrimmon, K. R., & Larsson, S. (1979). Utility theory: Axioms versus paradoxes. In M. Allais & O. Hagen (Eds), *Expected-utility hypotheses and the Allais paradox* (Vol. 21.) Dordrecht: Reidel.

March, J. G. (1978). Bounded rationality, ambiguity, and the engineering of choice. *Bell Journal of Economics, 9,* 587-608.

McGlothlin, W. H. (1956). Stability of choices among uncertain alternatives. *American Journal of Psychology, 69,* 604-615.

Nisbett, R. E., & Ross, L. (1980). *Human inference: Strategies and shortcomings of social judgment.* Englewood Cliffs, NJ: Prentice-Hall.

Payne, J. W., & Braunstein, M. L. (1971). Preferences among gambles with equal underlying distributions. *Journal of Experimental Psychology, 87,* 13-18.

Payne, J. W., & Laughhunn, D. J., & Crum, R. (1980). Translation of gambles and aspiration-level effects in risky choice behavior. *Management Science, 26,* 1039-1060.

Pratt, J. W., & Wise, D., & Zeckhauser, R. (1979). Price differences in almost competitive markets. *Quarterly Journal of Economics, 93,* 189-211.

Raiffa, H. (1968). *Decision analysis: Introductory lectures on choices under uncertainty.* Reading, MA: Addison-Wesley.

Savage, L. J. (1954). *The foundations of statistics.* New York: Wiley.

Simon, H. A. (1955). A behavioral model of rational choice. *Quarterly Journal of Economics, 69,* 99-118.

Simon, H. A. (1956). Rational choice and the structure of the environment. *Psychological Review, 63,* 129-138.

Slovic, P., & Lichtenstein, S. (1968). Importance of variance preferences in gambling and decisions. *Journal of Experimental Psychology, 78,* 646-654.

Slovic, P., & Tversky, A. (1974). Who accepts Savage's axiom? *Behavioral Science, 14,* 368-373.

Slovic, P., & Fischhoff, B., & Lichtenstein, S. (1977). Behavioral decision theory. *Annual Review of Psychology, 28,* 1-39.

Strotz, R., (1955-1956). Myopia and inconsistency in dynamic utility maximization. *Review of Economic Studies, 23,* 165-180.

Thaler, R. (1980). Toward a positive theory of consumer choice. *Journal of Economic Behavior and Organization, 1,* 39-60.

Thaler, R., & Shifrin, H. M. (1981). An economic theory of self-control. *Journal of Political Economy, 89,* 392-406.

Tversky, A., & Kahneman, D. (1974). Judgment under uncertainty: Heuristics and biases. *Science, 185,* 1124-1131.

von Neumann, J., & Morgenstern, O. (1947). *Theory of games and economic behavior.* Princeton: Princeton University Press.

CHAPTER 3

Decisional Variance

George Wright

INTRODUCTION

This chapter presents a selective review of studies of individual and situational influences on decision making that have been reported in the psychological and management journals. Various decision situations have been studied, various correlates of decision making have been obtained, and various decision styles have been proposed. The major difference between studies has been the relative emphasis on the decision maker or the decision situation as the main source of behavioral variation. Such research has implications for the design of management decision support systems.

Cognitive-style research, which has emphasized the decision maker, and contingent decision research, which has emphasized the decision situation, are viewed as alternative frameworks for research on decisional variance. The results of research conducted within each framework tend to be congruent with that framework because the methodologies of the frameworks tend to initiate fairly distinct lines of research and theory.

After outlining research and theory within the two frameworks, the last section of this chapter presents an overview of a methodology, taken from personality psychology, where similar issues have been of major concern. Adoption of this methodology may serve to moderate the two distinct approaches to decisional variance. In personality psychology, three main theoretical positions describe the individual and his or her interaction with the environment. *Personologism* advocates that stable intraorganismic constants such as traits or cognitive

George Wright • Decision Analysis Group, Department of Psychology, City of London Polytechnic, London E1 7NT, England. Preparation of this chapter was supported by the British Economic and Social Research Council project grant C0023037.

styles are the main determinants of behavioral variation (e.g., Alker, 1971). *Situationism* emphasizes environmental (situational) factors as the main sources of behavioral variation (e.g., Mischel, 1968). *Interactionism*, a synthesis of personologism and situationism, implies that the interaction between these two factors is the main source of behavioral variance (e.g., Endler, 1975).

It is argued that the methodology of personality psychology could be usefully used in an attempt to resolve the cognitive style/contingent decision-making issue.

PERSONALITY AND DECISION MAKING

The research to be reviewed in this section has usually taken a "personality" measure, a single decision situation, and a sample of people and attempted to see if any relationship exists between personality and decision making. For instance, the literature on authoritarianism, conservatism, and intolerance of ambiguity assumes that people who are high scorers on scales measuring these concepts see the world in "black and white," or as Souief (1958) conceptualizes it, they make extreme judgments or responses. As Bochner (1965) notes, the primary characteristics of an individual who is intolerant of ambiguity are "premature closure" and "need for certainty." An item from Budner's (1962) Tolerance–Intolerance of Ambiguity scale illustrates this; a negative response to "people who insist on a yes or no answer just don't know how complicated things really are" (p. 43) characterizes a person intolerant of ambiguity. Frenkel-Brunswik, writing in *The Authoritarian Personality* (Adorno, Frenkel-Brunswick, Levinson, & Sanford, 1950, p. 480), about high F-scale scorers, notes that "a simple, firm, often stereotypical cognitive structure is required. There is no place for ambivalence or ambiguities. Every attempt is made to eliminate them." Rokeach, writing in his book *The Open and Closed Mind* (1960, p. 56), noted that there is "relatively little differentiation within the disbelief system" of the high D-scale-scoring person. Indeed, Ertel (1972) has developed a measure of dogmatism based on the content analysis of "quantifiers" in the publications of writers; for example, dogmatic writers would be expected to use quantifiers such as *always*, *never*, *nothing but*, *completely*, *must*, and the like, whereas nondogmatic writers would use quantifiers such as *often*, *rarely*, *greatly*, *considerably*, *can*, and so forth. However, he has not, as yet, linked the content analysis to D-scale scoring.

From these orthodox conceptualizations of the personality/cognitive measures, Wright and Phillips (1979) anticipated strong relationships with their own measures of probability assessment that evaluate the tendency to use numeric probabilities or certainty assessments in response to questions concerning uncertain situations and the realism or calibration of the numeric assessments used.

A person is said to be "well calibrated" if the correct proportion is equal to the probability assigned. For instance, a well-calibrated probability assessor who said, in response to 10 questions, that he or she was 70% sure that he or she had picked the correct answer would have picked that answer seven times.

Wright and Phillips found that high-scale scoring authoritarianism was related to poor calibration with 100% assessments and to a less fine discrimination in probability assessed numerically, which is shown by little usage of intermediate probabilities. Also, dogmatic individuals were less likely to say that they did not know the answer.

In a study of the relationship between dogmatism and *dynamic* probability assessment, Brightman and Urban (1974) gave subjects a Bayesian probability revision task similar to that used by Phillips and Edwards (1966). Subjects were asked to imagine 10 opaque bags each containing 100 poker chips. Four of the bags contained predominantly blue chips. In each case the predominant color was allocated on a 70–30% basis. Subjects were told that 1 bag had been chosen at random from the 10 and that each bag had an equal probability of being the bag chosen. The experimenter then drew one chip from the bag, showed the subject the color, and then returned the chip to the bag, mixed the chips, and drew another. Subjects were required to make a subjective probability estimate that the bag that was being sampled was one of those that contained predominantly red chips. After each draw from the bag, subjects were able to revise their estimate. Brightman and Urban found that those subjects classified as high dogmatics showed different information processing than those classified as low dogmatics in that for ambiguous information sequences the low-dogmatic subjects' mean probability estimate was higher than the near estimate for the high-dogmatic group. This finding is in contradiction to most orthodox conceptualization of dogmatism where the tendency for "premature closure" would be expected to push probability estimates toward perceived certainty.

Taylor and Dunnette (1974) investigated the relationship between characteristics of the decision maker and decision processes using Taylor's (1972) Personnel Decision Simulation that requires a subject to play the role of a business manager making a promotion decision. In the simulation, the decision maker selects one of three hypothetical salesmen for promotion to sales manager. Various measures are taken during the simulation, including amount of information viewed, time required to reach a decision, and decision confidence. Using a battery of personality/cognitive measures, Taylor and Dunnette found that high-scale-scoring dogmatism had only a moderate relationship to decisional confidence. Similarly, risk-taking propensity, as measured by Kogan and Wallach's (1960) Choice Dilemma Questionnaire proved to account for a negligible proportion only of the variance in decision latency. Other decision-maker attributes, including age, experience in making personnel decisions, and intelligence made only minor contributions in accounting for decisional variance. Taylor and Dunnette (1974, p. 296) were thus led to conclude that "an even greater proportion of variance is not accounted for by the decision-maker attributes included in the present research."

Plax and Rosenfeld (1976) examined the relationship between scores on another battery of personality measures and three problems adapted from Kogan and Wallach's Choice Dilemma Questionnaire (CDQ). They found that

> Individuals exhibiting riskiness in decision-making were characterized as persistent, effective in their communication, confident and outgoing, clever and imaginative, aggressive, efficient and clear thinking, and manipulative and opportunistic in dealing with others. (Plax & Rosenfeld, 1976, p. 416)

However, they also noted that

> Even in the earliest research it was evident that the 12 items from the CDQ contributed to an overall risk-taking response in quite different ways.... In order to deal with this concern, a preliminary study was conducted...to isolate...risky items with similar and consistent initial means. (Plax & Rosenfeld, 1976, p. 414)

Indeed, Jackson, Hournany, and Vidmar (1972) have shown that there are four independent subdimensions of generalized risk taking. Their factor analytic study revealed the subdimensions to be monetary risk taking (gambling), physical risk taking, social risk taking, and ethical risk taking.

Steiner, Jarvis, and Parrish (1970) have argued that risk taking gives rise to high arousal levels and that the extent to which a person is willing to take risks depends upon his or her current level of arousal. According to these researchers, individuals attempt to maintain an optimum level of arousal by avoiding or accepting risks..Kozlowski (1977) measured preferences for simple gambles and found that subjects who showed a high demand for stimulation in Strelau's temperament inventory were found to prefer gambles with higher risk, that is, low probability of winning a high payoff, than gambles equivalent in expected value but with higher probabilities of winning lower payoffs. Kozlowski speculated that individual demand for stimulation may be the determinant of Coombs and Pruitt's (1960) ideal level of risk.

McInish (1982) investigated the relationship between Rotter's locus of control and real investment decision making using actual investors as subjects in his mailed survey. *Locus of control* refers to whether an individual sees rewards resulting from his or her own efforts and behavior (internal control) or as the result of luck, chance, or fate. McInish hypothesized that internal-scoring individuals would choose riskier portfolios than external-scoring individuals. However, he found the opposite to be true in his study; externals were found to choose more risky portfolios. This result contradicts a similar but unpublished study by Filer, Maitel, and Simon (1978), using student subjects.

Schoemaker (1979) had subjects rate duplex gambles in terms of hypothetical bids to play the bets. He used two groups of subjects. The members of the first group were unfamiliar with statistics and were "unable to give a proper definition or example of expected value," (p. 10), whereas the members of the second group, who were taking an introductory management course in which elementary statistics had been covered, were able to express understanding of expected value. Schoemaker found that the statistically trained subjects used more consistent decision rules in evaluating the gambles than the untrained subjects. The statistically trained subjects tended to use expected value as an evaluation criterion, and in answer to protocol questions also said they focused equally in all parts of the gamble compared to the untrained subjects. The untrained subjects, by contrast, tended to focus differentially on parts of the gambles such as the amount to win, probability of losing, and so forth. Schoemaker concluded that

> variations in decision strategies...can, in part, be understood from such individual differences as statistical knowledge...the explicit use of expected values, as reported by the trained subjects themselves, strongly suggests that training itself played an important role. (1979, p. 15)

COGNITIVE STYLE AND DECISION MAKING

Driver and Mock (1975) have identified two dimensions of information processing in decision making, the *focus dimension* and the *amount of information utilized*. There are two extremes of the focus dimension. At one pole are processors who view the data as suggesting a single course of action or solution, whereas at the other pole are processors who view solutions as multiple.

The amount of information used in reaching a decision also varies from decision maker to decision maker. At one extreme is the minimal data user who "satisfices" on information use, and at the other extreme is the maximal data user who processes all the available information that is perceived to be of use for the decision.

By combining these two dimensions of information processing in decision-making, Driver and Mock (1975) derived four basic decision styles. The *decisive style* is "one in which a person habitually uses a minimal amount of information to generate one firm option. It is a style characterized by a concern for speed, efficiency and consistency" (p. 493). The *flexible style* "also uses minimal data, but sees it having a different meaning at different times. . . . It is a style associated with speed, adaptability and intuition" (p. 493). In contrast, the *hierarchic style* "uses masses of carefully analyzed data to arrive at one best conclusion. It is associated with great thoroughness, precision and perfectionism" (p. 494). Similarly, the *integrative style* "uses masses of data, but will generate a multitude of possible solutions. . . . It is a highly experimental, information-loving style—often very creative" (p. 494). Driver and colleagues have developed two main psychometric measures of decision style that have apparently predicted such behavior as decision speed, use of data, information search, and information purchase on experimental tasks. However, most if not all of these empirical studies, including the psychometric measures themselves, are contained in unpublished reports, and so the quality of this research is difficult to evaluate. For instance, Driver (1974) has apparently shown that some persons use one style predominantly, whereas others employ one style as often as another.

McGhee, Shields, and Birnberg (1978) have published a study examining the relationship between Driver's decision styles and information processing in decision making. They used a decision situation in which their subjects were to make recommendations about whether to include certain companies in the investment portfolio of a large insurance company. Information about the companies included information about eight cue variables including sales, net income, and primary earning per share. For each set of eight cues presented, subjects were required to provide (a) a recommendation for or against further consideration of that company by their superiors; (b) an assessment of their confidence in their recommendation; and (c) an indication of the amount of *additional* information needed in order for the subject to increase confidence in his or her recommendation.

By constructing a multiple linear regression model of each subject, McGhee *et al.* were able to operationalize "use of information" by counting the number of significant betas in a subject's model because a significant beta means that when a cue is systematically varied the subject's judgment is affected. No significant difference in the number of significant betas was noted for those subjects classified as *maximal* or *minimal* data users on the basis of Driver's (1971) Integrative Style Test. Also, those subjects who showed low or high Tolerance of Ambiguity on Budner's (1962) Tolerance of Ambiguity scale did not have significantly different levels of confidence in their recommendations or a differential desire to seek additional information in order to increase their confidence in a recommendation. In conclusion, McGhee *et al.* concluded that "personality variables do not appear to be useful in describing, understanding or predicting human information processing" (McGhee *et al.*, 1978, p. 696).

The Myers–Briggs type indicator (Myers, 1962) has also been used to discriminate decision styles. This indicator follows the psychology of types developed by Jung. According to Casey (1980, p. 605), individuals categorized as *sensors* "prefer to analyze isolated, concrete details in making a decision," whereas *intuitors* "focus on relationships, or gestalt." In Casey's study, bank loan officers made "predictions" of the possible corporate failure of each of 30 firms based on the information contained in six financial ratios, such as net income/total assets for each firm. The ratios were real ones, belonging to 15 firms that had already filed for bankruptcy and to 15 randomly chosen nonbankrupt firms.

Casey describes the way in which Jung's information-processing styles were hypothesized to be related to performance on his task.

After an explanation and discussion of Jung's theory between me and the expert panel of bankers, the panel predicted that the intuitors would perform significantly better than the sensors in the prediction task. In the panel's opinion, analysis of financial ratios to predict failure accurately required that the levels and trends of the ratios, as well as the possible trade-offs among them (e.g. liquidity for profitability), be economical. (Casey, 1980, pp. 605–606).

Casey's prediction was confirmed in that he found a moderate biserial correlation, in the expected direction, between overall predictive accuracy and the two information-processing types.

Davis (1982) also utilized the Myers–Briggs instrument to differentiate individuals' performance on a computer simulation of a production function. Individual decision makers acted as operations managers. One of the tasks faced by his subjects was to develop a production plan for a 5-week production period with the objective of minimizing the firm's total costs. Davis found that sensing subjects obtained significantly lower costs than intuitive subjects. He argued that this was because his decision task was analytical and moderately well structured, whereas other tasks involving tactical and strategic decisions would be less well structured and would tend to favor good performance by intuitive types.

According to the Subjective Expected Utility (SEU) theory of decision making, optimal choices under uncertainty are made on two independent dimensions of information: probability and utility. Early research attempted to see if human decision making could be adequately described by this normative model. Most studies found that, in detail, it could not (e.g., Coombs & Pruitt, 1960; Edwards, 1961; Slovic, 1966; Tversky, 1967). Nevertheless, Peterson and Beach (1967, p. 31) concluded that

experiments that have compared human inferences with those of statistical man show that the normative model provides a good first approximation for a psychological theory of inference. Inferences made by subjects are influenced by appropriate variables in appropriate directions.

Those studies focusing on the probability dimension have found humans suboptimal in many ways; for example, Phillips and Edwards (1966) found that people do not extract as much information from probabilistic data as Bayes's theorem would allow; this phenomenon was labeled *conservatism*. Similarly, Lichtenstein, Fischhoff, and Phillips (1977) have found "overconfidence" in probability assessments, and Tversky and Kahneman (e.g., 1974) have outlined heuristics and biases that affect people's judgments of likelihoods in some situations.

Slovic (1972) and Hogarth (1975) have marshaled this evidence in support of the notion that limited capacity in terms of memory, attention, and reasoning capabilities leads the decision maker to be suboptimal. Running through these studies is the implicit notion that people think in terms of probability but are not very good at it. As long ago as 1957, Simon, in his "bounded rationality" theory, argued that human cognitive limitations often result in poor decision making due to the use of inappropriate models of the task.

> [The decision maker] behaves rationally with respect to this model, and such behavior is not even approximately optimal with respect to the real world. To predict his behavior, we must understand the way in which this simplified model is constructed, and its construction will certainly be related to his psychological properties as a perceiving, thinking, and learning animal. (Simon, 1957, p. 513)

It is not easy to interpret this decision theoretic research as either personologist, situationist, or interactionist. As a whole, it could be interpreted as supporting any of those positions.

Nevertheless, Wright and Phillips (1983) argued that is was possible to define alternate cognitive styles of probabilistic and nonprobabilistic thinking and predict performance across a variety of decision tasks. Specifically, they argued that a probabilistic thinker with no cognitive limitations would take a probabilistic rather than nonprobabilistic view when confronted with uncertainty, would value information that could reduce uncertainty, would revise probabilities in light of new information, would be less prone to violate a normative axiom of decision theory, would take account of future uncertainties when making plans, and would show no bias for certain over uncertain events just because the former are certain. On the other hand, the nonprobabilistic thinker would translate uncertainty into yes–no or "don't-know" terms, would put little value on fallible information, would show little revision of probabilities when fallible information was presented , would be prone to violate a normative axiom of decision theory, would make plans on the basis of best guesses, and would be biased toward opinions with certain consequences.

Wright and Phillips's predictions for performance were expressed entirely in terms of expected differences between nonprobabilistic and probabilistic cognitive styles, even though they did not have an independent measure that would distinguish people adopting these styles. The purpose of their research was to discover whether these two styles were consistently adopted by people over a variety of decision and inference tasks.

However, they found little evidence of cross-situational consistency of their hypothesized cognitive styles and they were led to conclude that

> probabilistic and non-probabilistic thinking, at least with the sample and measures used here, do not appear to be undimensional cognitive styles. (Wright & Phillips, 1984, p. 386)

In earlier studies, Slovic (1962, 1964) found no relationship between various questionnaire risk-taking measures, including those of Kogan and Wallach, and measures derived from a preference for long shots in hypothetical bet situations. Slovic (1962, p. 69) concluded that the implications of the present study for the existence and measurement of a general risk-taking trait are, (a) none or only a few of the variables analysed actually measure the trait; or (b) willingness to take risks may not be a general trait at all but rather one which varies from situation to situation within the same individual.

COGNITIVE STYLE AND THE DESIGN
OF DECISION SUPPORT SYSTEMS (DSS)

The preceding sections have given, I hope, a flavor of current research and theorizing on the relationship between personality/cognitive measures and decision making and also on the existence, or otherwise, of distinct cognitive styles of decision making.

From an applied point of view, other researchers have attempted to extract, from the results of this type of research, methods of presenting information or aiding decision making that match or complement the decisional styles of the decision makers.

Zmud (1979) surveyed and evaluated empirical research that might have relevance for this purpose. He concluded that

it is becoming increasingly realized that cognitive behaviors are dependent on contextual, i.e. task and environmental, factors as well as individual differences. In order for the results of research studies to be interpretable and generalizable, experimental designs for individual difference research must incorporate relevant contextual variables. To neglect to do so will result in ambiguous, inconsistent, and, possibly, meaningless findings. (Zmud, 1979, p. 974)

Huber (in press) takes the argument further.

The multitude of measuring instruments for assessing cognitive style, in combination with the variety of behaviors and performance measures that have been studied, causes there to be a limited number of precisely comparable studies. . . . Thus the literature must be labeled as inconclusive, since either (1) the sparseness of comparable studies prohibits precise comparisons, or (2) the aggregation of non-comparable studies leads to the identification of apparent inconsistencies.

Huber concludes on the basis of this argument that present research is insufficiently sound to be a basis for designing "individualized" decision support or management information systems. He also concludes that further cognitive style research is unlikely to lead to operational guidelines for the design of such systems because

(1) there are many individual differences related to decision-making behavior, and the task of constructing an empirically-based normative design model that accounts for all their effects is overwhelming, and (2) even if we could build such a model, it would be inapplicable to any one decision-maker because there are individual differences in the nature and extent of association among individual differences.

Huber's (in press) resolution of these problems is clear cut.

> This means that the DSS design effort should be directed towards creating a DSS that
> is flexible, friendly, and that provides a variety of options. If this focus is adopted,
> the matter of an a priori determination of the user's style as a basis for identifying
> the most appropriate design becomes largely irrelevant.

CONTINGENT DECISION BEHAVIOR

Other researchers have placed emphasis on the contribution of task characteristics to decisional variance.

For instance, Pitz (1977) has demonstrated that very small charges in the task can produce evidence of poor or good judgment. Pitz gives an example of a situation in which poor probabilistic judgment is evident. He operates a question from Tversky and Kahneman (1971, p. 107).

> The mean IQ of the population of eighth graders in a city is known to be 100. You
> have selected a random sample of 50 children for a study of educational achievements.
> The first child tested has an IQ of 150. What do you expect the mean IQ to be for
> the whole sample?

Tversky and Kahneman reported that a large number of subjects responded with an estimate of 100. They concluded that these subjects expected samples in the long run to generate extreme values in one direction that would cancel extreme values in the other direction, one version of the gambler's fallacy. Pitz noted (p. 106) however, that it is possible that subjects are simply using a well-learned rule: "Given a known population mean and a randomly selected sample from that population, the expected sample mean is equal to the population mean." Pitz hypothesized that other rules may exist, for example, "Given two random samples, the expected mean of the second sample is independent of information about the first sample," but that they had a lower priority. Pitz (1977, p. 260) demonstrated this by rewording Tversky and Kahneman's example in this manner:

> The mean IQ of the population of eighth graders in a city is known to be 100. You
> have selected a random sample of 50 children for a study of educational achievements.
> The first child tested has an IQ of 150. What do you expect the mean IQ to be for
> the *remaining* 49 children?

As Pitz notes, people who have given an answer of anything other than 100 are rare, and usually turn out to have misunderstood the question. From this finding, Pitz developed a theory of a "production system" of decision rules within the individual that produces responses. In order to show the presence of a rule in a person's production system, it is, of course, necessary to prevent a response from being generated on the basis of higher order productions.

Kahneman and Tversky (1982) in their "prospect theory" of decision making argued that the subjective valuation of the possible outcomes of a decision is contingent upon the decision maker's *reference point* or *frame of reference*.

> Framing effects—consumer behaviour may be particularly pronounced in situations that have a single dimension of cost (usually money) and several dimensions of benefit. An elaborate tape deck is a distinct asset in the purchase of a new car. Its cost, however, is naturally treated as a small increment over the price of the car. The purchase is made easier by judging the value of the tape deck independently and its cost as an increment. Many buyers of homes have similar experiences. Furniture is often bought with little distress at the same time as a house. Purchases that are postponed, perhaps because the desired items were not available, often appear extravagant when contemplated separately: their cost looms larger on its own. The attractiveness of a course of action may thus change if its cost or benefit is placed in larger account. (Kahneman & Tversky 1982, p. 140)

In another study that emphasized the contingent nature of decision making, Lichtenstein and Slovic (1971) had subjects evaluate gambles by a choice procedure and also by a bidding procedure. The choice procedure required subjects to indicate which of a pair of gambles they preferred, whereas the bidding procedure asked subjects to name an amount of money at which they would be indifferent between playing a specified single gamble or of having that amount of money. When they compared the results of the choice and bidding procedures they found, surprisingly, that for the same subject the results of the two procedures were not correlated. Specifically, they often found that subjects would indicate a greater preference for one gamble when a choice procedure was used and that they would bid more for another gamble when a bidding procedure was used. When asked to choose between gambles, people tended to prefer those containing a higher probability of winning, whereas higher bids were made for gambles containing the larger amounts to win.

Svenson (1983) has investigated the relationship between decision rules or strategies and choice between alternatives. His review demonstrated that most decision problems are solved without complete search of available information, whereas verbal protocols, obtained from individual problem solvers, revealed that many different decision rules are used in simple choice situations. One general conclusion is that less information is obtained when the number of alternatives or the number of value attributes describing the alternatives is increased. In addition, there seems to be a general tendency toward increased intraalternative search and decreased intraattribute search when the number of alternatives in a choice set is increased.

Svenson (1983) also speculated on the role of factors, other than those contained in the task, in determining decisional variance.

> Although the results seem to indicate the existence of individual search patterns in some of the investigated decision situations, little is known about the consistency of rules across situations. However thought provoking the idea, it is much too early to allege the existence of individual decision habits at present. (Svenson, 1983, pp. 139–140)

Payne (1982, p. 400) summarized most of this situation-oriented research.

> The present review strongly suggests the conclusion that decision making is a highly contingent form of information processing. The finding that decision behavior is sensitive to seemingly minor changes in task and context is one of the major results of years of decision research. It will be valuable for researchers to continue to identify task and context effects. Nevertheless, the primary focus of decision research should now be the search for some general principles from which contingent processing would follow.

Payne has identified three major theoretical frameworks for dealing with task and context effects on decision making. The first, *production systems*, has been described earlier. Payne notes further that the decision maker's testing of conditions for a production is considered to be automatic and unconscious. Also, the production system framework is very general, and one implication is that there could be large individual differences in response to a particular task environment. A second framework, *cost/benefit analysis*, views choice of strategy in decision making as a conscious process. Benefits could include

> the probability that the decision strategy will lead to a ''correct'' decision, the speed of making the decision, and its justifiability. Costs might include the information acquisition and computational effort involved in using a strategy. Decision rule selection would then involve consideration of both the costs and benefits associated with each possible strategy. (Payne, 1982, pp. 382–383)

A third framework is in terms of a *perceptual view*. This framework is explicit in Kahneman and Tversky's work on the framing of decisions (see Chapter 2). Tversky and Kahneman argue that people are often unaware of framing effects and, once they are made aware, they are unable to see decision problems in a veridical way. The analogy is with nonveridical perception in research on the psychology of illusion. Because the illusory effect produced by line drawings, for example, the Müller Lyer, have been shown to be fairly consistent across subjects, the implication is that task and context effects on decision making will also be fairly consistent across subjects. Because illusory effects have been shown to be predominantly cognitive rather than motivational it follows that the costs and benefits of a particular decision strategy will have a minor effect on strategy choice.

However, more data need to be collected before the relative dominance of any one of these three frameworks is shown to be the better explanation of task influences on choice behavior.

DECISIONAL STYLE OR CONTINGENT DECISION MAKING?: SOME USEFUL METHODOLOGY FROM PERSONALITY PSYCHOLOGY

A major topic in the study of personality is a concern with identifying the determinants of behavior. Cross-situational consistency versus situational specificity has been, and still is, an important issue in personality theory and research. Early personality research was dominated by trait and psychodynamic theories that *assumed* the existence of transsituational consistency (e.g., Cattell 1946; Guildford, 1959; McClelland, 1951). Later, social learning theorists emphasized the importance of the situation as a determinant of behavior. Although there have been attempts to classify situations (e.g., Sells, 1963), there has been little in the way of systematic attempts to study the situation *psychologically*. Endler (1975, p. 326) has pointed out that "situations do not exist in a vacuum but have psychological meaning and significance for people." Wachtel (1973) has gone further and argued that people select, create, and construct their own psychological environments. These arguments have led to a study of the *interaction* between persons and situations in an attempt to identify the locus of behavioral variation.

Bowers (1973) has noted that almost all recent studies investigating the source of behavioral variation have concluded that interactionism is more important than either personologism or situationism. In short, interactionism would seem to be the major contemporary conceptualization of personality.

Two major methodologies have been used for investigation of the relative contribution of the person, the situation, or an interaction of the two. The first strategy has been simply to correlate measures of a personality trait or behavior. As Endler (1975) pointed out, this strategy has usually yielded correlations of .30, and such results have usually been taken to support the situationist position. However, it must be noted that whereas such low correlations do not support a personologist or cognitive style, they do not differentiate between situationism and interactionism. This is because correlations may be attenuated by interactions and by less than perfect reliabilities of the measures correlated, in addition to situational specificity.

The second research strategy has been to use an analysis of variance (ANOVA) approach that allows the relative variance contributed by situation, persons, and an interaction of these to be evaluated. Endler and Hunt (1968,

1969) have provided one of the first demonstrations of this technique in an investigation of the person–situation issue. In essence, the development of the ANOVA approach has made possible fair comparisons between the personologist, situationist, and interactionist positions. Endler (1966) has presented an account of a variance components technique that surmounts the methodological problem of directly comparing mean squares from different sources of variance where the mean squares are not independent of one another.

However, more recently, some personality psychologists pointed to some potential problems with what would appear, at first sight, to be an ideal methodology for disentangling situationist, interactionist and personologist accounts of decisional variance. Olweus (1977) has noted that even if a large situation-by-person interaction variance is found, it may have arisen in many different ways. He argues that it is impossible to make a clear empirical test of the interactionist position. Nisbett (1977) has also argued that the major disadvantage of interaction hypotheses is that they are much more difficult to refute than main effect hypotheses. Also, interactions involving several levels on each of the independent variables can be extremely difficult to describe and comprehend.

> It is far from uncommon to discover that the results of a. . .design are virtually uninterpretable, because statements about main effects or interactions must be hedged around and constantly modified, in thought and communication, by qualifications necessitated by the presence of higher order interactions. (Nisbett, 1977, p. 421)

In other words, Nisbett is arguing that most reports of interactions are often post hoc. Another limitation with the analysis of variance approach would seem to be that the selective sampling of situations and persons can, perhaps unintentionally, alter the relative magnitude of the variance components. Perhaps a more acute problem is that ANOVA gives only an indication of *how much* the variance components contribute to behavioral variation. Deeper theoretical questions about *how* situations and individuals interact to produce observed behavior are not answered directly by the statistics of ANOVA.

Nevertheless, ANOVA methodologies do contain promise for the potential reconciliation of decision style and contingent decision research. Currently, taxonomies of decision situations, necessary for the best application of ANOVA, are little developed compared to the multiplicity of personality types that have been described. However, pairwise similarity scaling of situations and input into a multidimensional scaling analysis would seem to offer promise in establishing a taxonomy of situations based on individuals' perceptions. Other multivariate techniques, such as factor analysis, could also be used much more extensively to aid the systematic development of taxonomies of decision styles and decision situations.

REFERENCES

Adorno, T. C., Frenkel-Brunswick, E., Levinson, P. J., & Sanford, R. N. (1950). *The authoritarian personality.* New York: Harper.

Alker, H. A. (1971). Relevance of person perception to clinical psychology. *Journal of Consulting and Clinical Psychology, 37,* 167–176.

Bochner, S. (1965). Defining intolerance of ambiguity. *Psychological Record, 15,* 393–400.

Bowers, K. S. (1973). Situationism in psychology. An analysis and a critique. *Psychological Review, 80,* 309–336.

Brightman, H. J., & Urban, T. F. (1974). The influence of the dogmatic personality upon information processing: A comparison with a Bayesian information processor. *Organizational Behavior and Human Performance, 11,* 266–276.

Budner, S. (1962). Intolerance of ambiguity as a personality variable. *Journal of Personality, 30,* 29–50.

Casey, C. J. (1980). The usefulness of accounting ratios for subjects' predictions of corporate failure: Replication and extensions. *Journal of Accounting Research, 18,* 603–613.

Cattell, R. B. (1946). *The description and measurement of personality.* New York: World Books.

Coombs, C. H., & Pruitt, D. G. (1960). Components of risk in decision making: Probability and variance preferences. *Journal of Experimental Psychology, 60,* 265–277.

Davis, D. L. (1982). Are some cognitive types better decision makers than others? An empirical investigation. *Human Systems Management, 3,* 165–172.

Driver, M. (1971). *Integrative Style Test.* Unpublished manuscript, University of Southern California, Los Angeles.

Driver, M. J. (1974). *Decision style and its measurement.* Unpublished manuscript, Graduate School of Business Administration, University of Southern California, Los Angeles.

Driver, M. J., & Mock, T. J. (1975, July). Human information processing, decision style theory, and accounting systems. *The Accounting Review,* pp. 490–508.

Edwards, W. Behavioral decision theory. (1961). *Annual Review of Psychology, 12,* 473–498.

Endler, N. S. (1966). Estimating variance components from mean squares for random and mixed effects analysis of variance models. *Perceptual and Motor Skills, 22,* 559–570.

Endler, N. S. (1975). The case for person–situation interactions. *Canadian Psychological Review, 16,* 319–329.

Endler, N. S., & Hunt, J. McV. (1968). S-R Inventories of hostility and comparisons of the proportions of variance from persons, responses, and situations for hostility and anxiousness. *Journal of Personality and Social Psychology, 9,* 309–315.

Endler, N. S., & Hunt, J. McV. (1969). Generalizability of contributions from sources of variance in the S-R investigations of anxiousness. *Journal of Personality, 37,* 1–24.

Ertel, S. (1972). Erkenntnis und dogmatismus. *Psychologische Rundschau, 23,* 241–269.

Filer, R. S., Maitel, S., & Simon, J. (1978). *Risk-taking and risk aversion: A game simulation of stock market behavior.* Unpublished manuscript, Princeton University, Princeton, NJ.

Guildford, J. P. (1959). *Personality.* New York: McGraw-Hill.

Hogarth, R. M. (1975). Cognitive processes and the assessment of subjective probability distributions. *Journal of the American Statistical Association, 70,* 271–294.

Huber, G. P. (in press). Cognitive style as a basis for MIS and DSS designs: Much ado about nothing? *Management Science.*

Jackson, D. N., Hournany, L., & Vidmar, N. J. (1972). A four dimensional interpretation of risk taking. *Journal of Personality, 40,* 483–501.

Kahneman, D., & Tversky, A. (1982). The psychology of preferences. *Scientific American, 39*, 136–142.

Kogan, N. & Wallach, M. A. (1960). Certainty of judgment and evaluation of risk. *Psychological Reports, 6*, 207–213.

Kozlowski, C. (1977). Demand for stimulation and probability preferences in gambling decisions. *Polish Psychological Bulletin, 8*, 67–73.

Lichtenstein, S., & Slovic, P. (1971). Reversals of preference between bids and choices in gambling decisions. *Journal of Experimental Psychology, 89*, 46–55.

Lichtenstein, S., Fischhoff, B., & Phillips, L. D. (1977). Calibration of probabilities: The state of the art. In H. Jungermann & G. de Zeeuw (Eds.), *Decision making and change in human affairs*. Amsterdam: D. Reidel.

McClelland, D. C. (1951). *Personality*. New York: Dryden.

McGhee, W., Shields, M. D., & Birnberg, J. G. (1978, July). The effect of personality on a subject's information processing. *The Accounting Review*, pp. 681–697.

McInish, T. H. (1982). Individual investors and risk-taking. *Journal of Economic Psychology, 2*, 125–136.

Mischel, W. (1968). *Personality and assessment*. New York: Wiley.

Myers, I. B. (1982). *Manual: The Myers–Briggs Type Indicator*. Princeton, NJ: Educational Testing Service.

Nisbett, R. E. (1977). Interaction versus main effect as goal of personality research. In D. Magnusson & N. S. Endler (Eds.), *Personality at the crossroads*. Hillsdale, NJ: Erlbaum.

Olweus, D. (1977). A critical analysis of the "modern" interactionist position. In D. Magnusson & N. S. Endler (Eds.), *Personality at the crossroads*. Hillsdale, NJ: Erlbaum.

Payne, J. W. (1982). Contingent decision behavior. *Psychological Bulletin, 92*, 382–402.

Peterson, C. R., & Beach, L. R. (1967). Man as an intuitive statistician. *Psychological Bulletin, 68*, 29–46.

Phillips, L. D., & Edwards, W. (1966). Conservatism in a simple probability inference task. *Journal of Experimental Psychology, 72*, 346–354.

Pitz, G. F. (1977). Decision making and cognition. In H. Jungermann & G. de Zeeuw (Eds.), *Decision making and change in human affairs*. Amsterdam: D. Reidel.

Plax, T. G., & Rosenfeld, L. B. (1976). Correlates of risky decision-making. *Journal of Personality Assessment, 40*, 413–418.

Rokeach, M. (1960). *The open and closed mind*. New York: Basic Books.

Schoemaker, P. J. H. (1979). The rate of statistical knowledge in gambling decisions: Moment versus risk dimension approaches. *Organizational Behavior and Human Performance, 24*, 1–17.

Sells, S. B. (Ed.). (1963). *Stimulus determinants of behavior*. New York: Ronald.

Simon, H. A. (1957). *Models of man: Social and national*. New York: Wiley.

Slovic, P. (1962). Convergent validation of risk-taking measures. *Journal of Abnormal and Social Psychology, 65*, 68–71.

Slovic, P. (1964). Assessment of risk taking behavior. *Psychological Bulletin, 61*, 330–333.

Slovic, P. (1966). Value as a determiner of subjective probability. *IEEE Transactions in Human Factors in Electronics, 7*, 22–28.

Slovic, P. (1972). From Shakespeare to Simon: Speculations—and some evidence—about man's ability to process information. *Oregon Research Institute Bulletin*, (12).

Souief, M. I. (1958). Extreme responses set as measures of intolerance of ambiguity. *British Journal of Psychology, 49*, 329–333.

Steiner, J., Jarvis, M., & Parrish, J. (1970). Risk-taking and arousal regulation. *British Journal of Medical Psychology, 43*, 333–348.

Svenson, O. (1983). Decision rules and information processing in decision making. In L. Sjöberg, T. Tyszka, & J. A. Wise (Eds.), *Human decision making*. Bodafors, Sweden: Doxa.

Taylor, R. N. (1972). An empirical investigation of managerial information-processing strategies. *Proceedings of the American Institute of Decision Science, 10,* 54–57.

Taylor, R. N., & Dunnette, M. D. (1974). Relative contribution of decision-maker attributes to decision processes. *Organizational Behavior and Human Performance, 12,* 286–298.

Tversky, A. (1967). Additivity, utility and subjective probability. *Journal of Mathematical Psychology, 4,* 175–210.

Tversky, A., & Kahneman, D. (1971). Belief in the law of small numbers. *Psychological Bulletin, 76,* 105–110.

Tversky, A., & Kahneman, D. (1974). Judgment about uncertainty: Heuristics and biases. *Science, 185,* 1124–1131.

Wachtel, P. (1973). Psychodynamics, behavior therapy and the implacable experimenter: An enquiry into the consistency of personality. *Journal of Abnormal Psychology, 8,* 324–334.

Wright, G. N., & Phillips, L. D. (1979). Personality and probabilistic thinking. *British Journal of Psychology, 70,* 295–303.

Wright, G. N., & Phillips, L. D. (1984). Decision making: Cognitive style or task-related behavior? In H. Bonarius, G. van Heck, & N. Smid (Eds.), *Personality psychology in Europe*. Lisse: Swets & Zeitlinger.

Zmud, R. W. (1979). Individual differences and MIS success: A review of empirical literature. *Management Science, 25,* 966–979.

CHAPTER 4

Cognitive Approaches to Decision Making

A. John Maule

INTRODUCTION

Decision making is such a fundamental part of human activity that a satisfactory explanation of how people choose between various courses of action would seem to be a central problem for psychology. Though there has been much research addressing this problem, until recently it has remained comparatively independent of other areas of psychology with little evidence for the exchange of ideas that has occurred between these other areas. In trying to explain this separate development, one may point to the fact that the intellectual tradition informing research in decision making was rather different from the traditions informing other areas of psychology. Until recently, decision theory has provided the dominant perspective and because this has its origins in economics and statistics, it differs from other areas of psychology that are founded on such intellectual traditions as associationism.

Edwards (1954) has discussed the implications of decision theory, considering a number of issues likely to be important for developing a psychological theory of decision making. An important aspect of this discussion was the distinction between normative and descriptive theories. The former were the province of decision theory and they prescribed the "rational" or "best" course of action for the decision maker, whereas the latter were developed to explain the choices people do make and they were assumed to be the domain of psychological theory. In practice, the distinction between the two was blurred because the former often provided the basis for developing the latter. An example is subjective expected utility (SEU) theory, a normative approach prescribing how peo-

A. John Maule • Department of Behavioural Sciences, Huddersfield Polytechnic, Huddersfield, West Yorkshire, HD1 3DH, England.

ple should make decisions under conditions of risk. It applies to situations where an individual must choose between various courses of action each of which is associated with a number of possible outcomes. It is assumed that the decision maker assesses each outcome along two dimensions—its subjective value or utility and its perceived likelihood of occurrence or subjective probability. The overall attractiveness or SEU of a particular course of action is calculated by summing the products of the utilities and probabilities associated with each outcome. It can be shown that for any individual who accepts the axioms of the theory, the rational or best course of action is the alternative with the highest SEU. Much of the research in behavioral decision theory evaluated the extent to which SEU and similar theories were descriptive of human decision making.

In recent years, decision theory has become a less dominant influence, and research has shown an increasing awareness of developments in other areas of psychology, particularly cognitive psychology. Given the increasing importance of the cognitive approach, there is a need for a systematic evaluation of the contribution that it may have for an understanding of individual decision making. The aim of this chapter is to make this appraisal, and this will be achieved in three ways. Initially, a review of major developments in cognitive psychology wil be undertaken with some consideration of the appropriateness of these for a psychology of decision making. Following this, there will be a review of two areas where the cognitive approach has been applied with a critical evaluation of the contribution that it has had on our understanding in these areas. In the final section, some suggestions for future research will be outlined.

DEVELOPMENTS IN COGNITIVE PSYCHOLOGY

A primary aim of cognitive psychology has been to identify and explain the mental processes that underlie human behavior. Much of the research has adopted an information-processing approach that Haber (1974) argued was founded on two major assumptions. The first was that cognitive activity can be analyzed conceptually into a number of separate stages. The second proposes a limit to the amount of processing that can occur at any moment. Within the information-processing approach it has been possible to identify two general directions in which research has developed. One direction has been concerned with identifying the separate stages and explaining how each operates, whereas the other has taken a broader view, focusing on complex cognitive skills like problem solving and considering how stages operate and interact in the execution of these skills. There has been much research in each of these areas, and in the sections that follow a brief discussion of each area will be presented, indicating its relevance for a cognitive approach to decision making.

Identification of Separate Stages

A major issue for this area of research has been to determine what constitutes a stage and this has been resolved in two ways. One view has conceptualized the stage as an elementary process that performs basic cognitive functions, often just a single operation like comparing two symbols in memory. A particular simple cognitive task is extensively investigated so as to identify and describe the elementary information-processing stages that underlie it. The second view has conceptualized the stage at a more general level in an attempt to identify all the major stages in the cognitive system. Models of this kind have been developed to explain cognitive activity across a variety of different situations. Because both approaches are relevant, each will be considered in more detail.

Elementary Stage Models

Although this approach involves intensive experimentation on a single cognitive task, proponents of this view believe that as the number of tasks investigated in this way increases so research will gradually uncover a set of elementary operations that can "combine to produce the myriad of performances of which the human is capable" (Posner & McLeod, 1982, p. 479). One of the major problems in this area has been to develop an appropriate methodology to uncover these putative processing stages, and this has been limited to cognitive tasks requiring speeded performance. It is assumed that because each stage is independent and takes time to complete its operations, the overall response time can be used to identify these stages. S. Sternberg (1969) provided an example of this approach in his investigation of the probe digit task using the additive factor method. Subjects were required to determine whether a digit was a member of a predesignated target set. Subjects responded as quickly as possible, and response times were used to identify the underlying stages. Sternberg argued that each stage was likely to be affected by a particular independent variable with levels of the variable affecting the time to complete that stage. He argued that by combining these independent variables in a multifactor design, it was possible to interpret additivity between variables as indicating that the variables were affecting different stages. To date, six stages have been identified, and in a review, Sanders (1980) has defended this approach against a number of criticisms, concluding that the weight of evidence supports Sternberg's analysis.

The additve factor method is only one of a number of techniques developed to investigate elementary information-processing stages. Chase (1978) presented an extensive review of the area and concluded that it was possible to isolate a number of stages common to different tasks, giving examples like finding the next location in memory, comparison of two symbols in memory, and so on.

However, the approach has not been without its critics. Newell (1973a) came to the opposite conclusion to Chase, suggesting that the details of each model were so different that it was not possible to develop a set of primitive operations underlying all cognitive activity. A review by Posner & McLeod (1982) has attempted to combat these criticisms by presenting a taxonomy of mental operations in an attempt to bring together and identify similarities between the elements of different models. This scheme appears to be a useful development toward achieving the aim of identifying common processing stages.

R. Sternberg (1977) has recently developed componential analysis, which is a different and more sophisticated procedure for investigating underlying processing stages. It has been applied to cognitive tasks of greater complexity than other procedures, including analogical reasoning tasks of the form $A:B::C:D$. The analysis is developed in three phases, the first of which involves the recording of "interval scores." These scores represent the time taken to complete the task when given as a whole and when it is presented in parts; for example, the subject is given A alone and is told to request the rest of the problem $B::C:D$ when ready. From this it is possible to record the time taken to process A and to complete the rest of the task. This procedure is used to investigate other subtask combinations. It is assumed that breaking the task down in this way does not fundamentally alter it, an assumption that appears to hold for analogical reasoning tasks.

The second phase involves the formulation and testing of component models expressed in mathematical terms. The components of each model are elementary information processes, and the interval scores recorded in the first phase provide the basis for testing the models. If a model is found to account satisfactorily for the data, the third phase is used. In this phase parameters are estimated for individual components and these are correlated with performance on a series of reference ability tests like verbal and spatial abilities. It is argued that those components that correlate highly and meaningfully with the ability tests are of general significance, whereas those that do not are task specific. The distinction between general and task-specific components is important because it provides a way of identifying those processes likely to be a feature of cognitive activity across different tasks.

A second issue for elementary stage models concerns limits to the amount of information processing that can take place at any moment. In general, these models assume that each stage is associated with a particular processing limit that is not exchangeable with other stages. Thus the demands on one stage cannot be alleviated by the spare capacity available from another stage (see Shiffrin, 1976).

The relevance of these approaches for decision research initially appears limited, given that the methodology is based on speeded cognitive tasks. A particular problem is the requirement that subjects should respond quickly because

Wright (1975) has shown that this can affect the way people make decisions. Although Wright's experiment was rather different from those considered previously in that it involved a complex input and response times in 10s of seconds rather than parts of a second, nevertheless the results did suggest that there may be important differences in the way people behave with and without the requirement to respond rapidly. Such a finding may also have important implications for cognitive psychology because current cognitive theory has relied heavily on data from speeded mental tasks.

Despite these methodological problems, the notion of elementary processing stages may be useful for a psychology of decision making. For instance, there has been much recent interest in decision strategies with differences between strategies represented in terms of information search and evaluation. If it were possible to reduce each strategy to a set of elementary processing stages, this might provide an important basis for explaining how and why these are used. This issue will be developed further in later sections.

General Stage Models

These models conceptualize the notion of a stage at a more general level and have been developed to explain the architecture of the complete cognitive system. The system is represented in terms of a flow diagram in which each box is a particular cognitive component or processing stage and the functions associated with each are more complex than the elementary stages described in the previous section. Figure 1 presents a simple flow diagram depicting some of the stages included in most models. The stages are arranged in the order in which they operate on the input. The first stage or sensory store is assumed to retain information from the sensory input for a brief period of a quarter of a second or so, with the information retained in its original sensory form. During this retention interval, it must proceed to the pattern recognition stage or it will be lost. In the pattern recognition stage the incoming information accesses previously stored information in order that the act of recognition can take place. Having recognized the input, it may have a more permanent representation in the system by being retained in memory. Two memory stores are identified, differing in terms of their capacities and their temporal characteristics. The short-term store is assumed to retain a limited amount of information for a short period, whereas the long-term store has no measurable capacity limits and may retain information for as long as a lifetime.

The model is much simpler than most on two accounts. First, many models include more stages in an attempt to represent the complexity of the cognitive system. Second, the model assumes that the flow of information is in one direction from input to output, suggesting that it is by successive analysis of the sensory input that a response is determined. This is a data-driven view of process-

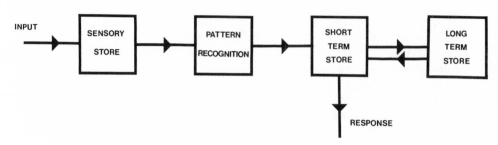

Figure 1. A general stage model of information processing.

ing. Recently, there has been an appreciation of the importance of information flowing in the other direction or conceptually driven processing, with stages later in the system affecting the way earlier stages operate. For instance, the effects of context on reading are well known, and contextual information associated with later parts of the system can influence the way a word is recognized (Rumelhart, 1977).

A second assumption underlying information-processing models concerns limits to the amount of processing that can take place at any moment. Though there have been many explanations of this limit, there are two broad classes of theory. Bottleneck theories assume that some stages have large data-handling capacities, whereas others have relatively low capacities. As a result, the input to a stage may exceed the data-handling limits, and a bottleneck occurs in the system, with the need to select some aspects of the input for analysis and a rejection of the rest. There has been some controversy as to where this bottleneck may occur. Some have argued that it occurs at the pattern recognition stage and have identified a selective mechanism between this stage and the sensory store (e.g., Broadbent, 1958). Others have argued that the bottleneck occurs at the short-term store, putting the selective mechanism between this stage and pattern recognition (e.g., Deutsch & Deutsch, 1963). The evidence suggests that there may be a bottleneck at both locations.

The second-class, or capacity theories, assume that processing at some or all of the stages makes demands on a central resource that is in limited supply (e.g., Kahneman, 1973). Thus, rather than limited processing being associated with the operation of a particular stage, it is the overall demand made by all the stages and how this relates to the capacity of this central resource that is the important issue. There is strong evidence in favor of both classes of theory, and it seems likely that together they illustrate the different ways in which processing is limited. In addition, both theories assume that it is only those inputs that are allocated these limited resources that reach later stages of the cognitive system and are likely to influence responding. However, recent experiments investigating automatic processing suggest that this assumption may not be strictly true.

LaBerge (1980) has reviewed evidence showing that some information processing may occur automatically and not make demands on the limited resources of the system, yet it influences responding. The studies reviewed by LaBerge suggest that there may be two different kinds of processing, controlled processing that requires capacity and automatic processing that may not. Shiffrin & Dumais (1981) considered the problems that emerge when trying to distinguish between these two, and they provide a definition and ways of testing for automatic processing. An important implication of this work is the need to consider automatic processing when assessing the capacity requirements of any cognitive task because any element that is automatic will not make demands on capacity.

Having considered both the stages and processing capacity, discussion of the model is now complete. Much of cognitive psychology has involved a detailed investigation of these and other stages as well as the nature of capacity limitations. Though there has been some discussion of general models of the kind illustrated in Figure 1, most research has focused on the individual stages, trying to explain how each operates. This research has been dominated by the use of a relatively small number of laboratory tasks each of which has been extensively investigated. This approach has been criticized because it has led to rather separate areas of investigation, with little attempt to integrate findings to produce more general cognitive theories. In addition, the laboratory tasks have often been unrepresentative of the kinds of situations people confront in the everyday world, and their relevance has been questioned (Neisser, 1976).

The general stage model raises a number of issues of relevance to decision research. The first of these concerns whether there ought to be a decision-making stage included in these models. Reed (1982) argued against this, suggesting that decision making is better thought of as a higher cognitive skill that depends on these other stages. This implies that a cognitive approach should use current knowledge about individual stages and see what implications this has for decision research. For instance, much is known about human pattern recognition and in a later section concerned with the perceptual aspects of decision making, we will see how this has been used to increase our understanding of human choice behavior. A second issue concerns the implications of man as a limited capacity processor and the importance of determining how this affects decision behavior. Recent evidence indicating automatic processing complicates this issue and suggests that any attempt to assess the capacity demands of decision behavior needs to take account of the distinction between controlled and automatic processing.

Complex Processing Models

Simon (1979) was critical of using the stage approaches to investigate complex behaviors like decision making and problem solving. He argued that it focused interest on activities within particular stages, whereas a more important feature of these high-level cognitive skills was the coordination and interaction of activities between stages. There was a danger that, by considering the problem stage by stage, these other features were neglected. To investigate these skills, Simon suggested the use of computer simulation because developing a program that "makes" decisions or "solves" problems insures that these issues are directly confronted. This approach assumes that a cognitive theory can be tested by representing it in a computer and comparing the performance of the computer with that of a human being when both are presented with a relevant experimental task. Over the last few years, there has been growing interest in the use of computer simulation with many claiming that it overcomes some of the shortcomings of the stage approaches (e.g., Norman, 1981).

The development of the simulation approach raises a number of important issues. The first of these concerns the development of an appropriate control system to determine the sequence in which the various stages operate. The system needs to be highly flexible because this is an essential feature of human cognition, and to meet this specification the notion of the production system was developed (Newell, 1973b, 1980). This system is constructed from a set of instructions or productions each of which has two parts, a condition and an action. Whenever the conditions of a particular production are satisfied, the action is executed. Very powerful processing systems can be built from these simple units, and in addition to providing a control system for running simulations, the production system has been developed as a theoretical scheme in which to explain the control of human cognition.

A second problem for this approach has been the development of a methodology for analyzing human behavior so that it can be compared to the simulation. This presents a considerable problem because in the cognitive skills being considered, the time elapsing between input and response may be several seconds or even minutes, and during this period many operations will have occurred, each taking some small part of a second. The aim of any method should be to identify as many of these different operations as possible, thereby increasing the number of comparisons that can be made with the simulation. The solution has been to take verbal protocols with subjects thinking aloud as they make decisions or solve problems. It is assumed that the protocol provides an accurate record of underlying processing activity.

Simon (1979) has provided a brief review of recent developments, showing that this approach has been successfully applied to a number of different areas of psychology. Though there is no consideration of decision making, some of the problem-solving research is of interest. Of particular relevance are findings emphasizing the importance of identifying the knowledge a person uses when solving a problem. This knowledge affects both the way the problem is internally represented and the subsequent procedures the person uses to solve the problem. These findings are important for decision research in that they emphasize the need to consider how an individual internally represents a decision problem rather than simply assuming that it is isomorphic with the problem as presented. The influence of these ideas is already evident in contemporary decision research, and this will be illustrated in a later section concerned with the perceptual aspects of decision making.

However, there are certain difficulties associated with this area, not least of which concerns the extent to which computer simulation provides an appropriate procedure for testing a theory of human behavior. There has been a protracted debate concerning the equivalence between man and computer that is needed before simulation is an acceptable approach, but the issue is difficult to resolve (see Cohen, 1977, Chapter 7, for a brief review). A second problem concerns the use of verbal protocols and the extent to which they accurately represent underlying processing activity. It has been suggested that the taking of a protocol might interfere with ongoing behavior, changing it qualitatively. In addition, Wason and Evans (1974–1975) suggested that key processing stages might not be open to introspection, and they showed this was the case in certain problem-solving situations. Finally, there are difficulties associated with coding the protocol because a long and often complicated set of verbal utterances must be organized in a way that allows comparison with the computer simulation. Despite these problems, a review by Ericsson and Simon (1980) concluded that in certain situations protocols provide an appropriate measure of information processing.

An important element of this area of cognitive psychology has been the development of the production system to represent the means by which control may be established over the sequence of operations underlying a particular task. Pitz (1977) discussed the use of production systems as a way of developing theories of decision making. Although he argued that there was considerable potential in this approach, there has been comparatively little interest from other decision researchers. One exception is a study by Fox (1980) using a simulated medical decision task. Medical students were given a ''presenting'' symptom of a hypothetical patient and were instructed to investigate further symptoms to determine the disease the ''patient'' had. Fox measured both the pattern of search for symptoms and how much the students could remember of the symptom/disease relations. The performance of subjects was compared with two computer simulations. One simulation was based on Bayes theorem, which is a normative theory prescribing how probabilistic information should be combined, and the other was based on a production system. Although the former provided a reasonable account of the behavior of subjects, the latter was as good, if not better. Fox argued that his results showed that the notion of the production system had considerable potential for decision research. However, until further research is forthcoming, it is difficult to evaluate the contribution that this approach may make to decision research.

In this section, we have reviewed major developments in cognitive psychology, indicating their relevance for decision research. However, the importance of the cognitive approach has already been recognized, and in the next section we will review the contribution that this approach is currently making to our understanding of human decision making.

APPLICATIONS OF THE COGNITIVE APPROACH

In recent years there has been a recognition of the fact that the methods and theories of cognitive psychology may provide a basis for developing decision research. In this section, there will be detailed consideration of two areas where this approach has been adopted. The areas chosen are concerned with decision strategies and perceptual aspects of decision making. Payne (1982) identified these as important areas of contemporary decision research, and they illustrate the application of methodological and theoretical issues discussed in the previous sections.

Decision Strategies

Simon (1955) discussed the psychological implications of individuals making decisions as prescribed by normative theories, suggesting that carrying out the mental operations implied by SEU theory would exceed the processing limits of the individual. He proposed that people may use simpler decision strategies that reduce the processing load to within manageable limits. As an example, Simon has considered "satisficing," a strategy where the indivdual chooses the first course of action that meets a minimum set of requirements on all dimensions. Satisficing was assumed to involve less processing capacity because the number of alternatives evaluated is likely to be less and the operations involved in evaluation are simpler. However, these assumptions have not been directly tested.

In the years that followed, other strategies were identified. For instance, Einhorn (1971) has discussed the conjunctive strategy (CON), which is essentially the same as satisficing, and the disjunctive strategy (DIS) where the individual chooses the first alternative to meet minimum requirements on any dimension. He investigated these, comparing their use with a third based on a linear model, which assumed that all relevant information was processed. To assess which of these strategies people were using, he formulated each in mathematical terms and investigated the extent to which performance on a laboratory-based decision task correlated with these strategies. He considered the performance of subjects averaged across a number of similar decision problems and showed a high correlation between this and both CON and the linear model. This led Einhorn to suggest that both strategies were being used by subjects. There was a relatively low correlation between behavior and DIS, though there was some suggestion that one or two subjects occasionally used this strategy.

Though Einhorn provided evidence that people use simpler strategies like CON, there are some difficulties with his methodology. The behavior of subjects was considered in terms of averages of performance across different problems; yet strategies are dynamic elements of behavior likely to be used interchangeably from problem to problem and with different frequencies by different subjects. Averages of performance may be combining a number of different strategies of the kind originally considered or others not considered, and it is not clear whether they provide a sound basis for investigating this aspect of decision behavior. A further complication arises because each strategy is defined in mathematical terms, and this allows only the pure version of each one to be evaluated, whereas individuals may use parts of each strategy or several in parallel. A second difficulty concerns the interpretation of significant correlations between mathematical models and behavior. Dawes (1979) has reviewed evidence suggesting that certain models are highly predictive of human behavior even when the basis for developing the model is inappropriate. Thus, the high correlations in Einhorn's study may be due to the particular class of the mathematical models being tested rather than the validity of the psychological principles underlying these models. Taken together, these criticisms suggest that testing mathematical models may not provide an appropriate basis for investigating decision strategies.

Although the notion of strategy is an important issue for decision research, studies like Einhorn's have been comparatively rare. It was not until recently, with the introduction of methods associated with the cognitive approach, that there has been a sustained effort to investigate this area. These recent developments were founded on an appreciation that a vital element in all strategies is a specification of both the amount and order in which information is processed. As we have seen, within cognitive psychology there has been much interest concerning the way people search and evaluate information, and the methods developed within this area have been used to investigate decision strategies. Two methods have been used, based on observing responses and verbal protocols. Research concerned with each will be considered separately.

Observing Response Methods

This technique depends on all information being continuously available and presented in an organized way so that the subject can immediatley locate any element. To identify an element a subject makes an observing response that in some instances involves turning over a card (e.g., Payne, 1976) and in other instances an eye fixation (e.g., Russo & Dosher, 1983). In either case, the pattern of observing responses is recorded and assumed to be indicative of the order in which information is processed.

Payne (1976) used this technique in a laboratory experiment on how people choose apartments, each being described along a number of dimensions like noise level and rent. Each alternative×dimension value was printed on a card that had to be turned over for the information to be seen. At the outset, Payne suggested that subjects might adopt either compensatory strategies that assume that all available information is processed or noncompensatory strategies like CON where less information is used and is processed in a simpler way. Observing behavior was analyzed in a number of different ways, and these all supported the view that subjects were using a variety of compensatory and noncompensatory strategies. A critical feature of strategy use was the level of task complexity, and as this was increased by adding alternatives and/or dimensions, so subjects showed an increased use of noncompensatory strategies. In the complex conditions, it was common for subjects to initially adopt a noncompensatory strategy to eliminate some of the alternatives quickly and then, when only a few alternatives remained, to use a compensatory strategy to make the final choice.

In explaining these results, Payne argued that as complexity increased so the processing load associated with the use of compensatory strategies became too great and necessitated the use of their simpler noncompensatory counterparts. Payne's study suggests that a careful analysis of observing responses can provide a basis for identifying the decision strategies people use.

Russo and Dosher (1983) used eye movements to evaluate observing behavior and found broadly similar results to those reported by Payne. Although the details of the experiment were different, results showed that subjects used either compensatory and noncompensatory strategies with an increased use of the latter as task complexity increased. In general, these results suggest that the observing response provides a useful way of investigating how a person behaves when confronted by a decision problem. There are, however, a number of difficulties associated with this methodology. One important problem concerns the constraints that are necessary if observing responses are to measured. In Payne's study, subjects had to turn over cards, whereas eye movement studies often require the use of head clamps and that information be presented in widely disparate areas of the display so that it is possible to determine which element is being fixated. Both of these are artificial constraints that may affect strategy selection.

A second problem concerns the observing response and whether it is a reliable indicator of underlying information processing. Though it would not be appropriate to assume that any particular fixation or act of turning over a card was itself indicative of underlying processing, it seems likely that most will be, making the observing response a reasonably reliable measure. Perhaps, the most important problem is the requirement that subjects know what information is available at the outset and that it remains available throughout the experimental session. Intuitively, such characteristics are not common to everyday decision situations and may well influence the strategies used by subjects. Englander and Tyszka (1980) present data that show that task characteristics like this crucially affect strategy selection. In addition, Payne (1982; Chapter 1, this volume) has presented a review that shows that decision behavior is highly sensitive to many features of task structure, highlighting the importance of developing designs that are similar in structure to everyday situations.

Verbal Protocols

Payne, Braunstein, and Carroll (1978) have provided an extensive review of the use of the verbal protocol in decision research, and they concluded that it is a useful method for uncovering underlying cognitive processes. The use of this method to investigate decision strategies has been illustrated by Montgomery (1977) who used a task in which subjects were required to choose one of a pair of gambles defined in terms of a probability, p, to win a certain amount, and a second probability, $1-p$, to win nothing. Analysis of the protocols was based on a coding system that identified the kinds of statements subjects made about comparing elements of the gambles because these were assumed to provide a basis for discriminating between strategies. Results indicated that subjects used both SEU and simpler noncompensatory strategies with statements like ''a high probability of winning x'' taken to indicate a compensatory strategy, whereas statements like ''the probability is higher in the second gamble'' were taken to indicate noncompensatory strategies. The results demonstrate that the verbal protocol may provide an appropriate method to identify different decision strategies. In addition, the choices made by Montgomery's subjects were similar to those reported in an earlier study that was the same in all respects except there were no verbal protocols (Tversky, 1969). Montgomery argued that this showed the taking of the protocol had not disrupted choice behavior, thereby supporting the appropriateness of this method. However, in the section Complex Processing Models, we saw there may be problems with the use of verbal protocols, and until these are resolved, there will be doubt surrounding results using this method.

The application of the methods of cognitive psychology to decision research has provided strong support for the view that people adopt a variety of different decision strategies and has also indicated some of the features of task structure that influence which strategy is adopted. Though we have identified difficulties with each method, similar results have emerged from studies using the different methods, thereby allowing greater confidence in the reliability of these findings. In addition, certain studies have used the two methods in the same experiment (e.g., Payne, 1976; Russo & Dosher, 1983) and have found similar results with each. Future studies should attempt to use the two methods simultaneously because this provides a more powerful analysis and produces convergent validation of particular processes.

An additional advantage of this approach is its flexibility because the methods allow one to identify how a single subject behaves in a particular situation rather than being dependent on averaging across situations as in the case of the mathematical modeling approach. However, the mathematical approach has its virtues, not least of which is its precision, and Einhorn, Kleinmuntz, and Kleinmuntz (1979) have made a strong appeal for multimethod investigations using mathematical and cognitive methods because each can complement the other in developing understanding of decision making.

Theoretical Considerations

The dominant theoretical explanation of why people adopt one strategy rather than another has developed on the assumption that some decision strategies make less demands on processing capacity and are therefore associated with less "cost" to the individual. Because simpler strategies involve less processing, the benefits to decision makers from using them may also be reduced in terms of a decreased likelihood of making a "correct" choice and one that may be justified to themselves or others. It may be a trade-off between costs and benefits that determines which strategy is adopted for a particular task, and in one formulation of this approach, Beach and Mitchell (1978) suggested that the trade-off is resolved according to characteristics of both the decision maker and the task. Further, it is assumed that the evaluation of strategy cost occurs consciously. An evaluation of this theory of strategy selection depends on being able to identify the cost of each strategy in processing terms, a problem that is at the heart of cognitive psychology.

Within cognitive psychology, there has been much interest in the notion of the capacity requirements of different tasks. This has involved identifying the momentary demands on capacity of one task in terms of its effect on the performance of a second task. However, the capacity demands of decision strategies have been approached from a different standpoint. Most discussion has centered on the total demands from input to response rather than momentary demands. It is not clear whether these different ways of conceptualizing processing demands are in any way related, or if one is more appropriate than the other. One consequence of this difference in interpretation is that the large body of cognitive research concerned with momentary processing demands is of little relevance for current theories of decision strategy selection. This highlights the need for future research to clarify the relation between these different interpretations.

Within decision research there have been several different attempts to evaluate the processing cost of different strategies. Shugan (1980) suggested that cost depended on the frequency with which a particular elementary processing stage was used in the execution of a strategy. For Shugan, this stage was a comparison process and used whenever two alternatives are compared along a single attribute. Such a view is clearly untenable in that strategies include other elementary processes each of which are likely to make demands on capacity, and there appears to be little justification in selecting one as the only determinant.

Klayman (1983) approached the problem of demands on capacity from rather a different standpoint. He considered a number of different decision strategies, developing a computer model of each. These models were constructed from a number of elementary information processes, and though they were associated with computer operations, they were assumed to have some psychological reality. He identified two categories of elementary processes, computational and executive. The former included such operations as calculation, counting, storing, and recalling, whereas the latter involved program control functions like looping and branching. Having constructed these models, all were presented with a decision problem, and simulation performance was measured in a similar manner to that outlined by Payne (1976) when investigating human performance. In general, the simulated search and evaluation associated with particular strategies was similar to the performance of human subjects using those strategies. Klayman discussed capacity in terms of the frequency with which all elementary operations were used. He found, as predicted, that there was a difference between compensatory and noncompensatory strategies with the former involving a greater use of these operations, and this was intepreted as evidence for greater capacity requirements.

Though Klayman showed that, in priniciple, strategies can be reduced to a number of elementary processing stages, there are two problems associated with this work. The first problem concerns the stages identified by Klayman because these were intuitive and developed for the convenience of the computer model rather than as elements representative of human information processing. It would be interesting to adapt some of the methods for uncovering elementary processing stages reviewed earlier and to see whether they could identify the basic processes that underlie decision strategies. Such a discovery would considerably enhance the approach advocated by Klayman. A second problem concerns the assumption that all elementary processes make demands on capacity; within cognitive psychology there is no evidence to substantiate this view (Shiffrin, 1976). Recent developments, discussed earlier, indicate an additional difficulty because it is known that some processing occurs automatically without making demands on capacity. This indicates how important it is for cognitive approaches to decision making to be developed in full knowledge of current developments in cognitive psychology. The notion of strategy cost may be better explained by a careful consideration of the wealth of theory and data concerning processing capacity that has been developed in cognitive psychology (e.g., Duncan, 1980; Eysenck, 1982, Chapter 3; Shiffrin, 1976).

Perceptual Aspects of Decision Making

A second area of decision research showing the influence of cognitive psychology is illustrated by considering some of the perceptual aspects of decision making. Much of behavioral decision theory has been dominated by the view that choice was determined by maximizing SEU. This highlighted the importance of identifying how a decision maker made judgments about the probabilities and values associated with the courses of action available in a situation. Estes (1980) argued that this was identified as a scaling problem with the major research effort directed toward developing scales of measurement of subjective probability and utility. Estes suggested that there was a belief that, once this scaling problem had been solved, the development of a descriptive theory would almost be complete because maximization of SEU or something similar was assumed to be a universal principle of decision making.

At that time, there were already indications that difficulties arise when scaling stimulus dimensions. Psychophysical investigations of the relation between stimulus magnitude and human judgment had shown that judgments were affected by immediate context. For instance, Campbell, Lewis, and Hunt (1958) found that judgments of the pitch of middle range piano notes were different depending on whether they were preceded by a set of high-pitch or low-pitch notes. To account for findings like this, Helson (1964) developed adaptation-level theory. In simple terms, the theory assumes that when people make a series of judgments along a dimension, these are not independent but themselves form an interconnected scale. Somewhere along this scale is a neutral point that is a weighted average of this set of stimuli. This neutral point becomes an important reference point for future judgment, and in the Campbell *et al.* study subjects experiencing an initial set of low tones would have a lower neutral point than those experiencing high tones and would, therefore, judge the middle range as higher.

These findings are highly relevant to present considerations because much of the research in behavioral decision theory has required subjects to make repeated choices among alternatives defined in terms of their probability and utility. It seems likely that judgments of probability and utility would crucially depend on context effects of this kind, and although Fryback, Goodman, and Edwards (1973) found support for this view, there has until recently been little account taken of these findings. We will see later how recent developments associated with prospect theory (Kahneman & Tversky, 1979) have been concerned with issues like this, and we will show how important it is to take account of the perceptual aspects of decision making.

Within cognitive psychology, there has been a large volume of work investigating a variety of perceptual issues. We will select two areas, pattern recognition and problem solving, and consider aspects that are relevant to decision research.

Pattern Recognition Studies

The pattern recognition stage of information processing was discussed earlier in General Stage Models where it was shown that current theoretical approaches highlight the importance of both data-driven and conceptually driven processes in the act of recognizing a stimulus. This distinction is important in that it suggests that the recognition of a stimulus depends crucially on the context in which that stimulus is presented and on other kinds of knowledge, not simply on the characteristics of the input. Chase and Simon (1973) have illustrated this issue in their research on recognition of chess pieces on a chess board. Subjects were asked to look at the pieces on one board and reproduce them on a second board. This involved glancing at the first board, putting some pieces on the second board, and so on. Results showed that more experienced chess players were able to place more pieces on the second board per glance, suggesting that increased knowledge about chess was used to produce a more complex internal representation of board positions. It seems likely that experienced players perceive the board differently, with recognition organized around small groups of pieces. This is in contrast to less experienced players who apparently recognize board positions by identifying individual pieces. Studies like this are important for decision research in that they highlight the need to consider the knowledge a person uses in constructing an internal representation of a decision problem.

Problem-Solving Studies

Investigation of human problem solving has provided a productive area of research for cognitive psychology. An important element of this research is an application of the issue raised in the previous section concerning the nature of the internal representation of a problem, or what is often called the *problem space*. Since Newell and Simon (1972), it has been recognized that the problem space crucially depends on the knowledge that a person brings to the situation and that for any individual the problem space may be different from the problem as presented to that individual. This has been illustrated in a study by Simon and Hayes (1976) in which subjects solved a series of problems that had a similar formal structure. It was argued that if the problem space accurately reflected the task structure, then solution of problems early in the series should facilitate solution of those later in the sequence. Results showed little evidence for improvement across the series, suggesting that the formal structure was not a major element of the problem space.

There are a number of important issues raised by these findings. One issue concerns possible differences between the decision problem as presented and the problem as internally represented by the individual. Whereas decision research has tended to assume that these two are equivalent, studies like the one reported by Simon and Hayes highlight the need to identify the way a problem is internally represented. A second issue concerns the apparent insensitivity of individuals to the formal structure of problems. Much of the research in behavioral decision theory has been dominated by formal models with choice behavior interpreted in these terms. The present results suggest that formal models may be an inappropriate way of conceptualizing individual decision making.

Findings from studies of pattern recognition and problem solving indicate the need to examine the perceptual aspects of decision making, in particular the internal representation adopted by the individual and the way in which this is constructed. The influence of these ideas on contemporary decision research is evident in a new descriptive theory of decision making called *prospect theory* (Kahneman & Tversky, 1979), which attempts to formalize some of the rules governing the way people construct an internal representation of a decision problem. The theory is an interesting combination of cognitive and traditional approaches in that it takes account of both the processes involved in representing and evaluating information and assumes maximization of some derivative of probability and utility.

It is assumed that there are two phases in the decision-making process. The initial phase involves adopting a ''decision frame'' that is the ''decision maker's conception of acts, outcomes and contingencies associated with a particular choice'' (Tversky & Kahneman, p. 25, this volume). This is equivalent to the notion of problem space considered earlier, and it is assumed that a particular decision problem may be framed in a variety of different ways. The particular frame adopted is critical in determining the subsequent phase in which the alternatives or prospects are evaluated. The theory specifies some of the priniciples governing the way a decision frame is constructed, identifying a set of editing procedures that, if applied, produce a simpler internal representation that simplifies subsequent evaluation and choice.

Fischhoff (1983) discussed three of the more important editing operations. In the first of these, called *coding*, it was assumed that when people evaluate the outcomes associated with prospects they do so by assessing them as gains or losses from a current reference point, rather than as final states of wealth. This reference point may be the individual's current state of wealth or some such psychologically significant point. This view of how people evaluate outcomes shows the influence of the work reviewed earlier on context effects in judgment and is formulated in a similar way to Helson's adaptation-level theory. In the second operation, called *segregation*, it is assumed that if a risky prospect has a riskless component embedded in it, then it is isolated as a separate element. As an example, Kahneman and Tversky (1979) argued that a gamble that involved either winning $300 with a .8 probability or $200 with .2 probability would be decomposed into a sure gain of $200 and the risky prospect of winning $100 with .8 and $0 with .2. The significance of this editing procedure lies in the fact that people are assumed to attach special importance to certainty and framing the gamble in this way allows this to be attributed. In the third editing operations that are elementary information processes and are very much within by prospects are eliminated and ignored for the purposes of evaluating those prospects.

Once the information presented to an individual has been edited to form a decision frame, the second or evaluation phase occurs. It is assumed that there are two scales along which evaluation occurs, one relating to probability, the other utility. The former assumes that for each value of p, the stated probability, there is a term $*p$, the decision weight that is similar to, but not the same as p. It is argued that $*p$ is generally lower than p and that special importance is attributed to certainty. The second scale, $v(x)$, represents the subjective value of an outcome, and given the coding procedure described previously, it is represented in terms of changes in wealth or welfare from the current neutral point. Kahneman and Tversky showed how prospect theory can explain certain findings that have been major difficulties for previous theories like SEU. The notion of the decision frame has recently been extended to a variety of different problems in decision research (Slovic, Fischhoff, & Lichtenstein, 1982).

In contrast to previous theories, prospect theory takes account of the important role played by cognitive factors. The notion of the decision frame demonstrates an appreciation that there may be crucial differences between the problem as presented and how this is internally represented by an individual. The theory also specifies how the decision frame is constructed by positing editing operations that are elementary information processes and are very much within the tradition of cognitive psychology. Unfortunately, in a recent experiment, Fischhoff (1983) found little support for the editing operations outlined by the theory. Despite this, the theory does highlight the importance of considering the perceptual aspects of decision making and should encourage researchers to look closely at current developments in cognitive psychology in order to develop theory and methodology in decision research.

FUTURE DEVELOPMENTS

The previous section illustrated the contribution that cognitive psychology has made to our understanding of issues in decision research. However, the full potential of this approach has not been fully realized and in this section some suggestions for future research will be outlined. Two aspects will be considered, relating to notions of limited capacity and elementary processing stages.

Notions of Limited Capacity

The implications of man as a limited-capacity processor have become increasingly important in decision research, and in Decision Strategies we saw how this has become a major element in explanations of why people adopt different decision strategies. However, there are two problems with this interpretation, each of which highlights the need for further research.

One problem concerns automatic processing because, in the discussion of Elementary Stage Models, research was reviewed indicating that some processing occurs automatically and without making demands on limited capacity. This suggests that whenever the capacity requirements of particular activities are being evaluated some account needs to be taken of this kind of processing. It is important to determine which processes underlying decision behavior may become automatic and under what circumstances this may occur. Although Shiffrin and Dumais (1981) have considered these issues, they have done so only in the context of simple detection tasks. There is a need for these to be clarified in the context of decision behavior. For instance, one important aspect of automatic processing is the increased likelihood of its occurring with practice. Research concerned with decision strategies has shown little concern for the nature of practice, and whereas experiments are limited to ''naive'' student subjects presented with one or two laboratory decision tasks, understanding of the processing load associated with different strategies will remain limited. The roles of automatic processing in particular and of practice in general need to be clarified in the context of decision making, and this may be achieved using the methods developed by cognitive psychologists interested in this area.

A second problem arises from recent developments in decision research that assess the capacity requirements associated with the execution of particular decision strategies. In the section, Theoretical Considerations, a number of criticisms were made of the view that this could be achieved by estimating the frequency with which a set of elementary information processes were used in the execution of a strategy. This view assumes that it is the total demands from input to response that is important. This is different from the notion of processing load developed by cognitive psychologists that assumes that it is the momentary demands that are important. Future research is urgently needed to clarify the relation between these different interpretations and to determine which, if any, is likely to be a determinant of strategy cost.

Although the issue of assessing processing demands remains open, it seems likely that a fruitful development for decision research would be to consider the capacity requirement of decision strategies from the standpoint of recent developments in cognitive psychology concerned with working memory (Baddeley & Hitch, 1974). Working memory is assumed to be a limited-capacity mechanism that has facilities for storing and processing information. It has been identified as an important element in such activities as arithmetical calculation (Hitch, 1978), probability judgments (Brainerd, 1981), and in a variety of reasoning tasks (Baddeley & Hitch, 1974). This theoretical framework has considerably increased our understanding of the nature of information processing underlying these and other cognitive activities and is likely to benefit decision research. For instance, conceptualizing the execution of a particular decision strategy in terms of its storage and processing requirements is likely to provide a new way of comparing the information processing underlying different strategies. Within this area of cognitive psychology, there are already a set of methods developed that can be adapted for this purpose.

Elementary Information-Processing Stages

Decision research has become increasingly concerned with identifying the elementary information processing stages that underlie decision behavior. However, it has made little use of the procedures developed by cognitive psychologists to investigate these processes. In Elementary Stage Models, it was suggested that this may be due, in part, to the fact that these procedures are overly dependent on speeded cognitive tasks. A recent development, componential analysis (R. Sternberg, 1977), however, does appear to have much greater potential. This procedure was briefly reviewed in the aforementioned section and because it has been successfully applied to reasoning tasks taking several seconds to complete, it seems likely to be relevant to decision research.

Componential analysis could be applied to many of the tasks traditionally used in decision research, for example, choice between duplex gambles, and thereby it could provide a way of identifying the underlying stages of information processing. There are two benefits likely to occur if this procedure is used. First, it may be possible to identify the general stages of information processing that underlie different decision tasks, thereby providing a sound basis for developing cognitive theories of decision making. Second, Sternberg has argued that correlating individual stage parameters with standard ability tests provides an effective way of investigating individual differences. A systematic investigation of individual differences in decision making is much needed, and this procedure may well provide a satisfactory basis for this to take place.

CONCLUSION

This chapter has considered the contribution that cognitive psychology may have for decision research. The general review in Developments in Cognitive Psychology, revealed a number of different ways in which a cognitive theory of decision making might develop. There appears to be considerable scope for developing elementary stage models, and new techniques like componential analysis suggest it may be possible to identify processing stages of general significance across different decision situations. The general stage models have increased our understanding about such components as the pattern recognition stage of information processing and because this is one of the many stages presumed to underlie decision behavior, such knowledge is highly relevant to decision research. Finally, the complex processing models highlight the importance of conceptualizing decision making as a complex cognitive skill, with the need to consider how stages are coordinated in the determination of choice.

In Applications of the Cognitive Approach, we saw how these ideas have already permeated through to decision research and have increased our understanding of decision strategies and the perceptual aspects of decision making. However, the full potential of the cognitive approach has not been fully realized, and some possible future developments have been outlined in the section, Future Developments, focusing on problems associated with notions of limited capacity and of identifying processing stages that underlie decision behavior.

Although useful, cognitive psychology is no panacea, and any contribution it can make will be tempered by the problems known to be a feature of this area. Some of these difficulties have been outlined in previous sections. In addition, cognitive psychology has tended to depend too heavily on abstract laboratory experiments and to neglect important issues such as motivation, emotion, and social processes. Despite this, it seems likely that a cognitive approach will make a positive contribution to decision research. Apart from providing new ways to investigate and interpret decision behavior, adopting an approach that is closely linked to other areas of psychology increases the opportunity for the exchange of ideas between areas. Also, this exchange of ideas should take place in both directions and allow the influence of decision research to be extended, making it more available to other areas of psychology and to become a more important element in general psychological theory.

REFERENCES

Baddeley, A. D., & Hitch, G. J. (1974). Working memory. In G. Bower (Ed.), *The psychology of learning and motivation* (Vol. 8). New York: Academic Press.

Beach, L. R., & Mitchell, T. R. (1978). A contingency model for the selection of decision strategies. *Academy of Management Review, 3,* 439–449.

Brainerd, C. R. (1981). Working memory and the developmental analysis of probability judgements. *Psychological Review, 88,* 463–502.

Broadbent, D. E. (1958). *Perception and communication.* London: Pergamon.

Campbell, D. T., Lewis, N. A., & Hunt, W. A. (1958). Context effects with judgemental language that is absolute, extensive and extra-experimentally anchored. *Journal of Experimental Psychology, 55,* 220–228.

Chase, W. G. (1978). Elementary information processes. In W. K. Estes (Ed.), *Handbook of learning and cognitive processes* (Vol. 5). Hillsdale, NJ: Erlbaum.

Chase, W. G., & Simon, H. A. (1973). Perception in chess. *Cognitive Psychology, 4,* 55–81.

Cohen, G. (1977). *The psychology of cognition.* London: Academic Press.

Dawes, R. M. (1979). The robust beauty of improper linear models in decision making. *American Psychologist, 34,* 571–582.

Deutsch, J. A., & Deutsch, D. (1963). Attention: Some theoretical considerations. *Psychological Review, 70,* 80–90.

Duncan, J. (1980). The locus of interference in the perception of simultaneous stimuli. *Psychological Review, 87,* 272–300.

Edwards, W. (1954). The theory of decision making. *Psychological Bulletin, 51,* 380–417.

Einhorn, H. J. (1971). Use of nonlinear, noncompensatory models as a function of task and amount of information. *Organizational Behavior and Human Performance, 6,* 1–27.

Einhorn, H. J., Kleinmuntz, D. N., & Kleinmuntz, B. (1979). Linear regression and process tracing models of judgement. *Psychological Review, 86,* 465–485.

Englander, T., & Tyszka, T. (1980). Information seeking in open decision situations. *Acta Psychologica, 45,* 169–176.

Ericsson, K. A., & Simon, H. A. (1980). Verbal reports as data. *Psychological Review, 87,* 215–251.

Estes, W. K. (1980). Comments on directions and limitations of current efforts towards theories of decision making. In T. S. Wallsten (Ed.), *Cognitive processes in choice and decision behavior.* Hillsdale, NJ: Erlbaum.

Eysenck, M. W. (1982). *Attention and arousal.* Berlin: Springer-Verlag.

Fischhoff, B. (1983). Predicting frames. *Journal of Experimental Psychology: Learning, Memory and Cognition, 9,* 103–116.

Fox, J. (1980). Making decisions under the influence of memory. *Psychological Review, 87,* 190–211.

Fryback, D. G., Goodman, B. C., & Edwards, W. (1973). Choices among bets by Las Vegas gamblers: Absolute and contextual effects. *Journal of Experimental Psychology, 98,* 271–278.

Haber, R. N. (1974). Information processing. In E. D. Carterette & M. P. Friedman (Eds.), *Handbook of perception* (Vol 1). New York: Academic Press.

Helson, H. (1964). *Adaptation-level theory.* New York: Harper & Row.

Hitch, G. H. (1978). The role of short-term working memory in mental arithmetic. *Cognitive Psychology, 10,* 302–323.

Kahneman, D. (1973). *Attention and effort.* Englewood Cliffs, NJ: Prentice-Hall.

Kahneman, D., & Tversky, A. (1979). Prospect theory: An analysis of decisions under risk. *Econometrica, 47,* 263–291.

Klayman, J. (1983). *Simulation of six decision strategies: Comparisons of search patterns, processing characteristics and response to task complexity.* Center for Decision Research Report, Graduate School of Business. Chicago: University of Chicago.

LaBerge, D. (1980). Automatic information processing: A review. In J. Long & A. Baddeley (Eds.), *Attention and performance* (Vol 9). New York: Academic Press.

Montgomery, H. (1977). A study of intransitive preference using a thinking aloud procedure. In H. Jungermann & G. de Zeeuw (Eds.), *Decision making and change in human affairs.* Dordrecht, Holland: Reidel.

Neisser, U. (1976). *Cognition and reality.* San Francisco: Freeman.

Newell, A. (1973a). You can't play twenty questions with nature and win. In W. G. Chase (Ed.), *Visual information processing.* New York: Academic Press.

Newell, A. (1973b). Production systems: Models of control structures. In W. G. Chase (Ed.), *Visual information processing.* New York: Academic Press.

Newell, A. (1980). Harpy, production systems and human cognition. In R. Cole (Ed.), *Perception and production of fluent speech.* Hillsdale, NJ: Erlbaum.

Newell, A., & Simon, H. A. (1972). *Human problem solving.* Englewood Cliffs, NJ: Prentice-Hall.

Norman, D. A. (1981). Twelve issues for cognitive science. In D. A. Norman (Ed.), *Perspectives on cognitive science.* Hillsdale NJ: Erlbaum.

Payne, J. W. (1976). Task complexity and contingent processing in decision making: An information search and protocol analysis. *Organizational Behavior and Human Performance, 16,* 366–387.

Payne, J. W. (1982). Contingent decision behavior. *Psychological Bulletin, 92,* 382–402.

Payne, J. W., Braunstein, M. L., & Carroll, J. S. (1978). Exploring pre-decisional behavior: An alternative approach to decision research. *Organizational Behavior and Human Performance, 22,* 17–44.

Pitz, G. F. (1977). Decision making and cognition. In H. Jungermann & G. de Zeeuw (Eds.), *Decision making and change in human affairs.* Dordrecht, Holland: Reidel.

Posner, M. I., & McLeod, P. (1982). Information processing models—In search of elementary operations. *Annual Review of Psychology, 33,* 477–514.

Reed, S. K. (1982). *Cognition: Theory and applications.* Monterey, CA: Brooks/Cole.

Rumelhart, D. E. (1977). Toward an interactive model of reading. In S. Dornic (Ed.), *Attention and performance* (Vol. 6). Hillsdale, NJ: Erlbaum.

Russo, J. E., & Dosher, B. A. (1983). Strategies for multi-attribute binary choice. *Journal of Experimental Psychology: Learning, Memory and Cognition, 9,* 676–696.

Sanders, A. F. (1980). State analysis of reaction processes. In E. Stelmach & J. Requin (Eds.), *Tutorials in motor behavior.* Amsterdam: North Holland.

Shiffrin, R. M. (1976). Capacity limitations in information processing, attention and memory. In W. K. Estes (Ed.), *Handbook of learning and cognitive processes* (Vol. 4). Hillsdale, NJ: Erlbaum.

Shiffrin, R. M., & Dumais, S. T. (1981). The development of automatism. In J. R. Anderson (Ed.), *Cognitive skills and their acquisition.* Hillsdale, NJ: Erlbaum.

Shugan, S. M. (1980). The cost of thinking. *Journal of Consumer Research, 7,* 99–111.

Simon, H. A. (1955). Behavioral model of rational choice. *Quarterly Journal of Economics, 69,* 99–118.

Simon, H. A. (1979). Information processing models of cognition. *Annual Review of Psychology, 30,* 363–396.

Simon, H. A., & Hayes, J. R. (1976). The understanding process: Problem isomorphs. *Cognitive Psychology, 8,* 165–190.

Slovic, P., Fischhoff, B., & Lichtenstein, S. (1982). Response mode, framing and information processing effects in risk assessment. In R. M. Hogarth (Ed.), *New directions for methodology of social and behavioral science: Question framing and response consistency* (Vol 11). San Francisco: Jossey-Bass.

Sternberg, R. J. (1977). *Intelligence, information processing, and analogical reasoning: The componential analysis of human abilities.* Hillsdale, NJ: Erlbaum.

Sternberg, S. (1969). The discovery of processing stages: Extension of Donder's method. *Acta Psychologica, 30,* 276–315.

Tversky, A. (1969). Intransitivity of preferences. *Psychological Review, 76,* 31–48.

Wason, P. C., & Evans, J. (1974–1975). Dual processes in reasoning? *Cognition, 3,* 141–154.

Wright, P. (1975). The harassed decision maker: Time pressure, distraction, and the use of evidence. *Journal of Applied Psychology, 59,* 555–561.

PART II

SMALL-GROUP DECISION MAKING

CHAPTER 5

Social Interdependence
and Decision Making

David M. Messick

When we think about social interdependence and decision making we often tend to think about game theory in contrast to decision theory. Game theory, after all, is the analysis of decision making and strategic planning in environments that are not neutral or indifferent to our goals and actions. These environments consist of others who have their own plans, intentions, and strategies, and of others with whom we must effectively cope to be effective decision makers. Game theory is limited, however, in that is normally *begins* with assumptions about the preferences of the persons involved, about what the persons know about each other, and about the form of the interdependence that exists among the participants. It does not deal with the problem of how the preferences came about in the first place, for example, or the conditions under which people will opt to change the nature of their interdependence. These two issues are the two foci of this chapter.

Specifically, this chapter will examine two phenomena that are unique to situations involving social interdependence. The first of these is the phenomenon of interdependent preferences—the fact that we are not indifferent to the outcomes received by others. I will note two conflicting ways in which others' outcomes influence our preferences, and I will indicate several directions one can take to study the general problem.

The second issue is only indirectly related to the first. Social institutions and arrangements that define the structure of interdependence are rarely fixed and immutable. I will describe some research that sheds a little light on the ques-

David M. Messick • Department of Psychology, University of California, Santa Barbara, California 93106.

tion of when it is, at least in one specific context, that people will opt to change the pattern of their interdependence. Part of this answer will involve interdependent preferences.

INTERDEPENDENT PREFERENCES

The study of human preference lies at the heart of the study of decision making. Utility theory, either in its older trappings (e.g., Davidson, Suppes, & Siegel, 1957; Mosteller & Nogee, 1951) or in more modern garb (e.g., Tversky & Kahneman, 1981), represents an effort to systematically describe human preferences in situations in which outcomes are known with certainty or in situations involving known or unknown probabilities.

Traditional utility theory has focused on a decision maker's preferences for outcomes, often monetary, that affect only the decision maker. Yet, in most interesting decision situations, one's choice not only influences one's own outcomes but the outcomes of others as well. If people were generally indifferent to the outcomes received by others, then decision theorists could safely ignore these dimensions in studying human preferences.

Nature, however, has made other arrangements. We are not indifferent to the consequences of our behavior for others or to the outcomes that others receive. We are often curious to discover the outcomes of others, and we are rarely indifferent when we have done so. Moreover, we can deviate from indifference in our preferences in two opposite directions: another's good fortune can either please us immensely, or it can make us wretched. How this can be so is the question at hand.

I propose that there are two qualitatively different processes by means of which we are affected by the outcomes received by others. The first of these processes is a sympathetic or empathetic process in which one vicariously registers the pleasure or the pain of others. Such a process of sympathetic responding implies that one will gladly alleviate the distress of another (to simultaneously reduce the sympathetic distress) and that one will try to please another in order to experience vicarious pleasure.

The good fortune of others may not produce vicarious pleasure in one, on the other hand. One person's good fortune may, by contrast, make another's lot appear insufficient and undesirable and thus make the other unhappy rather than vicariously pleased. Symmetrically, one's misfortune may make another feel fortunate, privileged, and happy, regardless of whether one feels sympathetic distress to the victim's plight. The relativity of one's outcomes to those of others around one creates a situation in which one's relative outcome drops as others do well and rises as others fare poorly. Thus, one's pleasure should be negatively correlated with other's outcomes, not positively correlated as would be the case if one were exclusively empathetic.

These two processes, empathetic responding to the outcomes of others and outcome comparisons with others, are two basic social psychological processes that have important implications for a theory of human preferences in interdependent situations. We will look at each briefly in turn.

Empathy and Altruism

One of the earliest, and still one of the most thoughtful and eloquent discussions of empathy was written by capitalism's articulate defender, Adam Smith. In 1759, seventeen years before Smith published his monumentally influential *An Inquiry into the Nature and Causes of the Wealth of Nations*, he published his first book *The Theory of Moral Sentiments*. In the opening paragraph of this book, Smith proclaims:

> How selfish soever man may be supposed, there are evidently some principles in his nature, which interest him in the fortune of others, and render their happiness necessary to him, though he derives nothing from it except the pleasure of seeing it. Of this kind is pity or compassion, the emotion which we feel for the misery of others, when we either see it, or are made to conceive it in a very lively manner. That we often derive sorrow from the sorrow of others, is a matter of fact too obvious to require any instances to prove it; for this sentiment, like all the other original passions of human nature, is by no means confined to the virtuous and humane, though they perhaps may feel it with the most exquisite sensibility. The greatest ruffian, the most hardened violator of the laws of society, is not altogether without it. (Smith, 1759/1976, p. 7)

This concern with the fortune of others, Smith calls *fellow feeling* and it is, he asserts, universal.

Recent research in social psychology tends to paint a somewhat different picture in that it has focused upon the conditions that either facilitate or inhibit fellow feeling from being expressed in action. The general finding is that, although the feeling *may* be universal, and there is considerable doubt about that, its behavioral expression is by no means so. Indeed, the first systematic research that investigated the determinants of peoples' willingness to help others in emergencies was described in a book entitled *The Unresponsive Bystander: Why Doesn't He Help?* (Latané & Darley, 1970).

What are the conditions under which fellow feeling will be aroused and manifested in helpful behavior? Two other approaches to this question, one espoused by Harvey Hornstein (1972, 1976) and the other by Dennis Krebs (1975), have come to similar conclusions.

Hornstein (1976) articulates a theory in which people partition their social environment into "we-groups" and "they-groups." The boundaries between these groups may be relatively permanent, or they may shift like cloud formations, but the essential feature of the groups is that we treat people quite differently depending on which group they are in. Although the boundary between a person and a member of that person's they-group is clear and well defined, 'the boundary is somewhat more obscure between the person and a member of the person's we-group. There is a bond among the members of a we-group that makes the welfare of each the concern of all others.

This bond is referred to by Hornstein as *promotive tension*. Promotive tension is the tension experienced by an individual as a result of witnessing an unfulfilled need or goal state in another, typically a member of a we-group. Promotive tension is a vicarious tension experienced by an observer that presumably parallels the primary tension of the person observed. The goal of altruistic behavior or of providing help is to reduce the promotive tension. Hence, altruism is transformed hedonism, a hedonism that is associated with the goal attainment of another person.

Promotive tension should not be aroused, according to Hornstein, unless the other is assumed to be a member of a we-group *and* the other's need appears strong. In a clever test of this hypothesis, pedestrians in a predominantly Jewish part of Brooklyn, New York, found two open letters, one of which identified the sender as having either a pro-Israeli (we-group) or anti-Israeli (they-group) attitude. The second letter contained a money order contribution to a medical charity. The second letter also contained a form indicating that the sender had agreed to make 10 such contributions and that the one in the lost envelope was either the first or the last of these. The rationale for this manipulation was that more tension would be aroused if the stranger were believed to be very close to fulfilling the goal of sending 10 contributions than if he or she were believed to be far from it. Thus, Hornstein's prediction was that the most promotive tension would be aroused and, hence, most contributions sent, when a member of the we-group was believed to be close to goal completion.

The results of the experiment provided clear support for this prediction. Although approximately 50% of the contributions were sent for the anti-Israeli senders and for those sending in their first contribution, nearly 90% of the last contributions lost by the pro-Israeli senders were forwarded. Thus, it appears that we-group membership *and* relatively intense need are required to create promotive tension and to increase the rate of helping.

Although Hornstein's approach to the fellow feeling phenomenon centers around promotive tension, a Lewinian field theoretic concept, Krebs's (1975) approach employs the related concept of *empathy*. Krebs (1975) proposed that, under certain circumstances, people experience the vicarious pleasure or pain of another. We enjoy others' happiness and are distressed by their sadness. Hence, in order to maximize our own happiness we must take account of factors that directly influence the happiness of others because those factors indirectly influence our own happiness. Whereas Hornstein's model is a homeostatic, tension-reduction model, Krebs conceives of people as more or less rational hedonic maximizers.

This empathetic response, however, does not occur to just anyone's emotional state. The crucial variable that determines whether one will experience a vicarious empathetic response to another is the person's *perceived similarity* to the target. Those people to whom we believe ourselves similar elicit an empathetic response, whereas those to whom we do not believe ourselves similar do not. Thus, similarity plays an analogous role in Kreb's conceptualization to that played by we-group membership in Hornstein's. The causal sequence, according to Krebs, is *similarity leads to empathy that causes altruism.*

Krebs (1975) reported an unusual experimental test of this hypothesis; it was unusual in that it included a test of the proposed intervening role of empathy. In this study, Krebs had adult male subjects watch a stimulus person (in actuality an experimental confederate) perform some tasks for a series of trials. By providing false feedback regarding the performer's responses to an attitude questionnaire, each subject was led to believe either that the performer held very similar or very dissimilar attitudes. Part of the performer's task was to play a roulette game in which the outcome purportedly depended on the number resulting from the spin of the roulette wheel. Half of the subjects were told that the performer either won money or was shocked as a result of the wheel spin—outcomes that were expected to be affectively important to the performer. The other half of the subjects were told that the only thing that depended on the outcome of the spin was whether the performer would perform a cognitive task or a reaction time task, outcomes presumably having little affective content for the performer.

The similarity–dissimilarity manipulation in combination with the high versus low-affect manipulation created four experimental conditions. In only one of these conditions did Krebs predict empathetic responding to the performer and that was the one in which subjects believed themselves similar to the performer who was experiencing affect-laden outcomes. As a test of this prediction, Krebs recorded several indices of emotional arousal from the subjects, that is, heart rate, blood volume, and skin conductance, and found that the similar, high-affect subjects did indeed display the predicted evidence of vicarious emotionality to a significantly greater extent than the other subjects.

To test whether empathy resulted in enhanced altruism, the subjects witnessed the performer being told that there would be one final "bonus" trial on which the performer could win up to $2.00 if the ball landed on an even number or a shock that could be intensely painful if the ball landed on an odd number. The exact amount of money or the intensity of the shock would be determined by the subject. The subject was asked to choose one of 21 possible ways to assign the $2.00 reward and the 100% shock to himself and the performer. The most altruistic of these allowed the performer to keep the entire $2.00 if an even number occurred but at the cost to the subject of having to accept the full 100% maximum shock if an odd number resulted. The next most altruistic option gave $1.80 to the performer for an even number but reduced the subject's shock to 90% of the maximum. The midpoint of the set of options provided no monetary payoff for the performer nor a shock for the subject. On the other side of this neutral midpoint were "selfish" options that provided the monetary payoff to the subject in the event of an even number and a shock to the performer. The most selfish provided the full $2.00 to the subject with the 100% maximum shock being given to the performer.

The subjects in the similar, high-affect condition, on the average, chose an option on the altruistic end of the dimension, one that assigned themselves 30% of the maximum shock for an odd number and sixty cents to the performer for an even number. The average options in the other three groups, in contrast, were all in the selfish segment of the scale, fairly close to the neutral midpoint.

Krebs (1975) presents compelling evidence that empathy lies at the heart of Smith's fellow feeling, that perceived similarity and vicarious affect promote this fellow feeling, and that one behavioral consequence of this fellow feeling is self-sacrificial altruism. Yet, this is not the whole story, and even Adam Smith knew perfectly well that the fellow feeling that provided the bedrock for his theory of of moral sentiments could be diminished or eliminated.

> On the contrary, as we are always ashamed of our own envy, we often pretend, and sometimes really wish to sympathize with the joy of others, when by that disagreeable sentiment we are disqualified from doing so. We are glad, we say, on account of our neighbour's good fortune, when in our hearts, perhaps, we are really sorry. (1759/1976, p. 44)

Although Smith does not delve into this "disagreeable sentiment" and related phenomena, modern social scientists have.

Envy and Social Comparison

Social psychological research on interpersonal processes related to envy has appeared under the rubrics of distributive justice (Homans, 1961); social comparison theory (Festinger, 1954; Suls & Miller, 1977); relative deprivation (Crosby, 1982; Runciman, 1966; Stouffer, Lumsdaine, Lumsdaine, William, Smith, Janis, Star, & Cottrell 1949); equity theory (Adams, 1965; Messick & Cook, 1983); competition (Messick & Thorngate, 1967); and comparison-level theory (Thibaut & Kelley, 1959). One central idea in all of these formulations is that one's reactions to one's circumstances and outcomes in life depend not only on the outcomes and circumstances themselves but also on those of relevant others in the social environment. Whether we perceive our situation to be satisfactory, fair, just, or acceptable depends not only on the objective situation itself but also on the situations of those around us. In one fashion or another, we compare our outcomes to those of others and register pleasure or satisfaction if the comparison is favorable and dissatisfaction if it is not.

This is not the place to elaborate the similarities and differences among the various formulations. Pettigrew (1967) has made such an effort, and Martin and Murray (1983) have contrasted two of the more popular conceptualizations—equity theory and relative deprivation. The curious reader is referred to books by Crosby (1982), Suls and Miller (1977), and Messick and Cook (1983) for more detailed treatments. However, the essential consequence of most of the theories is that as the welfare of relevant others increases, our relative welfare drops, and this decline is registered as an unpleasant state of affairs.

One's relative outcome is the only important measure in purely competitve situations. Whether one finishes ahead of or behind another determines who wins and who loses. Thus, a runner may intentionally run a strategically slow race if by doing so he or she increases the chances of outkicking the competition and winning. Although maximizing speed is generally desirable, being first is even more so, and speed may be sacrificed for position.

There are other situations in which what gets sacrificed for position may have intrinsic value, so that one must pay a real cost for a competitive advantage. Many years ago, I did an informal experiment with my sons to illustrate this point. They were 5 and 8 years old at the time, and they devoured peanuts with a passion. In isolation from each other, I gave them a choice between a dish containing two peanuts and one containing three. With no hesitation, they both chose the three peanuts. The next step was to put one peanut next to the dish containing two and four peanuts next to the dish containing three. I then asked the boys to again tell me which dish they preferred, with the additional stipulation that the peanuts beside the dish that they chose would be given to their brother: if they chose three, the brother got four; if they chose two, the brother got one.

Needless to say, making their outcomes interdependent changed the choice situation dramatically. The younger boy chose the dish with two peanuts and explained that he did not want his brother to get four when he would only get three. He paid a peanut for relative position. The older boy still chose the dish with three but explained that he did not mind giving his brother four peanuts because he was sure that he would shortly be able to get some of them back for himself. He too was not indifferent to relative position.

The social comparison and evaluation of outcomes is a fundamental social psychological process (Festinger, 1954). A number of experiments have shown that in a variety of choice tasks, people are willing to trade-off money or points that are convertible to money in order to maintain or increase a relative advantage over another or others. Messick and Thorngate (1967), for example, provided a clear demonstration that in a two-choice, two-person game, being able to observe the outcomes of the other player led subjects to adopt a competitive, or relative gain, orientation rather than one in which they maximized the points (and hence money) that they won. These authors also presented evidence that the concern with relative position or relative gain was more a reflection of the desire to avoid falling behind the other than of a desire to excel or surpass the other. Experiments using decomposed games, choice situations like those presented to my sons in which each of a set of possible options specified an outcome to the chooser as well as an outcome to another person, have also found a high frequency of competitive or relative gain maximizing choices. Messick and McClintock (1968) estimated that roughly one-quarter to one-half of subjects' choices were competitive with the exact proportion depending on experimental arrangements. In an analysis of the data reported by McClintock, Messick, Kuhlman, and Campos (1973), Messick (1972) estimated that roughly 30% of all the choices in a three-choice game were competitively motivated choices with nearly twice as many competitive choices being made (roughly 40% vs. 20%) in situations where the subject was in a position of relative disadvantage rather than relative advantage. Again, the possibility of being disadvantaged seems to make relative position more salient than being advantaged.

The General Problem

The general problem in the study of preferences in interdependent contexts is to understand not only the dynamics of fellow feelings, on the one hand, and competitive impulses, on the other, but also to create a general theory that incorporates both of these components with other elements as well. Recent research indicates that considerations of fairness play an important role in interdependent decision making and that the determinants of perceived fairness may be quite different from the determinants of satisfaction (Austin, McGinn, & Susmilch, 1980; Messé & Watts, 1983). Messick and Sentis (1979, 1983a) have argued that choices made on the basis of fairness will be different from those that reflect preference without fairness considerations. Most choice situations involve normative considerations such as fairness in addition to competitive and/or altruistic tendencies.

The combination of empathic, equitable, or prosocial impulses with competitve ones can have complex and, at times, apparently paradoxical consequences. One fairly commonplace instance of such a combination is manifested by people who dislike competitive games because they do not like to lose and they feel sorry for others when others lose. The only kind of games that would not cause such people to feel bad would be ones in which there were no losers.

An experiment by van Avermaet (1974) provides a more systematic illustration of the interplay among individualistic, competitive, and prosocial impulses. In this experiment, subjects were to fill out questionnaires until the experimenter told them to stop. Depending on the experimental condition, subjects either worked for 45 minutes or for 90 minutes, and, crossed with this manipulation, they either completed three or six questionnaires.

When the subjects had finished, they were told that there had been another subject who had also been working on questionnaires but who had had to leave in a hurry. As a result, the experimenter explained, he had not been able to pay the other subject nor even to tell that subject that he or she was to be paid. The experimenter continued that he himself was late for an appointment and, as a result, he asked the subject to take care of getting the other's pay to him or her.

The experimenter told the subject that the research was being financed by a grant that allowed subjects to be paid $7.00 for each pair. Looking at a bogus record sheet, the experimenter announced that the other subject had either put in more, equal, or less time than the subject and had completed either more, an equal number, or fewer questionnaires than the other. The experimenter then gave the subject $7.00 (in six one-dollar bills, three quarters, two dimes, and one nickel) along with a stamped, addressed envelope, and asked the subject to put the appropriate amount into the envelope and to mail it.

The subjects left the laboratory with $7.00 of which they could send all, none, or any amount in between to the bogus other. The subjects did not know that the name and address on the envelope were those of a neighbor of the experimenter. The dependent variable in this experiment, of course, was how much, if any, of the $7.00 the subjects in the various conditions sent to the other (bogus) participant.

Van Avermaet's major hypothesis was that subjects would emphasize the performance dimension, either time worked or number of questionnaires completed, that would enable them to justify keeping the most money. The data provided strong support for this hypothesis: when the subject either worked longer or did more questionnaires than the other, the average number of dollars sent to the other was significantly less than $3.50. Furthermore, when the subject equaled the other on one dimension and was inferior on the second, the subject sent the other almost exactly $3.50 on the average. Finally, when the subject worked less *and* accomplished less than the other, the other received an average of $3.67, an amount that is not significantly different from $3.50. Thus, subjects in this study appear loath to part with more than half of the $7.00, even when there is no obvious justification for their keeping half.

On the other hand, of the 94 subjects tested, 1 refused to accept the money, 1 expressed doubt as to the authenticity of the request, and only 2 of the remaining 92 subjects failed to send *some* money to the other (or, less likely, had their envelopes lost in the mail). The obvious strategy of keeping the entire $7.00 (plus the stamp) was adopted by, at most, 2% of the subjects. Thus, one can view these results either as a reflection of the subjects' concern for others (so few simply kept it all) or as a manifestation of their greediness (so few sent more than they kept). Each view is partly correct, but the task facing the scientific study of interdependent preferences is to delve deeper than partly correct simplifications into a more basic layer of theory.

I will conclude this section by describing a recent and as yet unpublished effort in this direction that I made with Keith Sentis. The theoretical ideas that we were testing consisted of a model of the preference process plus an hypothesis about how different components of the model would change as a function of situational changes. The model simply asserted that in situations where pay is to be allocated to two strangers for work that they have done, one's preferences for amounts of pay to oneself and the other can be represented by a utility function having two components. The first component is simply a function of the payoff to oneself, the amount of money the decision maker obtains; and the second component is a function of the *difference* between the decision maker's payoff and that of the other. The model proposes that if x is the decision maker's payment and y is the payment to the other, then

$$u(x,y)=f(x)+g(x-y)$$

the utility or value of the pair (x,y) is simply the sum of the utility of x, $f(x)$, and some function of the difference, $g(x-y)$. It is this second component that carries the information about interdependence: If g is an increasing function of the difference it would represent a competitive addition to self-interest; if g were single peaked in the vicinity of zero, it would manifest an equalitarian component; and if g were decreasing it would imply a desire for the other to do well relative to oneself (or, if own outcome were held constant, it would imply an altruistic orientation).

Clearly, it is the g component that carries information about the interdependent aspects of the decision maker's preferences. Our hypothesis, therefore, was simply that changes in the social aspects of the decision-making task should change the function g but not the nonsocial function f.

We tested both the model and the hypothesis in a situation that was similar to the one described by Messick and Sentis (1979). University student subjects read a scenario in which they were asked to imagine that they had worked with another student as a reader for a psychology course. Roughly a third of the students was asked to imagine that both they and the other student had worked 10 hours (10,10); another third was asked to imagine that they had worked 10 hours, whereas the other student had worked only 7 hours (10,7); and the final group was told to imagine that they had worked only 7 hours, whereas the other had worked 10 (7,10).

After the subjects had read the instructions and the scenario, we obtained a ranking of 20 different payment allocations, each of which specified a payment in dollars to the student and to the other. The set of 20 payment allocations was constructed by crossing four levels of payment to self, $15, $25, $35, and $45, with five levels of difference between self and other. Thus, the pair represented by a difference of -$5 and payment to self of $35, say, would provide $35 to the student and $30 to the other. The subjects then ranked these 20 payment allocations in order of preference. (The details of the ranking procedure are available in Messick & Sentis, 1983b.) The ranks for each subject were next submitted to a 4 x 5 analysis of variance, the goals of which were twofold. First, we tested the accuracy of the hypothesis that the rank orders of the allocations could be expressed as an additive combination of some function of the decision maker's payoff and a function of the difference. These tests have been described by Messick and Sentis (1983b), and they were overwhelmingly supportive. Thus, the next step was to estimate the f and g functions for the subjects and to examine them.

These functions are simply and directly estimated for each subject from that subject's 4 x 5 matrix of ranks. The estimate for each of the nine points, four for f and five for g, are simply the marginal mean ranks for the appropriate row or column, minus the overall mean rank, 10.5. These estimated functions can be thought of as value or utility functions.

Our hypothesis was that changing the nature of the interdependence would change the social utility function, g, and leaving the individual one unchanged. In the context of our study, this meant that we expected the changes in the hours worked by the student and the other to influence the estimated g functions but to have little or no impact on the estimate f functions.

For each subject, we estimated both the f and g functions. Figure 1 depicts the mean of the f functions for subject's own payoff for each group, whereas Figure 2 displays the mean estimated g functions for the three groups. These data provide clear support for our hypothesis. In Figure 1, it is obvious that the mean f is monotonic, increasing from \$15 to \$45 and that the slope of the functions, a quantity that might be interpreted as an indicant of the importance of own payment, is very nearly the same in all three conditions.

In contrast to the very similar functions in Figure 1, the three average g functions in Figure 2 are markedly different. Clearly, the manipulation of the hours worked had a great impact on these social value functions. In each of the three experimental conditions, the point having maximum value is appropriate to the condition. That is to say, when the subject and the other worked an equal number of hours and read an equal number of exams, the most preferred *difference* in payments was zero, that is, equal payments. When the subjects had worked more, they thought they should be paid more—that is, the most preferred difference was positive; and when the subjects had worked less, they had a negative most preferred difference. They wanted the other to be paid more.

There are two asymmetries that should be noted in these data that tie in the previously mentioned findings by Messick and Thorngate (1967) and van Avermaet (1974). The first asymmetry is in the (10,10) function. Briefly put, even though equal outcomes are most preferred, departures of equal magnitudes but opposite directions from equality are not equally preferred. Inequality favoring the decision maker, differences of \$5 or \$10 are much better than inequality favoring the other, differences of −\$5 or −\$10.

The second asymmetry is evident from a comparison of the function for the

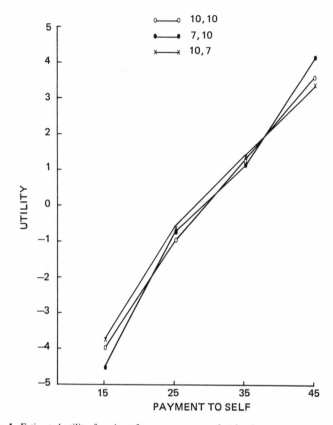

Figure 1. Estimated utility functions for own payments for the three experimental groups.

(10,7) group with that for the (7,10) group. If relative advantage had no influence on the judgments, the curves should form a pattern that would be bilaterally symmetric about zero. Although they are nearly so, there is one notable discrepancy. The highest point on the value function for the (10,7) subjects is at +$10, whereas the most preferred point on the (7,10) value function is −$5, not −$10, as would be required for symmetry. Both this asymmetry and the one discussed previously reflect a principle that people prefer to be advantaged rather than disadvantaged by a given amount.

One final comment about these functions deserves to be made. Siegel (1957), in an important article attempting a theoretical integration of decision theory and level of aspiration theory, proposed that one's level of aspiration for achievement-related outcomes can be represented as the outcome at the "upper bound of the largest distance on the utility scale" (p. 257). In other words, the level of aspiration is the point below which the utility function drops maximally. An inspection of Figure 2 reveals that for all three of the utility functions displayed, the level of aspiration, according to Siegel's (1957) definition, is zero. Thus, these functions have in common the property that equality of outcomes, zero difference, is the estimated level of aspiration, the minimally acceptable outcome in Siegel's theory.

We are not indifferent to the impact of our behavior on others' outcomes, and we are certainly not indifferent to the effect of others' behaviors on our own

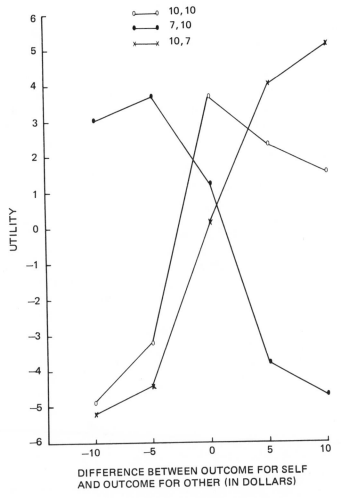

Figure 2. Estimated utility functions for the difference between own and other payment for the three experimental groups.

outcomes. Most of us would prefer to receive a bottle of Château Margaux to a poke in the eye with a sharp stick. Consequently, to the extent that our outcomes and others' are affected by the nature of our interdependence, it is to be expected that one would not be indifferent to the form or structure of our interdependence. It is to this issue that we will next turn.

INTERDEPENDENCE STRUCTURES: CHANGING THE RULES

The *structure* of interdependence refers to the rules, institutions, and procedures that coordinate or integrate a set of individual choices or behaviors. In an abstract sense, one can think of the structure of interdependence characterizing a group of people as a system for mapping a set of individual choices, behaviors, or preferences into a set of individual and/or collective consequences. The analysis of interdependence structures and their social and psychological consequences is one of the central problems in all of the social sciences. Books by Arrow (1951), Brams (1975, 1976), Colman (1982), Cross and Guyer (1980), Davis (1969), Hamburger (1979), Kelley and Thibaut (1978), Olson (1965), Schelling (1978), Sen (1970), Steiner (1972), Riker and Ordeshook (1973), and von Neumann and Morgenstern (1944) convey both the breadth and depth of investigations into interdependence structures in economics, political science, psychology, and related disciplines.

Most of the theoretical and experimental work that has been done on structures of interdependence has focused either on the properties of the structures themselves under a variety of conditions, or on the behavior of individuals in such structures and the consequences of that behavior. The large body of research that followed Arrow's (1951) pioneering work on social choice illustrates the first type of endeavor, and the massive amount of experimental data accumulated by social psychologists and others on two-person mixed-motive games exemplifies the latter. There is one important set of questions, however, that has received relatively little attention.

The nature of our collective interdependence in work environments, in the political domain, in organizational contexts, and in many other facets of modern urban society is often itself an issue about which we must make decisions.

A timely example has been provided by Brams and Fishburn (1983) in their proposal that political elections, particularly primary elections in which the number of candidates may be quite large, be held by *approval voting*. Unlike the current system of plurality voting in which each voter is allowed to vote for only one candidate, with approval voting, each voter may cast a vote for, or approve of, as many of the candidates as the voter wishes. As with the plurality system, the candidate receiving the largest number of votes is declared the winner. Brams and Fishburn (1983) argue that approval voting represents a major advance over plurality voting and urge its widespread adoption. In fact, they report that bills have been introduced in the state legislatures of New York and Vermont to require approval voting if more than two candidates are on the ballot. Although there are some who question the superiority of approval voting to plurality voting (e.g., Reynolds, 1983), its adoption would clearly change the structure of voters' interdependence in that it would change the way in which sets of individual preferences are mapped into collective outcomes.

The question that is raised here is: How will voters decide, if they are offered the opportunity to vote on the issue, whether to vote in favor of plurality voting or approval voting? Are the processes that are involved in evaluating political candidates within either of the voting systems, the same processes that will be involved in evaluating the systems themselves?

This is the question that we have been studying in a different context, and the answer that we are getting is that decisions made *within* an interdependence structure are made on different bases from decisions *about* the structure itself. The situation that we are interested in was described by Hardin (1968) as the *tragedy of the commons*. In this story, a number of herdsmen share a common pasturage for their flocks. There is an incentive for each of the herdsmen to increase the size of his herd because the profit yielded by a grown animal belongs to the herdsman, whereas the cost of feeding the beast, a cost measured in usage of the common grazing lands, is distributed across the herdsmen. As each of the herdsmen increases the size of his herd, the carrying capacity of the common pasturage is inevitably exceeded, the grazing land becomes overused and unable to replenish itself, and tragic collapse of the commons occurs.

Hardin (1968) and many others have argued that the processes underlying the tragedy of the commons are at work in a variety of interconnected contemporary problems including overpopulation, increasing pollution of the environment, and the growing depletion of natural resources. The solutions to these problems, according to Hardin, will involve not only fundamental changes in morality but also institutional changes that eliminate each individual's free access to the common resources and the individual's incentive to abuse them.

One solution mentioned by Hardin and proposed by others (Cross & Guyer, 1980; Platt, 1973) involves the establishment of a superordinate authority that would have the responsibility for the allocation or use of the resource. Governmental regulatory agencies, at least in prinicple, constitute such authorities, as do agencies in the United States like the National Park Service, which regulates and allocates access to wilderness areas and camping facilities. The recognition that a superordinate authority may be sufficient to "solve" the tragedy of the commons is not the same thing as specifying the means by which such an authority could be established. Who would have the authority to establish such an agency? How would it obtain legitimacy?

Probably the most direct route to the establishment of a superordinate authority would be through its election or approval by a vote of the persons whose interests are at stake. This was the mechanism, for example, that permitted the introduction of water allocation and of a moratorium on new water hookups in many areas of California during the drought years of 1976 and 1977. Candidates for election to water boards expressed their support for policies that would severely curtail free access to water, and in many parts of the state these candidates were the ones elected to office.

What are the conditions under which people will voluntarily relinquish their free access to a resource? When will they approve of a change in their interdependence structure, a change that may result in a reduction of their own level of well-being as well as that of others? How does this willingness to change the decision structure relate to a willingness to exercise self-restraint with regard to the consumption of a resource? Do factors that encourage one type of "solution" also promote the other?

The research that we have been conducting is designed to answer these and some related questions. Our experimental task allows university student subjects to participate in what Messick and Brewer (1983) have called *replenishable resource traps* or *dilemmas*. In these experiments, subjects in groups of up to six can share a common pool of a hypothetical resource. On each of a series of trials, the subjects are allowed to "harvest" or extract some quantity of the resource that becomes the subjects' own. Subjects' individual resources at the end of an experiment are potentially exchangeable for money, so it is in the best interest of each subject to accumulate as much of the resource as possible.

The common resource pool is capable of replenishing itself by growing at some constant rate after each trial. If subjects jointly harvest too much from the pool, it will not be able to replenish itself up to its previous level. Clearly, if overharvesting persists, the pool, like Hardin's commons, will be depleted, and subjects will be unable to make any harvests. The subjects' joint task, therefore, must be to try to extract as much as possible from the common pool without depleting it. (See Parker, Lui, Messick, Messick, Brewer, Kramer, Samuelson, & Wilke, 1983, for a fuller description of the task and its supporting software.)

We hypothesized that people would be willing to relinquish access to a resource in favor of establishing a superordinate authority for one of two general reasons. First, if people believe that free access to a resource leads to large inefficiencies in use of the resource, and, in particular, if the inefficiencies result in the overuse of the resource with the concomitant depletion of it, then people will be likely to want to change the system of resource allocation for a more efficient one, and, especially, for one that might prevent complete resource depletion. After all, losing free access to a resource because the resource has ceased to exist is worse than losing access to an agent who will have the responsibility of allocating the resource.

The second factor that we considered to be important was whether the distribution of the resource across the members of the group was perceived to be fair and equitable. Our reasoning here was based on issues raised in the first section of this chapter regarding the use of other people's outcomes as standard for evaluating one's own. If there are large differences in the amount of the resource harvested by the different group members, with some taking much and others relatively little, then we might expect that those taking less would be relatively dissatisfied with their outcomes, even though they could increase their harvests if they wished to. Moreover, such wide discrepancies in harvests, we proposed, would lead to a perception that the distribution of resources was unfair and to a dissatisfaction with free access that would express itself as a desire to change the system, to discard free access in favor of establishing a superordinate authority to harvest and allocate the resource.

In our first experiment (Messick, Wilke, Brewer, Kramer, Zemke, & Lui, 1983), subjects in groups of six were led to believe that they shared a common resource pool that replenished itself at a rate of about 10% per trial. On each trial, the subjects independently could harvest from 0 to 10 units from a pool that had an initial (and maximum) size of 300 points. The subjects were told that the sum of their harvests would be subtracted from the current pool size on each trial and that the pool would then be incremented or replenished by 10% to determine the pool size for the following trial. The optimum harvest size, the one that takes the largest amount per trial without reducing the pool for the subsequent trial, was 4.54 points per trial.

In this experiment, the efficiency and homogeneity of the resource use were manipulated by providing the subjects with false feedback regarding the harvest decisions of the other five group members. Because the subjects were seated in individual cubicles, visually isolated from each other, and because all decisions were typed into individual computer terminals, it was possible to give each subject different feedback about the behavior of the others. Thus, at the end of each decision trial, the subjects were told how many points each of the others harvested and what the pool size was for the next trial.

Efficiency was manipulated by varying the average amount the subject was told that the others took on each of a series of trials. There were three levels of this variable. In the *overuse* condition, the subjects were given feedback that the average harvest per other was nearly 8 points per trial; in the optimal use condition, the subjects' feedback implied that the others took an average of 4.60 per trial; and in the underuse condition, the feedback indicated that the others, on the average, took 3.28 points per trial. In the overuse condition, naturally, the pool size was displayed as falling from one trial to the next. It remained at or close to the maximum in the other two conditions.

In each of these three conditions, we varied the homogeneity of the group by manipulating the variance of the others' harvests. In the low-variance conditions, the subjects' harvests tended to cluster rather closely around the mean harvest. The range in these conditions was around 2 to 4 points per trial. In the high variance conditions, in contrast, there were always some extremely high harvesters and some extremely low ones. The ranges were from 7 to 9 points per trial.

In each group of six, there was one subject in each of the six experimental conditions. The subjects made harvests on each of 10 trials, after which they were told that the first part of the experiment was over. After answering a series of questions regarding their own and their group's performance, they were told that some groups had felt that they could have done a better job if they had been allowed to have just one person from the group make one harvest for the entire group on each trial and allocate that harvest to the individual group members. The subjects were then allowed to vote on whether they preferred to conduct the second session as they had the first, with each person's having the freedom to make an individual harvest, or to elect a leader from among the group members who would make a group harvest and allocation on each of a series of trials. If they opted for the latter, the subjects were told, those who were not elected leader would be given a different task on which to work.

Our predictions with regard to the vote to elect a leader for the second session are straightforward. We expect more votes to change the system in the overuse and underuse than in the optimal use condition and more votes for a leader in the high-variance than the low-variance condition. Predictions for the effects of these manipulations on the trial-to-trial harvests of the subjects, however, are not so clear. Messick et al. (1983) hypothesized that at least three considerations should affect subjects' harvest decisions—a desire to accumulate as much of the resource as possible, a concern for using the pool sensibly, and, finally, a desire not to deviate from perceived group norms. As Messick et al. (1983) have pointed out, the latter two goals are in conflict in this experiment. In the overuse condition, for example, perceived group norms should be in the direction of high harvests because that is the average level of harvest of the others. On the other hand, reasonable pool use would lead a subject to decrease harvest size because the others are overharvesting. Similarly, in the underuse condition, conformity considerations should lead to low levels of harvest, whereas sensible pool use as well as a desire to accumulate the resource should produce higher levels. Because these different goals were in conflict, no clear prediction could be made regarding the effect of the efficiency variable on harvest size.

It was somewhat easier to make predictions about the effects of the variance variable. We assumed that when the harvests of the other group members were homogeneous, the influence of group norms or conformity pressures would be stronger than when the harvests were heterogeneous. This assumption led to different predictions for the overuse and underuse conditions. In the underuse condition, as was just mentioned, the only factor keeping harvest levels low was the normative pressure. If that pressure is reduced in the high-variance conditions, then harvests should increase. In the overuse condition, conformity impulses should tend to keep harvests relatively high; if the strength of those impulses are reduced in the high-variance condition, harvests can be expected to drop. These considerations lead to a prediciton of a statistical interaction between the efficiency manipulation and the variance manipulation.

To summarize, although we expected the efficiency and variance manipulations to have had a rather straightforward impact on subjects' decisions on whether or not to vote for a leader, we expected that the effects on harvest decisions would be rather more complex.

An analysis of the vote for a leader provided clear support for the prediction that perceived inefficiency would promote a desire for changing the interdependence structure. Sixty-eight percent of the subjects in the overuse conditions voted to have a leader in the second session, whereas only 39% and 28% of the underuse and optimal-use subjects did so.

Our prediction that a high variance among the others' harvest would also enhance the desire for change was not supported on the other hand. Although 51% of the subjects in the high-variance condition voted for change in comparison to 38% in the low-variance condition, the difference was not statistically reliable.

Despite the fact that the efficiency manipulation had a large impact on the desire for structural change, there was no corresponding impact on the individual harvest decisions. Statistical analysis of the harvest decisions indicated that the average harvest size increased over the 10 trials and that the predicted interaction between efficiency and variance (and trials) occurred. The pattern for this interaction only partly supported our analysis, however, in that the expected *increase* in harvest size in the high-variance underuse condition was obtained but the expected decrease in the high-variance overuse condition was not obtained.

This experiment has been replicated, with one major change and several minor ones, both in the United States, at the University of California, Santa Barbara, and in The Netherlands, at the University of Groningen (Samuelson, Messick, Rutte, & Wilke, 1984). We need not be concerned with the minor changes, but the major change is important. In the first study, we manipulated the efficiency variable by holding the replenishment rate constant and varying the purported harvests of the others in the group to create the overuse, underuse, and optimal-use conditions. Overuse and underuse are, of course, relative concepts that describe the *relationship* between the availability of a resource and the consumption of it. It is therefore possible to create conditions of overuse, underuse, and optimal use by holding behavior constant and manipulating resource availability. In our experimental setup, this would mean varying the replenishment rate. This is what we did.

In these experiments, subjects were given false feedback about the harvests of the other subjects, but this false feedback was exactly the same in all three efficiency conditions. The mean harvests of others were constructed so as to be optimal for a replenishment rate of 10%. In the overuse condition, the subjects were instructed that the replenishment rate was 3%; in the underuse condition they were told it was 17%; and in the optimal-use condition they were told that the replenishment rate was 10%. As in the first experiment, the pool size dropped over trials in the overuse condition but not in the other two. Procedurally, these experiments were identical to the first one.

Our predictions regarding the subjects' decisions to change the interdependence structure, to eliminate free access in favor of electing a leader, are precisely the same as in the first experiment. The predictions with regard to individual harvests are different, however. Because the false feedback about the others' behavior is constant across the efficiency conditions, the conflict between conformity and intelligent pool use that characterized the first study is eliminated. Of the three sources of influence that we proposed only one, the desire to use the pool wisely, should be influenced by the efficiency manipulation. Consequently, unlike the first study, we predicted that individual harvests would be lowest in the overuse condition, next in the optimal-use condition, and greatest in the underuse condition. Out expectations regarding the affects of the variance variable were very similar to those in the first study.

To both the Dutch and the American experiments, our predictions with regard to the efficiency manipulation were confirmed, both for the leader vote and for individual harvests. In the overuse conditions, 60% to 70% of the subjects voted to conduct the second session with a leader who would have exclusive access to the resource. Only 20% to 40% of the subjects in the other conditions did so. Moreover, in both locations, subjects in the overuse condition harvested less than subjects in the optimal-use or underuse conditions. Thus, it appears that subjects in these resource dilemmas will opt to change the nature of their interdependence, to replace a system of free individual access to the resource with a leader with exclusive authority, when the resource is being overused causing its level to decline. However, the perceived overuse only results in *individual* decisions to curtail harvest size when the overuse is a result of a drop in the replenishment rate, an environmentally caused overuse, and not when it is produced by an increase in others' harvests, a socially caused shortage—as in the first experiment.

The effects of the variance manipulation, on the other hand, were quite different in the Santa Barbara experiment than in the Groningen study. The former experiment closely replicated the findings of the first study (which was also done in the United States). There was evidence that the high-variance conditions weakened the pressures for subjects to conform their harvests to the average of others in their groups in that there were larger harvests in the high- than low-variance underuse and optimal-use conditions. However, as with the first experiment, there was no evidence that the relative homogeneity or heterogeneity of the harvests influenced the subjects' desire to alter the nature of the interdependence. The difference between the 37% of the high-variance subjects who preferred a leader and the 47% of the low-variance subjects expressing this preference was not statistically significant.

In the Dutch study, in contrast, 46% of the high-variance and 26% of the low-variance subjects voted to elect a leader, and the difference between these figures is statistically reliable. On the other hand, there was absolutely no evidence that the variance manipulation influenced the individual harvest decisions to the slightest degree. So this variable appears to have influenced *only* individual harvests in Santa Barbara and *only* preferences for structural change in The Netherlands. Samuelson, Messick, Rutte, and Wilke (1984) have speculated that the Dutch subjects viewed the high-variance condition as morally objectionable, whereas the American students viewed the same condition as justification for increasing their own harvests. Thus, depending on the cultural interpretation of the heterogeneity, it can lead to structural solutions to the dilemma, as in The Netherlands, or to an exacerbation of it, as in the United States.

In either case, these results and our other findings highlight the fact that the problems of interdependence that characterize resource dilemmas can be solved by individual changes in behavior within the existing structure, that is, by adjusting individual harvest sizes or by changing the structure itself, that is, by electing a leader representing a superordinate authority to replace the system of free individual access. In studying decision making in interdependent contexts, like the resource dilemmas that we have focused on, it is important to try to understand not only the determinants of decisions *within* the context but also the determinants of decisions *about* the context.

Will approval voting become widely adopted, and, if so, how will it happen? If not, why?

CONCLUSION

This chapter has focused on but two of a number of issues that have been raised by the study of decision making in situations of human interdependence. Virtually nothing has been said about strategic interaction like bargaining, negotiation, competition, or conflict resolution, nor has space permitted discussion of other central problems like processing information from and about social sources, using others to accomplish one's ends (power, influence, persuasion), or the multitude of issues involved in studying group decision making. A number of these topics have been addressed directly or indirectly in other chapters in this book. I have focused on interdependent preferences and changing interdependence structures in part because they represent current research interests, but also because I believe they are both fundamentally important processes. Interdependent preferences are arguably one of the most basic social psychological phenomena, appearing in rudimentary form in very young infants as sympathetic distress (Hoffman, 1975), the tendency for infants to cry in response to the sound of another infant's crying. The focus on conditions under which we will want to change interdependence structures is profoundly important because it reminds us that although we cannot avoid interdependence, we can often choose how the interdependence will be structured.

REFERENCES

Adams, J. S. (1965). Inequity in social exchange. In L. Berkowitz (Ed.), *Advances in experimental social psychology* (Vol. 2). New York: Academic Press.

Arrow, K. J. (1951). *Social choice and individual values.* New York: Wiley.

Austin, W., McGinn, N. C., & Susmilch, C. (1980). Internal standards revisited: Effect of social comparisons and expectancies on judgments of fairness and satisfaction. *Journal of Experimental Social Psychology, 16,* 426–441.

Brams, S. J. (1975). *Game theory and politics.* New York: Free Press.

Brams, S. J. (1976). *Paradoxes in politics.* New York: Free Press.

Brams, S. J., & Fishburn, P. C. (1983). *Approval voting.* Boston: Birkhäuser.

Colman, A. (1982). *Game theory and experimental games.* Oxford: Pergamon.

Crosby, F. J. (1982). *Relative deprivation and working women.* New York: Oxford University Press.

Cross, J. C., & Guyer, M. J. (1980). *Social traps.* Ann Arbor: University of Michigan Press.

Davidson, D., Suppes, P., & Siegel, S. (1957). *Decision making: An experimental approach.* Stanford: Stanford University Press.

Davis, J. H. (1969). *Group performance.* Reading, MA: Addison-Wesley.

Festinger, L. A. (1954). Theory of social comparison processes. *Human Relations, 7,* 117–140.

Hamburger, H. (1979). *Games as models of social phenomena.* San Francisco: Freeman.

Hardin, G. (1968). The tragedy of the commons. *Science, 162,* 1243–1248.

Hoffman, M. L. (1975). Developmental synthesis of affect and cognition and its implications for altruistic motivation. *Developmental Psychology, 11,* 607–622.

Homans, G. C. (1961). *Social behavior: Its elementary forms.* New York: Harcourt, Brace & World.

Hornstein, H. A. (1972). Promotive tension: The basis of prosocial behavior from a Lewinian perspective. *Journal of Social Issues, 28,* 191–218.

Hornstein, H. A. (1976). *Cruelty and kindness.* Englewood Cliffs: Prentice Hall.

Kelley, H. H., & Thibaut, J. W. (1978). *Interpersonal relations: A theory of interdependence.* New York: Wiley.

Krebs, D. (1975). Empathy and altruism. *Journal of Personality and Social Psychology, 32,* 1134–1146.

Latané, B., & Darley, J. M. (1970). *The unresponsive bystander: Why doesn't he help?* New York: Appleton-Century-Crofts.

Martin, J., & Murray, A. (1983). Distributive justice and unfair exchange. In D. M. Messick & K. S. Cook (Eds.), *Equity theory.* New York: Praeger.

McClintock, C. G., Messick, D. M., Kuhlman, D. M., & Campos, F. T. (1973). Motivational bases of choice in three-choice decomposed games. *Journal of Experimental Social Psychology, 9,* 572–590.

Messé, L. A., & Watts, B. L. (1983). Complex nature of the sense of fairness: Internal standards and social comparison as bases for reward evaluations. *Journal of Personality and Social Psychology, 45,* 84–93.

Messick, D. M. (1972). A stochastic model of preference in decomposed games. In Sauermann, H. (Ed.), *Contributions to experimental economics* (Vol. 3). Tübingen: Mohr.

Messick, D. M., & Brewer, M. B. (1983). Solving social dilemmas: A review. *Review of Personality and Social Psychology, 4,* 11–44.

Messick, D. M., & Cook, K. S. (Eds.). (1983). *Equity theory.* New York: Praeger.

Messick, D. M., & McClintock, C. G. (1968). Motivational bases of choice in experimental games. *Journal of Experimental Social Psychology, 4,* 1–25.

Messick, D. M., & Sentis, K. P. (1979). Fairness and preference. *Journal of Experimental Social Psychology, 15,* 418–434.

Messick, D. M., & Sentis, K. P. (1983a). Fairness, preference, and fairness biases. In D. M. Messick & K. S. Cook (Eds.), *Equity theory.* New York: Praeger.

Messick, D. M., & Sentis, K. P. (1983b). Estimating social and nonsocial utility functions from ordinal data. Unpublished manuscript.

Messick, D. M., & Thorngate, W. (1967). Relative gain maximizations in experimental games. *Journal of Experimental Social Psychology, 3,* 85–101.

Messick, D. M., Wilke, H., Brewer, M. B., Kramer, R. M., Zemke, P. E., & Lui, L. (1983). Individual adaptations and structural change as solutions to social dilemmas. *Journal of Personality and Social Psychology, 44,* 294–309.

Mosteller, F., & Nogee, P. (1951). An experimental measurement of utility. *Journal of Political Economy, 59,* 371–404.

Olson, M. (1965). *The logic of collective action.* Cambridge, MA: Harvard University Press.

Parker, R., Lui, L., Messick, C., Messick, D. M., Brewer, M. B., Kramer, R., Samuelson, C., & Wilke, H. (1983). A computer laboratory for studying resource dilemmas. *Behavioral Science, 28,* 298–304.

Pettigrew, T. F. (1967). Social evaluation theory: Convergence and applications. In D. Levine (Ed.), *Nebraska Symposium on Motivation* (Vol. 15). Lincoln: University of Nebraska Press.

Platt, J. Social traps. (1973). *American Psychologist, 28,* 641–651.

Reynolds, H. T. (1983). A proposal for elections (Review of *Approval voting*). *Science, 221,* 450–451.

Riker, W. H., & Ordeshook, P. C. (1973). *An introduction to positive political theory.* Englewood Cliffs, NJ: Prentice-Hall.

Runciman, W. G. (1966). *Relative deprivation and social justice: A study of attitudes to social inequality in twentieth-century England.* Berkeley: University of California Press.

Samuelson, C. D., Messick, D. M., Rutte, C. G., & Wilke, H. (1984). Individual and structural solutions to resource dilemmas in two cultures. *Journal of Personality and Social Psychology, 47,* 94–104.

Schelling, T. C. (1978). *Micromotives and macrobehavior.* New York: Norton.

Sen, A. K. (1970). *Collective choice and social welfare.* Edinburgh: Oliver & Boyd.

Siegel, S. (1957). Level of aspiration and decision making. *Psychological Review, 64,* 253–262.

Smith, A. (1976). *The theory of moral sentiments.* Oxford: Clarendon Press. (Work originally published in 1759)

Steiner, I. D. (1972). *Group process and productivity.* New York: Academic Press.

Stouffer, S., Lumsdaine, A., Lumsdaine, M., William, R., Smith, M., Janis, I., Star, S., & Cottrell, L. (1949). *The American soldier.* Princeton: Princeton University Press.

Suls, J. M., & Miller, R. L. (1977). *Social comparison processes.* New York: Wiley.

Thibaut, J. W., & Kelley, H. H. (1959). *The social psychology of groups.* New York: Wiley.

Tversky, A., & Kahneman, D. (1981). The framing of decisions and the psychology of choice. *Science, 211,* 453–458.

van Avermaet, E. (1974). *Equity: A theoretical and experimental analysis.* Unpublished doctoral dissertation, University of California, Santa Barbara.

von Neumann, J., & Morgenstern, O. (1944). *Theory of games and economic behavior.* Princeton: Princeton University Press.

CHAPTER 6

Combining Individual Judgments

William R. Ferrell

INTRODUCTION

It is often assumed that n heads are better than one, that a judgment obtained from a group will be of higher quality than could be expected from an individual. This chapter considers the effectiveness of methods that have been proposed for combining individual quantitative judgments into a group judgment. For the most part, it will be found that n heads are, indeed, better than one, and at least one investigator has concluded that it does not much matter how they are combined. But the potential for improving performance is so great and the problems of achieving it so subtle that a clear understanding of the issues is essential.

Why Groups?

The importance of quantitative judgments as inputs to decision processes has increased with the growing use of decision analysis and its extension to social issues and to large-scale system design. Judgmental input is needed because of such factors as (a) lack of objective data, (b) high levels of uncertainty about future conditions and the efficacy of actions, and (c) the desire to include in the analysis factors that are in priniciple difficult or impossible to measure, things that are essentially matters of judgment. The most common approach taken to attempt to assure the quality of such judgments is to seek multiple opinions, to use a panel of experts.

There are, of course, other reasons for obtaining a group opinion. The group itself may be the decision maker, attempting to choose an alternative that best

William R. Ferrell • Systems and Industrial Engineering Department, University of Arizona, Tucson, Arizona 85721.

satisfies the entire group. The problem of combining individual opinion for the group as a decision maker is quite different from that of the group as an expert. If the group must live with the decision, there are complex questions of equity among individuals, of satisfaction with the process by which the judgments are obtained, and of commitment to carrying out the action finally decided on. Group decision making itself is beyond the scope of the present chapter. So, too, are many kinds of judgments that are of vital importance to decision making, such as invention of alternatives, generation of hypotheses, and solving problems. The focus will be on aggregation of quantitative judgments to provide a group judgment of potentially higher quality according to such criteria as consistency or agreement with an objective standard.

There is ample evidence that human judgment, even group judgment should not be relied upon when there are objective measures and hard data, even very little of them, from which to infer the desired quantities. Expertise, especially about matters in the future, is usually overrated (Armstrong, 1980, provides an amusing review). When weighing the cost-effectiveness of judgment relative to taking data, it is probably wise to retain a healthy bias in favor of empirical observation.

Aggregation Methods

There are two basic kinds of aggregation of opinion—mathematical and behavioral. An example of mathematical aggregation is the simple averaging of the judgments of separate people. Purely behavioral aggregation is the process whereby the individuals discuss the matter and agree upon a value. Mixtures of the two are possible, and many methods have been proposed to attempt to improve behavioral aggregation by formal means. In the following sections, mathematical aggregation will be considered first; it will be followed by behavioral aggregation, and then methods that combine both types of aggregations.

MATHEMATICAL AGGREGATION

Mathematical methods of aggregation are especially attractive for practical decision problems because of their relative ease of use and apparent simplicity. The individuals need not be in the same location and can be queried by mail, telephone, or computer. Moreover, differences in such factors as status, personality, and assertiveness do not influence the judgments.

But the simplicity is, in part, only apparent because the mathematics of aggregation can produce complexities and paradoxical results in decision situations. Some of these problems are due to the mathematical properties of the aggregate's not completely representing the reality it purports to summarize. Two opposed zealots do not combine to a bland indifference. Other difficulties are rooted in the interaction between the axiom system for the measure being assessed, for example, probability, and the mathematical properties of the aggregation method. For example, averaging probabilities destroys their multiplicative properties. Finally, some of the difficulties are due to intractable measurement problems, such as the interpersonal comparison of values.

To see how complexities of aggregation can potentially affect decisions, consider the decision matrices for three members of a group shown in Table 1. Each individual prefers a different action on the basis of expected utility, so it seems appropriate to aggregate their opinions to find a decision for the entire group. But different formal methods give different results.

If a group decision matrix is formed as in Table 2, by averaging the probabilities and summing the individual utilities to give a group utility, Action A3

Table 1. Hypothetical Decision Matrices for Individuals

Person A		Action		
State	A1	A2	A3	Probability
B1	0	.5	1.0	.3
B2	1.0	0	.5	.2
B3	.5	1.0	0	.5
Expected utility	.45	.65	.40	1.0
Rank	2	1	3	

Person B		Action		
State	A1	A2	A3	Probability
B1	0	1.0	.75	.1
B2	1.0	.5	0	.6
B3	.5	0	1.0	.3
Expected utility	.75	.4	.375	1.0
Rank	1	2	3	

Person C		Action		
State	A1	A2	A3	Probability
B1	0	.5	1.0	.55
B2	.5	1.0	0	.15
B3	1.0	0	.5	.30
Expected utility	.375	.425	.7	1.0
Rank	3	2	1	

Table 2. The Group Decision Matrix Obtained by Averaging the Individual Probabilities and Summing the Individual Utilities from Table 1

Group State	Action A1	A2	A3	Probability
B1	0	2.0	2.75	.317
B2	2.5	1.5	.5	.317
B3	2.0	1.0	1.5	.367
Expected utility	1.527	1.477	1.580	1.0
Rank	2	3	1	

is preferred on the basis of the expected group utility. If the members vote on pairs of actions or sum the ranks of their individual preferences based on their own expected utilities, Action A2 wins. Finally, if the members agree to accept the average of their probabilities as a best estimate for the group and recalculate their own expected utilities, Person A's opinion does not change, but B's and C's rankings change completely. If they then vote, Action A1 would win. That would also be the result of averaging the individual expected utilities for each action and choosing on the basis of the highest average. Raiffa (1968) gives examples to show that the paradox can arise even when all the members agree in preferring one action; the "group" opinion can favor a different action after aggregation.

Estimation of Unknown Quantities

Point estimates of unknown quantities are frequently required in decision analysis. Forecasts of parameters such as interest rates or labor cost and estimates of quantities such as process yield or efficiency are very often judged as fixed values rather than as probability distributions to keep the analysis of the decision mathematically tractable. And even when distributional estimates are required, the judged means or expected values can usually be thought of as point estimates of unknown true values.

Random Error Model for Judgment

If the individual estimates are modeled as being true values with an added zero-mean, independent random error, results from mathematical statistics show that the best aggregation method is the simple average over the n individuals because its expectation is the true value and its standard deviation is a minimum.

One can get as accurate a group estimate as necessary by combining the estimates of a sufficiently large number n of individuals because the standard deviation is proportional to $1/\sqrt{n}$. However, the additional number required for a given percentage reduction in the standard deviation increases in proportion to the number of individuals. Thus, there will generally be an optimum number, depending on the cost of obtaining independent judgments and on the cost of error in the final group judgment.

Much of the early research on group task performance compared average judgments based on perception, for example, of numerosity or the weight of objects, with individual judgments. Group averages consistently outperformed individuals, and for such judgments the zero-mean error model is probably quite good. For judgments involving more complex information, this was not always the case (Rohrbaugh, 1979).

Correlated Judgments

In most practical situations, the individual judgments are not independent in the statistical sense, that is, the probability that two judges will both be in error by given amounts is not the product of their individual probabilities of doing so. The usual case is for a positive correlation between judgments so that when one judge has under- or overestimated, the others are more likely to have done the same. It seems reasonable to expect that experts will tend to agree on matters within their field of expertise.

Hogarth (1978), following Ghiselli (1964), has examined this situation in detail. Accuracy of the group judgment can be measured by the correlation between the true value and the average of the estimates of the n individuals. If this is done, accuracy will not increase to 1 as n increases. It will be strictly limited, depending on the intercorrelation among average individual estimates and on the average individual accuracy. When the average individual accuracy is low but the average intercorrelation of judges is even lower, the performance of the group average improves strongly with group size n. Small amounts of independent knowledge do add up. But when the intercorrelation of the individuals is greater than their average accuracy, the limit to group performance is reached with quite small groups, as can be seen in Figure 1.

Hogarth (1978) has derived the condition for a new member to increase the group performance. Because the new member can increase the average intercorrelation among individuals even when increasing the average individual performance, it is possible to have a case in which a less expert individual with independent knowledge is preferred to a more expert one whose judgments correlate highly with the others'.

There is substantial evidence that people's ability to judge quantities that depend on a variety of casual factors is relatively poor and that their judgments tend to be highly intercorrelated. In those cases, the performance of the group

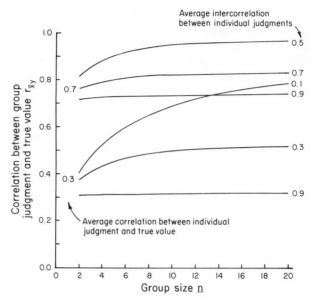

Figure 1. The quality of the group judgment as a function of group size for groups of different expertise and independence. After "A Note on Aggregating Opinions" by R. M. Hogarth, 1978, *Organizational Behavior and Human Performance*, 21, pp. 42–43.

judgment, the average of the individual judgments, will be limited to a rather low value, and the limit will be approached with quite small groups.

Biased Judgments

People often consistently over-or underestimate such quantities as cost, time to complete a project, or anticipated production. A simple model for judgments that are biased is that they consist of the true value plus an error that is random but with mean B rather than zero. Aggregation by averaging n individual judgments will give a group judgment with a variance smaller than that of the individual estimates, but it will not eliminate the mean error B. Under these circumstances, it would be valuable to be able to determine the individual with the smallest error on any particular occasion. For example, Ferrell and Curtis (1983) have found that the error of expert auditors' judgments of account balances can be predicted with fairly high accuracy from their uncertainty about them.

If the most accurate response could be identified, it should be the group judgment. The larger the group, the better the best response can be expected to be. However, if one individual were selected from the group at random to give the group judgment, performance would be poor; there would be no effect of group size at all if the group is a random selection of individuals. In between the performance of the best and of a random member is that of the average of all the group members. Although the average can be more accurate than the best member some of the time, it cannot be so on the average. A weighted average of the members that weights more heavily those who are more likely to be more accurate falls between the performance of the equally weighted average and the best member, closer to the latter to the extent that those with more accurate responses can be identified reliably. The simple weighted average is just

$$x_G = \sum_{i=1}^{n} w_i x_i \qquad (1)$$

where w_i is the weight given to individual i's estimate x_i and the sum of the weights is 1.

Weighting Individual Judgments

General Approaches

There are three approaches for obtaining the weights for weighted aggregations of individual judgments: self-rating, rating by the entire group, and methods based upon performance. In self-rating, the ith member gives an assessment v_i of personal expertise with respect to the judgment in question, say on a scale from 0 to 5. Normalized weights that sum to 1 are then calculated by dividing each individual assessment by the total of all the individual assessments.

In weighting by the entire group, each member judges all the members. There is then the problem of how to aggregate these individual judgments of expertise. Different methods have been employed, such as summing the ratings for each individual and then normalizing, or else normalizing first to give weights assigned by each individual and then averaging these. The latter is preferable if individuals seem to have different scales of ratings.

DeGroot Weighting

A conceptually elegant solution to the problem of aggregating the members' judgments of each other's expertise has been provided by DeGroot (1974). The ratings given by each member i to all the members j are first normalized to weights p_{ij} that sum to 1 for each member i. One can then interpret these weights as specifying a weighted linear combination of opinions about an unknown quantity that member i would accept as a better opinion than his or her own initial opinion. Consistent application of this principle requires that member i apply it not only to the initial opinions of all the members j but also to the opinions they each form in the same manner.

Conceptually, then, each member weights all the members' initial opinions to arrive at a new opinion; then he or she takes that opinion and the new opinions of all the others and weights them in the same way to get a still further revised opinion, and so on.

Under certain conditions, this iterative process will converge on a unique group opinion. For this, it is suffficient that at least one member be given some weight by all the members. When this is the case, it is only necessary to find a set of weights w_i that would have produced the group judgment in the first place. These can be found by solving the set of equations

$$\mathbf{w}P = \mathbf{w} \quad \text{subject to} \sum_{i=1}^{n} w_i = 1 \tag{2}$$

where $\mathbf{w}$ is the vector of weights being sought and P is the matrix $[P_{ij}]$ of weights assigned by member i to member j.

Although the concept can be used to derive weights, it may not be a good model of the way in which actual consensus takes place in a group (Hogarth, 1980).

SPAN

SPAN (successive proportionate additive numeration) is a method of weighted voting that applies to discrete judgments (McKinnon, 1966). It has considerable intuitive appeal and is readily understood by people without mathematical ability. Each member has, in effect, an equal number of votes, say 100, that may be divided among one or more of the other members of the group and/or among one or more of a set of discrete alternatives. The votes a member receives from others are passed on, according to the same initial allocation. Under suitable conditions, this iterative process converges with everybody's votes assigned to the alternatives, thereby ranking them or selecting one alternative to be the group choice. A sufficient condition for this to occur is for each individual to assign some portion of votes to at least one of the alternatives.

An important feature of the SPAN method is the variety of each member's options for participation. A member's influence on the outcome is maximized by putting all the votes on one alternative or is minimized by dividing them equally among the alternatives. But one also has the option of giving one's influence to those persons one thinks are better qualified to judge. If they do not think they are well qualified, they will have allocated their votes to others. Ideally, the influence of those who do not consider themselves to be qualified ends up being exercised by those who do and who also have the confidence of others.

The mathematics of SPAN is that of absorbing Markov chains. The alternatives are the absorbing states. The members of the group are the nonabsorbing states, and the transition probabilities from each member to every other state are the fraction of votes assigned by that member to that state. Thus, one can easily compute the final totals as the probabilities of terminating in each absorbing state. But, as in its initial application by McKinnon, apportioning votes can be carried out by computer, or even by hand, to determine the final vote totals.

Performance Weighting

Weights based on subjective judgments presumably embody the perceived ability of the individual being judged to perform the task in question. A more direct approach but one for which there may not always be adequate data is to weight the individuals' contributions on the basis of measured past performance. There are many such schemes because there are many ways to measure performance. Such methods apply to all kinds of estimates, not just the judgments of individuals, and most of the work on the problem has been motivated by the desire to improve statistical forecasts by combining different estimates.

One very general approach has been to treat the set of forecasts or judgments as an observed sample of data and then to try to obtain the conditional distribution of the true value given the observed sample. The mean of that distribution is then taken as the group judgment. To do this, one needs to make assumptions about the statistical properties of the judgments. If they are assumed to be normally distributed about the true value and if their variances and covariances are known or can be estimated, Bordley (1982a) shows that the mean value of the conditional distribution is a weighted sum of the individual judgments. If the judgments are independent, the weights are inversely proportional to the judgment variances about the true value.

If the same approach is taken with judgments assumed to be lognormal, the group judgment is a weighted geometric mean rather than a linear combination. Still other assumptions yield other results.

When judgment performance changes with time, the weights need to change with it. For example, Bates and Granger (1969) compared several differential weighting methods for linearly combining two forecasts from different sources when there was a history of forecast errors. To account for change in error with time, they used weights that differentially emphasized more recent performance.

Roberts (1965) has suggested, for a linear combination of probability judgments, weighting each member in proportion to the product of that person's past probability judgments for events that actually occurred. Thus, the member who consistently gives the highest probabilities to those events that actually happen would get the most weight. Giving a zero probability to an event that happens, gives that member a zero weight from then on because of the zero factor in the product of probabilities.

Performance of Differential Weighting Methods

Both behavioral and performance-based differential weighting methods have been tested in a number of contexts but mostly in connection with assessment of probabilities and with methods for aiding group opinion aggregation. The results have consistently shown only slight or no improvement over equal weighting. Some of these studies will be described later.

The reasons for such lackluster performance from a method that seems so intuitively appealing are perhaps several.

1. The improvement in performance over equal weighting that can be obtained by identifying even the best judgment in a relatively small group may not be very large, and the probability of selecting the best must be quite high to obtain an advantage if the best is not known for sure.
2. In practical groups, individuals are likely to be of almost equal expertise. Were they aware of large discrepancies of abilities to do the task, the group would probably be constituted differently.
3. Judgment tasks are frequently information limited, rather than expertise limited. Skilled professional groups, for example, weather forecasters, usually have access to the same information.
4. Equal or even random weights perform remarkably well in comparison with optimal ones in multiple linear regression (Wainer, 1976), and perhaps the simple average performs similarly to weighted averages because of the general insensitivity of linear models to weighting.

Differential weighting would be expected to have the most advantage for a moderately large group of well-acquainted individuals that frequently works together and has a wide range of different types of expertise to bring to bear on questions that require an equally wide range of knowledge. Few experimental situations provide these conditions.

The SPAN method has shown advantages over equal weighting. Aguilar (1980) compared it with simple plurality voting and with percentage voting with a 7-member group. In percentage voting, one allocates 100 points among the alternatives. The questions were four alternative multiple choice and were designed to tap a wide range of general knowledge such as sports, cooking, business, history, and the like. The group was comparably heterogeneous, and the members were all well acquainted. SPAN consistently gave higher weight to the correct answer and achieved a significantly higher percentage of correct answers. In earlier tests, Willis, Hitchcock, and McKinnon (1969) found SPAN better than equal weighting methods but not better than an alternative method in which individual weights were established by the group.

Discrete Probability Judgments

To find methods that give a group probability judgment that is better than individual judgments, it is necessary to specify ways in which one such judgment can be better than another. Seaver, von Winterfeldt, and Edwards (1978) suggest the following criteria:

1. consistency with the rules of probability, including those for modification in the light of evidence;
2. ability to discriminate between events that do occur and those that do not, with events that do occur being assigned relatively high probabilities and those that do not relatively low probabilities;
3. good calibration in that the relative frequency of occurrence of all the events assigned a given probabilty should be equal to that probability; and
4. high scores when evaluated by proper scoring rules, ones that give the best score when the judgments correspond to the beliefs of the respondent.

Probability is constrained by its axioms to be a measure on an absolute scale. Just as with numerosity, the number of discrete items, there is no transformation of probability, no function $g(p)$, that is also a probability and that preserves all its information. If subjective probabilities are to have the properties of probabilities, then one cannot in principle find for a given individual a general function relating that person's subjective probability judgments to their objective counterpart, the relative frequency of occurrence of the events to which they are applied. That relationship must necessarily depend upon the events. Nevertheless, calibration curves that give the relation between judged probabilities and relative frequencies for specified sets of events are useful indicators of judgment quality, even if they do not generalize to other sets of events.

In a similar way, there is no nontrivial single function of any vector of n probabilities, for example, the judgments of n group members, that involves all n components and that is itself a probability. As a result, there is no single function $p(p_1, p_2, \ldots p_n)$ that can consistently be used for aggregation independently of the events being judged. This was pointed out by Dalkey (1975).

The kinds of problems involved are easily demonstrated. The average of consistent probability judgments of individuals will not obey the rules of probability. Let A and B be independent events so that their joint subjective probability is the product of their subjective probabilities for each individual, $p(A,B)=p(A)p(B)$. However, the average $p(A,B)$ does not equal the product of the averages of $p(A)$ and $p(B)$.

Bayesian Aggregation with Independent Observations

A theoretically sound approach to the problem of aggregating individual probability estimates is to treat the individual probabilities as if they had resulted from a process of Bayesian revision of prior opinion based on evidence. From this, the nature of each member's evidence is inferred, and the group probability is obtained by pooling the evidence.

Bayesian revision of the probability of an event $p(E)$ and of its nonoccurrence $1-p(E)$ can best be thought of in terms of the odds in favor of the event $O(E)=p(E)/[1-p(E)]$. When evidence is obtained, the prior $O(E)$ is revised by multiplying it by a number L, the likelihood ratio, to give a new value, the posterior $O(E)$. The likelihood ratio L measures the impact of the evidence. It is 1 if there is no impact, greater than 1 if the evidence favors E, and less than 1 if it favors the nonoccurrence of E.

The value of L can thus be inferred from the resulting change in the probability of E. If evidence is independent, the value of L depends only on each individual piece of evidence and not on any previous evidence obtained. Thus, the impact of n pieces is just the product of the n values of L.

If one assumes that the probability given by each member of a group has been obtained by observing independent evidence and revising a prior probability, one can obtain a group judgment that takes all the evidence into account by multiplying together all the individual values of L implied by the individual probabilities. This group's posterior odds is then converted to a group probability $p_G(E)$. In terms of the indivudal probabilities p_G is the multiplicative relation

$$p_G = \frac{\prod_{i=1}^{n} p_i(E)}{\prod_{i=1}^{n} p_i(E) + \prod_{i=1}^{n} [1-p_i(E)]} \tag{3}$$

The group probability will be more extreme than the individual probabilities even if all the members agree on a single value because they all supposedly have independent evidence as to whether E will occur so that the pooled evidence is stronger. But, reasoning that if the experts agree on a probability, the group probability ought to be that value, Morris (1983) rejects this formulation in favor of a weighted average. He shows that a weighted average is the correct Bayesian result if the probability being estimated is the parameter of a Bernoulli process. In that case, the evidence provides an estimate of the value of an unknown quantity, like the proportion of red balls in an urn, rather than discriminating between mutually exclusive hypotheses such as which of two differently filled urns is being drawn from. It is thus important to take into account the nature of the probability being judged (but that is not always easy, for example, the probability of the stock market's going up).

Bayesian Approach with Dependence and/or Miscalibration

Individuals seldom have entirely independent information, and in most cases they tend to be overconfident rather than well calibrated. As a result, it may be necessary to provide for these factors in the aggregation, and more information is needed than just the probability judgments themselves.

One way to think of a group probability judgment is as the opinion of a decision maker based on the advice of n experts. Viewed in this way, the information about the experts' interdependence and calibration can be considered to be the decision maker's opinion about the experts—the group members. With this premise, Bordley (1982b) has rigorously derived a multiplicative aggregation formula for discrete events that does not require the individuals to have independent information but that does assume that the decision maker's opinion of each of the individuals is independent of the probabilities given by the others.

Bordley's aggregation rule is most simply stated in likelihood ratio terms

$$L_G = L_1^{w_1} L_2^{w_2} \ldots L_n^{w_n} \tag{4}$$

where L_i is the likelihood ratio that would revise the prior probability of event E from its (common) prior value to the value p_i stated by the ith individual, and where w_i is a weight reflecting the decision maker's opinion of that individual's knowledge. L_G is then the likelihood ratio that the decision maker should use to revise the same common prior probability into a group probability.

Equation 4 can be rewritten as in Bordley (1982b), in terms of the prior P_o and the individual judgments p_i as

$$p_G = \frac{\prod_{i=1}^{n} \left(\dfrac{p_i}{p_o}\right)^{w_i}}{\prod_{i=1}^{n} \left(\dfrac{p_i}{p_o}\right)^{w_i} + \prod_{i=1}^{n} \left(\dfrac{1-p_i}{1-p_o}\right)^{w_i}} \tag{5}$$

If the $w_i = 1$ and $p_o = 1/2$, this is just the independent case of Equation 3. If the sum of the weights equals 1, it is as if all the individuals share one observation among them, and if they agree, that is also the group judgment. If the sum of the weights is between 1 and n, it is as if the indivudals are somewhat independent or somewhat underconfident or both, and the results of agreement is a group judgment farther from the prior than the common individual judgment. When the sum of weights is less than 1, the opposite is the case, and it is as if the individuals' common judgment were to be considered overconfident. Actually, of course, the effects of both calibration and independence are combined in the weights.

Linear Combination

Probably the most commonly used method of aggregation for discrete event probabilities is the weighted linear combination, that is, the weighted average. It is a theoretically consistent method when the judgments can be modeled as estimates of the parameter of a probabilistic process based on binomial samples. However, it is a good choice, even when it is not a theoretically consistent method (Einhorn & Hogarth, 1975). Many reward functions, for example scoring rule scores, are concave with respect to probability so that the reward for using the average probability will be greater than the average of the rewards obtained using the individual probabilities.

Performance of Probability Aggregation Methods

There have been a number of attempts systematically to test aggregation methods for discrete probability judgments. Staël von Holstein (1970) used weighted linear combinations of the probability judgments of people who were not expert. They gave probabilities for weather conditions and stock prices. Evaluation was by proper scoring rules. Weighting schemes based on measures of individual performance were tried, for example, weights proportional to the average score for previous judgments, weights proportional to performance rank, weights based on a moving average of scores, weights based on Roberts's (1965) method, and random weights.

Because the scoring rules were all concave on probability, the aggregated judgments outperformed individual judgments. However, there was very little difference in the performance of different weighting methods. The random weights even did better than the average of the other methods, and the performance-weighted methods only occasionally did better than equal weights.

Winkler (1971) used Roberts's weighting method along with equal weights, self-weighting, and weights based on past scores for linearly combining individual probabilities of football teams' winning. Again, the averages performed better than the average individuals, but only minor differences were noted among the weighting methods when evaluated by scoring rules. If one gives a zero probability to an event that happens, Roberts's method produces a weight of zero. This eliminated all but 2 of the 10 individuals very quickly. Treating a judgment of zero probability as if it were a small value retained a larger group size, but the score for the group was worse.

Seaver (1979) evaluated judgments both by scoring rules and by calibration. He compared individual judgments with the aggregated judgments of groups of four people. The task was to choose one of two answers to a general knowledge question and to give a subjective probability on [.5,1] that it was correct. For aggregation, this probability was transformed into the probability for the correct answer on [0,1].

Aggregation methods were weighted linear combination, weighted geometric mean (Equation 5 with $p_o = 1/2$), and likelihood ratio (Equation 3). The weighting methods were equal, self-weighting and DeGroot. However, there were no significant differences in performance due to the weighting method.

There were significant differences in calibration but not in score due to the aggregation method. The calibration results are shown in Figure 2. Individuals are overconfident as indicated by the responses being more extreme than the relative frequencies. The linear combination reduces this the most; the likelihood ratio not at all; and the geometric mean an intermediate amount. The differences in calibration with aggregation method can be attributed to two factors: (a) improvement in the proportion correct with all aggregation methods due to the fact that respondents were more often right than not, and (b) increase in the extremeness of the judgments. An increase in proportion correct tends to raise the calibration curve, producing relative underconfidence, and an increase in extremeness moves the curve to the right, producing relative overconfidence.

In the case of linear aggregation, there is no increase in extremeness, only

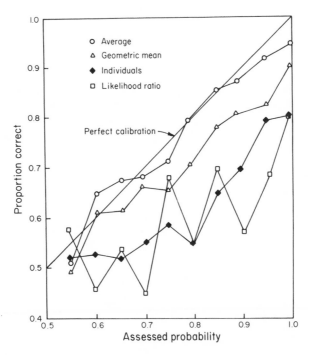

Figure 2. The effect on calibration of different methods of mathematical aggregation of discrete probability judgments. From "Assessing Probability with Multiple Individuals" by D. A. Seaver, unpublished doctoral dissertation, University of Southern California. Copyright 1979 by author. Adapted by permission.

in proportion correct. But the likelihood ratio aggregation assumes that the individuals are independent, and it causes a substantial increase in extremeness that cancels the effect of the increase in proportion correct. The geometric mean with weights summing to 1 is less extreme, and so is intermediate in calibration.

The fact that the linear combination gives good calibration is almost certainly an artifact of the overconfidence of individuals. One would expect the same relative ordering of conditions if the individuals were well calibrated to begin with, but then the aggregation would move the curves above the line of perfect calibration. This expectation was borne out in the simulation by Ferrell and Rehm (1980). They used the model of the way people generate subjective probabilities proposed by Ferrell and McGoey (1980) to produce individual judgments and combined them mathematically to simulate Seaver's (1979) experiment.

Probability Density Functions for Continuous Quantities

Uncertainty about continuous variables is described by probability density functions with the property that the area under the function between any two values of the variable is the probability that the true value of the quantity will lie in that interval. It is generally assumed that subjective uncertainty can be represented by a subjective probability density function (SPDF). There are a number of ways to specify the shape of such functions, and there are a corresponding number of ways to assess an individual's SPDF. Methods can be roughly classified as (a) those that ask for the probabilities corresponding to given values of the variable; (b) those that ask for fractiles, that is, values of the variable that correspond to specified probabilties; and (c) those that ask for parameters of an assumed functional form of an SPDF. In the first two types of assessments, a particular form of distribution may or may not be assumed.

Aggregation Methods

When the assessment method gives probabilities, the aggregation methods already described for discrete probabilities can be applied. Otherwise, there are again basically two approaches for continuous quantities—Bayesian methods and linear combination.

Bayesian Combination. The general Bayesian approach is exemplified by the work of Morris (1977, 1974, 1983). Using the general continuous form of Bayes's rule, he derives a theoretically correct multiplicative formula for combining individual SPDFs, $f_i(x)$. The individual SPDFs are taken as data with which to revise a diffuse prior that represents complete uncertainty. The result he obtains is

$$f_G(x) = kC(x) \prod_{i=1}^{n} f_i(x) \tag{6}$$

where k is a normalizing constant to make the SPDF integrate to 1, and $C(x)$ is a function that accounts for miscalibration and dependence among the individuals. If they are calibrated and independent, its value is 1. Obtaining a theoretically correct and intuitively meaningful value for $C(x)$ is very difficult, which has probably inhibited the practical application of Morris's excellent work.

When the posterior PDF resulting from Bayesian revision is of the same form as the prior, that form is said to be a *natural conjugate family*. The parameters of the posterior PDF are then functions of the parameters of the prior PDF. Winkler (1968) has proposed using the revised conjugate with weights on the individual parameters to obtain the aggregated group SPDF. Beta distributions represent a conjugate family. If the indivudal SPDFs are beta distributions with parameters r_i, $(n_i - r_i)$, the posterior group SPDF will be beta with parameters r_G, $(n_G - r_G)$ where

$$r_G = \sum_{i=1}^{n} w_i r_i \ , \ n_G = \sum_{i=1}^{n} w_i n_i \tag{7}$$

The normal is also a natural conjugate family, but the parameters of the aggregated distribution are not just the weighted sums of the individual ones.

Winkler (1981) has also developed a normal model for aggregation that explicitly assumes that the individual SPDFs are correlated. It is likely that correlations among individual assessments are high. For example, Winkler (1971) found pairwise correlations between sportswriters' errors of prediction of point spreads for football games to be between .73 and .97. Under the assumption that individuals are well calibrated and give normal SPDFs, Winkler's model correctly gives the weights to account for the intercorrelation among them. The result is the same as that derived by Bordley (1982a) for application to point estimation of unknown quantities. Agnew (1983) has developed a more general solution giving weights that adjust for both calibration and dependence based on past judgments.

Linear Combination. When values $f_i(x)$ of the individual's SPDF for the quantity X can be inferred directly from the judgments, one of the simplest methods is to obtain a group SPDF as a linear combination of the individual SPDFs.

$$f_G(x) = \sum_{i=1}^{n} w_i f_i(x) \tag{8}$$

If the weights sum to 1 and if the individual functions are proper probability densities, the aggregate will be, too. But, it will be a mixture distribution. It may even be multimodal if the individual SPDFs disagree sufficiently on the mean value. Typically, too, the variance of the group SPDF will be larger than the variances of the individual ones. This may be an advantage and lead to better calibration as will be indicated later.

Frequently, SPDFs are assessed by asking for specific fractiles. The p fractile is the value of the variable such that there is a probability p that the true value falls below it. When fractiles are assessed, they are sometimes simply averaged to give fractiles for the group SPDF. If the individual SPDFs are normal, then the group SPDF will also be normal with mean and standard deviation that are the average of the individual means and standard deviation.

Performance of Aggregation Methods of SPDFs

There have been few reported comparisons to date of mathematical methods of aggregation for continuous distributions. Evaluation is difficult and requires much data. Winkler (1968) compared self-weighting and equal weighting for linear combination of SPDFs of students assessing general knowledge questions. The quality of the resulting group distributions was not studied, but the differences between the results from the two weighting methods were slight.

Seaver (1979) has conducted the most comprehensive experiment. He asked inexpert subjects to judge the mode and an equivalent sample size to obtain subjective beta distributions for various unknown percentages requiring general knowledge. The mode is essentially a best guess, and the sample size a measure of spread. Subjects were carefully trained so that they could give those parameters accurately for pictures of different beta PDFs.

The resulting beta SPDFs were aggregated by a linear combination of the density functions and by the conjugate method of Equation 7, a linear combination of the individual parameters. In both cases equal, self- and DeGroot weights summing to 1 were used, but all weighting methods gave essentially the same results.

Calibration results are shown in Figure 3. On the calibration graph the abcissa is the area under an SPDF for the unknown percentage from 0 to some value x. It represents the subjective probability that the true value is less than x. The ordinate is the actual proportion of times the true value was less than x. As with discrete probabilities, overconfidence is represented by values being too near 0 or 1, that is, the SPDFs have too little spread. Departure of the curve from the (.5, .5) point indicates bias, consistent over or underestimation. Individuals were, on the average, overconfident and tended to underestimate the true values. Linear combination of their SPDFs produced group SPDFs with larger spread and thereby reduced the overconfidence, but it did not affect the underestimation much. The conjugate method had little effect on calibration, just as its counterpart, the likelihood ratio method, did in the discrete case.

In contrast to Seaver's (1979) inexpert subjects, those of Solomon (1982) were highly skilled accountant auditors who gave the .01, .10, .25, .50, .75, .9, and .99 fractiles of their SPDFs for the values of six accounts on the basis

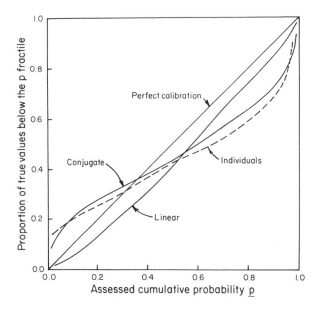

Figure 3. The effect on calibration of different methods of mathematical aggregation of subjective probability density functions. From "Assessing Probability with Multiple Individuals" by D. A. Seaver, unpublished doctoral dissertation, University of Southern California. Copyright 1979 by author. Adapted by permission.

of standard accounting information. The fractiles were averaged in groups of three to give group fractiles. The resulting .50 group fractile, taken as an estimate of the true value, had an average absolute error 20% less than that of individuals. By taking the actual best judgment in each group, the error would have been reduced by about 65%. As shown in Figure 4, calibration of individuals was fairly good, with a moderate underestimation bias and slight overconfidence. But the group calibration was substantially underconfident relative to individuals.

Because of the high consistency and expertise of the auditors, Ferrell and Curtis (1983) were able to predict each auditor's absolute error on each account with some accuracy. They found that the fractile judgments closely fitted the normal distribution and used a regression equation on the subjective standard deviation and the .50 fractile to predict the error. Selecting the predicted best individual from groups of three by this means led to an improvement in accuracy of 46% over individuals and calibration that was better than with the averaging of fractiles.

Evaluative Judgments and Preferences

The viewpoint taken here on aggregation of individual evaluations and preferences is that of achieving a better informed and more "correct" evalua-

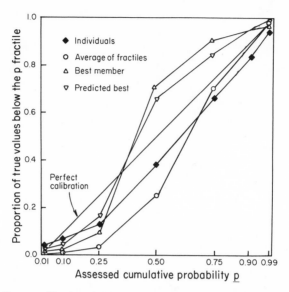

Figure 4. The effect on calibration of different methods of obtaining a group subjective probability density function. Data from "Probability Assessment by Individual Auditors and Audit Teams: An Empirical Investigation" by I. Solomon, 1982, *Journal of Accounting Research, 20,* p. 702.

tion by taking into account opinion from different sources. The problem of obtaining a group utility, which should be equitable and otherwise satisfactory to the members for use in a group decision is avoided insofar as is possible. But the line between is not entirely clear.

Preference Order

Arrow's famous "impossibility theorem" shows that there is no transitive group rank ordering that is a function of a set of *n* individual orderings when certain assumptions are made that guarantee that each individual's opinion will count and that misstating an opinion will not give one more influence. The axioms are (from Olnick, 1978):

1. Each individual may have any preference order on the (3 or more) outcomes.
2. The aggregation function produces a unique transitive group preference order.
3. If every individual prefers one outcome to another, so does the group.
4. The group ordering of any two outcomes depends only on the members' preferences for that pair. (This is sufficient to insure that no individual can unduly affect the group ranking by misstating opinion.)

5. There is no one whose preference between a given pair of outcomes is always the group's preference.

Many schemes, such as the summing of ranks and the like, are commonly used even though they are not consistent with these axioms and lead to paradoxical results in some cases.

The most popular method for selecting a group alternative or indicating a group rank order is voting. The study of voting methods is exceedingly complex and technical. The effectiveness of methods depends critically on the type of mathematical order represented by the outcomes, the temporal order of voting, the possibility of coalitions, the possibility of voting contrary to one's opinion, and so on.

As Arrow's work dramatically points out, there can be no one best method, and thus all methods will be found defective in some respect. There are two recent approaches to the problem that are simple and robust, however. The simplest is approval voting. Each individual votes for all of the alternatives that are at least just acceptable. The group ranking is in order of the number of votes each alternative receives. It has been carefully studied by Brams and Fishburn (1982) who find it superior to many other methods. And its simplicity recommends it for actual use in elections. By ignoring most information about individual preference orders, it achieves sensitivity to collective opinion and avoids paradoxical results.

An alternative to using less information about individual preferences is to use rules to make just enough alteration in their expressed preferences in order to enforce consistency. Marcotorchino and Michaud (1982) use pairwise comparison of alternatives to generate a table showing the number of individuals who prefer alternative i to alternative j. They then apply constraints to this table, such that it must represent a transitive order and apply an optimization algorithm to perturb the entries, but as little as possible, until such an order is reached.

Cardinal Utility

Arrow's impossibility theorem does not hold when individual preferences for outcomes can be described by cardinal (i.e., interval scaled) utility functions. Keeney (1976) shows that a set of five axioms that are essentially the same as Arrow's, but substituting utilities for orderings, is consistent and that there are many such group aggregation functions when the outcomes are certain, that is, when lotteries among the outcomes are not included in the set of outcomes.

For uncertain outcomes, Keeney (1976) proves that only the weighted linear combination of individual utilities is consistent with the axioms. The weights can be thought of as being the product of two factors, as Brock (1980) points out. The first factor scales the different utilities after they have been normalized to $[0,1]$ so that the unit of measurement is the same size for each individual. The second factor weights the importance of the individual. In the evaluation situation considered here, this would represent the relative capacity of that person to contribute to a sound evaluation. In a strict sense, there can be no group utility function because obtaining the weights requires interpersonal comparison of utilities, a process for which there is no formally correct algorithm.

Other, more general methods for combining individual utilities have been proposed of which the weighted linear combination is a special case, for example, multiplicative aggregation (Keeney & Kirkwood, 1975). The principle objective of such aggregations is to provide equity among individuals with respect to decisions under uncertainty. For example, they could work to prevent an option in which Individual 1 gets everything and Individual 2 gets nothing from being equal in group utility to one in which each person has an equal chance.

Evaluating Aggregations of Evaluative Judgments

It is difficult to specify criteria to test the effectiveness of methods for mathematically aggregating evaluative judgments. In part, this is because value is inherently a subjective judgment, and in part it is because of the ill-structuredness, complexity, and high dimensionality of the situations for which aggregated judgments are desirable. Mathematical aggregation may function largely as a formal way of proving that one has taken a variety of opinions into account, and its main technical advantage may be to reduce the variability of the evaluation, to make it more repeatable.

Aggregation of Verbal Judgments

Subjective judgments are often given in verbal form. An event is "quite likely," quality is "very high," or a quantity is "more than a little." Language designates categories to which things may not belong absolutely, but only to some degree, that is, it designates fuzzy sets. Fuzzy set theory (Kaufmann, 1975) has been proposed as the mathematical basis for aggregation of verbally expressed judgments (Cooley & Hicks, 1983).

Linguistic Variables

A fuzzy set is a set of elements each of which has associated with it a membership value m on the interval $[0,1]$ indicating the degree to which that element is characteristic of or belongs to the set in question. Ordinary nonfuzzy sets have elements with membership values of 1. A notation for a fuzzy set x is

$$X = \bigcup_{i \in B} \{m_x(i), [i]\} \tag{9}$$

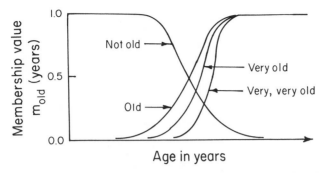

Figure 5. Membership functions for the fuzzy linguistic category *old* and related categories.

where U means the union of, *i* indexes the elements, and $m_x(i)$ is the membership value. *B* is the base set of elements. For ordinary sets, $m_x(i)=1$.

A linguistic variable, such as *old,* can be defined on the base set age in years by a fuzzy set that specifies how characteristic any particular age is of the category *old* (Zadeh, 1975). The imprecision of the meaning of the term, the fact that there is no specific age at which one becomes old, is thereby given precise specification (see Figure 5 for a graphical representation).

The base scale for a linguistic variable need not be a physically measureable quantity; it can also be a generalized scale of the attribute in question. For computational tractability, the scale is almost always discrete, so that the fuzzy set has a relatively small number of elements. Linguistic variables are also normalized so that their maximum membership values are 1.

As a qualifying adverb modifies an adjective or adverb, a linguistic hedge modifies a linguistic variable. *Very, somewhat, more or less, indeed,* and the like can be defined as operations on fuzzy sets that change them in accord with the linguistic meaning of the hedge. For example, *very* should result in a more extreme or concentrated fuzzy set. The operation of squaring the membership values is a possible method. Several hedges are also illustrated in Figure 5.

Binary operations of addition, subtraction, multiplication, and division have been defined for fuzzy sets, so that one can aggregate a collection of verbal judgments expressed in terms of hedged linguistic variables by taking, for example, a weighted average with verbally expressed weights. The definition of the binary operations on fuzzy sets has the same form for all four binary operations $+$, $-$, x, and /. If * represents a binary relation and x and y are linguistic variables

$$X*Y = \bigcup_{i \in B} \{m_x(i),[i]\} * \bigcup_{j \in B} \{m_y(j),[j]\}$$
$$= \bigcup_{i*j} \{MAX[MIN(m_x(i),m_y(i))], [i*j]\} \qquad (10)$$

The output of a binary operation is also a linguistic variable defined on the same base scale, and although it may not correspond exactly to a previously defined variable, it may be translated into a verbal judgment by finding a hedged version of a defined linguistic variable that is close to it (Eshragh & Mamdani, 1979).

Cooley and Hicks (1983) proposed evaluating the strength of control over accounts in a business firm by aggregation of verbal judgments of all the component parts of the system. They suggest several ways to do this. The priniciple is the same for aggregation over individual judgments. One of their examples shows that the average of *weak* and *strong* is *medium*. If *weak* is defined on a base scale of 1 to 9 as $\{1.[1],.875[2], .5[3],.125[4]\}$, and if *strong* is $\{.125[6],.5[7],.875[8],1.[9]\}$, then application of Equation 10 gives $(weak + strong)/2 = \{.125[3.5],.5[4],.875[4.5],1.[5],.875[5.5],.5[6],.125[6.5]\}$. These fuzzy sets are shown in Figure 6.

Evaluation

Although the literature of fuzzy sets has become very large (Gaines & Kohout, 1977), there have been only a very few empirical tests of the ability of fuzzy sets to capture natural language usage, for example, Hersh and Caramazza (1976) and Kochen and Badre (1974). There have also been relatively few attempts to evaluate application to practical situation. But the general trend of results has been encouraging and suggests that even if linguistic variables do not model actual natural language very well, they can still be usefully applied.

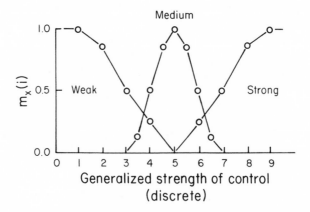

Figure 6. Membership functions for the fuzzy categories *weak, medium,* and *strong.* After "A Fuzzy Set Approach to Aggregating Internal Control Judgments" by J. W. Cooley and J. O. Hicks, 1983, *Management Science, 29,* pp. 321–322.

BEHAVIORAL AGGREGATION

Behavioral aggregation is the process whereby members of a group communicate among themselves and arrive at a group judgment. Potentially it can (a) increase resources by combining the knowledge and intelligence of the members and thereby obtain a judgment better than any member could produce; (b) increase members' motivation and their attention and effort directed toward the task; and (c) facilitate creativity, watchfulness for errors, and resolution of ambiguous and conflicting knowledge. In their review of the problem, Hackman and Morris (1975, p. 75) stated:

> Although literally thousands of studies of group performance have been conducted over the last several decades, we still know very little about why some groups are more effective than others.
>
> We know even less about what to do to improve the performance of a given group working on a specific task. Moreover, the few general findings that have emerged from the literature do not encourage the use of groups to perform important tasks. Research has shown, for example, that for many tasks the pooled output of noninteracting individuals is better than that of an interacting group.

They conclude that the group interaction process is critical to performance quality and that the challenge lies in identifying and controlling those aspects of it that can lead to optimum performance.

Group Process and the Judgment Task

Task characteristics are a prinicipal determinant of group performance. Judgment tasks are ones that Steiner (1972) describes as having the following properties relevant to group interaction. They are *unitary* in that the task cannot generally be divided into subtasks that members can perform individually. They are *optimizing* in the sense that there is a preferrred result that is to be sought. Finally, they are *discretionary* because the procedure followed and the manner of integrating the contributions of individuals is not strictly set by the task but is determined by the group itself. For tasks of this kind, the quality of the interaction process is expected to have a major influence on performance quality.

Effectiveness at judgment tasks will depend on the group's ability to use the group interaction process to find appropriate strategies to give suitable weight to the best knowledge and opinions that emerge and to encourage members to do their best with respect to both the problem at hand and the process itself (Hackman & Morris, 1975). An example of a strategy would be to decompose an estimate into judgments of component quantities from which the desired quantity can be computed.

Three factors have substantial and predictable effects on group judgment: (a) input variables that have potentially negative effects on group process; (b) conformity; and (c) polarization.

Input Variables

It is useful to think of group performance in terms of process gains, the extent to which the potential for better performance than that of the best member is achieved, and process losses, the degree to which the interaction intended to realize that potential actually reduces performance. There is wide agreement among researchers on those major input variables that influence group process and on their ability to cause process losses. A few of them are:

1. *Task norms.* Incorrect expectations about the task, for example, misconceptions about statistical reasoning in probability assessment, reduce performance quality.
2. *Process norms.* Many norms for behavior in ad hoc groups, such as avoiding disagreement, minimizing interaction and not taking initiative, inhibit effective group process.
3. *Group size.* Although increased group size improves the likelihood of having the requisite information or skill, it also makes communication more difficult and less effective.
4. *Group communication patterns.* Seating arrangements and procedural rules can strongly inhibit the flow of information.
5. *Perceived status of members.* When perceived status does not accord with an individual's potential to contribute, it can cause a misallocation of attention and misweighting of information.
6. *Individual personality characteristics.* Talkative and extroverted members generally have more influence, and even when they do not, can cause process losses. Personal needs and behaviors that do not coincide with task requirements detract from group effectiveness.
7. *Group experience.* Established and experienced task groups generally have the advantages of practice and of members knowing each others' strengths and weaknesses; however, they may also overemphasize behavior that is not task related.

Input variables also interact in complex ways. For example, those individuals with high perceived status carry more weight in established groups than those equally high in status do in *ad hoc* groups.

Conformity

The tendency for the individual responses of group members to conform more closely to those of the group following exposure to the group's opinion has been demonstrated in many situations. (For a review, see Insko & Schopler, 1972.) The strength of the effect depends on many factors. It appears to be strongest in two circumstances. When one is uncertain about how to respond and is in consequence receptive to information from others, one may tend to accept their judgment. Also, when one desires the good opinion of the group or to avoid possible censure, one may be disposed to act more in concert with it.

Experiments with the Delphi technique for obtaining a group opinion (which will be described in the next section) clearly show the effect on individual opinion of information about the opinions of others (Dalkey, 1969). Members individually and privately made estimates of an unknown quantity. They were then given information such as the median and interquartile range of the responses of the entire group and asked to estimate again. The second estimates moved significantly closer together. Both the likelihood of moving and the amount moved were greater when the initial estimate was farther from the median. Repetition of this process led to further conformity but only up to a point.

When the group task is to reach a consensus, there is the additional stimulus to assent to a group position, even if one does not entirely agree with it. In such a circumstance, the group can be thought of as having a decision rule for combining the individual views to eliminate residual differences. The relative weight given to each individual's opinion will depend upon such factors as the group's norms, the vehemence or cogency of indiviudal arguments, and the perceived status and attractiveness of the individuals, as well as on all the personal factors that affect each individual's disposition to compromise. Whether the resulting consensus is a good one will depend on the degree to which the influence of all these factors coincides with the real contribution of the various individuals.

Polarization

There is a widely reported tendency for the average of group members' responses to polarize, to shift further in the direction of the group's initially dominant tendency after interaction or discussion. For example, a jury going from "probably guilty" to "definitely guilty."

Polarization has been studied most extensively with attitudes and preferences and less often with judgments of fact. (For a review, see Lamm & Myers, 1978.) It was initially observed with judgments of acceptable levels of risk. Because the stimuli reflected socially desirable risktaking, the shift was almost always in the direction of greater risk and was mislabeled *risky shift*.

Various processes can lead to polarization. The one most supported by evidence is the effect of information. The predominant influence of argument and facts emerging in discussion will be in the direction of the initial tendency and will reinforce it, moreso because of the usual bias to be more receptive to information supporting one's own views and because such attention will stimulate new ideas in support. Active espousal of a position also tends to reinforce belief in it.

Although polarization is widely observed it does not always occur. One factor that can inhibit, or even reverse it, is a strong societal norm that is opposite to the initial tendency.

Effectiveness of Behavioral Aggregation

There have been few systematic studies that would provide the basis for a definitive comparison of purely behavioral and mathematical aggregation for the kinds of judgments considered here. The results of early research suggest that behavioral aggregation effectively produces a weighted average. At best, the group judgment approximates the judgment of its most accurate member. Although it generally falls short of that, it is usually better than an equally weighted average (Lorge, Fox, Davitz, & Brenner, 1958).

For example, Einhorn, Hogarth, and Klempner (1977) had students judge the population of their city first as individuals and then in groups of three. The group judgments fitted the "best member" model better than any of the other models considered, including the equally weighted linear combination. Uecker (1982) obtained the same result with accountants who chose sample sizes for statistical auditing.

If groups have repeated, difficult judgments, they may adopt heuristic but nonetheless well-defined rules for making them. In Goodman's (1972) study of individuals and groups judging the relative odds of oberved data, each of the six groups invented and used its own rule. However, she found the group judgments only slightly superior to individual ones.

In the work described earlier, Seaver (1979) included group consensus in his studies of subjective probability judgment for both discrete events and continuous quantities. In the discrete case, conformity and averaging effects due to the consensus process will have an effect similar to that of voting, so that, if individuals are right more often than not, groups will, as a result, be right even more often. As previously noted, this will tend to move the calibration curve toward underconfidence. Polarization, on the other hand, leads to group judgments being more extreme and thus more overconfident than the individuals' judgments. Seaver found, indeed, that the calibration of the discrete consensus probabilities was intermediate betwen the highly overconfident individuals and the good calibration of the linear mathematical combinations in which there is only the effect of averaging and none of polarization.

For continuous quantities, Seaver found that discussion to consensus had the effect of increasing the underestimation characteristic of the individual judgments and of slightly increasing the overconfidence and the tightness of the assessed distributions. This also suggests polarization, or group-induced accentuation of the dominant tendencies of its individual members.

Fischer (1981), in a test of several mixed aggregation methods, to be described later, compared consensus probabilities with equally weighted linear combinations. Students judged the probability of other students' grade point averages on the basis of sex and test scores. There was no significant difference between the methods.

Solomon (1982) had teams of three experienced, professional auditors generate consensus fractiles for SPDFs over account values. The teams performed very well in comparison to both individuals and mathematical aggregation. Calibration was somewhat better than that for individuals in Figure 4. Moreover, the average absolute error between the judged median and the true audit values was only 49% of the average individual error.

This is less than the 65% improvement that selecting the best individual could obtain, but it is about the same as the improvement using the mathematically predicted best of three found by Ferrell and Curtis (1983). The high performance of the auditors in contrast to that of the students in the Seaver (1979) and Fischer (1981) studies is very likely due to their substantive knowledge and professional orientation. Auditors often work in teams of three and must come to agreement about various aspects of the audit, although the use of SPDFs is not yet common.

Avoiding the many potential negative influences in group discussion and helping the group identify the best judgments within it may be facilitated by instruction in good communication strategy. Hall and Watson (1971) have developed a set of guidelines that can be taught to groups in a short session. They have shown it to be remarkably effective in improving performance in tasks for which it is important to bring out as much relevant knowledge as possible and to use imagination in applying it to the problem at hand.

Summarized by Eils and John (1980), the guidelines for the group are:

1. Avoid arguing.
2. Avoid "win-lose" statements.
3. Avoid changing your opinion only to avoid conflict and to reach agreement and harmony.
4. Avoid conflict-reducing techniques such as the majority vote, averaging, bargaining, and coin flipping.
5. View differences of opinion as natural and helpful rather than as a hindrance in decision making.
6. View initial agreement as suspect.

Instruction in this strategy was tested by Eils and John (1980) for judging the creditworthiness of loan applicants. The standard was a statistical model used by a major bank. Groups did significantly better when they had been given instruction in communication.

Discussion leaders whose task is to see that all members express their opinions and who encourage consideration of all points of view also improve problem solving in groups. For example, Goitem (1983) found that groups with discussion leaders were less likely to make conceptual errors in statistical judgment.

MIXED AND AIDED AGGREGATION

The propensity for groups to fail to perform up to their potential has led to a great number of schemes aimed at improving performance. For the most part, they attempt to control the interaction process to avoid negative effects of input variables, or else they substitute mathematical processes for key behavioral ones such as achieving a final consensus.

Delphi is the name most often associated with structured group interaction. In its original form, as developed by Norman Dalkey, Olaf Helmer, and others at the Rand Corporation, a Delphi exercise consisted of an anonymous iterative process in which individuals made judgments, received a statistical summary of the group's responses, and reconsidered their judgments. After a suitable number of iterations, the group median, or sometimes the mean, was taken as the group judgment (Dalkey, 1969).

A great many variants were tried: self-weighting of individual judgments, different numbers of iterations, having to give a reason for persisting in a judgment outside the previous interquartile range, and so forth. The improvements effected by such modifications, if any, were never very large.

This original conception of Delphi severely restricts the amount of information individual group members share, and its advantage in performance over purely mathematical aggregation is doubtful. Much of the apparent improvement with iteration can be accounted for by the initial distribution of judgments and by conformity. The response distributions for the questions used in the initial tests of Delphi were lognormal. And the median was generally an underestimate of the true value. The median and the interquartile range were fed back to the participants, who then tended to make their revised judgments closer to the mean, and moreso if farther from it. This tends to shift the median upward and closer to the true value.

Early applications of Delphi were to prediction of the future. The general publicity that surrounded it and the methodological difficulty of evaluating such applications led to much criticism and countercriticism (Goldschmidt, 1975; Sackman, 1974). At present, practically any procedure for assessing opinion that uses anonymous responses, some kind of feedback, and at least one iteration is likely to be called a Delphi.

An approach with the same general intent, but richer in information, is the "nominal group technique," or NGT, investigated by Andre Delbecq and Andrew van de Ven at the University of Wisconsin. (The term *nominal group* is used by others in various ways in the literature, sometimes meaning just a mathematical aggregation.) NGT begins with individual assessments, then there is announcement and recording of these in a face-to-face group meeting, discussion of each judgment for clarification and evaluation, and finally mathematical aggregation to obtain a group judgment.

Table 3. Characteristics of the Type of Controlled Interaction
Investigated in Four Studies

Seaver	Fischer	Gough	Gustafson	Interaction type	Initial private estimate	Knowledge of others' opinion	Knowledge of source of others' opinion	Oral information exchange	Discussion	Consensus required
*	*	*	*	None	*					
*	*	*	*	Delphi	*	*				
*				Mix	*	*	*	*		
*	*	*	*	NGT	*	*	*	*	*	
*	*	*		Con	*	*	*	*	*	*
			*	Talk estimate	*	*	*	*		

Column group headers: Investigator[a] | Method | Method Characteristics

[a]Seaver (1979), Fischer (1921), Gough (1975), and Gustafson *et al.* (1973).

Both Delphi and NGT have been expanded in their application by their origi-
nators and others to include judgments in the widest sense, generation of ideas,
policies, and solutions to problems. Variations on the procedures are made to
suit the circumstances. A tutorial on both methods has been given in Delbecq,
van de Ven, and Gustafson (1975).

The comparative effects of different methods of controlled interaction on
judgments of uncertainty have been studied systematically by Gustafson, Shukla,
Delbecq, and Walster, Gough (1975), Fischer (1981), and Seaver (1979). Their
experimental conditions are shown in Table 3, based on one given in Seaver
(1979).

Gustafson *et al.* (1973) had individuals make judgments of likelihood ratios,
the relative odds of observations under different hypotheses, for which there were
objective values. They did so individually and interacting in groups of four. The
NGT result was the most accurate in every case, whereas the Delphi was usually
the worst. Fischer (1981) reanalyzed those results in terms of the probabilities
implied by the likelihood ratios. He found that, on the average, NGT judgments
were only .038 closer to the true probability than Delphi, a negligible difference.

Gough (1975), as reported by Seaver (1979), had individuals and groups
judge fractiles of SPDFs. Group judgments were formed from individual ones
by linear combination and evaluated by a proper scoring rule. Again, the NGT
came out best, but the advantage was slight.

Seaver (1979) also found that NGT scored highest for discrete probability
judgments, but although interaction had an effect, there were no significant differences among the types of interactions. After interaction, the calibration of individual subjective probabilities became less overconfident, but that of the mathematically aggregated judgments become more overconfident. Ferrell and Rehm
(1980) were able to duplicate this effect in their simulation of Seaver's work by
assuming that interaction produces a linear combination of polarization and con-

formity effects on subjective confidence. Polarization was movement of individual confidence toward full confidence in the answer favored by the average confidence of the rest of the group. Conformity was movement toward the average confidence of the rest of the group.

For the task of judging the parameters of beta distributions to represent SPDFs for unknown percentages, Seaver (1979) again found a significant effect of interaction on scores, on calibration, and on agreement of the mode with the true value but no differences among the interaction types. Again, NGT was slightly but not significantly better.

Fischer (1981) had students judge the probabilities that other students' freshman grade point averages would fall into four mutually exclusive and exhaustive intervals, given the student's sex and other academic scores. On the basis of a scoring rule, there were no significant differences among the different methods. Fischer (p. 97) concluded that

> at the risk of overgeneralizing, I suggest that all research to date on methods for aggregating probability forecasts from a panel of experts points to a single conclusion. From a practical standpoint it makes little or no difference how one aggregates the conflicting opinions of experts. Any reasonable approach is likely to be as good as any other.

This conclusion is certainly warranted for Fischer's experiment, though it should be noted that his subjects were not experts at all. More generally, it probably does not matter much which method of controlled interaction is used if it is highly controlled. But, as has been shown, the method of mathematical aggregation of probabilistic judgments does indeed matter. There are strong, predictable effects on calibration and accuracy.

It would also be incorrect to infer that the method is unimportant for other kinds of judgments. The research surveyed clearly indicates that it is necessary to take into account the nature of the judgment task, the composition of the group, and the expertise of its members in order to identify cases in which a particular method will be better than another.

CONCLUSION

Although necessarily tentative and imprecise given the present state of research, a few practical conclusions can be drawn from the work to date. Broadly speaking, if there is heterogeneity of opinion, aggregation is a good practice. It will generally produce somewhat better judgments with less variability, but there is seldom an advantage to a large group. Three to five is probably sufficient.

The performance of the group judgment cannot be expected to be much better than that of individuals unless individuals have substantive expertise. Ignorance cannot be averaged out; it is only made more consistent by aggregation.

Expertise and its role in judgment, though long neglected, is beginning to be studied seriously.

The potentially best method for real experts is face-to-face interaction. But if one suspects that nontask factors will interfere with judgment in a group, a mixed method such as NGT or, if enough information is exchanged, Delphi should be used.

A purely mathematical aggregation will probably do very well compared with face-to-face interaction and probably just as well if the judgment is one about which there is not much expertise.

Unless the special conditions for its effectiveness are met, it is not worthwhile to attempt differentially to weight the individual opinions. But when a judgment of an unknown quantity may be biased and there is adequate expertise in the group, a method that attempts to select the most accurate judgment on the basis of past performance is likely to prove effective.

The type of mathematical aggregation is particularly important with subjective probability and subjective probability density functions because the methods affect both calibration and accuracy. The choice of method depends on the nature of the probabilistic quantity being assessed, the calibration of the individuals, and the extent to which the individual judgments are correlated.

But for most judgments, when no individual is clearly most knowledgeable, a simple average is probably the best method.

REFERENCES

Agnew, C. E. (1983). *Multiple probability assessments by dependent experts.* (Report No. 36J). Stanford: Stanford University, Economic Systems Department (Program in Information Policy).

Aguilar, D. L. (1980, December). *SPAN: An improvement in group decision making.* Unpublished project report, Industrial Engineering Department, University of Arizona, Tucson.

Armstrong, J. S. (1980). The seer-sucker theory: The value of experts in forecasting. *Technology Review, 83,* 18–27.

Bacharach, M. (1975). Group decisions in the face of differences of opinion. *Management Science, 22,* 182–191.

Bates, J. M., & Granger, C. W. J. (1969). The combination of forecasts. *Operational Research Quarterly, 20,* 451–468.

Bordley, R. F. (1982a). The combination of forecasts: A Bayesian approach. *Journal of the Operational Research Society, 33,* 171–174.

Bordley, R. F. (1982b). A multiplicative formula for aggregating probability assessments. *Management Science, 28,* 1137–1148.

Brams, S., & Fishburn, P. C. (1982). *Approval voting.* Cambridge, MA: Birkhauser Boston.

Brock, H. W. (1980). The problem of "utility weights" in group preference aggregation. *Operations Research, 28,* 176–187.

Cooley, J. W., & Hicks, J. O., Jr. (1983). A fuzzy set approach to aggregating internal control judgments. *Management Science, 29,* 317–334.

Dalkey, N. C. (1969, June). *The Delphi method: An experimental study of group opinion* (RM-588-PR). Santa Monica, CA: The Rand Corporation.

144   William R. Ferrell

Dalkey, N. (1975). Toward a theory of group estimation. In H. A. Linstone & M. Turoff (Eds.), *The Delphi method: Techniques and applications*. Reading, MA: Addison-Wesley.

DeGroot, M. H. (1974). Reaching a consensus. *Journal of the American Statistical Association, 69*, 118–121.

Delbecq, A. L., van de Ven, A. H., & Gustafson, D. H. (1975). *Group techniques for program planning*. Glenview, IL: Scott, Foresman.

Eils, L. C., & John, R. S. (1980). A criterion validation of multiattribute utility analysis and of group communication strategy. *Organizational Behavior and Human Performance, 25*, 268–288.

Einhorn, H. J., & Hogarth, R. M. (1975). Unit weighting schemes for decision making. *Organizational Behavior and Human Performance, 13*, 171–192.

Einhorn, H. J., Hogarth, R. M., & Klempner E. (1977). Quality of group judgment. *Psychological Bulletin, 84*, 158–172.

Eshragh, F., & Mamdani, E. H. (1979). A general approach to linguistic approximation. *International Journal of Man-Machine Studies, 11*, 501–519.

Ferrell, W. R., & Curtis, P. E. (1983, December). *A model of calibration of auditors' subjective probability distributions and it's application to aggregation of judgments* (Working paper 83-023). Tucscon: University of Arizona, Systems and Industrial Engineering Department.

Ferrell, W. R., & McGoey, P. J. (1980). A model of calibration for subjective probabilities. *Organizational Behavior and Human Performance, 26*, 32–53.

Ferrell, W. R., & Rehm, K. (1980, May). A model of subjective probabilities from small groups. *Proceedings of the Sixteenth Annual Conference on Manual Control*. Cambridge: Massachusetts Institute of Technology.

Fischer, G. W. (1981). When oracles fail—A comparison of four procedures for aggregating subjective probability forecasts. *Organizational Behavior and Human Performance, 28*, 96–110.

Gaines, B. R., & Kohout L. J. (1977). The fuzzy decade: A bibliography of fuzzy systems and closely related topics. *International Journal of Man-Machine Studies, 9*, 1–68.

Ghiselli, E. E. (1964). *Theory of psychological measurement*. New York: McGraw-Hill.

Goitem, B. (1983, June). *An application of techniques for improving group problem solving to increasing the use of statistical reasoning by groups assessing uncertainty*. Paper presented at the Third International Conference on Forecasting, Philadelphia.

Goldschmidt, P. (1975). Scientific inquiry or political critique? *Technological Forecasting and Social Change, 7*, 195–213.

Goodman, B. C. (1972). Action selection and likelihood ratio estimation by individuals and groups. *Organizational Behavior and Human Performance, 7*, 121–141.

Gough, R. (1975). The effect of group format on aggregate subjective probability distributions. In D. Wendt & C. Vlek (Eds.), *Utility, probability, and human decision making*, Dordrecht, Holland: Reidel.

Gustafson, D. H., Shukla, R. K., Delbecq, A., & Walster, G. W. (1973). A comparative study of differences in subjective likelihood estimates made by individuals, interacting groups, Delphi groups and nominal groups. *Organizational Behavior and Human Performance, 9*, 280–291.

Hackman, J. R., & Morris, C. G. (1975). Group tasks, group interaction process and group performance effectiveness: A review and proposed integration. *Advances in Experimental Social Psychology, 8*, 45–99.

Hall, J., & Wason, W. H. (1971). The effects of a normative intervention on group decision-making performance. *Human Relations, 23*, 299–317.

Hersh, H. M., & Caramazza, A. (1976). A fuzzy set approach to modifiers and vagueness in natural language. *Journal of Experimental Psychology: General, 105*, 254–276.

Hogarth, R. M. (1978). A note on aggregating opinions. *Organizational Behavior and Human Performance, 21*, 40–46.

Hogarth, R. M. (1980). *Judgment and choice*. New York: Wiley.

Insko, C. A., & Schopler, J. (1972). *Experimental social psychology*. New York: Academic Press.

Kaufmann, A. (1975). *Introduction to the theory of fuzzy subsets* (Vol. I). *Fundamental theoretical elements.* New York: Academic Press.

Keeney, R. L. (1976). A group preference axiomatization with cardinal utility. *Management Science, 23,* 140-145.

Keeney, R. L., & Kirkwood, C. W. (1975). Group decision making using cardinal social welfare functions. *Management Science, 22,* 430-437.

Kochen, M., & Badre, A. N. (1974). On the precision of adjectives which denote fuzzy sets. *Journal of Cybernetics, 4,* 49-59.

Lamm, H., & Myers, D. G. (1978). Group induced polarization of attitudes and behavior. *Advances in Experimental Social Psychology, 11,* 145-195.

Lorge, I., Fox, D., Davitz, J., & Brenner, M. (1958). A survey of studies contrasting the quality of group performance and individual performance. *Psychological Bulletin, 55,* 337-372.

Marcotorchino, J. F., & Michaud, P. (1982). Preference aggregation and cutaneous melanoma. *Perspectives in Computing, 2,* 34-39.

McKinnon, W. J. (1966). Development of the SPAN technique for making decisions in human groups. *American Behavioral Scientist, 9,* 9-13.

Morris, P. A. (1974). Decision analysis expert use. *Management Science, 20,* 1233-1241.

Morris, P. A. (1977). Combining expert judgments: A Bayesian approach. *Management Science, 23,* 679-693.

Morris, P. A. (1983). An axiomatic approach to expert resolution. *Management Science, 29,* 24-32.

Olnick, M. (1978). *An introduction to mathematical models in the social and life sciences.* Reading, MA: Addison-Wesley.

Raiffa, H. (1968). *Decision analysis: Introductory lectures on choices under uncertainty.* Reading, MA: Addison-Wesley.

Roberts, H. V. (1965). Probalistic prediction. *American Statistical Association Journal, 60,* 50-62.

Rohrbaugh, J. (1979). Improving the quality of group judgment: Social judgment analysis and the Delphi technique. *Organizational Behavior and Human Performance, 24,* 73-92.

Sackman, H. (1974). *Delphi critique.* Lexington, MA: Lexington Books.

Seaver, D. A. (1979). *Assessing probability with multiple individuals.* Unpublished doctoral dissertation, University of Southern California, Los Angeles.

Seaver, D. A., von Winterfeldt, D., & Edwards, W. (1978). Eliciting subjective probability distributions on continuous variables. *Organizational Behavior and Human Performance, 21,* 379-391.

Solomon, I. (1982). Probability assessment by individual auditors and audit teams: An empirical investigation. *Journal of Accounting Research, 20,* 689-710.

Staël von Holstein, C-A. S. (1970). *Assessment and evaluation of subjective probability distributions.* Stockholm: The Economic Research Institute at the Stockholm School of Economics.

Steiner, I. D. (1972). *Group process and productivity.* New York: Academic Press.

Uecker, W. C. (1982). The quality of group performance in simplified information evaluation. *Journal of Accounting Research, 20,* 388-402.

Wainer, H. (1976). Estimating coefficients in linear models: It don't make no nevermind. *Psychological Bulletin, 83,* 213-217.

Willis, J. E., Hitchcock, J. D., & McKinnon, W. J. (1969). SPAN decision making in established groups. *Journal of Social Psychology, 78,* 183-203.

Winkler, R. L. (1971). Probabilistic prediction: Some experimental results. *Journal of the Ameri- 15,* 61-75.

Winkler, R. L. (1971). Probabilistic prediction: Some experimental results, *Journal of the American Statistical Association, 66,* 675-685.

Winkler, R. L. (1981). Combining probability distributions from dependent information sources. *Management Science, 27,* 479-488.

Zadeh, L. A. (1975). The concept of a linguistic variable and its application to approximate reasoning (Parts I, II, III). *Information Science, 8,* 199-249, 301-357; *9,* 43-80.

PART III

ORGANIZATIONAL DECISION MAKING

CHAPTER 7

Organizational, Group, and Individual Decision Making in Cross-Cultural Perspective

George Wright

INTRODUCTION

This chapter reviews research that has investigated decision making in a cross-cultural perspective. Work has concentrated on three main areas:

1. Studies of Japanese versus American organizational decision-making processes
2. Studies of the group polarization phenomenon, which has shown that following group discussion, both individual and group decisions differ significantly from the average of the previous individual decisions
3. Studies of individual decision making under uncertainty between groups of students and managers in Southeast Asia and Britain

Because, as we shall see, the research has tended to be sparse, diverse, and unsystematic, very few firm conclusions can be drawn. The Japanese management process has been characterized as consensus orientated, whereas the Americans seem more autocratic. However, the evidence for consensus or simply consultation within Japanese organization decision making is blurred. The group polarization phenomenon has been demonstrated successfully cross-culturally, but a precise test of its cause is more elusive. In the context of individual decision

George Wright • Decision Analysis Group, Department of Psychology, City of London Polytechnic, London E1 7NT, England.

making, research suggests that people from Southeast Asia may view uncertainty in a nonprobabilistic manner. The implication is that probabilistic decision analysis may not have universal applicability.

JAPANESE VERSUS AMERICAN DECISION-MAKING PROCESSES

Managerial Communication

Many studies have argued that there are two main differences between Japanese and American management methods. The Japanese, it is held, utilize a consultative decision-making process using extensive communication between all levels of the work force, whereas Americans tend to formalize job descriptions such that each individual has a specified role within the decision-making process and the resulting organizational structure tends to be more autocratic and delegative, involving little upward communication of information.

Because of interest, mainly American, in efficient organizational structures, studies have attempted to describe and evaluate differences between American and Japanese decision-making processes in organizations. The reason for this interest is obvious to Rehder (1979).

> There is growing concern on the part of some American scholars, government officials and managers that the Japanese corporate structure and management system may prove to be superior in our high technology, post industrial era. Can we now learn as much from their managers and organizations as they have learned from us since World War II? Apparently, if the Japanese comparative edge in productivity, balance of payments and world-market share continues to grow. (Rehder, 1979, p. 22)

However, to quote Pascale (1978), early research has been methodologically very poor.

> A close look at the methodology of these studies as they pertain to the Japanese managerial process indicates that they are not based upon empirical measures of Japanese management practices but rather upon (1) researcher impressions, (2) attitudinal measures, and (3) decision-making experiments in laboratory settings. (Pascale, 1978, p. 92)

Evan (1974) argued in a similar fashion that

> no systematic comparisons are made between the cultural values of a sample of the population of the country and of a sample of employees of one or more organizations in order to ascertain the import of "societal culture" versus "organizational culture" in organizational systems variables. (Evan, 1974, p. 10)

In his own study, Pascale (1978) investigated possible cultural differences in the empirical frequency of autocratic and participative decision making among managers of Japanese and American companies. A total of 13 Japanese firms participated in the study, representing 10 different industries. A sample of American firms was then matched to the Japanese sample. There was substantial similarity between the Japanese and American firms in terms of the number of organizational levels and the number of functional departments. All firms were involved in "highly routine, noncreative production activities."

Measures of the managerial communication process included respondents' day-to-day reports of the number of incoming and outgoing phone calls, written communications, face-to-face interactions (including the extent to which these were initiated by the respondent or others), and the percentage of those various types of contact that were made with subordinates, peers, and superiors. In all, 34 measures of the communication process were taken.

Decision-making style was measured by use of a modified form of Vroom and Yetton's (1973) scales.

> Respondents were requested to indicate the percent of decisions in which (1) they made decisions essentially by themselves, (2) they gathered the facts from relevant subordinates but ultimately decided themselves and (3) they consulted with subordinates in making the decision. Respondents were also asked to describe their boss's decision-making profile using the same three categories. (Pascale, 1978, p. 101)

Pascale's results came as a surprise to him. Although there was a greater amount of lower to higher communication in Japanese firms compared to the American firms, there were *no* significant differences noted in the style of decision making. Managers in Japanese firms were not found to utilize consultative decision making more extensively than American managers. However, managers of the Japanese firms in Japan perceived a higher quality of decision making in recent decisions made by others, above the respondent's level in the organization, which affected the respondent in some way. This result tends to confirm Vroom and Yetton's (1973) suggestion that personal involvement in a firm's decision-making process increases the acceptance of decisions and increases the likelihood of successful implementation.

However, Rehder (1979) disputes Pascale's view and argues that Japanese organizational decision making is consensus orientated, one decision-making style that was not investigated directly by Pascale.

> The Japanese believe it is crucial to first debate the question or problem in order to truly understand it in its overall corporatewide context, and then develop a consensus in order to deter groups from prematurely taking sides on one solution or another. Thus, group conflict between a victorious group and losing groups, which tends to undermine implementation, is minimized.... Implementation is quite rapid, and, according to the Japanese, more than makes up for time lost in the consensus decision-making process. (Rehder, 1979, p. 23)

Is the Japanese organizational decision making, whether based on extensive communication or consensus, worth exporting? Johnson and Ouchi (1974) studied 21 Japanese companies operating in the United States and attributed their high performance to the flow of information and initiative from the bottom up, with stress on consensus as the way of making decisions, using management as the "facilitator of decision making rather than the issuer of edicts" (p. 279). Involvement in decision-making processes may also lead to higher job satisfaction and less employee turnover for Japanese firms operating in the United States. However, although a positive relationship between participation and job satisfaction is often assumed, Locke and Schweiger (1979) found no evidence for this in nearly half of the 43 studies they reviewed.

Yoshio Maruta, the president of a large Japanese corporation, the Kao Soap Company, suggests that there are background reasons for the prevalance of consensus decision making in Japanese companies.

> We make all the management information available to everybody who wishes to have it through the use of computer terminals. Maybe it is worthwhile to mention that a majority of Japanese stay in one company all of their working career. So we have rather good security. Even if there might be a little leakage, we consider such a loss is well covered by the gains resulting from the practice of open information access.... The doors of our executives are always open for anybody to come in and talk without appointment. Even the people who are not related to the discussion are encouraged to come in and hear.... In order to improve productivity, they even discuss ways to eliminate their jobs. For example, we are introducing a non-operator method of detergent packaging. All the people who worked in the packaging line cooperated and positively contributed to realizing the goal. They knew they would be given new jobs afterwards. (Maruta, 1980, pp. 40-41)

Gordon and Kikuchi (1970) have also noted that although vertical bureaucratic structures typify Japanese social structure, the leader is a symbol of group effort rather than an authority figure. They argue that "status is primarily institution or group related rather than professionally or societally based, and harmony and cooperation are the prevailing norms" (Gordon & Kikuchi, 1970, p. 133). However, Hesseling and Korren (1969) found, in a simulation decision exercise, strongly critical remarks between experts within organizations and a refusal to consider decisions realistically in the presence of foreigners or nonorganizational members. This result suggests that consensus is only reached after forceful debate.

Gestenfeld and Sumiyoshi (1980, p. 31) have also identified strong differences between Japanese and American decision making.

> Managers change jobs over a relatively short time in the United States and rewards associated with risks are often not realized. Equally true in the United States, the punishments associated with failure are severe and often mean loss of employment. In Japan the risk is shared (the employment guaranteed), and as such the propensity for risk taking is high.... In Japan industry workers often receive bonuses as much as half again their annual income...on a group basis so there is wide participation and general enthusiasm for the program.

Managerial Values

Several attitudinal studies have bearing on Japanese/American comparisons of the decision-making process. Kelley and Worthley (1975) note, from their questionnaire study of managerial attitudes in Japan and the United States, that whereas 60% of American managers thought that the ability of an individual to play "company politics" was an important factor in career progress, only 13% of Japanese managers thought this was true. England and Lee (1974), in their study of the values of American, Australian, Indian, and Japanese managers found all successful managers (where success was measured as managerial pay, standardized using Z scores, relative to age) placed high value on productivity, profit maximization, ability, aggressiveness, achievement, success, and competition. However, the Japanese managers placed a greater emphasis upon "loyalty" and relatively less emphasis upon "me" than did managers in the other three countries studied.

In a major piece of cross-national research, Hofstede (1980) has identified four dimensions of national culture on the basis of a statistical analysis of 116,000 questionnaires completed by members of one large U.S.-based multinational corporation located in 40 countries around the world. Hofstede matched employees in terms of job, age, and sex and argued that he had thus isolated natural culture as an independent variable. Only the first three of Hofstede's dimensions of *power distance, uncertainty avoidance, individualism/collectivism*, and *masculinity* are relevant to our analysis of differences between American and Japanese decision making. The first dimension of national culture, power distance, is "the extent to which society accepts the fact that power in institutions and organizations is distributed unequally" (p. 45). *Small* power distance is measured by questions based upon attributes such as "superiors are accessible," "all people should be interdependent," and "people at various power levels feel less threatened and more prepared to trust people" (p. 45), whereas *large* power distance is measured by questions based upon the converse of these statements. Employees of the firms in America and in Japan were found to score similarly on this dimension, a finding that may at first sight appear contradictory to the majority of the research discussed earlier. However, it is important to note that the firm Hofstede studied is a U.S.-based corporation operating in Japan, and, as such, the U.S.-based organizational structure may have been imposed on the Japanese subsidiary.

The second dimension of national culture, uncertainty avoidance, is concerned with "the extent to which a society feels threatened by uncertain and ambiguous situations" (p. 45). *Strong* uncertainty avoidance is measured by questions based upon attributes like "a strong need for consensus is involved" and "great concern for security in life." However, although the Japanese show stronger uncertainty avoidance than the Americans, other attributes belonging to this pole of Hofstede's dimension of national culture, such as "deviant persons and ideas are dangerous; intolerance holds sway," are less easily reconciled with our earlier discussion of Japanese organizational decision making.

Finally, on the third dimension of national culture, individual/collectivism, where collectivisim is defined as "a tightly knit social framework in which individuals can expect their relatives, clan, or other in-group to look after them, in exchange for unquestioning loyalty," the Japanese show greater evidence of collectivism than the Americans, as might be anticipated on the basis of our earlier discussion.

Is there a relationship between culturally determined managerial values and managerial success? England and Lee (1974) caution against the drawing of causal links between managerial values and managerial success, whereas Smith and Thomas (1972) question the link between managerial value and managerial behavior, at least in India.

> Indian managers, at both middle and senior levels in organizations, profess a belief in group-based, participative decision making, but have little faith in the capacity of workers for taking initiative and responsibility.... A belief in participation may be highly utilitarian in that a major benefit to be gained from these methods would be decreased resistance to the leadership of the superior.... Since this does not imply real delegation of influence, such a belief is not incompatible with the attitude that individual subordinates cannot handle increased responsibility. (Smith & Thomas, 1972, pp. 39–40)

Cascio (1974) argues that participative management practices may not be superior in all cultures.

> In cultures where relatively, and even absolutely, more satisfaction is reported by superiors and subordinates with supervisory direction and subordinate submission, we should seriously question whether we are justfied to try...participative management practices.... In a traditional society employing status differences and dominance-submissive relations between superiors and subordinates, the manager may continue to exhibit the directive authoritarian style with which he is more comfortable. Likewise his subordinates may be more comfortable with him. (Cascio, 1974, pp. 594–595)

In summary, differences between American and Japanese organizational decision making are blurred. Perhaps Smith and Thomas's (1972) cynical view of "participative" decision making in India applies also to Japan. This would explain Pascale's (1978) apparently contradictory conclusion that although there is a greater amount of lower to higher communication in Japanese firms compared to American firms, there are no significant Japanese/American differences in self-reported styles of decision making.

Perhaps the contradiction between Pascale's conclusions and those of most other investigators of Japanese/American organizational decision-making processes can be resolved by a consideration of the type of decision-making task the manager is involved with. Recall that all of Pascale's sample of Japanese and American firms were involved in "highly routine, non-creative production activities."

INTERACTION BETWEEN THE TASK
AND DECISION-MAKING STYLE

Frank Heller and his colleagues have made a close investigation of the influence of the decision-making task upon the type of decision making undertaken. Heller, Drenth, Koopman, and Rus (1977) note that most studies of decision making in organizations assume that participative behavior is most appropriate in all decision situations and that this is associated with increased job satisfaction. However, these researchers have identified a

> substantial variety of decision styles used by managers in every sample investigated. The decision styles varied with level of organization, type of decision, skills and qualifications of staff etc. (Heller *et al.*, 1977, p. 570)

The importance of individual and situational moderators in the relationship between participative leadership and job performance and satisfaction has also been stressed by Abdel-Halim and Rowland (1976). Locke and Schweiger (1979) have identified other moderator variables such as task knowledge, motivation, group characteristics, and leader characteristics.

Using samples of managers in Britain and Germany who were questioned about their decision-making styles in 12 different decision situations, Heller and Wilpert (1977) were led to conclude that

> the findings show that senior, experienced and presumably successful managers do not use the same decision method in all circumstances. A manager will use a "democratic" method on one occasion and an "autocratic" one on another. The terms democratic and autocratic are really inapplicable because they pretend to describe *personality* whereas our findings suggest that the *situation* or *task* is the real differentiator. (Heller & Wilpert, 1977, pp. 77–78)

Heller and Wilpert's conclusions tend to confirm those contained in an earlier study by Vroom and Yetton (1973). Interestingly, Heller and Wilpert's matched sample of German and British managers show similar responses on a decision situation by decision situation analysis.

Using artificial decision problems based on problem attributes such as "if you make the decision yourself it is reasonably certain that it will be accepted by your subordinates" and derived from Vroom and Yetton's (1973) model of decision making, Hill and Schmidt (1977) found that between-subject variance was four times outweighed by situational variance in their managers' decisions. Using decision problems similar to those of Hill and Schmidt, Jago and Vroom

(1977) explored differences in disposition toward power sharing within managers at differing organizational levels. They found a consistent tendency of increasing participativeness with increasing hierarchical level. Indeed, attempts by organizations to implement employee participation in decision making may often fail due to opposition by managers who were expected to adapt participative management. Long (1982) found that low authoritarianism, internal locus of control, and high length of time in the same job were related to a higher desire, on the part of managers, for greater participation in policy decision making.

Interest in cross-cultural comparisons of group decision making has also been evident in the social psychological literature where questionnaire and laboratory-based tasks have been utilized. This research has centered around the finding of "group polarization."

GROUP POLARIZATION

Over the last 15 years it has been shown that, following group discussion, both individual and group decisions differ significantly from the average of the previous individual decisions. The decision-making task typically used in these studies has been Kogan and Wallach's (1964) Choice Dilemma Questionnaire. This questionnaire gives respondents a choice between a "sure thing" and a risky option with two possible consequences, one worse than the sure thing and one better. The respondent is asked to choose a probability for the better consequence so that the risky option is perceived as good as the sure thing.

Why do decisions made after group discussions differ from the average of previous individual decisions? The most widely held cause is the cultural value hypothesis which was first elaborated by Brown (1965). Carlson and Davis (1971) have summarized the cultural value hypothesis.

> The approach seems to rest on three assumptions: (a) Individual decisions are influenced by and are generally consistent with widely held values; (b) individuals consider their own behaviour to be more consistent with widely held values than that of their peers; (c) group discussion, or any other source of information that others are as consistent with or more consistent with on cultural value, will result in greater conformity to that value. Thus the risky shift should occur when the cultural value favours risk and the subjects learn that they are not riskier than others in the group. Conversely a cautious shift should occur when the value favours caution. (Carlson & Davis, 1971, p. 392)

There have, however, been few cross-cultural tests of this hypothesis. Carlson and Davis (1971) argued that on the basis of "extensive anecdotal evidence and personal observation...many African societies do not evaluate risk positively" (p. 392). This observation led Carlson and Davis to undertake one of the first cross-cultural studies of the group polarization phenomenon using samples from the United States and Uganda. They argued that if cultural values determine the direction of the postdiscussional polarization and Ugandan subjects do indeed place less value in risk, a risky shift should be reduced or eliminated relative to their risk-valuing American counterparts. Their results, consistent with the cultural value hypothesis, were based on a sample of Ugandan secondary-school children.

However, Gologov (1977) criticized Carlson and Davis's study, noting that some of Kogan and Wallach's questions, notably those concerning visiting marriage counselors and dilemmas over blue chip stocks, may not be decision situations previously encountered, or indeed, potentially encounterable by Ugandan secondary-school children!

Also, characterization of divergent groups of people from a single culture as risk valuing or caution valuing on an *a priori* basis is arguable. At first glance, Stoner's (1968) value assessment procedure would seem to offer a method of circumventing this problem. Essentially, Stoner's questionnaire obtains an individual ranking of the alternatives from the choice dilemmas in terms of personal importance. The alternatives to be later presented as "risky" can be rated relative to those presented as sure things in the choice dilemmas. However, Spencer, Williams, and Oldfield-Box (1974) found that Stoner's suggested method for predetermining the nature of choice shifts was unsuccessful. These researchers argued that the method is too abstract in practice. Regarding one choice dilemma problem, concerning a man about to embark on a holiday abroad who experiences stomach pains and must choose between abandoning his holiday to see his doctor and boarding the plane, Spencer *et al.* note:

> Subjects were agreed that the phrase corresponding to the cautious alternative ("physical comfort and health") was clearly more important than the value-phrase representing the risky alternative ("going away for a good holiday"), when the phrases appear on the Value Ranking Instrument. Yet, when these abstract concepts are put into the context of a dilemma facing the holidaymaker... their relative importance would seem to be reversed, and significant shifts towards the risky position occurred. (Spencer *et al.*, 1974, p. 380)

Indeed, Finney (1978) has argued that risk as a cultural value is also contextual. The American culture values success as well as risk, and risky individuals must succeed in their ventures *before* they are viewed favorably.

In another attempt at a cross-cultural test of the risk-as-value theory of group polarization, Hong (1978) tested Chinese college students from Taiwan and American students. Hong argued that traditional Chinese culture is a cautious culture because the "Confucian ethic values moderation, equilibrium and avoidance of extremes in thought and actions" (p. 343). Hong's results confirmed that the Taiwan Chinese students were more cautious in their solitary and group decisions than their American counterparts. Because the Chinese come from Taiwan, "one of the last strongholds of Chinese values" (p. 345), he argued that his result confirmed the risk-as-value theory. However, Hong had no direct measure of the Confucian ethic, and it may be that other differences between his samples may account for this result. Indeed, moderation, equilibrium, and avoidance of extremes in thought and action have been taken by some authors as evidence of the Protestant ethic!

In another study, Harrison (1975) investigated betting behavior of black and white Zimbabweians at a racetrack in Zimbabwe. He found that the average of bets made individually and then restated after group discussion, with other gamblers, differed between the two Zimbabweian groups; the whites shifted to caution and the blacks to risk. However, he was unable to account for his results.

In one of the most rigorous studies of group polarization, Gologov (1977) investigated decision making with a Liberian sample. After 6 months living in Liberia, he changed Kogan and Wallach's original problems in such a way as to make them have more face validity for his subjects. Gologov then tested his culturally appropriate dilemmas on Liberians who, he argued, were a cautious or conservative people.

> When Liberians were obliged to choose between two alternatives, keeping things the way they were—such as a method of growing rice—was, in most instances preferred to change. (Gologov, 1969, pp. 338–339)

However, Gologov's results turned out to be inconclusive; on some items his sample of high school students shifted to risk, on others, they shifted to caution. Gologov's findings should themselves be viewed with caution as he neglected to test the reliability of his revised questionnaire.

Currently then, the results from studies of the group polarization phenomenon are inconclusive, and Brown's (1965) risk-as-value hypothesis is as yet unproven. Clearly, individual decisions made after group discussion differ from those made before the discussion. This effect has been identified cross-culturally. However, there has been no attempt to provide an independent measure of risk-as-value in the studies so far undertaken. Anecdotal justifications of "cautious" or "risky" cultural values may be of dubious value.

INDIVIDUAL DECISION MAKING UNDER UNCERTAINTY

In two studies (Phillips & Wright 1977; Wright, Phillips, Whalley, Choo, Ng, Tan, & Wisudha, 1978), we identified cultural differences in probabilistic thinking between British, Hong Kong, Malaysian, and Indonesian student samples. We defined probabilistic thinking in terms of the tendency to adopt a probabilistic set, discrimination of uncertainty, and realism or "calibration" of assessments of probability. For an individual to be perfectly calibrated for events assessed as having a .xx probability of occurrence, xx% of all such events should actually occur. The largest cultural differences were found between Asian and British student groups. The British students adopted a more finely differentiated view of uncertainty, both verbally and numerically, than did the Asians in response to uncertain situations. These differences were not predictable on the basis of the relative abundance of probability expressions in the Indonesian language or the Malay samples' ability to discriminate English probability words on a meaningful probability-discrimination dimension. For numerical probabilities assigned to almanac questions, the British were less extreme and better calibrated than the Asian students.

We have recently examined the generality of these cross-cultural differences using a far wider range of samples (Wright & Phillips, 1980). Malaysia, Indonesia, Hong Kong, and Britain were again chosen as countries to extend the research, with samples selected on the basis of subculture, religion, arts/science orientation, sex, and age. Because our earlier research had suggested that the strong cultural differences in probabilistic thinking might be related to the "fate orientation" of a culture, we anticipated that Rotter's (1966) internal/external control scale, conceptualized as one measure of this orientation, would show some relationship with probabilistic thinking; high "external" scoring was presumed to be an indication of a fatalistic attitude (Kriger & Kroes, 1972; Parsons & Schneider, 1974). However, we found that Indian Malaysian students, Chinese Malaysian students, and Malay Malaysian students performed very similarly on the measures of probabilistic thinking but differing strongly from a sample of British students. Because Indians have been found to be highly "internal" relative to representatives of most other cultures (Carment 1974; Parsons & Schneider 1974), this result suggests that probabilistic thinking may be unrelated to external/internal control. This conclusion was reinforced by strong similarities on the measure of probabilistic thinking between Moslem and Christian Indonesians; the former were presumed to be more passively "external" than the latter. Arts/science and sex differences in probabilistic thinking were apparent across cultures, although these differences were not systematic. Intracultural differences in probabilistic thinking between students and managers from Britain, Hong Kong, and Indonesia were found to be smaller than intercultural differences. Our major conclusion was that strong differences in probabilistic thinking exist between Asians and British and that these differences outweigh any influence of subculture, religion, occupation, arts/science orientation, or sex. Generally, Asians adopt a less finely differentiated view of uncertainty, both numerically and verbally, than do the British. In cases where a numerical probabilistic set is adopted by Asians, the probabilities assessed are much more extreme and much less realistic. This finding has clear implications for communication of uncertainty across cultures and for the applicability of decision analysis to Asian culture.

We also closely examined the response of Asian and British managers to uncertain situations. The data indicated that a "yes/no" versus "don't-know" style of dealing with uncertainty, previously identified in a factor-analytic study using a British sample (Wright & Phillips 1979), was prevalent within Asian culture. The cognitive processes involved in answering a question show three stages (Phillips & Wright 1977): a certainty response (either "yes" or "no" or a probability estimate of 0 or 1) in Stage 1; a response consequent on a refusal to respond probabilistically (either "don't know" or a .5 probability estimate) in Stage 2; and a truly probabilistic response (either a probability estimate between 0 and 1 or a corresponding verbal expression) in Stage 3. Asians tend to respond to judgmental tasks by stopping at Stage 1 or Stage 2.

We developed a model of differential Asian and British ways of dealing with uncertainty (Wright & Phillips, 1980) in which the Asian tendency to view the world in terms of certainty or total uncertainty, with any elicited probabilities being poorly calibrated, was labeled *nonprobabilistic thinking*, and the British tendency to view the world in terms of degrees of probability that are fairly well calibrated was labeled *probabilistic thinking*.

Are cultural differences in probabilistic thinking reflected in management decision making in the "real world" as well as on our questionnaire tasks? Anecdotal evidence seems to confirm the generality of our research findings. For instance, Redding and Martyn-Johns (1978, p. 7) have noted that

> the commonest of the phrases used by the Western practising manager dealing with his Asian equivalent—"they think differently" [and] if probability is seen differently, then this will materially effect the process of management thinking and in turn it will effect management action.

Nonprobabilistic thinking may result in a lack of long-term future planning. Events in the future may be seen as "uncertain" rather than "probable" or "improbable." For instance, Penny (1967, p. 43) commented about Indonesian agricultural planning: "Too great a willingness on the part of the government to forego future gains for the sake of smaller immediate ones can mean the rejection of extremely profitable development opportunities." The successful nonprobabilistic thinker, realizing his or her inability to think probabilistically, may remain flexible in response to an uncertain future. The unsuccessful nonprobabilistic thinker may make confident predictions of the future and often be wrong. Conversely, the probabilistic thinker may predict the future in terms of probabilities assigned to events but still be unprepared for actual events due to lack of perfect calibration.

Redding (1978, p. 48) remarked on the subject.

> Why is it that the Chinese form of business is predominantly the small scale, owner-dominated enterprise, with a *reputation for flexibility* and a capacity for survival?. . .Instead of surveys of product markets, it relies instead for its strategic thinking on personal recommendations, keeping an ear to the ground, having a highly developed sense of the complete context in which it operates, the *following of hunches*. It

takes risks but not based on probability theory.... It goes without saying the Chinese have a flair for business. It also seems evident that their managerial methods are not the same as are found in a Western company. The contrast seems to be between the Western sense of order and rationality and the Oriental sense of all-embracing contextual thinking in which the *options are always open, the view can change* and sense or feel takes over from calculation. It is arts versus science.

I believe that it is clear from this analysis that probabilistic and nonprobabilistic thinking may be qualitatively different ways of dealing with uncertainty, at least in calibration studies. Our findings do not imply cultural deficit. Indeed, in an age of rapid and unpredictable change, the nonprobabilistic thinker may be at an advantage over the probabilistic thinker. Consider an example of the failure of a probabilistic decision analysis undertaken by Watson and Brown (1975) and reported in Humphreys (in press). Watson and Brown recounted the results on decision analysis facing the Neer motor company (a pseudonym!) in 1972. Neer's parts division wanted to decide whether or not to become involved in car tires. Humphreys succinctly summarizes Neer's options.

Neer had to choose between four immediate acts: (i) *do nothing,* (ii) accept a *deal* with a major tyre manufacturer to supply their product at a discount, (iii) investigate the possibility of Neer producing its own *private brand* of tyre, (iv) *wait about three years* before making a decision. Neer considered the key uncertain events to be (i) whether or not Trimark Motors (a major competitor) would decide to make their own brand of tyre, (ii) whether the government would exert pressure on motor manufacturers to include tyres in their warranties, and (iii) what the increased cost to Neer of using private branded tyres would be.

As you will have appreciated, the problem was quite complex with many act-and-event linkages represented in the form of a "bushy" decision tree. The result of the decision analysis prescribed that Neer should investigate private branding immediately, which it did. However, as it turned out, the decision analysis was what Humphreys calls a "fantasy of the future." It turned out that not *one* tire manufacturer was willing to bid for Neer's contract, and Neer was forced to choose the act that they would have to have done anyway if no decision analysis had been performed: wait for 3 years. In this example, the consequences of an inappropriate representation of the decision problem facing Neer were not catastrophic, but it is not hard to imagine decision situations where inappropriate problem representation may have more serious consequences. To quote Fischhoff (in press):

Decision Analysis is orientated to picking the apparent best alternative rather than to assessing the adequacy of our knowledge, it may encourage us to act where ignorance dictates hesitation or continued information gathering.

Bowonder (1981) has examined the related topic of cultural differences in risk assessment of damage to the soil, malnutrition and health hazards, deforestation, and water pollution, all of which are examples of environmental degradation that require risk management. Environmental risk assessment is the first stage in managing risks. Moreover, as Bowonder (1981) notes, the process of risk assessment may be culturally determined.

> Some Indian societies, especially Hinduism and Buddhism, view disasters as fated or predetermined. They consider a disaster as something that cannot be avoided and attribute it to natural causes.... When people are poor and live on a day-to-day basis their thought horizon is very short.... Culture has a strong bearing on the existence of forward looking attitudes, and hence environmentalism.... There are literally hundreds of institutions in the developed world concerned with technological forecasting...but not in the most developed of the underdeveloped countries, for example, India or Jamaica. (Bowonder, 1981, p. 109)

Although our investigations have not yet extended to Japan, Stewart (1981, p. 8) suggests that the Japanese may also be nonprobabilistic thinkers.

> Despite the wide use of statistical control in industry and business, Japanese managers do not readily draw ideas or conclusions from statistical analysis. They prefer a more intuitive process.... The use of objective probabilities are difficult anywhere, but in Japanese culture there appears to be a greater preference for categorical predictions...Japanese managers seem reluctant to make calculated estimates relying on probability, avoiding these estimates if possible...Japanese preference for adapting to and adopting existing conditions...he [the Japanese manager] places his ultimate trust in personnel rather than in ideas and analysis.... American decision making generally relies on a conceptual base that anticipates future events.... Instead, the Japanese are likely to perceive a continuously unfolding train of events to which they can accommodate.

PRACTICAL IMPLICATIONS OF CROSS-CULTURAL RESEARCH ON DECISION MAKING

The practical implications that have been drawn from cross-cultural research on decision making are not world shattering. Granner (1980, p. 103) notes that "A country should be able to send its trade negotiations into an international business negotiating session anywhere in the world." But his advice is less specific.

> Be very aware of the significance of the Japanese negotiating process. Before going to Japan in person a salesperson should devote ample attention to the ways in which Japanese decision-making groups seem to have a singular cohesion from which differences are resolved into consensus. (Granner, 1980, p. 106)

Guttentag and Sayeki (1975) are a little more helpful.

> It is often different to pin down subtle differences in the values of different national groups. Pervasive but often unspoken values colour how events are valuated.... Differences in beliefs and values, though they are usually implicit, play a powerful role in shaping the dialogue between individuals and groups. (Guttentag & Sayeki, 1975, p. 203)

In their paper, they illustrate the use of a heuristic method for eliciting the dimensions and weightings of the utilities or subjective valuations of possible outcomes of a decision from the decision maker. This method, formally called *multiattributed utility decomposition,* is widely used in decision analysis, but Guttentag and Sayeki's use of the method in a cross-cultural context is innovative. Those authors showed that Japanese and American social scientists, their subject sample, held different values (and gave different weightings to similarly held values) in their view of "international issues of probable importance to the future of communication and peace in the Pacific" (p. 209). Guttentag and Sayeki concluded the following:

> Concrete feedback in similarities and differences between the values and importance weights of the other national group were useful in throwing light on each group's own image of itself and the other national group, and served as a spur to more pointed discussion. It was also interesting to members within each group to see other members' importance weights and to hear the reasons for their choices. The technique appears to be a promising heuristic for the illumination of cultural differences, and a useful device for structured dialogue. (Guttentag & Sayeki, 1975, p. 216)

In essence, the results of research on decision making from a cross-cultural perspective have few applied implications. In the case of investigations of Japanese versus American organizational decision-making processes the research results are contradictory. Although all researchers hold that there are cross-cultural differences between the two countries, it is unclear whether the Japanese utilize either consensus or participative or consultative decision making. Perhaps in Japan there is an interaction between the task and the decision-making style similar to that found in Western organizations. It may be that any form of consultation within an organization results in a greater likelihood of the successful implementation of a decision. However, other differences in the structure of Japanese organizations, for example, lifetime employment, may aid organizational change and the implementation of what may be viewed as potentially threatening decisions.

The results of work on the group polarization phenomenon have, as yet, no applied implications because the cause of the polarization is still open to question.

My own work on individual decision making suggests that people from some cultures may not view uncertainty in terms of probability. This result may have implications for the universal acceptability of probabilistic decision analysis as a single best way of aiding decision making. But as yet, this conclusion is based on the results of a restricted range of questionnaires combined with anecdotal confirmation of differences in managerial decision making.

REFERENCES

Abdel-Halim, A. A., & Rowland, K. M. (1976). Some personality determinants of the effects of participation: A further investigation. *Personnel Psychology, 29,* 41–55.

Bowonder, B. (1981). Environmental risk assessment issues in the third world. *Technological Forecasting and Social Change, 19,* 99–127.

Brown, R. *Social psychology.* (1965). New York: Free Press.

Carlson, J. A., & Davis, C. M. (1971). Cultural values and the risky shift: A cross cultural test in Uganda and the United States. *Journal of Personality and Social Psychology, 20,* 392-399.

Carment, D. W. (1974). Internal versus external control in India and Canada. *International Journal of Psychology, 9,* 45-50.

Cascio, W. F. (1974). Functional specialization, culture, and preference for participative management. *Personnel Psychology, 27,* 593-603.

England, G. W. & Lee, R. (1974). The relationship between managerial values and managerial success in the United States, Japan, India, and Australia. *Journal of Applied Psychology, 59,* 411-419.

Evan, W. M. (1974). Culture and organizational systems. *Organizational and Administrative Sciences, 5,* 1-16.

Finney, P. D. (1978). Personality traits attributed to risky and conservative decision-makers; culture values more than risk. *The Journal of Psychology 99,* 187-197.

Fischhoff, B. (in press). Decision analysis—Clinical art or clinical science? In L. Sjöberg, T. Tyszka, & J. A. Wise (Eds.), *Decision analyses and decision processes.* Bodafors (Sweden): Doxa.

Gestenfeld, A. & Sumiyoshi, K. (1980). The management of innovation in Japan—Seven forces that make the difference. *Research Management, 23,* 30-34.

Gologov, E. (1977). Group polarization in a non-risk-taking culture. *Journal of Cross-Cultural Psychology, 8,* 331-346.

Gordon, L. V., & Kikuchi, A. (1970). The measurement of bureaucratic orientation in Japan. *International Review of Applied Psychology, 19,* 133-140.

Granner, B. (1980). Cross-cultural adaption in international business. *Journal of Contemporary Business, 9,* 101-108.

Guttentag, M., & Sayeki, Y. (1975). A decision theoretic technique for the illumination of cultural differences. *Journal of Cross-Cultural Psychology, 2,* 203-217.

Harrison, D. E. (1975). Race track shift: A cross cultural study. *South African Journal of Psychology, 5,* 10-15.

Heller, F. A., & Wilper, B. (1977). Limits to participative leadership: Task, structure and skill as contingencies—A German-British comparison. *European Journal of Social Psychology, 7,* 61-84.

Heller, F. A., Drenth, P. J. D., Koopman, P., & Rus, V. (1977). A longitudinal study in participative decision-making. *Human Relations, 30,* 567-587.

Hesseling, P., & Korren, E. (1969). Culture and subculture in a decision-making exercise. *Human Relations, 22,* 31-51.

Hill, T. E., & Schmitt, N. (1977). Individual differences in leadership decision-making. *Organizational Behaviour and Human Performance, 19,* 353-367.

Hofstede, G. (1980). Motivation, leadership, and organization: Do American theories apply abroad? *Organizational Dynamics,* 42-63.

Hong, L. K. (1978). Risky shift and cautious shift: Some direct evidence on the culture-value theory. *Social Psychology, 4,* 342-346.

Humphreys, P. C. (in press). Decision aids: Aiding decision. In L. Sjöberg, T. Tyszka, & J. A. Wise (Eds.), *Decision analyses and decision processes.* Bodafors (Sweden): Doxa.

Jago, A. G., & Vroom, V. H. (1977). Hierarchical level and leadership style. *Organizational Behaviour and Human Performance, 18,* 131-145.

Johnson, R. T., & Ouchi, W. G. (1974, September). Made in America (under Japanese management). *Harvard Business Review,* pp. 61-69.

Kelley, L., & Worthley, R. (1975, August). Managerial philosophy and its relation to culture: An empirical study of Caucasian-American, and Japanese-American, and Japanese managers. *Academy of Management Proceedings,* pp. 243-245.

Kogan, N., & Wallach, M. (1964). *Risk taking: A study of cognition and personality.* New York: Holt, Rinehart & Winston.

Kriger, S. F., & Kroes, W. H. (1972). Child-rearing attitudes of Chinese, Jewish and Protestant mothers. *Journal of Social Psychology, 86:* 205–10.

Locke, E. A., & Schweiger, D. M. (1979). Participation in decision-making: One more look. In B. M. Staw (Ed.), *Research in organizational behaviour.* Greenwich, CT: JAI Press.

Long, R. J. (1982, July). *Determinants of managerial desires for various types of employee participation in decision-making.* Paper presented at the Twentieth Congress of Applied Psychology, Edinburgh, England.

Maruta, Y. (1980). The management of innovation in Japan—The tesuri way. *Research Management, 23,* 39–41.

Parsons, O. A., & Schneider, J. M. (1974). Locus of control in university students from Eastern and Western societies. *Journal of Consulting and Clinical Psychology, 42:* 451–61.

Pascale, R. T. (1978). Communication and decision-making across cultures: Japanese and American comparisons. *Administrative Science Quarterly, 23,* 91–110.

Penny, D. M. (1967). Development opportunities in Indonesian agriculture. *Bulletin of Indonesian Economic Studies, 8,* 35–64.

Phillips, L. D., & Wright, G. N. (1977). Cultural differences in viewing uncertainty and assessing probabilities. In H. Jungermann and G. de Zeeuw (Eds.), *Decision making and change in human affairs.* Amsterdam: Reidel.

Redding, S. G. (1978). Bridging the culture gap. *Asian Business and Investment, 4:* 45–52.

Redding, S. G., & Martyn-Johns, T. A. (1978). *Paradigm differences and their relation to management functions, with reference to Southeast Asia.* Hong Kong: University of Hong Kong Centre for Asian Studies.

Rehder, R. R. (1979). Japanese management: An American challenge. *Human Resource Management, 18,* 21–27.

Rotter, J. B. (1966). Generalised expectancies for internal versus external control of reinforcement. *Psychological Monographs, 609* (80), 1–28.

Smith, B. E., & Thomas, J. M. (1972). Cross-cultural attitudes among managers: A case study. *Sloan Management Review, 13,* 35–51.

Spencer, C., Williams, M., & Oldfield-Box, H. (1974). Age group decisions on risk-related topics and the prediction of choice shifts. *British Journal of Social and Clinical Psychology, 13,* 375–381.

Stewart, E. C. (1981). *The Japanese model of modernization: Present and future.* Paper delivered in Seoul, Korea.

Stoner, J. A. F. (1968). Risky and cautious shift in group decisions: The influence of widely held values. *Journal of Experimental Social Psychology, 4,* 442–459.

Vroom, V., & Yetton, P. (1973). *Leadership and decision-making:* Pittsburgh: University of Pittsburgh Press.

Watson, S. R., & Brown, R. V. (1975). *Case studies in the value of decision analysis* (Technical Report 75-10). Maclean, VA: Decisions and Designs, Inc.

Wright, G. N., & Phillips, L. D. (1979). Personality and probabilistic thinking: An exploratory study. *British Journal of Psychology 70,* 295–303.

Wright, G. N., & Phillips, L. D. (1980). Cultural variation in probabilistic thinking: Alternative ways of dealing with uncertainty. *International Journal of Psychology, 15,* 239–257.

Wright, G. N., Phillips, L. D., Whalley, P. C., Choo, G. T., Ng, K. O., Tan, I., & Wisudha, A. (1978). Cultural differences in probabilistic thinking. *Journal of Cross-Cultural Psychology 9,* 285–299.

CHAPTER 8

Contexted Decision Making
A Socio-organizational Perspective

David Weeks and Sam Whimster

INTRODUCTION

The central purpose of this chapter is to consider the role of decisions and the nature of decision-making processes within large-scale organizations in advanced capitalist societies from a sociological viewpoint. We shall start, in the section, Decision Making in Organizations, by outlining the major conceptualizations of organizational decision making that have been predominant in the research literature and ask how effective and realistic such analyses are in describing and understanding the nature and role of decisions.

A key concept that emerges in the discussion of decision making in organizations is that of rationality. It will be seen that there are broad similarities between what constitutes rational action within an organization and the notion of an optimum or best choice in decision-making theory. However, in succeeding sections of this chapter we will go on to show that different concepts of rationality may obtain when the wider environment of society and social interaction is considered. We feel it is particularly important to place "rational" decision making in relation to the exercise of control within the organization and the distribution of power in society. Viewed from such a standpoint, decision making can be seen to be inextricably linked to a political process, and therefore, appropriate decision-making techniques must be viewed in this light.

This kind of analysis falls squarely within a sociological approach. It is a basic tenet of the sociological perspective to focus on the social structures and

David Weeks and Sam Whimster • Department of Sociology, City of London Polytechnic, London E1 7NT, England.

social processes that surround an outcome or event, in this case the event being a decision or decision-making procedure. A major result of adopting a sociological stance is to refocus the analytical lens to concentrate not on the individual decision or decision maker but instead to view the decision outcome as part of a wider social pattern in which individuals, although significant, cannot be divorced from their social context in any attempted explanations. Thus, it is not a prime concern of a sociological analysis to investigate the cognitive processes of the individual decision maker but rather to look to those aspects of the social environment that require that a decision be made, stipulate how the decision is to be reached, determine who is to be held responsible, say what is to count as relevant information, and limit what ends and means are to be regarded as acceptable.

In this complex web of social demands and expectations the individual decision maker (assuming one can be identified) in a large organization is likely to be but a small cog in a huge machine. The extent to which an individual can be said to exercise decision-making choice in relation to a significant range of alternatives needs to be questioned. Under these circumstances, the model of decision making that locates the explanation of decisions as the outcome of "individual best choice," given the relevant information and a clear set of organizational priorities, leaves out of account the influence of socially generated and sustained constraints. The goals, information, and environment are dynamic elements in a developing social process in which any actor is both a recipient of reality and a contributor to that reality. We would argue that any adequate account of decision making needs to reflect this dynamic and be alert to any analysis that objectifies or reifies decision making by reducing it to a study of techniques.

Before turning to a consideration of specific decision making in organizations, we must say something about how the social forces mentioned previously might be conceptualized. Within sociology two distinct, but not necessarily contradictory, theoretical perspectives have developed. The first of these is commonly termed a *structural approach*. This tends to stress the way in which all social actors are recipients of social reality. It highlights the point that as individuals, or even when acting collectively with others, there is often very little that we are able to do to change or effectively challenge a situation. Many of the most important features of our social environment seem to exist as rules and constraints "out there" that we are powerless to alter. These *social facts,* as Durkheim (1938) termed them, are nonetheless constraining even if we fail to perceive them in a conscious way as impositions on our actions. Indeed, most of the time we come to view such restrictions as normal or natural and even essential to achieving valued goals. Consider, for example, the link that is usually deemed necessary between increasing formal authority and increasing levels of remuneration in organizations. Without such a background of taken-for-granted assumptions, it is hard to imagine how a consistent and persistent social order could be maintained. Within this approach, it is but a short step from viewing structural elements as a part of the social context to seeing them as the whole of social reality. This can easily give rise to an account of decision making that limits any analysis to an instrumental concern of matching given ends to appropriate means.

The second theoretical approach, which we term the *social process approach* (Douglas, 1974), places greater emphasis on the manner in which the social environment is constantly changing due to the contributions of individuals and groups engaged in social interaction. It is important to stress that this approach is not a return to the reductionist accounts based on individual actors. The key difference is the way in which all definitions of social ends and social means are seen as social constructions. Thus, what might be seen as unproblematic and categorical rules and conditions of social reality in the structural approach now become contingent social meanings in loose confederation with each other, and conflict and change are common features. Within this approach, decisions and decision-making procedures can be viewed as a temporary social consensus seen as appropriate at a particular conjunction of social factors but that might easily have been decided differently and may indeed be so in the future. From this viewpoint, the stress in any analysis needs to be placed on the emergent qualities of social reality that is conceived as a constantly developing process.

Bearing in mind these two approaches within the sociological perspective, we shall see how they can lead to different definitions of decision making and how they jointly challenge conventional analyses of the nature and role of decision making in organizations.

DECISION MAKING IN ORGANIZATIONS: CONVENTIONAL ANALYSES

When considering decision making in large organizations, we need to be clear about the object of our analysis, that is, what constitutes a decision. At its simplest, a decision represents a choice between alternative courses of action in relation to an end or purpose. This broad definition covers a very wide range of possibilities from the trivial to those decisions with the most profound social and individual consequences. What is needed is a means of stratifying or classifying types of decisions to make possible a manageable analysis. A widely used distinction is that between *routinized* or *programmed* decisions and *nonroutinized* or *nonprogrammed* decisions (March & Simon, 1970). These terms are almost self-explanatory, and the essential idea is that some decisions rely on the exercise of considerable discretion (nonroutinized),whereas others simply require the recognition that a particular and already specified (programmed) action be taken.

Routinized decision making is usually part of the standard operating procedures of an organization, and thus any deviation from the appropriate rules poses a threat to the administrative order. To minimize such threats, suitable checks and controls are typically built into the organizational structure through supervision procedures, bureaucratic referral, or, increasingly, computer-based monitoring. Thus if things go wrong at this technical level, organizational safety nets should detect and minimize the damage. Although these semiautomatic decisions are of vital concern to the operation of all organizations, they are themselves dependent on the first type of decision making, the nonroutinized/nonprogrammed variety.

Nonroutinized decision making has been the major focus for analysts of the individual decision maker. Not only does this kind of decision determine the routine decisions, but it also represents a way of assessing the direction in which the whole organization is heading. Thus, these decisions are of strategic importance and tend to be reserved for those organizational positions relatively high in the hierarchy of formal authority. However, we need to be aware that even these decisions are restricted in important ways by the organization's internal structure and external environment. These restrictions arise from the limited influence, both spatial and temporal, that affects all organizational decisions, the need to take account of particular contingencies (such as available technology and labor power), and perhaps most important, the uncertainties and limitations relating to the information available about resources and environment. Each of these elements must be assessed and interpreted in the light of past experience and anticipated developments in the decision-making process. (For a more complete discussion of these aspects, see Weeks, 1980.)

When considering strategic decision making, the problems just mentioned have been tackled in ways that partially correspond to the two approaches outlined in the previous section. Those who have adopted a predominantly structural approach have tended to conceptualize the problems involved in strategic decision making as a set of common functional issues that confront all organizations in their varied contexts and that can, therefore, be tackled to a considerable extent on a common basis. The corollary of this view is to seek for general technical solutions to the problems of assessing technology, information verification, and the like in the hope that at least some of the uncertainties in decision making may be reduced if not eliminated.

In opposition to this view are those theorists who favor an approach focusing on social process. According to this set of assumptions, the problems of strategic decision making are not to be overcome by technical prescriptions but can only be understood by conceptualizing the organization as a more or less unique cultural whole with its own peculiar set of interpretive procedures that must be analyzed independently from the circumstances of other organizations. This results in a tendency to take a case study approach to the explanation of strategic decision making.

This theoretical and methodological divide on the approach to strategic decision making is reflected in the way in which research is conducted, the overall manner in which organizations are conceived, and the kind of knowledge that is thought to result. Thus, structural theorists tend to concentrate on objective evidence in terms of quantifiable inputs and outputs, to regard different organizations as fundamentally more similar than distinctly different, and they aim for a form of explanation about decision making that is potentially universal in application. Social process accounts, in contrast, tend to rely on subjective evidence in the form of social meanings, to view organizations as distinct cultural wholes, and to claim knowledge that is essentially idiographic or partial in its range of application.

Before the full critical implications of the structural and process approaches are developed in the following sections, it has to be established that even within conventional analyses the central concept of rationality receives different interpretations. Rationality is inextricably linked to the process of making a choice and, according to Pfeffer,

> [it] is generally construed to mean choosing that course of action which will maximize the chooser's expected utility. The concept of utility recognizes that outcomes may have different values to different persons, and the concept of expectation recognizes that decisions may be made under conditions of uncertainty. (Pfeffer, 1978, p. 8)

Thus the role of rationality is to act as a justification for a particular decision or decision-making prescription.

When considering how rationality is conceived in relation to decision choices, we need to identify how different models of decision making take account of the variations in the definitions of utility that might be at work and also how they deal with the problem of uncertainty, or how to assign probabilities to possible outcomes. In other words, we need to investigate how ends or goals are defined and what influences beliefs about which are the appropriate means to choose. In a key distinction, Simon (1965) suggests that we can usefully separate "economic man" and "administrative man" models of decision making.

The model of economic man has much in common with the rational actor of neoclassical economic theory. The sole aim of this rational actor is to maximize his or her utility by a comparative analysis of alternative means and outcomes and to choose that combination that yields the highest return. This account depends on a number of important assumptions.

First, it assumes that the actor has clear preferences and that the outcomes can be scaled according to some order of priorities. For those taking decisions within, and on behalf of, large-scale organizations it might be argued that the goals are given in commercial environments by the need to respond to market signals. If the prices of the constituent factors of production are known together with the likely demand for the product, then a simple computation should reveal the decision(s) required to yield the highest return. For organizations not directly linked to market forces (e.g., public corporations, state agencies, and voluntary associations), then bureaucratic directives on policy and objectives might be seen as the sources of goals. In either case, the identification of goals is regarded as relatively unproblematic, and hence the choice of utility is given.

A second assumption is concerned with the fit that pertains between goals and the means available. Here we can observe a tendency to rely on definitions of formal authority and bureaucratic structure as efficient means for achieving the goals sought. The information about these internal structures is taken to be sufficiently accurate to allow a high probability in predicting the outcomes from their utilization. Predictions about environmental influences are likely to be more difficult and variable, but the feedback on performance available through the communication and information systems of an organization may be assumed to provide the necessary inputs to allow corrective decisions to be taken if necessary.

In many ways the decision maker is seen as a fairly passive actor in this model. She or he responds to the demands of the organization by assembling and activating the established mechanisms. We are nearly back to a situation of routinized decision making because the image presented here is one of a narrow range of decisions operating in a stable, known, and probabilistically predictable environment.

Simon (1965) describes this model of decision making as subscribing to an "objectively rational" view. It involves defining decision making as the pursuit of optimal or maximum utility as measured by the actual outcome. It furthermore requires that we are able to quantify, in a fairly precise manner, all the inputs and outputs involved in the decision process so that the necessary predictions and choices can be made. This attempt to measure and map in mathematically accurate terms the contributory elements to the decision-making process is typical of normative decision making as exemplified by such techniques as decision analysis. It is this form of analysis of decision making that tends to be favored by those who strongly support the view that organizational success depends on the maintenance and exercise of managerial prerogative. This approach is further characterized by an almost asocial definition of the situation because little or no account is included of exactly *how* decisions are taken or implemented. It is deemed sufficient to uncover the economic or bureaucratic logic of the situation.

The "administrative man" approach takes as its starting point the obvious deficiencies of the "economic man" model in providing a description of decision making as an organizational practice. Lindblom has pointed out that "the usefulness of an analytic method cannot be understood in isolation from the social processes through which it is applied" (Lindblom 1958, p. 305). The social processes he refers to influence both the identification of utility and the knowledge about appropriate means. If organizational goals are ambiguous and in competition, then no clear-clut priority can be assigned nor an objectively rational choice of means be made. Although in principle the notion of *highest economic return* may seem a simple test to apply, when it comes to operationalizing the concept in a complex social world characterized by uncertainty, irregularity, and unintended consequences, achieving this goal becomes extremely problematic. Questions such as whether long- or short-term perspectives should be employed and the basis upon which the return should be calculated are real difficulties with no unambiguous answers. If the goal is in dispute, so also are the means likely to be. Organizations are social constructs made up of the interaction of individuals and groups holding a variety of ideas (beliefs and values), which may be very difficult to define and harder to predict, particularly when mixed together with a dynamic external environment.

In this situation, we need to recognize that our rationality is *bounded* and that our search for alternatives and our ability to discriminate between probable outcomes is limited. Simon (1965) describes this state of affairs as typifying *subjective rationality*. In these circumstances, the search is not for the optimal solution but rather the satisfactory outcome. Thus, performance may be assessed on a variety of criteria and success judged according to an acceptable range of end results. With unclear goals and imperfect knowledge about how to achieve them, the possibility of defining universal decision-making techniques is remote and needs to be replaced by approaches that recognize, to some extent, the social complexity of the problems. It is in this context that we can observe the development of *contingency theory* (Perrow, 1974). Contingency theory is an approach that acknowledges that there is no one best way to manage or make decisions. Instead, we must look to the range of contingent factors that impinge on a particular organization at specific moments. Although we may have many ideas about which general features are likely to be important, their significance in a particular context cannot be derived from abstract models based solely on economic or mathematical logic. Rather, a situational logic obtains.

In these two models, labeled economic man and administrative man, we can observe competing logics for understanding organizational decision making. Although they are opposed in many ways, they also share a common thread in their commitment to the analysis of decision making through a concentration on the goal–means relationship. Both see the rationality of decision making in terms of predicting outcomes that are largely restricted to those that organizations define for themselves and that rely on the analysis of individual decision makers in the last instance. Thus, we would argue that the two models differ more in degree than kind and that both share inadequacies as accounts of decision making. In the remainder of this chapter we will consider three forms of critique that can be applied to what we have covered so far. All these critiques derive from a sociological perspective and we have labeled them the *social process critique*, the *structural power critique*, and the *communicative rationality critique*.

THE SOCIAL PROCESS CRITIQUE

A major advance contributed by the administrative man model is to bring into focus a range of social factors that crucially influence all forms of judgment in the decision-making context. In this respect, the administrative man model has clear links with the social process approach described previously. However, as we have also noted, the administrative man paradigm still takes as its central object the individual decision maker. The social process critique can both extend the criticisms offered by the administrative man model of economic man, by analyzing the social influences operating on the decision-making process and push the critique further by questioning the goal–means approach to the understanding of decisions.

In terms of the social influences affecting individuals, the social process critique notes that individuals within large organizations invariably belong to distinct groups. Indeed, the bureaucratic structures of large organizations positively rely on some aspects of this process to ensure conformity and consistency. However, this dependence on the power of the formal structure is unlikely to prove a satisfactory explanation of organizational functioning. This is because we now know that organizations develop specific cultural environments and subcultural ideologies that are often confused and inconsistent when viewed from the perspective of the organization as a whole.

Under these circumstances, the identification of unambiguous organizational goals becomes an almost hopeless task. The idea of rationality also breaks down as an organizational attribute when there is no clear agreement on what the organization is trying to achieve. Instead, we must speak of several rationalities in relation to the different objectives sought. Indeed, where the commitment to a particular organizational practice reaches such a level that it seems to run counter to the more general goal which that practice is designed to serve, we may speak of *goal displacement*. In other words, the means becomes an end in itself, a goal in its own right.

Of course, there may be an attempt to impose one rationality or ideology by a particular group, but the extent of its success cannot be prejudged by the application of some external and independent criterion of organizational rationality. An interesting discussion of this issue is provided by Child (1972) in his analysis of the role of "dominant coalitions" in organizations. It is perhaps a weakness of all social process accounts that they fail to provide any systematic treatment of the basis of power and influence within organizations that might be linked to the distribution of power in the wider society.

If organizational cultures are so important, then we need to have a vocabulary on which to base an analysis. Pettigrew (1979) suggests that we need to concentrate our attention on the symbols, languages, beliefs, visions, ideologies, and myths that are generated and sustained by organizations in order to understand the actions and commitments of individuals and groups in the decision-making process. We might expect such studies to adopt an ethnographic approach to the investigation of organizations along the lines pioneered by Donald Roy (1952, 1953, 1954, 1958).

A somewhat more radical argument from the social process critique questions the whole approach to the study of decision making that works within the framework of a goal–means account. It suggests that the assumption that behavior is always goal directed be questioned. At first glance, this may appear somewhat absurd, for it would seem to suggest that decisions could be seen as preceding the identification of the purposes or goals that they are designed to achieve, almost a case of the cause following the effect. But this is not a far-fetched account at all. Consider how often we pursue a course of action for no very clear reason and only retrospectively justify it in relation to the outcome that emerges, when we had no obvious intention to pursue that outcome at the start of our actions. In such circumstances, we talk of a *rationalization* rather than the exercise of *rationality*.

This justificatory process is likely to be determined to a great extent by our social perceptions and expectations in a given social environment. Although this may be viewed as an individual adaptation to a social situation, it is unlikely to be sustainable in a complex organization unless it is consonant with the views of others who form parts of the interlocking organizational structure. Pettigrew (1973) gives a nice example of how advice on the purchase of a computer system was mainly determined by the expectations the advisers had of the views presumed to be held by those who would ratify the decision. The actions of the advisers were not governed by the goal of making the best choice of computer system *per se* because the advice procedure merely provided a justification for behavior that was based on other grounds.

In relation to the administrative man approach, the social process critique is skeptical concerning both the focus on individuals and with respect to the exclusive employment of a goal–means analytic framework. However, the social process account has its own limitations because, if carried to its extreme, it would seem to posit the possibility of organizational anarchy, typified by uncontrolled conflict and inconsistencies within the organization's structure. Clearly, that does not often occur, and this suggests that some broader controls must be operative to maintain organizational functioning. It is to these controls that we can now turn.

THE STRUCTURAL POWER CRITIQUE

If the social process critique emphasizes that the goals pursued by organizations are difficult to define and that our knowledge of the social mechanisms involved is imperfect, then the structural power critique sets out to elucidate those forces that do operate to hold organizations together by pointing to the relationship that intraorganizational decision making has to the wider social environment. The main message here is that the goals that organizations need to achieve to survive are not ones that they are free to choose themselves, but rather that they are derived from the distribution of power in the wider society. (A further discussion of the role of power can be found in Chapter 9, this volume.)

This general approach returns us to the perspective linked with Durkheim's notion of social facts referred to previously and has been taken up in more specific terms by those working within a Marxist framework. For the Marxist, organizations are not to be seen as collective actors attempting to act rationally in relation to whichever goals they choose, but rather they are elements within a capitalist system that is typified by an unequal distribution of economic, social, and political power where the interests of the few are dominant over those of the majority. The internal decision making of organizations cannot be divorced from this broader context.

One problem for the Marxist account is that not all organizations seem to be directly involved in the market relationships central to the process of capitalist production and exchange. Thus, state agencies answer to political forces rather than to market forces. For Marxists, this is to view the situation too simply. Although state agencies may not be directly governed by market logic, they may be essential supports to sustain the continuation of the free enterprise system. Thus education, health, welfare, and social services are necessary elements in the overall system for the reproduction of capitalism from one generation to the next. Moreover, there have been signs recently in some capitalist countries, notably Great Britain, of attempts to return state-owned industries to private hands and thereby extend the logic of capitalist production.

In relation to those organizations that are privately owned, Marxists argue that the major goals that they pursue are forced upon them by the demands of the system. The one goal that predominates is that of profit. Unless production takes place on this basis (except for perhaps in the relatively short term), the organization cannot survive. The question then arises as to the basis of this profit and how this is likely to affect our understanding of decision making within the organization.

For Marxists, profit does not result from the almost accidental success that a product may enjoy in the marketplace. In terms of number of units sold, almost any good or service may be successful if it is sold at a sufficiently low price. Marxists argue that the origins of profit are to be found in the production process itself and particularly that aspect referred to as the *labor process*. The primary aim of capitalist production is to so organize the utilization of labor power that it generates the greatest amount of surplus value for the capitalist. Whether or not this surplus can be realized, that is, converted into a monetary return, depends on the exchange conditions that prevail in the market and that may be outside the control of any one producer. Whatever the state of the market, the organization will maximize its probability of realizing its surplus by ensuring that the costs of production are kept low and the level of productivity kept high.

In relation to organizational decision making, the major concern for managers is how to organize and control the effort contributed by the work force. In working out the *effort bargain* (Baldamus, 1961), a number of strategies might be employed. According to Braverman (1974), the major strategy in the twentieth century has been one that has relied on the principles of "scientific management," which was first enunciated by F. W. Taylor. This is a form of management control that seeks to minimize the discretion left in the hands of the individual worker by divorcing, as far as possible, the elements of conception and execution in the work process. Conception is an activity that is reserved for those in managerial positions whose commitment to the goals of profitability and capitalism is not in doubt. Thus, the whole planning process is taken from the hands of the production worker whose job becomes one of simply executing the orders passed down from others. Typically, this arrangement results in a deskilling of work tasks, making jobs increasingly monotonous and repetitive with firm controls on the efforts expended by the worker. Thus, the role of decisions is not simply to ensure production and that cost targets are met in the short term but also to maintain the integrity of the control process to permit surplus to be accumulated in the future.

There have been important challenges to Braverman's account of how the labor process has developed in capitalist societies, stressing in particular that the dominant position of managerial decision making has not gone unchallenged. (A good review of this whole debate can be found in Wood, 1982.) In particular, the countervailing power of trade union organization has been highlighted. However, what evidence we have of trade union influence on decision making does not contradict the assumptions of managerial dominance. Thus, Hickson and Mallory have concluded that "our panorama of 150 strategic decisions suggests an unchanging scene in which management's 'prerogatives' are maintained by both managers and union officers" (Hickson & Mallory, 1981, p. 59).

Opponents of the Marxist view have suggested that to deny that changes have occurred in decision-making procedures is to take a blinkered ideological stance. It has been pointed out that various forms of participative decision making have emerged that differ markedly from the direct forms of control that are associated with deskilling practices. The question thus arises of whether these developments are to be seen as a denial of the forces of a broad capitalist logic operating on decision making or rather merely a change in the way in which the same control is exercised. This is clearly a very complex issue, but we can at least note how Marxists have analyzed the situation.

Their view remains based on the premise that the logic of capitalist production will always prevail whatever the means used to achieve the cooperation of the work force. Changes in decision-making procedure are, therefore, superficial rather than fundamental in their influence. In Herman's terms, the real subordination of labor exercised through direct control is merely replaced by what he labels *hegemonic control*. He argues that

> the hegemonic mode is characterized by relations of consent and legitimation between labour and management rather than coercion. The essence of the hegemonic mode is . . . that commitment and participation replaces alienation and domination as the *modus vivendi* of labour process control. (Herman, 1982, p. 14)

This new form of control is made possible by changes in the nature of the capitalist system itself. The crucial change is the development of monopoly capitalism, which is "characterized by high concentrations of capital and large corporations which have a predominant hold over particular product markets" (Littler, 1983, p. 172). Once free from some of the competitive forces of the market system, large organizations can adapt their decision-making procedures to focus more on maintaining the possibility of generating long-term surplus than on the earning of a short-term profit. The constraints on the goals that organizations must pursue remain despite any changes that occur in the decision-making means that are employed.

STUDYING DECISION MAKING IN ORGANIZATIONS

So far in this chapter the distinction between structural explanations of the organization and accounts of social process within the organization have represented two separate approaches to the study of decision making. On the one hand, structural explanations, either Marxian or Durkheimian derived, emphasize external determination—that the nature and course of decision making runs along predetermined lines and the extent of choice implied by the very term decision making is (in a structurally determined reality) very much narrower than decision-making theory or the actual actors involved are prepared to admit. On the other hand, the social process model opens up the decision-making process to a whole range of sociological factors within the organization that are formally excluded by normative decision-making theory.

Having made this review of the major directions within sociology in respect to decision making, we can now make some sort of assessment between these two approaches, which, as they stand, point in opposite and conflicting ways. It is not possible within the limited space of the chapter to make choices between what are fundamental schools of thought within sociology. However, neither can we leave the matter of decision making and its appropriation by one approach or the other still "up in the air."

Let us consider the stance of the sociologist Tom Burns. His conceptualization of organizations does not fall in either camp. Neither does he attempt a reconciliation of the two. Instead, he demands a degree of agnosticism in the study of organizations. There are structures outside the organization, and there is more than one form of social process within. What has to be recognized is that these structures and processes coexist and, most importantly for Burns, there is no necessary coherence between them.

In Burns's terminology (Burns, 1969), there are three social systems operating and interacting with one another. These are the working organization, the political system, and the career structure. Although they interact, they are not functionally interdependent. We have seen in the case of the administrative man theorists the attempt to reconcile organizational goal achievement with the degree of goal displacement attributable to social processes within the organization. For Burns, this is an unrealistic assumption. Managers in organizations may well want to effect such a reconciliation between what the organization should be achieving and the sometimes less than helpful actions of individuals and groups within the organization. But, as a basis of research, Burns argues that it is more realistic to assume that people's career aspirations, the way politics operates within the organization, and the working organization are, in fact, three separate and different dimensions. For instance, career structures in the case of the professional accountant, solicitor, or computer person do not fit within the organization. The organization may well be simply a stepping stone within a career structure that lies beyond the organization.

The distinction between within and without the organization is not paramount here. In his study of the BBC, Burns (1977) shows that the career path and the work role can be at odds with each other. The ambitious producer, in order to ascend the career hierarchy within the BBC, will have to abandon his or her job as producer and so the basis of his or her previous professional competence: leading and coordinating a production unit.

Treating the political system as separate to the working organization likewise has important consequences for decision making. Conventionally, decision making would be considered as part of the working organization. Organizational goals are achieved through decisions being made at various levels within the organization and the coordination of those levels. If, however, one introduces a political system operating parallel to the work organization, then it is possible to perceive that decisions made within the work organization will be interpreted politically and reacted to according to political calculation.

In any large organization, personnel are liable to form competing groups. Factory managers may, in terms of company organizational charts, be able to command the services of their various managers: the production manager, sales manager, and management services manager. In practice there may also be rivalries between managers so that factory managers are not treated as ultimate authorities, even though they may claim such authority. For example, the management services manager may consider his or her department's and his or her own expertise distinct from the factory that they serve and seek an identification with management services elsewhere in the company.

Pursuing this hypothetical example a little further, what might be the possible reactions to a plan for production reorganization that originated from management services? The acceptability of the plan derives in one respect from the professional expertise or competence of management services. They are able to deploy certain skills—operations research, systems analysis, or whatever other techniques—to argue a case for reorganization. This acceptability may be challenged by production management who could dispute the plan on the basis of an on-the-ground knowledge of the complexities and practicalities of the production process. As it stands, there could be a conflict between two different sorts of knowledge—one practically acquired and one based on certain decision-making techniques. If, let us say, the management services plan effected a rationalization in the production process, then the members of the production management team may well interpret this as a loss of their autonomy and what they consider to be the sphere of their decision-making competence. It does not take much imagination to see that what overtly is a dispute over the rational way of organizing production becomes instead a political conflict between different sections of management. Moreover, such political jockeying for power and influence will, to return to Burns, be an already existing social system.

This has important consequences for the status of decision analysis. Although various analyses are put forward on the basis of politically neutral claims of expertise, know-how, and so forth, their interpretation and reception will be essentially political. This can have a serious impact on the particular knowledge status of decision analysis; it will not be viewed as neutral objective knowledge but will be gauged according to the political structure and process. The upshot for decision analysis is that its claim to validity by virtue of a rational analysis of goal achievement by the company is unlikely to be accorded a respect solely in terms of rational consideration. If an analysis goes against the current political stream, then it could suffer a damaging undervaluation, or even worse, simply be shelved and ignored. In the case of overvaluation, things are no better; an encouraging endorsement by higher management may be regarded by others as an attempt to use decision-making analysis as the rationalistic legitimation of changes already in progress within the political structure.

The question arises: How then *do* organizations act in a goal-directed manner? Burns's answer is open ended; individuals make calculative decisions, weighing valued ends and the possible means for their attainment. However, the researcher has to be clear that the individual may invoke any one of the three "dominant reference systems for this action, decision or plan" (Burns, 1969, p. 247). So, for Burns, the problem is not that of rationality because individuals do calculate what actions have utility for them but that there exists more than one dimension for valuing such calculations and there is no necessary fit between organizational goal attainment and individual interest. What constitutes a decision has a much wider scope than the set frame of reference of decision-making analysis.

It is in the nature of Burns's position that organizational goal achievement cannot be rigidly defined. This is reflected in his relaxed definition of organizations: "All organizations are cooperative systems assembled out of the usable attributes" (Burns, 1977, p. 257). This would seem to imply that people at some point are prepared to come together to hammer out common solutions and that there is a level of sociality that contains the separate subsystems. However, what Burns has to say about the way decisions are reached in the political subsystem effectively rules out this line of speculation: that the decisions made by an organization reflect in part the operation of common understandings that mediate between individual or group interest. (We will have more to say on this later.) What Burns has to say about the influence of power on the cooperative, consensual aspects of organizational life may appear cynical but no doubt can be defended on grounds of realism.

> Decisions of this kind [over organizational goals] are reached through the organizing of consensus and the manipulation of sanctions, legitimate and illegitimate, within a systematic framework of political action; and such organizing and manipulative activity may be regarded as in the interests of the organization as a whole or of interested individuals, or, indeed both. (Burns 1969, p. 241)

A final note on Burns's approach to studying organizations: he does not abandon the notion of individual rationality. Indeed, quite the reverse, for he seeks to extend its scope to spheres usually ignored by formal decisionmaking analysis. In the last section we will consider a sustained attack on the notion of subjective rationality.

THE COMMUNICATIVE RATIONALITY CRITIQUE

On the one side, we have seen those organizational theorists, namely the administrative man school, who have sought a structure of the organization that is compatible with the rationality of decision making; others, however, have considered it erroneous to effect such a reconciliation and instead have emphasized the multiplicity of the social context, noting that decision-making analysis is one of several competing rationalities within the organization.

A radical approach to these problems is to reconsider the nature of rationality. We have already established at the beginning of this chapter that decision-making theory, best seen in theories of economic man, employs the concept of individual rationality whereby the optimum choice is the selection by the individual of certain goals having a measurable amount of utility for the individual and the calculation of the probabilities of various means by which the goals can be attained.

Jürgen Habermas (1981) has subjected this concept of rationality to a profound critique and has counterposed an alternative model of rationality, which he terms *communicative rationality*. It must be said, at once, that Habermas does not address his critique to decision-making theory itself but rather to the underlying concept of rationality. This is not exclusive to decision-making theory, for the concept of individual rationality was first developed to explain individual maximizing behavior in the market. The same concept of rationality is also to be found in sociology where Max Weber (1968), who formulated a classification of the basic concepts of sociology, made it the starting point for his analysis of social action.

> Action is instrumentally rational when the end, the means, and the secondary results are all rationally taken into account and weighed. This involves rational consideration of alternative means to the end, of the relation of the end to the secondary consequences, and finally of the relative importance of different possible ends. (Weber, 1968, p. 26)

What Habermas proposes is very simple. This concept of rationality, which, following Max Weber, we will term *instrumental rationality*, is not, according to Habermas, a form of *social* action. It represents individual maximizing behavior, but this is not the basis for explaining social interaction or what we, in this chapter, have been calling social processes. Goal-directed behavior of the individual is oriented to achieving individual success in the world. It is not oriented toward reaching social understanding with other actors in the social world. Hence, instrumental rationality is essentially *nonsocial*. It either attempts to get the best result for the individual, or, where this involves interacting with other people, the basis of this interaction is using other people to achieve one's own ends. Although the latter alternative does involve social interaction with other people, it is tied to a perspective of individual rationality. Communicative action occurs on the basis of common understandings reached and created by individuals as participants in a group.

> I speak of communicative action when the action plans of participating actors are conducted not on the egocentric calculation of ends, but are coordinated through acts oriented to reaching understanding. (Habermas, 1981, p. 385)

The basis of such acts for reaching understanding is communication.

This produces, for Habermas, the following classification of types of action shown in Table 1. Table 1 can be related directly to the earlier sections of this chapter. The premises of normative decision making fall into the category of non-

Table 1. Types of Actions

Action situation \ Action orientation	Success	Reaching understanding
Nonsocial	Instrumental action, e.g., normative decision making	
Social	Strategic action (e.g., political subsystem)	Communicative action

social instrumental action. Strategic action[1] relates directly to Burns's account of rational action by individuals, especially in the political subsystem. Instrumental action involves the adherence to technical rules of action and the estimation of the effects of such actions. Strategic action again follows rules of rational choice but also takes account of the effects of action on the behavior of other competing actors or opponents, who are presumed to act in a likewise rational manner.

We have seen the problems posed by both types of action; instrumental action simply ignores the whole question of social processes because, as Habermas shows, it is premised on a nonsocial view of the world. Strategic action, as we have seen in the case of Burns, treats people in an essentially expedient and manipulative manner and opens the organization up to the dynamic of power and influence. (Other theorists [Lindblom, 1965] have attempted to formalize the nature of political decision making, but these attempts fall firmly within the category of strategic action.) What Habermas suggests is that a new notion of rationality be formulated that is predicated upon agreed understandings common to all actors involved in a group. Seen in this light, decisions or acts reached by the group are derived from a communicative rationality and already presuppose the operation of social processes within the group. Whereas previous conceptualizations of decision making provide clear technical rules for reaching correct decisions, they then have to encounter in the organization the problematic nature of political and social processes. Is it not then possible to build these social processes into decision making itself rather than try and accommodate them with the conceptualization of instrumental rationality?

Habermas provides no direct answer; that is not the purpose of his book. But he does provide a fairly precise specification for the attainment of com-

---

[1]Strategic in this usage refers to a type of action and not a class of decision as in Decision Making in Organizations, this chapter.

municative rationality against which any new form of decision making can be adjudged.

Because Habermas's classification of action is based on the juxtaposition of instrumental and communicative actions, securing the conditions of the latter necessitates the rejection of the sociological assumptions of the former. Hence communicative action cannot include individuals acting in a means–end manner, and secondly it excludes the operation of power; that is, of the person's trying to manipulate another by virtue of superior power. The play of power and instrumentality effectively dissuades action oriented toward reaching common social understandings of a situation. If the former predominates, the latter cannot be achieved. At the empirical level, there is some doubt as to how categorical Habermas wishes his distinction between action oriented to success and action oriented to reaching understanding to be. If they are mutually exclusive categories, then there is little scope for the development of the notion of communicative rationality. (There are very good reasons for this being so, especially if one argues that the structures of or ganizations, as both work and power structures, are forced to express the capitalist logic inherent in capital accumulation; see The Structural Power Critique.) However, we will adopt the stance that at the empirical level some degree of overlap in certain circumstances is feasible. This is in line with what we have said previously on the coexistence of structure and social processes within the organization, even though this is clearly a problematical relation.

What then is communicative action? It is a situation where the participant members are able to have regard for one another's communicative acts on the basis of some sort of consensually agreed definition of their situation. This basis is not explicitly arrived at or noted by the actors, but it does make possible a regard to the communicative acts of others in the following respects: A statement will be accepted as rational by the participants if it fulfils three tests of validity. These are that there is some way of checking the truth of a statement against the objective world; that what is said or how it is said is correct in terms of the understood norms and values of the group; and lastly, that the speaker is held to be sincere in his or her communicative regard to the group. Statements that do not pass these three tests do not fulfill the conditions of communicative rationality.

Let us choose a simple example to illustrate how decisions might be reached on the basis of communicative rationality. A headmistress of an infants' school is pondering whether to change the set up of classes. At present there are five regular classes and one *nurture* class. (The term *nurture class* is a usage employed by teachers in certain English metropolitan areas to describe a special class composed of children who are seen to exhibit difficult and nonintegrative behaviors.) Should the nurture class be disbanded and six equal classes be created? If the headmistress acts purely in a *strategic* manner, she will assess the advantages and disadvantages of the various outcomes, each of which can be estimated with some degree of probability. She makes her decision on the overall balance of advantages and disadvantages, informs her staff, pupils, and parents, and takes steps to implement her decision. Empirically, the decision may not occur in this step-by-step basis. For instance, the headmistress may well consult her staff members and even give the impression that she will be governed by their advice. From a strategic perspective, consultation would be prudent; further information is gained, and the grounds for acceptability of the decision are being prepared. In Burns's terms, the grounds for consent are being created and, if necessary, manipulated. But the decision reached will be that of the headmistress on the basis of her authority.

In the case of communicative action, the headmistress cannot make the decision on the basis of authority. Instead, this has to be set aside to the extent that her will does not distort the consensual basis upon which the group members reach their decision. The participants in the group, which we will arbitrarily define as the teachers in the school, then have to argue the case. They have to do this in a way that enables some sort of assessment of each outcome proposed; in other words, it is not an ideal discussion but relates to the world insofar as it is known. If the decision is to be one arrived at by the group, each participant has to keep within the socially defined boundaries of how a topic such as this is discussed. Finally, there has to be a sincerity of intent behind what each speaker contributes; for instance, if the calculation of individual interest lies behind what is said, then such behavior reverts to strategic action.

The major potential advantage of this model of communicative rationality is that decision making on the basis of individual rationality does not then have to be squared with the social processes of the organization. It also highlights a fundamental distinction between information and communication. Conventionally in decision making, information is a constantly updated input that is essentially passive. It is data to be acted upon but does not in itself effect the process of decision making. In the communicative model, the grounds on which information is fed into a discussion presumes a recognition that is socially produced; that is, it is not a neutral datum absorbed from the environment "out there," but the act of presenting information imposes a social evaluation. One of the arguments against merging nurture classes with the other classes is that it causes *disruption* in all the classes. And one of the arguments for merging the nurture class is that children are not singled out and labeled (with its implication of self-fulfilling prophecy) as *difficult*. Either way, the assessment of the information is highly evaluative, and different teachers will, because of their own views of the world, weight each argument differently. However, because the decision has to be made as a group, these valuations are forced into the open, and a contribution may be excluded as violating the agreed basis for the acceptance of a statement.

Another advantage of this model is that there need be no divide between reaching a decision and its implementation. The decision has been reached on a common basis of understanding, and, moreover, the meaning and implication of the decision should have undergone a communicatively rational validation. The decision reached should be correct for it has been empirically assessed, and the valuations involved have been hammered out through mutual agreement. Unlike the case of strategic action the decision analysis cannot be construed as an *ex post facto* rationalization or a legitimation of some foregone conclusion.

It is a little too early to formulate judgments on Habermas's concept of communicative rationality and whether or not it can form the basis of a new way of reaching decisions. However, we can point to its obvious strength, which at the same time is a limiting condition. It provides the theoretical grounds for judging the truly sociological nature of all those forms of decision making that claim to be participatory or democratic. For example, any forum of industrial democracy that exists within the context of interest calculation or power structure is merely a sophisticated version of strategic action.

The distinction between participatory versus strategic action does not correspond to the distinction between consensual and conflictual behaviors. Habermas is saying that the basis on which communicative rationality is achieved is that of understandings held in common. Once that basis is taken for granted, it is very much in the nature of the social world for conflict and disagreement to occur (see the case of the nuture group discussion). Consensus and the apparent absence of conflict do not warrant the inference of noninstrumental behavior. Sophisticated manipulation of interests (Burns, 1977), or the maintenance of traditional values to authority such as deference (cf. Chapter 7 in this volume), may well produce consensus, but it also rules out communicative rationality.

Whether decision-making theory can be developed according to the model of communicative rationality remains to be seen, for as yet no one has explored this approach. We note in conclusion that Habermas's model within an organizational context is essentially precarious; one wonders in how many types of organizations and for how long can a space be cleared free from the play of instrumentality and power.

CONCLUSION

To answer the question posed at the end of the last section is in many ways to answer the more general sociological question: What degree of latitude should we allow to subjective rationality and social processes in the face of wider, structural factors? Each of the major positions outlined in this chapter takes a stand on the question. Economic man theories assume a free play to subjective rationality. Administrative man theories seek to accommodate social processes to organizational structure, and structural power critiques heavily circumscribe the grounds for individual choice. Burns suggests a working model for the study of organizations, and finally Habermas provides a radical critique of instrumental rationality and offers in its stead a communicative model of rationality predicated on higher levels of social interaction.

To pursue matters further would require a deeper awareness of the sociological issues involved and a deeper acquaintanceship with the literature than this chapter permits. Although a conclusion common to all approaches cannot be drawn together, the following checklist, although unsystematic, should be used in any assessment of decisions, that is, if it is the intent of the researcher to take into account social factors.

1. Has the decision been reached after the event, so that decision analysis is only confirming an already existing state of affairs?
2. To what extent is a decision freely made? This is not only a question of assuming that choice actually exists but of addressing the further question: Are the set of choices pregiven by a wider structure?
3. What is the evaluation of a decision by other individuals or groups in an organization who are not directly involved in the decision analysis?
4. Is the rationality of a decision premised solely on decision analysis, or does it express some other calculative rationality, for instance, of power or career. Question 3 should be used as an indicator for 4.
5. When the term *information* is used, is it referring to data gathered from the surrounding environment and as such neutral, or is it an *active* ingredient in the decision-making process reflecting the culture and levels of understanding existing within the organization? Decision-making analysis based on the former usage of information would be ill-suited for the latter situation.

Clearly this checklist is only of pragmatic use and does not represent a summation of our theoretical arguments. The reader, we hope, is by now aware of the ambivalence sociology has in regard to normative decision making. Many of the difficulties of some of the positions reviewed in this chapter stem from their tendency to ignore the dimension of social interaction or their attempts to incorporate the social to a pregiven notion of what is rational behavior within the organization.

Decision making is a relatively new and certainly vigorous offshoot of the quantitative side of the social sciences. In its future development it will surely have to encounter and to conceptualize the interrelation between individual and social behaviors. We trust that this review of organizational behavior indicates some of the problems involved and that in the continued expansion of decision making some of the lessons from organizational theory may be taken on board.

REFERENCES

Baldamus, W. (1961). *Efficiency and effort.* London: Tavistock.

Braverman, H. (1974). *Labour and monopoly capital.* London: Monthly Review Press.

Burns, T. (1969). On the plurality of social systems. In T. Burns (Ed.), *Industrial man.* Harmondsworth: Penguin.

Burns, T. (1977). *The BBC public institution and private world.* London: Macmillan.

Child, J. (1972). Organization structure, environment and performance: The role of strategic choice. *Sociology, 6,* 1–22.

Douglas, J. (Ed.). (1974). *Understanding everyday life.* London: Routledge & Kegan Paul.

Durkheim, E. (1938). *The rules of sociological method.* New York: The Free Press.

Habermas, J. (1981). *Theorie des kommunikativen Handelns* (Vol. 1). *Handlungsrationalität und gesellschaftliche Rationalisierung.* Frankfurt am Main: Suhrkamp.

Herman, A. (1982). Conceptualizing control: Domination and hegemony in the capitalist labor process. *The Insurgent Sociologist, 11,* 7–22.

Hickson, D., & Mallory, G. (1981). Scope for choice and strategic decision making and the trade union role. In A. Thomson & M. Warner (Eds.), *The behavioural sciences and industrial relations.* Aldershot: Gower.

Lindblom, C. (1958). Policy analysis. *American Economic Review, 48,* 298–312.

Lindblom, C. (1965). *The intelligence of democracy: Decision making through adjustment.* New York: The Free Press.

Littler, C. (1983). A comparative analysis of managerial structures and strategies. In H. F. Gospel & C. R. Littler (Eds.), *Managerial strategies and industrial relations.* London: Heinemann.

March, J., & Simon, H. (1970). Decision-making theory. In O. Grusky & G. Miller (Eds.), *The sociology of organizations.* New York: The Free Press.

Pettigrew, A., (1973). *The politics of organizational decision-making.* London: Tavistock.

Pettigrew, A., (1979). On studying organizational cultures. *Administrative Science Quarterly, 24,* 570–581.

Perrow, C. (Ed.). (1974). *Perspectives on organizations.* Milton Keynes: Open University Press.

Pfeffer, J. (1978). *Organizational design.* Artlington Heights: Harlam Davidson.

Roy, D. (1952). Quota restriction and goldbricking in a machine shop. *American Journal of Sociology, 57,* 427–442.

Roy, D. (1953). Work satisfaction and social reward in quota achievement. *American Sociological Review, 18,* 507–514.

Roy, D. (1954). Efficiency and the fix: Informal intergroup relations in a piece-work machine shop. *American Journal of Sociology, 60,* 255–266.

Roy, D. (1958). "Banana time": Job satisfaction and informal interaction. *Human Organization, 18,* 158–168.

Simon, H. A. (1965). *Administrative behavior.* New York: The Free Press.

Weber, M. (1968). *Economy and society.* New York: Bedminster Press.

Weeks, D. (1980). Organizations and decision-making. In G. Salaman & K. Thompson (Eds.), *Control and ideology in organizations.* Milton Keynes, The Open University Press.

Wood, S. (Ed.). (1982). *The degradation of work?* London: Hutchinson.

CHAPTER 9

Sociological Approaches to Power and Decisions

Roger King

INTRODUCTION

This chapter examines differing concepts of power presented by sociologists and political scientists in recent accounts of political processes. Consequently we will be less concerned with terminological definitions of power and associated concepts, such as authority, influence, force, coercion and the like than with exploring the different philosophies or values—ways of seeing the world–that underpin various approaches for understanding political decision making. As we will see, this is no easy task, for social scientists are considerably at odds as to how to go about assessing power. Many share Steven Lukes's view (1974) that the concept of power itself is an "essentially contested concept" that rules out a universally accepted agreement because different conceptions of power are tied to quite fundamental differences of values. Nonetheless, it is possible to identify three or four major approaches for studying power that elucidate the primary methodological issues involved.

Sociological approaches to power in decision making raise what ought to be a central concern in human decision theory, more generally: Whether behaviorism or methodological individualism provides the best, or only, approach for the analysis of decision processes. Associated with this issue is the problem of "decisionalism"—to what extent, if at all, is it useful to consider outcomes as the consequences of choice(s) made by autonomous individual(s), perhaps in conflict or cooperation with others? Is the notion *decision making* itself predi-

Roger King • Department of Behavioural Sciences, Huddersfield Polytechnic, Huddersfield, West Yorkshire HD1 3DH, England.

cated on individualistic assumptions that are difficult to overcome in offering sensible accounts of "who gets what, when and how," to use one famous expression. How should we explain those situations of inequity or injustice, for example, that are not the consequence of any obvious "decision," or that provoke no objection? This, of course, raises even trickier problems, that of specifying "interests." Specifically, what are we to understand by an individual's or group's interests? Is the individual to be regarded as the sole judge of his or her interests and in what circumstances?

The sociological discussion of power cuts to the heart of these methodological dilemmas because in recent years the previously well-established behavioral or individualistic orthodoxy in conceptualizing power has been severely and persistently challenged. For many years the study of power seemed a relatively unproblematic exercise and was largely based on the work of one of the founding fathers of classical sociology—Max Weber. The central assumption was that power is a characteristic of conflictful, observable relationships between two or more individuals. The advantage of such an apparently commonsensical and simple approach was that it was perfectly congruent with the established methodological canons of social science. Power is assessed by requiring observation, empirical testability, and data on individual action. Moreover, although some theorists, such as Talcott Parsons, doubted the emphasis on conflict as the revelatory mechanism by which power relations were exhibited and argued that power was a collective resource usable on everyone's behalf, few theorists challenged the notion that the exercise of power usually involved a conflict of wills and preferences between knowledgeable individuals. Individuals were aware of their interests that became reflected in preferences articulated more or less strongly, depending on how intensely a person felt about a matter, in social and political arenas. The absence of preference articulation, that is, inaction, indicated satisfaction that interests were either being advanced or not endangered, whereas power was a reflection of success in the relatively public clash of policy preferences.

In recent years, however, a more "radical" approach to power has challenged a number of these assumptions. It rests largely on the claim that the positivistic, behavioral and conflictful conceptions of power ignored the role of ideology in human affairs. Ideas, beliefs, and values are not necessarily the fully voluntary or reflexive constructs of autonomous individuals but can be used as symbolic or cultural resources in securing or maintaining dominance by one group over another. The result of such an exercise of power is not necessarily conflict but its absence—not action but inaction. Perhaps most contentiously of all, the successful imposition by the powerful of its "definition of the situation" over the powerless leads to the view that, in some circumstances at least, individuals may not be aware of what is in their best interests and, therefore, may not be the best judge of them.

Some of these objections to established conceptions of power are not new. Marxists, for example, have long argued that individual consciousness was a social class product and not simply ideational reflection by free individuals. There is also a tradition in non-Marxist sociology, perhaps best exemplified by the work of Emile Durkheim and Talcott Parsons, that emphasizes the normative and value constraints on individual action and that questions the assumption that individual preferences are freely constructed. However, this view regards values as a collective, social resource, not the manipulative means for obtaining compliance from individuals in the interests of particular groups or classes. Nonetheless, recent critiques of behaviorist approaches to power lay greater emphasis on the need for empirical substantiation of claims about power relations that involve reference to inaction and the causal influence of ideology. That is, power is operational, empirically useful in that hypotheses can be framed in terms of it that are in principle verifiable. Mere assertions of "false consciousness," for example, are regarded as generally insufficient without an identification of those "counterfactuals" that open such assertions to tests of falsifiability. Moreover, recent critiques of orthodox conceptions of power differ in the extent to which they depart from methodological individualism and to the degree to which relevant counterfactuals are to be hypothetically constructed or empirically located. To understand this, we need to explore now in greater detail the different conceptions in sociological approaches to power in decision making.

THREE CONCEPTIONS OF POWER

A useful framework for discussing the analysis of power is provided by Steven Lukes (1974). He distinguished three "conceptual maps" that underlie three major models of power. First, there is the one-dimensional view, associated with the work of Max Weber but that predominated among political scientists in the United States in the post–World War II years, particularly in the work of the pluralists. Second, the two-dimensional view offers a critique of Weberian or pluralist behavioralism through the use of the notion *nondecision*, although it is clear that this provides only a partial critique. Consequently, a three-dimensional view has emerged that offers a more thoroughgoing challenge to the methodological and theoretical assumptions of decisionalism and that, it is claimed, gives a deeper and more satisfactory analysis of power relations than the first two models.

Decisional or Pluralist Accounts of Power

Although several British and other European writers have contributed to contemporary theoretical debates on power, most of the empirical work that has underpinned these discussions is derived from analyses of power relations in American local communities. Very few community power studies have been carried out in Britain, partly because of the view that community power analysis is based on the relative weakness of local political institutions compared with private community organizations and groups. In contrast to the United States, British local government is held to be both the formal and real source of power in local communities, which is relatively immune from control by external groups or individuals.

Whatever the accuracy of this view, the corpus of substantive power research is undoubtedly American and primarily local or urban. The seminal study of American community power is Hunter's (1953) study of Atlanta, Georgia, in which Hunter adopted a much more individualistic methodology than those of earlier studies. As Dunleavy (1980) points out, Hunter argued that power could be understood as the property of particular individuals and that this could be measured by the use of a "reputational" methodology. This involved the observer's asking a number of expert "judges" or "inside dopesters" in the city (e.g., newspaper editors, leading businessmen, and politicians) to nominate a small number of "community influentials" from lists drawn up by local organizations. Interviews were then carried out to discover the extent of personal interaction between influentials and also which individuals were the chief members in any elites or cliques that were unearthed.

The problem with this technique was that it tended to look for those individuals with the *reputation* for possessing power rather that for those who actually *exercised* it. It is possible for individuals to be falsely attributed with having power, for example, and although it may be argued that even false reputations provide the basis for power of a sort, this is not the intention of the methodology. An adequate conception of power should distinguish between dispositional (reputational or potential for power) and episodic (exercise of power) usages, and Hunter's approach did not. Moreover, it was a technique that tended inevitably to produce a picture of elitist, privately dominated community power structures when replicated elsewhere because it involved a step-by-step winnowing and narrowing of community leaders from ever-shortening lists of potential community influentials.

Consequently, an alternative methodology associated with pluralism developed that challenged both Hunter's reputationalist approach and also its elitist conclusions. A number of theorists, such as Dahl (1961), Polsby (1963), and Wolfinger (1971), argued that to study power, researchers should look at actual decisions involving cases of overt political conflict and reject reputationalism. The most influential work was Robert Dahl's study of New Haven, *Who Governs?* Dahl argued that any group with a serious grievance or goal could make it known in New Haven's relatively open political system. He suggested that the researcher could see whether a group was powerful or not by seeing how successful it was in the policy process. Dahl concluded that in New Haven power was widely diffused and that no group was significant across all issues, although some were in particular decisions.

Although the pluralist study of power structures aimed to demonstrate that power within the American political system was distributed less cumulatively than Hunter claimed, observers have generally failed to note the essentially similar conception of power employed by both Hunter and the pluralists. Hunter was criticized for ignoring *actual* behavior or the exercise of power in observable, concrete decision making but not for his view that power was to be conceived "individualistically." For both, power was interpreted as the capacity of one actor to do something affecting another actor that changes the probable pattern of specified future events (Polsby, 1963). We should be clear, therefore, that the notation *pluralism* refers to a type of power structure, to be distinguished from elitism, rather than a description of a methodology for studying power. The one-dimensional view is probably best characterized as the *issue-outcome* or the *decisional* approach, and although it is often associated with pluralist *findings,* this does not follow inevitably.

Dahl describes his "intuitive idea of power" as the successful attempt by A to get B to do something he or she would not otherwise do. This reference to a successful attempt is central, for it indicates that Dahl is referring to the exercise of power in a social relationship. Power is conceived episodically and is to be distinguished from dispositional conceptions of power as an individual's property or capacity in which the individual has a potential for power that may or may not be exercised. The operationalization of Dahl's concept of power, as found in *Who Governs?,* involves identifying a number of key decisions in the local community and then determining for each decision which participants had put forward proposals that were eventually accepted, which had successfully opposed proposals from others, and which had suggested proposals that were not adopted. Overall, the participants with the greatest proportion of successes out of the total number of successes were then considered to be the most influential.

The emphasis in this approach is seeing who wins or loses in actual decision making by studying concrete, observable behavior. This behavior may be observed directly by the researcher, or it may be reconstructed from documentation, newspapers, interviews, and other sources. Whichever, the approach rests on producing empirical data as evidence for propositions about the exercise of power that have been operationalized for particular settings in a way that enables these propositions to be verified or falsified. Moreover, these data are action based and exhibited by public policy preferences in decision making. A further central assumption, however, is that decision making involves actual and observable conflict. As Lukes (1974) notes, the pluralists speak of the decisions being about issues in selected (key) "issue areas"—the assumption being that such issues are controversial and involve actual conflict. For example, Dahl

(1961) argues that one can only strictly test the hypothesis of a ruling class if there are cases including key political decisions in which the preferences of the hypothetical ruling elite run counter to those of any other likely group that might be suggested, and in such cases, the preferences of the elite regularly prevail. However, as Lukes (1974) remarks, this focus on behavior in the making of decisions over key or important issues as involving actual or observable conflict is not required in Dahl's definition of power, which merely refers to A's successfully affecting what B does, and which presumably could occur in the absence of observable conflict. As we will see, critics of the decisional or issue-outcome view make use particularly of the possibility of nonconflict or inaction as part of a successful exercise of power in their critique of its behaviorist assumptions.

In summary, therefore, conflict over freely made and articulated preferences by individuals, which is accessible to the observer, provides the empirical test of power in the decisional approach. This raises the concept of *interests* employed in the analysis. Interests are defined as articulated policy preferences. To infer that an individual's interests may be unknown to the individual or mistakenly perceived is rejected as unscientific for it then becomes impossible to disprove any empirical proposition on power relations. The presumption by the observer of a set of "real" interests not recognized or articulated by an individual only involves a substitution by the observer of his or her own prejudices. But it is around these particular issues that alternative conceptions of power to that found in decisionalism have been constructed.

Nondecisionalism or the Two Faces of Power

An important group of critics of Dahl's approach are known as *nondecisionalists;* they are so described because of their stress on the importance of issues not discussed within the political arena. A problem with the issue-outcome approach is that the issues selected for decisional study are those already recognized by the political system as issues. Moreover, the definition of interests as articulated preferences suggests that issues involve conflict of policy preferences that are regarded as conflicts of interest.

Yet conflicts of interests may not be indicated by conflicts of articulated policy preferences for the possibilities for effective political action are not evenly distributed. Not only do individuals and groups differ in the resources that they possess (e.g., wealth, time, literacy, etc.), but they differ also in the way they are regarded by society. Those groups with low public or social esteem may have great difficulty in having their claims taken seriously. Some groups may find that a consideration of their wishes or interests never takes place in the political arena, and any analysis of the distribution of power based solely on the analysis of decisions would not detect this. The most powerless would not be those who did least well in having their preferences accepted but those whose wishes or interests were never considered at all.

The assumption of the decisionalists is that when people do not advance policy preferences then this is because they either do not particularly care about, or are generally satisfied with, existing or proposed arrangements. If they did feel intensely about a matter, then the political system is sufficiently open for people to be motivated to express their views. However, this raises the question of the process whereby the will to engage in political action becomes manifest. Moreover, as Saunders (1979) notes, if the objective possibility for such action is present (i.e., through access to the necessary resources), yet inactivity results, then we need to explain why the will to act has apparently failed to develop.

This clearly suggests that analysts of power may be as concerned with inaction as they are with action. Instead of assuming, with the decisionalists, that inaction indicates satisfaction or agreement with existing arrangements, inaction may reveal an inability to advance a set of interests that, over a period, may induce a fatalism or resignation about even trying. On the other hand, too, inactivity may not be a reflection of weakness or suppression but the reverse. The very powerful may rarely need to act to advance or maintain their interests because they are already taken into account by decision makers. The supreme exercise of power may be the capacity not to have to act at all.

One of the earliest attempts to challenge the one-dimensional or issue-outcome view that political inaction indicated unconcern or satisfaction is found in Bachrach and Baratz (1962, 1970). Referring to the "two faces of power," they suggest that whereas power may be reflected in concrete, observable decisions ("the first face"), it is also exercised when powerful individuals use social values and institutional practices to limit political discussion to only those issues that are relatively harmless to them ("the second face"). Not only may those in powerful positions simply ignore claims by the less powerful, but the less powerful people may not advance their claims because they anticipate that they will not succeed or, if they fail, invite retaliation.

Bachrach and Baratz develop the notion of *non–decision making* to criticize the issue-outcome approach for ignoring those areas of policymaking where certain interests have been prevented from having a public airing. One reason for this may be a "mobilization of bias," which refers to a set of predominant values, beliefs, rituals, and institutional procedures (rules of the game) that operate systematically and consistently to the benefit of certain persons and groups. For example, it is often argued that in capitalist societies, business and business groups have little difficulty in having their views or proposals accepted as legitimate matters for serious public discussions, whereas labor or the poor encounter much greater suspicion for their aims or objectives. Bachrach and Baratz, therefore, employ the notion non–decision making to criticize the behaviorist assumptions in the one-dimensional or issue-outcome approach to power for unduly emphasizing the importance of initiating, deciding, and vetoing, that is for stressing political *action*. Yet Bachrach and Baratz's position is a difficult one to maintain, particularly when it comes to operationalization, for it has been pointed out that when it comes to considering non–decision making, there is a multiplici.; of events that have not happened from which the researcher may choose. It is in response to such criticisms that Bachrach and Baratz moderate their antibehaviorism, for they assert that "nondecisions" that limit the area of decision making are themselves observable decisions. However, these nondecisions are more covert and less accessible to the investigator than decisions because opposition is thwarted before it reaches the formal stages of authoritative decision making. But signs of the "opposition" and its "thwarting" may still be empirically detectable if the analyst digs deep enough.

Yet, as Parry and Morriss (1974) argue, if nondecisions are actually observable practices (albeit harder to observe than decisions) the conceptual distinction between decisions and nondecisions tends to collapse. In many cases nondecisions are decisions, although not necessarily the sorts of "key decisions" studied by Dahl and the "decisionalists." What happens, they suggest, is a series of lesser decisions or choices, each of which forecloses other courses of action. Therefore, either nondecisions are observable, in which case they may be regarded as a type of decision, or else they are not observable and, therefore, not open to empirical enquiry. Parry and Morriss (1974) suggest that nonresponses by elites or the mobilization of bias against the powerless usually involve some form of visible behavior sufficient for the vigilant researcher to be alerted to inquire why claims were not followed through. However, these are properly recognized as decisions, for to do otherwise will be to collapse distinctions between very different political techniques. For example, the term *nondecision* includes both action and inaction, but some nondecisions involve conscious choices, whereas others may be the outcome of the unconscious acceptance of community values. Therefore, to understand the power and penetrability of any community it is better to replace blanket terms like nondecision with a more precise analysis of the many different patterns decision making can take.

The problem with Parry and Morriss's formulation (and also Bachrach and Baratz's) is that there are cases of non-decision making where the powerless take no action because, for example, they are aware of the futility of pressing a claim. Indeed, the utility of a notion such as non–decision making is that it points to the everyday or routinized nature of many power relationships. Also, it recognizes those situations where dominant interests exercise such a degree of influence over the beliefs of the less powerful that they effectively determine not only whether certain demands come to be articulated or taken into account but also whether people even conceive of such demands. It is not clear from Bachrach and Baratz's analysis whether their acceptance of a behaviorist interpretation of non–decision making is based solely on methodological or moral grounds. That is, it could be argued that although it may be difficult to empirically test false consciousness propositions, it does not follow that situations of false consciousness never occur; only that it is difficult to verify such propositions in a way that allows for their falsifiability. Thus, as with pluralism, observable conflict or action provides the test for power relations, and the assumption is that conflicts occur over interests that are consciously articulated as policy preferences, even if it is recognized that some preferences may never reach the formal agenda of public decision making. In the end, therefore, Bachrach and Baratz's notion of non–decision making reasserts positivism and the decisional paradigm and rests on the assumption that decisions are choices consciously made by individuals.

However, in criticizing Bachrach and Baratz's methodological individualism, Lukes (1974) argues that the bias of a system can be mobilized, recreated, and reinforced in ways that are neither consciously chosen nor the intended result of particular individual's choices but by the socially structured and culturally patterned behavior of groups and practices of institutions as a function of collective forces and social arrangements. Consequently, it has been argued that the two-dimensional view underestimates the significance of ideology, the imposition of beliefs, and the manipulation of values in securing stability, and the absence of conflict. Although an individual may exercise power over another individual by getting him or her to do what he or she would otherwise not do, he or she also exercises power over him or her by influencing, shaping, and determining his or her very wants. This takes us on to a consideration of the "radical" view of power.

Radical Approaches to Power

Radical approaches to power offer a critique of the behaviorist assumptions of both the decisionalists and the non–decision makers. They tend to rest on the claim that rather than actual conflict being necessary to power, the very absence of conflict may reveal the most thoroughgoing use of power in which potential grievances are prevented through the shaping of individual perceptions and wants. Social and political arrangements can be legitimated and accepted by the powerless despite a contradiction between the interests of the powerful, which are advanced or maintained by such arrangements, and the real interests of the powerless, which are not. The necessary methodological corollary is that the observer is able to distinguish between the subjective interests of the participants and their real or objective interests as these are theorized by the observer.

Clearly, such an assertion provokes scientific and moral indignation by those that regard notions of *false consciousness* or associated concepts as a shorthand way of saying that people do not know what is good for them. As we have seen too, if it is difficult enough to verify the claims made in Bachrach and Baratz's essentially behaviorist interpretation of non–decision making, how much harder it is to meet criteria of adequacy for propositions about the manipulation of cognitions and preferences. However, because such a task is methodologically difficult does not mean that claims for false consciousness should be theoretically ignored, or that, in the absence of conflict, we should assume the existence of consensus. Nonetheless, the identification of real or objective interests, as Lukes (1974) asserts, must rest on empirically supportable and refutable hypotheses.

It is interesting to note the seminal role played by Parson's work on power in the formulation of an empirically verifiable, nonbehavioral conception of power. An essential feature of power for Parsons (1967) is that it is less an individual capacity than a facility or system property for achieving collective goals. In liberal democracies, the inevitable asymmetry of power possession is justified if power is used for the benefit of society as a whole. That is, the legitimacy for wielding power is dependent on more than the subjective agreement of societal members but also on demonstrating that the objective interests of the powerless have also been met by the powerful. As Saunders (1979) notes, the approach necessarily rests on the central premise that it is possible to identify the real interests of a given individual or group independently of the way in which such interests may be subjectively conceived by those concerned.

But how are these real interests to be identified? First, by rejecting on philosophical grounds the behaviorist assertion that interests and wants are necessarily the same and that a concept of objective interests that is not consistent with people's own wants or perceptions of their interests is unacceptable. Not only is it possible for someone to want something that he or she recognizes is against his or her interests (e.g., a cigarette), but it is also possible for someone to mistake his or her interests. Individuals are often not aware of their motives for acting in a particular way. Scientists have long recognized the existence of unconscious wants. Similarly, theorists of the so-called Frankfurt School, such as Habermas (1976) and Marcuse (1964), have suggested that ideological distortion in advanced capitalism prevents individuals from necessarily wanting their true needs, although they accept that in the final analysis, in the appropriate circumstances, individual wants and needs should be synonymous. But these "appropriate circumstances" are where social and political mechanisms allow truly autonomous individuals to be the judges of their own interests, freed from the influence of dominant ideologies. These conditions do not presently obtain in the real or empirical world, for they require (for Habermas, 1976, at least) undistorted, rational communication within a context of ideological neutrality and political equality. To understand empirically unobservable but real individual interests requires the analyst to mentally recontruct or hypothesize the conditions of open discourse that allow autonomous will formation and the authentic individual identification of interests. (The method is similar to Weber's *verstehen*). However, such constructs or hypothecations are obviously difficult to verify or falsify empirically.

One step towards a methodology allowing empirical test of false consciousness claims may be to look for those situations in the empirical world where ideological constraints have been loosened and then seeing whether the hypothesized forms of action actually occur. These situations may be exceptional, but if individuals or groups do act in ways consonant with their real interests, that is, if subjective and objective interests converge, then it is possible to argue that the appropriate counterfactual has been adduced. Certainly, this notion of *relative autonomy* is more likely to be empirically available than the hypothesized situations of full individual autonomy or open, discursive will formation of the kind advanced by Habermas. Lukes (1974), for example, suggests that in the absence of observable conflict, situations where ideological or coercive power is weak or has been relaxed provide grounds (albeit indirect) for asserting that if A had not acted (or failed to act) in a certain way, then B would have thought and acted differently from the way he or she does actually think and act.

A number of writers have used Matthew Crenson's (1971) study of the politics of air pollution control in two American cities as one of the more successful analyses of the indirect exercise of power and as indicating that radical approaches to power are, in principle, open to empirical verification and falsifiability. The study seeks to explain inaction as well as action, that is, to explain why certain actions did not occur. Specifically, why was the issue of air pollution not raised as early or as effectively in some American cities as it was in others? Crenson starts with the reasonable axiom that individuals prefer clean air and good health to bad and explains the slower speed with which one of two similar towns adopts air pollution controls to its dominance by one company. In Gary, Indiana, which was a company town founded by U.S. Steel, the major employer in the town, the issue of air pollution surfaced slowly and spasmodically on the political agenda. In East Chicago, which was not dominated by one employer, the question of air pollution had a much higher political visibility. Legislation to restrict air pollution in the town was introduced after a relatively open, pluralist decision making process.

The advantage of Crenson's study is that he showed that where the steel industry enjoyed a reputation for power it could effectively prevent the issue of air pollution being raised through its power reputation operating on anticipated reactions. It did not have to enter into open, public discussion or overt policy processes. Moreover, as Lukes (1974) has noted, Crenson does not interpret non–decision making behaviorally because he emphasizes the importance of inaction, whereas he also considers institutional as well as individual power. Crenson is able to demonstrate, therefore, that local political institutions and political leaders may exercise considerable control over what people choose to care about and how forcefully they articulate their cares. Furthermore, Crenson's study provides both the relevant counterfactual and the identification of a power mechanism. That is, it is reasonable to suppose that people do not want to be poisoned, even if they do not articulate such a preference, and Crenson provides data indicating how institutions prevented people's interests not being acted upon.

This is not to ignore the possible objection that in many situations it is likely to be very difficult to justify the relevant counterfactual. Individuals' interests are not so readily adduced as they are in the case of air pollution, and it is hard to be sure that people would have acted differently but for the exercise of power. Charges that the observer is simply positing his or her values over those of the subject are difficult to rebut. Yet we have to recognize that exceptional or abnormal instances of relative autonomy do occur, and perhaps they occur more readily than we realize. For example, the intermittent periods of liberalism or relaxation of controls over individual freedom that have occurred in Eastern Europe indicate how differently people can behave when presented with an opportunity to do so. Even in normal times it may be possible for the observer to detect occasions when people escape from subordinate positions, from direct surveillance at work, for example, and to use such data to test propositions that people would act differently, in line with their "real" interests, if provided with the ideological autonomy and freedom to do so. For another example, Lukes (1974) has suggested that there is a significant difference between the caste system as it exists in the popular conception and as it actually operates. Although caste position is held to be ascriptive and unchangeable, lower castes do seek to rise within the system. When the opportunity arises, there is a marked change in behavior. Moreover, instances may also be available to the observer to detect the specifiable consequences of inaction when acting in a certain way was a reasonable, hypothesized expectation that would have had determinate effects.

However, in seeking empirical applications of notions of *relative autonomy,* we may forfeit some of its theoretical power. Bradshaw (1976), for example, argues that it is extremely difficult to determine at what stage we arrive at relative autonomy such that the level of influence being exercised by A over B is sufficiently reduced for B to act sufficiently autonomously so that his or her real interests are advanced or maintained. Moreover, B's hypothesized independence of A's power fails to rule out the likelihood of B's continued subjection to other sources of power that, even though opposed to A, may still be inimical to B. Further difficulties with "autonomy" solutions to problems of identifying power and interests follow from attempts to retain the individual as the final arbiter of his or her own interests in circumstances of (relative) freedom and equality. Saunders (1979) notes that not only do such solutions tend to lead to hypothetical analysis that is difficult to assess empirically, but they compel us to accept that a course of action is in an individual's interests, no matter how bad it is, provided that the individual made the choice in a situation of relative autonomy. Thus, he argues, we would be obliged to accept that if the inhabitants of the steel towns studied by Crenson actually opted for their air to be polluted, provided they made this choice in a situation of relative autonomy and with full access to all the relevant information, then poisoned air would be in their interests.

An alternative approach that rejects any individualistic conception of power and interests is found in certain theories in Marxist structuralism in which power is the capacity of a social class to realize its specific objective interests. Poulantzas (1973), for example, argues that the interests of a class are determined in the field of class practices by what it can achieve as a social force in conflict with other classes. Moreover, the members of a given class will not always be aware of the extent of their class interests, but this does not hinder class interests because interests are limited only by what can be achieved. However, such a position, rooted in Marxian historical materialism, is difficult to verify empirically, for it rules out, by definition, the possibilities of a genuine consensus and shared interests between the two principal classes within capitalism. Similarly, Lukes (1974) argues that within a system characterized by total structural determinism, there would be no place for power because to speak of power in social relations is inevitably to speak of agents, individual or institutional, who, although operating within structurally determined limits, have an autonomy and an ability to act other than in the way that they did. That is, in the case of a collective exercise of power, on the part of a group or institution, this is to imply that the members of the group or institution could have combined or organized to act differently.

Although accepting Lukes's strictures on structural deterministic accounts of power, it may not be necessary to go as far as he does in abandoning objective criteria for assessing whether or not interests have been met in any given situation. Lukes (1974) wishes to keep a subjective referent to the identification of interests for he believes that an attribution of power is at the same time an attribution of (partial or total) responsibility for certain consequences.

However, this raises questions as to whether power is being exercised when the consequences of an action on others is unintended. Moreover, following Saunders (1979), it may be possible to go further than Lukes by accepting a definition of interests that rests on the assumption that real interests refer to the achievement of benefits and the avoidance of costs in any particular situation and that the assessment of benefits and costs is to be determined independently of the desires and preferences of the individuals concerned. That is, benefits and costs are determined by the observer with reference to the context in which they are distributed. For example, Saunders points out that we can demonstrate which groups benefit from local authority density provisions and zoning policies, from welfare cutbacks, and the like, and we can identify which groups have lost out as a result, irrespective of whether they recognize or accept the fact.

A major objection leveled at the notion of *objective interests* and the claim that power is exhibited by the consequential costs and benefits of policies imposed on agents irrespective of their view of the matter, is that the definition of *costs* and *benefits,* like that of objective interests, is value determined. That is, it is argued that there are usually different views of what counts as a cost or benefit and no objective criteria for discriminating between these views. One response, offered by Saunders (1979) is to suggest that it is possible to assess costs and benefits in any empirical context once the nature of that context is identified. The context of lead poisoning, for example, is health. It is clear that the greater the level of poisoning, the greater the cost to those affected. Therefore, we can take certain "life chances," such as wealth or health, as providing objective indices of interests. One is able to say that a person's interests are advanced (benefits) or diminished (costs) to the extent that his or her position, in respect of such indices, also advances or declines. In political decision making, empirical analysis of the allocation of scarce resources indicates who gains and who loses (for example, who pays most, perhaps in the form of increased taxation, and who receives most, perhaps in the form of increased services). It may also be possible to determine the extent to which such gains or losses are cumulative or patterned.

Individuals, of course, may act deliberately against their own interests. For example, rich capitalists may vote for socialist legislation to introduce a wealth tax because they believe in greater equality. That course of action is perfectly rational and compatible with their beliefs. It is nonetheless, contrary to their objective interests as wealthy persons. Altruistic behavior, although rational and in accord with a person's values, is literally behavior against one's interests. Thus, costs and benefits do exist objectively, and within specified contexts they may be analyzed empirically.

CONCLUSION: THE CASE OF BUSINESS POWER

In this chapter we have emphasized some of the dangers in analyzing power behaviorally. That is, we have argued that action or participation (voice) in decision making, in which competing agents seek to resolve conflicts of interest exhibited as policy preferences, does not necessarily provide the best test of power. Instead, it is suggested that inaction or the absence of participation may indicate a supreme power accomplishment—the ability to have one's interests catered for without having to take action at all. To borrow a description employed by Friedland (1982, p.1), "political power may be silent, voiceless."

An obvious but still useful example of "voiceless power" is provided by the influence of major business interests. Not only do such interests find that their material or economic power may be sufficient to guarantee that their requirements are met by political decision makers without the necessity of participation, but when participation does occur it is to *communicate* existing dominance rather than to create it through the mobilization of political resources. Until recently, social scientists assumed that discovering business political influence lay in studying the political participation of individual businessmen. As we noted when examining elitist and pluralist approaches, whatever the different conclusions about the distribution of power, the empirical focus for both was on individual involvement by business people. However, the implicit assumption that the political power of business derives from the aggregated individual acts of participation has been criticized. Rather, as Friedland (1982) has noted, interpretation has rested recently on regarding both the participation and the power of individual businessmen as being determined by the organizational structures from which they are drawn. Thus, an individual businessman's source of power derives from his position in an organization and in the structure of organizational relations. Nonetheless, even with this approach, the emphasis is still on organizational *participation* as being necessary to the exercise of power.

A further view, in keeping with some of the radical or three-dimensional conceptions of power, is to suggest that the absence of political participation by business may not indicate a low level of business influence but rather the reverse. It may signify a taken-for-granted assumption by governmental decision makers that keeping business sweet is axiomatic for effective policymaking. Local governments, for example, invite businessmen to become involved in policy processes as a means of legitimating their own decisions and to give standing to claims to external agencies for local investment. It is control over economic production that may allow business to influence the determination and scope of publicly acknowledged "issues." As Friedland (1982) suggests, from this perspective the political power of businesses, particularly of dominant economic units, derives more from their locational flexibility and control of the material base of the city than from their present or potential political participation. Capital, particularly in its more liquid forms, is able to move quickly in response to locational variation in profitability, and it is this control over the investment process that is the source of its power. In comparison, labor is much more spatially "locked in" or tied to particular localities, and unions are less able to control the local economy or to adapt easily to local conditions through the mobility of their members. Moreover, because labor unions are not locally dominant economic organizations in the way businesses are, to generate power they are required to mobilize their members and participate in the political process.

There is, therefore, less imperative for business to organize politically than for labor. The latter seeks to "voice" its interests, whereas capital's power frequently may be silent. Furthermore, as Offe and Wiesenthal (1980) point out, although "labor" consists of individual men and women, "capital" consists of units of money. Units of capital can be added together, merged with each other, to provide single lumps of capital, but workers, even when united, remain individual human beings with separate needs and wants. Capital is in that sense always a collectivity and automatically has the advantage of organization, whereas, for workers, organization presents particular difficulties. Workers require organization to construct a collective identity out of separate individual identities.

This is not to suggest that business's political power is always voiceless. In

Britain, for example, the development of trade unionism helped to trigger business association as firms, in addition to their continued merging of capital, recognized political participation as a necessary means of promoting their collective interests against the challenge offered by labor organization and political representation in an era of mass democracy. However, business's preferred and most efficient form of action is to respond individually to the constraints and opportunities offered by the market. This is a less hazardous method of control than that offered by the political frame of action in which agents perform, however nominally in actuality, on equal terms. If it is accepted that organized political representation is a less preferred source of influence for capital than individual action in the market, this suggests that participation occurs when economic power is weakened and is no longer sufficient for controlling the political process.

Nonetheless, business appears uniquely privileged by political institutions in capitalist societies, and this influence is explained by the structural dependence of the state on a capitalist accumulation. This is not a view confined to Marxists. The distinguished American political scientist Charles Lindblom (1977), best known for his liberal-conservative positions, has suggested that government regards business not simply as another special interest but as an entity performing such an indispensable function that government grants it an exceptionally privileged status. He argues that decisions on incomes, production, and distribution are of momentous consequence for the welfare of any society, and in a private enterprise market system they are in large part decided not by government officials but by business executives. Delegation of these decisions to the business executives does not diminish their importance or their public aspect. In Lindblom's view, therefore, business executives become a kind of public official exercising "public" functions. Employment, production, and prosperity in a society rests in their hands, and a major requirement for government is to encourage businessmen to perform their tasks, for it is beyond the power of government to organize or control the process of accumulation. Moreover, in liberal democracies, this must be done by inducement rather than command.

Yet, Lindblom's observations on the structural rather than the behavioral locus of business power should be qualified. If business is inevitably privileged in the political systems of advanced capitalist societies, why does it need business interest associations? Nor should governmental institutions be regarded as always or inevitably following capitalist interests. Some sociologists, for example, regard the growth of public administration in modern society as providing state bureaucrats with the capacity to pursue their own interests in the determination of policy. Not only are such interests independent of capitalist interests, but they may be detrimental to them. The expansion of bureaucratic power can constitute a fiscal drag on accumulation as well as posing potential dangers for entrepreneurial sovereignty. Moreover, the political effectiveness and activities of business vary considerably over time. Vogel (1983), for example, argues that the decade from the mid-1960s to the mid-1970s witnessed a significant decline in the political influence of business in the United States, as a coalition of consumer, environmental, feminist, and civil rights organizations were able to influence the outcomes of government policy in a direction antithetical to the interests of business. The consequence was a mushrooming in formal association and representation by business in the late 1970s to counteract lack of influence.

Any analysis of power must recognize the limitations of a solely behaviorist framework. Our study of the special case of business indicates that power may follow from structural position rather than from political action. Yet we have also noted that totally voiceless or silent power is rarely achieved, even for business, and that more overt behavior or influence is also detectable and that this may vary from period to period. The nature of political action must still be analyzed in any account of power. However, the structural bases of action (and inaction) must form part of this analysis. Does action, for example, constitute the *source* of power, or does it, as with business associations, simply *register* or *communicate* that which already exists (e.g., as a consequence of economic position, although other statuses, such as religious, could conceivable operate in a similar fashion)? Consequently, any adequate approach to power in decision making must take account of both structure and action.

REFERENCES

Bachrach, P., & Baratz, M. (1962). Two faces of power. *American Political Science Review, 56,* 947–952.
Bachrach, P., & Baratz, M. (1970). *Power and poverty.* New York: Oxford University Press.
Bradshaw, A. (1976). A critique of Steven Lukes's *Power: A radical view. Sociology, 10,* 121–127.
Crenson, M. (1971). *The unpolitics of air pollution.* Baltimore: Johns Hopkins Press.
Dahl, R. (1961). *Who governs?* New Haven: Yale University Press.
Dunleavy, P. (1980). *Urban political analysis.* London: Macmillan.
Friedland, R. (1982). *Power and crisis in the city.* London: Macmillan.
Habermas, J. (1976). *Legitimation crisis.* London: Heinemann.
Hunter, F. (1953). *Community power structure.* Chapel Hill, NC: Chapel Hill Books.
Lindblom, C. (1977). *Politics and markets.* New York: Basic Books.
Lukes, S. (1974). *Power: A radical view.* London: Macmillan.
Marcuse, H. (1964). *One-dimensional man.* London: Routledge & Kegan Paul.
Offe, C., & Wiesenthal, H. (1980). Two logics of collective action. *Political Power and Social Theory, 1,* 67–115.
Parry, G., & Morriss, P. (1974). When is a decision not a decision? In I. Crewe (Ed.), *British political sociology yearbook* (Vol. 1). London: Croom Helm.
Parsons, T. (1967). On the concept of political power. In T. Parsons (Ed.), *Sociological theory and modern society.* New York: Free Press.
Polsby, N. (1963). *Community power and political theory.* New Haven: Yale University Press.
Poulantzas, N. (1973). *Political power and social classes.* London: New Left Books.

Saunders, P. (1979). *Urban politics.* London: Hutchinson.

Vogel, D. (1983). The power of business in America: A re-appraisal. *British Journal of Political Science, 13,* 19–44.

Wolfinger, R. (1971). Non-decisions and the study of local politics. *American Political Science Review, 65,* 1063–1080.

CHAPTER 10

Decision Making in Organizations
The Effective Use of Personnel

Humphrey V. Swann

This chapter reviews a number of topics in occupational psychology and shows how early attempts to develop unitary theories have been superceded by decision-making approaches. It should also become apparent that developing a universalistic decision-making theory, such as an expectancy theory, is itself questionable because the experience of both practitioners and theoreticians in occupational psychology (and most people in the field are a bit of both) is that any decision-making scheme must embrace both the context and purpose of the decision. In organizations, people do not make decisions in isolation; they make decisions about something or someone within a historical, political, social, legal, physical environmental, and economic context, and with some aim in mind. Furthermore, decisions need to be implemented and maintained, and because difficulties, hard work, and unpleasantness may accompany any decision, there is often considerable attractiveness in decision avoidance. Janis and Mann (1977) have described some of the decision avoidance ploys.

A BRIEF HISTORICAL BACKGROUND

Many current practices and hotly debated issues within organizations have a history that predates Christianity. Topics such as minimum wage rates, incentive schemes, division of labor, and transfer of skill were discussed by Babylonians, Chinese, Chaldeans, and Greeks (Marriott, 1968, p. 18). Nonetheless, psy-

Humphrey V. Swann • Department of Psychology, City of London Polytechnic, London E1 7NT, England.

chologists' interest in the field is usually traced to two impetuses: Taylor's scientific management (Taylor, 1911/1947) and Munsterberg's (1913) seminal book arguing that academic psychology could improve personnel selection, advertising, and working conditions. Although simultaneously a sociological literature was developing, its impact on psychology was relatively insubstantial until organizational psychology (Schein 1965) was established, and Khandwhalla (1977) describes lucidly how several disciplines can be drawn together when studying organizational design. All the three themes outlined by Munsterberg have since been pursued, although advertising has been hived off to the specialists in consumer psychology.

Occupational psychology's history reveals clear shifts in thinking about people and work, views that themselves reflect societal values. Taylor's scientific management was a rational scheme well suited to the rapid technological development of the U.S. in the 1980s. The assembly line was its apotheosis because it allowed hitherto poor peasants entry into capitalist society. It also fitted in with a class-oriented society.

Social man theories,[1] which arose in response to deficiencies in Taylorism, not only explored human relations at work but fitted in with significant changes in interwar societies reflected in the collapse of many monarchies, the rise in power of organized labor, and the development of social welfare programs. Social man theories, in turn were challenged after World War II by "self actualizing man," an approach that fitted with economic growth and the rise in "knowledge-based" work.

World War I saw the U.S. mass testing program of conscripts, and similar programs were used in Britain in World War II. Observational exercises (now assessment centers) were used by the Germans, the U.S. Office for Strategic Studies (OSS) and the British War Office Selection Board (WOSB). Civilian interest in selection grew between the wars, and since then there has been the rise in personnel selection consultancies.

Consistent with Taylorism, World War I saw an interest in studying fatigue. One famous study was that of U.K. munitions workers who increased their output in response to the shortening of the working week. Military technological requirements in World War II led to the study of man–machine systems and the development of ergonomics. Of most interest to decision making is systems thinking that views organizations as complex interacting systems. Once this approach is adopted, the researcher is seen as part of the system, and the emphasis turns toward issues of structural change not making single decisions. The last section on implementing decisions highlights some of the issues.

Finally, history has also changed the name of the discipline, for the original title, *industrial psychology*, is not appropriate to a field involved in studying so many nonindustrial working contexts.

---

[1]*Social man* was the term used in writings of the time (see Schein, 1965).

OCCUPATIONAL PSYCHOLOGY'S
DECISION-MAKING FRAMEWORK

Occupational psychology is both a science, seeking knowledge of how people experience and respond to work situations, and a technology trying to solve work-related problems. As a practitioner, the occupational psychologist operates as an advisor and enabler; he or she can only contribute when asked, and then often in areas of peripheral interest to those running organizations. An added limitation is that his or her approach and recommendations will be compared with contributions from other "management sciences." Also, an occupational psychologist is rarely a decision maker but an advisor to decision makers.

Rodger (1955) established useful guidelines for U.K. practice by pointing out that the discipline was concerned with effective use of the work force, understanding this to cover both employers' concerns with the satisfactoriness of employees' performance and employees' satisfaction/dissatisfaction with their work. This model is dynamic in that views about satisfaction and satisfactoriness and tolerance levels will vary with economic and other environmental conditions. In practice, problems are approached by using two polar contrasts. The first approach is to regard the demands of a job (i.e., its tasks, purposes, and context) as relatively fixed and to seek those who can and are willing to do the work (selection, vocational guidance) or who can be trained for it. The second contrasting approach is to seek a better fit between people and work by regarding people as relatively fixed in their capabilities, needs, and wants and to alter jobs and their contexts to match these constraints. Such alterations include equipment/methods/work design, structure of organization, rewards, and working conditions. This approach was labeled *fitting-the-man-to-the-job/fitting-the-job-to-the-man* or FMJ/FJM (Rodger 1955).[2] In the end, any recommendation is likely to draw on both FMJ and FJM strands, although one of these will probably predominate.

It is interesting to view the FMJ/FJM approach in the light of decision making. Successful use, it has been found, depends on adequate analysis of problems and careful communication with clients about possible improvements because of consideration of costs and political acceptability. With regard to problem analysis, many different procedures are available because different areas require different approaches, and some of these will be covered later. To be effective, Rodger, when professor at Birkbeck College, London University, taught his students to ask themselves whether their procedures were "technically feasible, administratively convenient, socially or politically acceptable." Because it is well known that psychological testing programs, job enrichment schemes, appraisal systems, and work method changes have all failed on occasion, this advice would seem wise. Often, also, failures have been for nontechnical reasons.

---

[2]*Man* here is used in its generic sense. Today, *person* would be more readily accepted.

Given that the FMJ/FJM approach relies on adequate analyses of problems and a sensitivity in application, it follows that the occupational psychologist is required to exercise considerable judgment over his or her proposals and requests for time and access to organizations. Also, a significant part of one's art involves using one's own disposition and capabilities to influence events. Not only this, but, in some cases, he or she knows that waiting for a suitable opportunity or for a group to admit they have reached an impasse is necessary. It follows, therefore, that although there exists a framework for making judgments and although clients, when presented with various analyses of work and talked through the FMJ/FJM system, find it acceptable and professional, the area in which it is applied makes it nearly impossible to reach specific decisions by recourse to a simple mathematical formula or mechanistic procedure. Although conceptually it can be viewed in terms of subjective expected utility (SEU) theory, the scheme provides little more than a *modus operandi*. Although this chapter follows the traditional FMJ/FJM approach, it should be observed that more recent approaches, such as organizational development, reveal a move from simple problem solving toward major changes within systems. Nonetheless, it is valuable for that because it does enable the psychologist to operate within a scheme that draws together many aspects and functions of organizations that, although they interlock, are treated separately. Having described the overall framework, there follows a summary of trends in various aspects of the discipline.

SCIENTIFIC MANAGEMENT—THE FORERUNNER

Although others had previously timed operators carrying out tasks, Taylor was the first to incorporate such studies within a system attempting to integrate human capacities, the arrangement of work, the structure of organizations, fitting people to work, and views of pay. Taylor observed that, whereas managers of his day could argue reasonably consistently about the capabilities and life span of plant and machinery, their estimates of people's capacities to contribute to effective work were lamentable. He sought to correct this by proposing scientific management that required managers to select the right employees for any task, to train them in correct ways of working, and to pay appropriate incentives. The correct way of working was established by carefully analyzing work into its components and timing them. Such a time and motion analysis enabled the expert to determine the one correct method for a task. The simpler form of analysis allows an observer to record all processes or movements of people using a classification of five activities: operation, inspection, delay, storage, and transport. More complex systems that depend on film analysis of human micromotions have used more units (see Blum & Naylor, 1968, p. 579).

It was Taylor's approach to pay that has aroused most ire and resistance, for, although he believed that employees should often be better paid than they were, improvements depended on their working to his efficient system and on individual incentives. Employees needed to be watched to prevent laziness; they should not be paid too much, otherwise they would dissipate it on their vices. No allowance was made for variations between people, for an individual wishing to change his or her work pattern during the day, for employees' concern to stabilize their earnings, or to keep within norms and limits established by work groups. Taylor also rode roughshod over any resistance to change. That he was forced to become aware of the all too human objections to his methods can be found in his writings as quoted by Brown (1963, p.14).

Many social scientists have castigated the scientific management school, but to reject it totally is unsound. First, the areas selection, training, and pay that concerned Taylor have all been taken up and are seen to be important today. Second, the techniques that Taylor and others developed are still widely used, and certainly more people are employed in "work study" or "O & M" (organization and methods) than in "occupational psychology." The techniques have also been used as a basis for other management sciences (systems analysts often use Taylor's symbols as well as others of their own), and it should be expected that Taylor would regard many of the management sciences' disciplines, aims, and procedures as being up-to-date versions of his thinking. (Whitmore, 1976, shows such links.) Third, many psychologists have found the need to study in detail the complexities of human movement and to develop methods analysis for use in ergonomics and skill training.

TAYLOR'S WORK IN RELATION TO OCCUPATIONAL PSYCHOLOGY

For the decision-making theorist, work study, despite its peripheral links to psychology, provides several important lessons.

1. It shows that decisions on improving working methods require an appropriate system, method study, for examining work and that this analysis must be related to observations of specific tasks. Thus, inherent in the approach is an understanding of industrial, commercial, or administrative functions for an uninformed practitioner will soon be disregarded.

2. Suggestions for improving working methods depend on applying various rules concerning the economy of human movement, work space, layout, and environmental features (Barnes, 1963), and such knowledge must develop from research into human capacities, not mathematical theorizing.

3. Although effective, there are many occasions when work study is not used or is conducted as part of a bureaucratic folderol. Managements may object to its use in areas that threaten their power or comfort; and employees, unless

offered some suitable inducement, may oppose or sabotage its application. Here is seen the political nature of work study.

4. Work study practitioners, aware of potential resistance to their recommendations, stress the importance of implementing and maintaining changes. Often, deciding upon a new method will be easy, but establishing it, especially when it is seen as negotiable by labor unions, may be difficult. This illustrates the need, expressed earlier, for decision makers to attend to more than the intellectual analysis of alternatives.

5. Many social scientists have challenged the appropriateness of "one-best-way" solutions because this overlooks individual differences. Also the use of expert observers to study staff is often unwelcome and precludes participatory methods.

6. Even if people were economically rational at work, work study is still trapped in the competing rationalities of employers seeking more output for less pay and employees wishing to increase their incomes. To conceive of a rationality divorced from this conflict is unrealistic; to develop a rational model that acknowledges the conflict would need a calculus that incorporated the ebbs and flows of political power at the workplace.

7. Scientific management was a rational system. If success depended exclusively on rational decision making, then Taylor provided the framework a hundred years ago. Although undoubtedly useful, scientific management is limited, and any formal rational economic decision-making scheme can be expected to reveal the same failings.

PERSONNEL SELECTION AND DECISION MAKING

Personnel psychologists' attempts to improve selection have followed several directions and, to date, have culminated in methods of job analysis and in ways of exploring applicants' past work-related behaviors. A brief overview of topics so far explored follows.

Validation Studies

Traditional psychometric validation studies have often established significant validity coefficients between test scores and performance measures (Ghiselli, 1966), but, in general, these are of such a size as to indicate clearly that other variables need to be considered.

Tests and Discrimination

Several cases have occurred where personnel selection practices have been challenged, and the law courts are not necessarily sympathetic to psychological as opposed to educational attainment tests. Tests valid for one purpose with one ethnic group may not be useful predictors for that same purpose with other ethnic groups. The fact that correlations between tests and criteria are not high means that many individuals may be excluded from certain jobs and hence have a legal case if selection decisions are based on test scores only.

In spite of these difficulties, legislation in the U.S. and U.K. does allow employers to use test scores and other information in selection, provided there is some relationship to specific occupational proficiency or occupational requirements (Byham & Spitzer, 1971). Even so, in the U.K. employers have been relatively slow to undertake validation studies (Sneath, Thakur, & Medjuck, 1976), preferring, one suspects, to rely on past practice and care in not giving explicit reasons for rejecting candidates.

The Criterion Problem

Any validation study, and hence decision-making approach, depends on establishing some correlation between predictors and criteria. Finding defensible and relevant criteria is difficult in selection for, whereas superficially it often appears relatively easy to obtain performance data such as errors, output, rates of absence, superiors' ratings, reported grievances, and labor wastage, yet, in many cases, variations in equipment or supplies of materials, differences in opportunities, and knowledge of predictor bias will distort apparently suitable measures. Furthermore, what may be easiest to put a number to may not be the measure most valued by employers. Thus output per operator may be easily recorded, but it could be that some operators with relatively low output are valued because they are good at problem solving, helping new trainees or for being peaceable employees! There may be a general consensus among operators about output norms that prevents the researcher ascertaining operators' capabilities. Also, reliability studies of many criteria would probably show them to be doubtful measures. This certainly can arise with superiors' ratings where research into appraisal procedures has shown the need to deal with many biases and distortions in ratings. In many cases, finding a criterion that is both relevant and meets reasonable standards of measurement is either elusive or time consuming. Reviews of the criterion problem are to be found in Blum and Naylor (1968, pp.174–194) and five articles in the journal, *Occupational Psychology* (Rodger, Thompson, Brolly, Vernon, & O'Neill, 1965).

Statistical Decision Methods in Selection

Various attempts have been made to improve on low-validity coefficients. These include estimating the increase in predictive value of using a test over not using one, according to the proportion of candidates selected (selection ratio). For example, one scheme (Taylor & Russell, 1939) argues that if, currently, no test is used, 80% of employees are satisfactory and there are two applicants for each post, adopting a test with a validity coefficient of 0.3 should result in 87% of staff being satisfactory and using one with a coefficient of 0.5 would result in 91% being satisfactory. Since Taylor and Russell's paper, several other statistical schemes have been devised (see Blum & Naylor, 1966, pp. 53–58 and McCormick & Ilgen, 1980, pp. 129–138).

Bass and Barrett (1981, pp. 319) have pointed out that personnel psychologists have accepted that validity coefficients are specific to the particular investigation in which they were obtained and so approach each validation study anew, even though the situation may be similar to previous contexts. This means there is no steady build up of information on tests, and Schmidt and Hunter (1977) have argued that a Bayesian approach could be applied to accumulate a body of knowledge on tests. Superficially, such an argument is attractive, but it still has to be acknowledged that many people, purportedly doing the same job, face very different requirements and styles of management as well as a host of other influences within and outside their employing organization.

Selection Interviewing

Research into this mainstay of nearly all selection procedures has clearly traversed from traditional psychometric studies, through decision making to counseling.

The reliability and validity of interviews have been investigated since early in this century, yet Wagner (1946) in a review of 106 articles found only 25 reporting any coefficients, and most of these were low. Ulrich and Trumbo (1965) in a further significant review article reported much the same story but went further and suggested that it was necessary to study components of the interview.

Webster and his coworkers at McGill University reported on a series of microanalytic studies into decision-making processes in selection interviews (Webster, 1964). It seemed that such features as the amount of time the interviewer talked and whether or not the interviewer received early favorable or unfavorable information about the candidate affected interviewers' decisions.

Undoubtedly, Webster's book exerted a significant influence on research into interviewing, and several themes such as stereotyping, visual cues, attitudes, sex, and ethnic background of the participants were studied. Schmitt (1976) has summarized research into 13 such variables. Mayfield (1964) also emphasized that research should concentrate on decision-making processes and that investigations should use carefully controlled studies of small sections of interviews. Despite some successes, the role of microanalytic decision-making studies has not gone unquestioned. Thus, Wright (1969) called for more macroanalytic studies and was concerned that microanalytic ones could so fragment the interview as to become meaningless.

This concentration on the processes in interviewing raises interesting issues, for an earlier standpoint in selection is well represented by Meehl (1954) who had argued that statistical decisions were to be favored over clinical ones because whenever interviewers interpreted their data clinically they did worse, or no better, than if they had used statistical analyses. Research into the interviewing processes allows for an incorporation of both structured data such as is obtained from biographical records and psychometric instruments and insights gained by interviewers. A study that applied this approach with a carefully worked-out role for the interviewer, as used in the Israeli armed forces, is that by Reeb (1969).

The part of the interviewee has been relatively neglected, and this is an important oversight, in that one argument often put in the interview's favor is that it allows the interviewee to examine his or her potential employing organization. Nonetheless, a few studies have reported interviewees' reactions, and the effect of the liking variable has been studied by Keenan (1977). Alderfer and McCord (1970) have gathered evidence to suggest that M.B.A.s value both supportive and confronting behavior from interviewers. An awareness of the interviewee's context can direct thinking away from decision making, and a start along the relationship between psychotherapeutic counseling and interviewing has been made by Lewis (1980).

From a decision-making viewpoint, several issues concerning interviewing arise. First, would participants accept a selection system that did not use interviews? Anecdotal evidence suggests that both employers and applicants like to meet, and applicants want to learn about their future employing organization. Thus, with regards to Rodger's dictum, the interview is socially acceptable. Second, the interview allows for lengthy discussion to topics, and skilled questioning can reveal much about applicants. It can be regarded as having a broad band width even if it lacks the depth of psychometric measures. Third, despite question marks over its effectiveness, there is research and a belief among personnel specialists that carefully planned interviews that incorporate information from application forms and tests can add to the validity of selection procedures (e.g., Reeb, 1969). Fourth, in a climate of sensitivity over discrimination, employers will want to stick by a procedure that allows them to make a decision on vague grounds rather than face court proceedings defending an "objective" measure. Last, within the interview itself, researchers can study decision processes. As has been mentioned, this theme has been explored quite thoroughly, but there is considerable doubt over the appropriateness of microanalytic studies.

PRACTICAL RECRUITING AND SELECTING OF STAFF

In practice, jobs, even those with the same title, vary considerably, and people's talents and tolerances are so different that professional practice requires selection to be based on an appropriate job analysis. Such an analysis requires the psychologist to have a usable, relevant model of people as workers that takes account of individual differences. In the U.K., undoubtedly the best known model in personnel selection and vocational guidance is Rodger's Seven Point Plan (Rodger, 1951). The scheme comprises a dynamic framework of questions that those in selection or guidance should put to themselves. The seven points include physical makeup, attainments, education, special aptitudes, occupational interests, disposition, and personal circumstances, and the model is that of a person having a relevant history, making adaptations to past experiences that may provide insights into future work adjustments, and operating within an environment that is both individual and significant. The plan is used in personnel selection and guidance by nonpsychologists as well as psychologists. The aim was to reduce the person–job fit information sought to the minimum number of relevant, independent, and assessable headings, while having a scheme that was open enough to include any new psychological findings. It is widely used and is standard teaching material in the U.K. on management and vocational guidance courses.

As well as having a model of people as workers, successful use requires an analysis of jobs. Although many methods exist for gathering the necessary information (McCormick, 1979), in principle, the focus is on what is done that differentiates successful performance from adjudged failure,environmental features of the work, and some picture of the attractions and repulsions of the job as perceived by job incumbents. As a means of information gathering, Flanagan's Critical Incidents Technique (1949) has often proved invaluable. This technique entails questioning employers on what distinguishes successful job incumbents from unsuccessful ones by focusing attention on behavioral evidence.

The information from job analysis is used as a basis for advertising, application forms, screening, and interviewing. A reading of a job analysis will often suggest other actions (training, work methods design, etc.) as well.

There is very little link between standard systems of job analysis and decision-making theory. Although some schemes detail those behaviors or attributes deemed essential or desirable (that is, utilities that must exist and those desired), no one would, in practice, find it worthwhile to put numbers to these qualitative assessments because the words *essential* and *desirable* express intentions satisfactorily.

Practice has shown psychologists that if systematic procedures can be developed for analyzing jobs, monitoring response to advertising, training those responsible for selection, and for following up selected candidates' progress, where these have not hitherto been undertaken, considerable benefits can be achieved for both employers and employees. (It should be noted that taking on employees who are unsuited can cause them considerable stress.) Plumbley (1976) provides a good account of U.K. recruitment and selection practice, and a useful case illustration is Livy and Vant's (1979) investigation into labor wastage and recruitment of oil roustabouts.

An examination of selection research and practice will show an underplaying of mathematic formulas and a concentration on specifying aims, being alive to environmental constraints, and a preparedness to monitor performance and adjust procedures in the light of outcomes.

Cronbach and Gleser (1965) have argued that decision theory as applied to selection can be comprehended at two levels, either at a formal optimizing level or as a set of notions to be borne in mind. Holdsworth (1971), after discussing most of the common decision theory approaches, argues that formal solutions demand unjustifiable assumptions and that a compromise strategy must involve applying mathematical calculations alongside ideas that are as yet unready for mathematical analysis.

There are two further complications for decision theory. The first, and one that could be surmounted with a good theory, is that clients do not turn to psychologists for mathematical analysis of their problems; they think that psychologists have ways of discovering aspects of people not available to them. This means that clients expect psychologists to help with interviewing or interpreting qualitatively psychometric test findings and to give a verbal not a numerical "picture" of the person. Second, it has to be observed that most of the more valued selection decisions (i.e., those where a personnel officer or selection consultant earns his/her reputation and keep) are those concerning single appointments to high-salaried posts. Here it is expected that the candidate will remain and progress within the organization for several years. To date, selection specialists have developed acceptable qualitative procedures, often drawing on normative psychometric data and ideas, but any quantitative approach will need to be a single-case one.

TRAINING STAFF

Just as academic studies of learning and cognitive processes are a major part of the psychological literature, so is training an important component of occupational psychologists' work. As with selection, training provides a useful entrée into organizations because it is acceptable and allows psychologists to introduce ideas over a long time scale. Unfortunately, training schemes are always subject to political maneuvering at both governmental and organizational levels, with the consequence that many technically sound schemes are lost or destroyed.

Training programs have, at one time or another, called on most academic ideas on learning. Thus programmed instruction, T-groups, lateral thinking, and transactional analysis have all excited attention.

An important contribution of occupational psychology to training is the work on developing systems of training needs analysis. This is because it has become clear that the effective way to design training courses is to analyze what has to be learned, where and by whom, and to concentrate on developing suitable objectives. All this requires training needs analysis. Seymour's manual skills analysis (Seymour, 1966) integrated work study techniques and a psychological model of skill (Crossman, 1964) and a classification of the technological demands on the operator. The CRAMP system (ITRU, 1977) tries to relate the demands of a task to recommended training strategies. For decision theorists, an interesting approach is the hierarchical task analysis of Annett, Duncan, Stammers, and Gray (1971). They asked what is the probability, without training, of inadequate performance and what is the cost (in a general sense) to the system of inadequate performance? Analysis is then undertaken into those areas where the product of probability × cost is high. In many cases the probabilities and costs are subjective estimates, and hence this is clearly an expectancy approach. The value of the approach lies not in the values of the estimates but in the fact that a bane of all training analyses is in knowing how detailed to make the analysis. The hierarchical system is valuable in providing such a criterion (the probability × cost one).

Another technique used in training, both as a means of analysis and as a training aid, is the algorithm or training flow chart (Lewis, Horabin, & Gane, 1967). Discovered serendipitously, this is a decision tree showing the trainee what actions or alternatives are available. It is particularly useful in diagnostic and legal contexts as people find it difficult to process conditional statements.

EMPLOYEE APPRAISAL

Logically, if organizations wish to deploy personnel effectively, some system of reviewing employees' past performance, discussing and planning their future, and relating their rewards to performance would appear necessary. In theory, employee reviews and appraisal schemes can do this, but, in practice, there are difficulties.

Much of the work on appraisal systems done by psychologists has been directed at devising appraisal report forms. This reflects some large organizations' desires for standardized reporting procedures and an opportunity for psychologists to practice their methodological skills. Although, undoubtedly, considerable ingenuity has been used (see texts such as Bass & Barrett, 1981, Chapter 8; Anstey, Fletcher, & Walker, 1976), it is widely recognized that other aspects of staff appraisal need attention. These include dealing with raters' biases, training raters, getting people to conduct appraisal interviews, and relating appraisals to organizations' aims.

Many of the preceding difficulties possibly emanate from the unsure basis of appraisal systems. Thus, Randell, Packard, Shaw, and Slater (1972) have argued that reward reviews, past performance reviews, and reviews of job holders' potential, because they serve different purposes, should be separated.

Given the importance of, and threats implicit within, many appraisal interviews, it is not surprising that the textbooks regale readers with tales of superiors who have spent several hours in such interviews with their subordinates without quite coming to the point. In practice, it is found that a workable appraisal system requires a major training program to initiate appraisers into how to use reporting forms and conduct interviews and a considerable administrative effort to maintain the system. (No little effort, sometimes, has to be expended on cajoling reluctant managers to complete their appraisal returns). Usually, it also proves advisable to establish some system whereby the appraiser's assessments are examined, and often this involves the appraiser's superior being involved (the "grandfather" system).

Putting to one side the problems of conducting them, can staff appraisal systems contribute significantly toward decision making? One standpoint to adopt is that, because appraisal reviews past performance and examines future potential of staff and because it can also be used to monitor training and selection procedures, it represents one of the best opportunities to integrate the human resources requirements and demands into the organization's functioning. This thinking underlies the system of management by objectives, MBO (Humble, 1965; Odiorne, 1970) where it is suggested that organizations can formulate specific objectives that state clearly what is to be achieved by a certain time, and these objectives can be written down for any activity. There is also an important motivational element in MBO, as it is believed that systems can be established where superiors and subordinates will work better together because they have jointly agreed on targets.

Logically attractive to decision making though MBO is, it has to be acknowledged that there are difficulties. Sometimes the system's paperwork swamps its overall aim. It is possible for superiors and subordinates to manipulate the scheme, and it has been argued that, in reality, far from there being joint agreement on objectives, subordinates are still being told what to do. MBO needs the whole of top management to be committed as well. The two most significant disadvantages are that, first, it removes the role of the opportunist who, by definition, is reacting to the unexpected in a way that does not fit into a master plan and, second, by assuming a cooperative approach to management, it pays little attention to the political nature of many organizations. Thus, in the private sector of the economy, the self-made man or woman might see himself or herself shackled by MBO; in the public sector those already with influence will be unwilling to abide by a system that appears to question or reduce their authority. For example, the public sector financial controllers will insist that it is sound financial governance that rules; the doctors and academics will argue that the Hippocratic oath and seeking knowledge are sufficient objectives and that their employers should ensure these objectives can be pursued.

Although many organizations use appraisal schemes, the impression can be gained that several of these carry very little clout. Among the reasons cited are reluctance to reward by merit, relatively little mobility between occupational groups, and trade unions' support for "collective" rather than "individualistic" treatment of staff. Also, Pym (1973) produced several damning political criticisms of formal appraisal schemes.

1. The systems emphasize achievement motives, yet are used in large complex organizations that are run on nonachievement lines.
2. Managers, knowing they must continue to work with their subordinates, are bound to favor the vague and devious verbal report over a full, frank written one.
3. An objective appraisal system, if it is used to control transfers and promotions, will take away some of the few powers left to managers in large organizations.

In the area of appraisal schemes and MBO can be seen a vital fundamental clash between the rational decision frameworks for monitoring staff performance and the political response to their use. To contribute significantly in this area, decision theory will need to be addressed to this rational/political clash.

PAYMENT FOR WORK

It is readily observable that people work for rewards and that intangible rewards such as status, pride, praise, craftsmanship, and feeling wanted are valued highly by some. Insofar as attitude surveys reflect employees' feelings, it appears that many are satisfied with, or tolerant of, their work situation and that factors other than pay are important. Indeed, pay often appears not to be the preeminent reward that might be expected (Herzberg, Mausner, & Snyderman, 1959; Tiffin & McCormick 1965, p.361). Nowadays, occupational psychologists are cautious in their readings of research findings about pay because so much depends on the methodology used, and there is also a question as to how people value what they have as opposed to what they do not have. Although undervalued so long as they are satisfactory, people may rate health and money as very important when confronted with the prospect of illness or poverty! Whether it is socially acceptable for workers to admit their striving for money (or for status or power) is also questionable.

How much could a salary administrator use a utility approach in determining rewards? The previous paragraph shows that such a person must evaluate not only what people say they want, but also what they are reluctant to forego and what they have not mentioned because it is taboo! Occasionally, also, the need would arise to assess the response to introducing new systems of payment of which employees hitherto had no experience.

Although a simple application of utility theory would be problematic, some research can be seen as utility based. Some instances are the use of a questionnaire, which in seeking employees' views on their current motivational needs, asked, for each need: How much is there now? How much should there be? and How important is this to me? (See Porter & Lawler, 1968, and studies of cafeteria reward systems.) Thus Nealey, (1964) asked 1,133 members of an electrical trade union to value six employee benefits, all equally costly to the employer. Generally, the most preferred benefit was for the company to pay hospital insurance premiums, but the older employees valued most an increase in their pension. Cafeteria reward schemes offer the chance to vary rewards according to employees' utilities, but such schemes are virtually untried.

Currently, one can imagine that many managers would dislike cafeteria schemes because of administrative costs and the implied challenge that they do not know what their staff value. Also one would expect the use of cafeteria reward systems to vary with economic conditions. They would appeal to employers when staff were difficult to retain, and they would become an annoyance when labor was plentiful.

Turning now to traditional pay practices, what issues stand out and what are the challenges to decision theory? Broadly, psychologists' research has covered employees' attitudes toward pay, development of payment systems, and reactions to pay practices. There has also been some discussion on the role of money. Is it a generalized conditional reinforcer? Or is it an anxiety reducer or an instrumental means to obtain certain outcomes? These are just some of the questions explored by Opsahl and Dunnette (1966) and Wernimont and Fitzpatrick (1972). This chapter, though, will be limited to the decision of deciding upon a payment system.

Commonly, incentive schemes (bonuses, commissions, etc.), either used alone or combined with guaranteed wages, have been seen as the way to link pay and productivity. Thus, Taylor argued for incentive schemes, but experience and research have shown that simple individual economic self-interest is not employees' only value. Employees are concerned about security; the balance between effort, leisure, and pay; protecting weaker or older colleagues; and other collective values. Employers also find that incentive schemes can lead to bitterness, unwillingness to undertake small extra chores, and resistance to work method changes and unsafe working practices because most safety precautions slow down work rates. Group incentive schemes have a long history and are not without problems. Nonetheless, despite their drawbacks, incentive schemes are often so attractive that only a foolhardy employer would drop them. Important reviews are those by Marriott (1968) and Lupton (1972), and Lupton and Gowler (1969) have provided a decision system for choosing between various incentive schemes.

Another type of scheme, popular in the U.K. following the pay freeze imposed by Wilson in 1966, was the productivity agreement. The basis of such agreements was that employees would forego hallowed restrictive practices in order to allow for greater productivity and would be paid a productivity bonus. In this way they could circumvent the pay freeze! Between 1967 and 1969 there were over 4,000 agreements in the U.K. (McKersie & Hunter, 1973); yet many of these were known to be "fudges" arranged by managements and unions to get round the pay freeze restrictions. Two major issues affect productivity agreements. One is the problem of measuring productivity and attributing this to employees' contributions as opposed to investment. The second is that productivity agreements can favor those groups of employees with the strongest restrictive practices at the expense of those who have cooperated to date and who genuinely can only increase their efficiency a little.

In attempts to avoid the problems of incentive schemes and to pay staff equitably, some employers have installed job evaluation systems. The basis of these is that it is possible to look at all the jobs within an organization and to assess their characteristics such as skill demand, responsibility, unpleasant working conditions, and the like, and to use the assessments to produce a rank order. Although many methods exist for evaluating jobs, the systems depend on agreed values about paying for work among employers, employees, and trade union representatives. Job evaluation has been used in many countries (Holland established a nationwide system after World War II) in all economic sectors, and it is accepted by many trade unions. Livy (1975) provides a comprehensive review.

At their extremes, the contrast between wage incentive systems and job evaluation schemes is that of individual economic self-interest versus equity among groups. Needless to say, in practice, many employers operate somewhere in the middle and have group incentive schemes or merit payments built into their job evaluation systems. There is, though, a third strand that has appeared, and that is the decision-making one. Thus, Paterson (1972) suggested the decision-banding job evaluation method, and perhaps the most revolutionary scheme, still, is that of Jaques (1970) who argued that people have firmly held concepts of felt-fair pay that are related to the time span of discretion. The time span of discretion, essentially, reflects the stress of decision-making because it is the time between a decision and its feedback's becoming evident. Decision makers might note, though, that Jaques's system is virtually untried, despite being quite widely discussed, and although it has been criticized on a number of counts (Livy, 1975), it suffers from the disadvantage of removing from trade unionists their role in pay bargaining. Such emasculation is not relished by members of these quite powerful institutions. So even if the scheme is technically feasible and would ease the burden of decision making significantly, it is not politically acceptable.

Looking at the problem of choosing a payment system from a decision theory perspective, one is forced to conclude that the attempt to theorize would be extremely difficult. No one has much understanding of how pay and productivity are linked, and the area of pay is inevitable one of conflict. Furthermore, the choice of any system reflects first the paymaster's values (belief in free labor market, equity for staff, what attributes should be rewarded) and secondly environmental constraints in that any employer must remain within the law and take account of competitors' practices and labor union demands. Perhaps, though, of most importance to decision theory is the realization that deciding on a payment system is not a once-and-for-all-time decision. What is required is something that will hold for 1, 2, or maybe 3 years. Today's practice may be out of fashion a few years hence, and acceptability reflects political pressures, social values, and people's emotions. All of this would suggest that an appropriate decision theory would be an irrational and fluid one!

IMPLEMENTING PERSONNEL DECISIONS

From a managerial orientation, research into implementing decisions embraces three directions: leadership, participation, and organization design. These orientations reflect political sensitivities and researchers' values. The first direction aims to find or train leaders; the second entertains the idea of employers and employees cooperating with the stimulus for cooperation spanning the whole spectrum from "all one happy family" to antagonistic symbiosis; and the last is founded on the belief that structuring the organization in response to political, economic, technological, social, and cultural constraints is appropriate.

Hitherto, little deference in the literature has been paid to the idea that employees might have separate interests and values from employers. Early studies concentrated on such phenomena as absenteeism, labor wastage, output restriction, and resistance to change. It is only recently that there has been any significant attention to bargaining, conflict, and power. Although there follows only a sketchy outline of work in the previously mentioned areas, this should suffice to show that research into implementing decisions is vital as that into arriving at them.

LEADERSHIP

Chronologically, theorizing about leadership has followed four stages: trait, style, situational, and decision-making approaches. Trait theories appealed to those with ideas of selecting those with particular characters or personalities. Extensive early research (Gibb, 1954; Stogdill, 1974, Chapter 5) produced a few usable guidelines, though there was some suggestion that certain traits might be associated with successful leading in certain situations.

The human relations school was influential in arguing that leaders could be trained to adopt more effective leadership styles. Research studies led to the formulation of two contrasting styles, employee and production centered (Michigan University) or consideration and initiation styles (Ohio University). Although early studies appeared to show that employee-centered or considerate styles of leadership gave rise to greater output, later investigations questioned this. It has also been found, on occasion, that training foremen to be more "considerate" in style can be counterproductive if their superiors do not use this style. Evaluative reviews are to be found in Korman (1966) and Stogdill (1974).

The failure to find a better style of leadership led to the situational or contingency theories. The best known is Fiedler's (1967), which classifies situations into eight categories defined by three dimensions (leader–member relations, task structure, and position power) and measures leadership style by the Least Preferred Co-Worker scale which is an enigma. Fiedler, Chemmers, and Mahar (1976) have suggested how leaders can be matched to tasks. Disquiet over the prescriptive nature of previous theories and their failure to allow for leaders to adapt their styles to different contexts led to the development of decision-making theories of which Vroom and Yetton's (1973) is best known. Despite some studies (Field, 1982; Vroom & Jago, 1978), this still remains largely unvalidated.

Leadership research is a confused field, and many issues such as leader's influence, the extent to which good management equates with leadership, and the classification of situations and tasks present major problems. What can be said, though, is that the trend is toward providing managers with aids to decision making rather than prescriptive guidelines. Partly, this is an acknowledgment of individual differences and variations in situations.

PARTICIPATION AT WORK

Rather than leading subordinates, some have thought that involving them in decision making through participation will be more effective. Although fitting in with the social and political climates of the 1960s and 1970s, the various interpretations of the word (Guest & Fatchett, 1974, pp. 9–12) and the host of diverse practices, ranging from improved communications, consultative procedures, and job enrichment to worker directors, has made participation a minefield for practitioners and academics.

Early studies into the links between participation and productivity have produced varied results, and summaries can be found in Stogdill (1974) and Wall and Lischeron (1977). Briefly, research results suggest that employees' participation in changes at work can make decisions more acceptable (Stogdill, 1974); rarely decreases satisfaction (Locke & Schweiger, 1979); and that one should differentiate between direct forms, where workers are influencing immediate working decisions and indirect forms of participation where employee representatives try to modify an organization's conduct. The former generally appear to be more important to employees (Wall & Lischeron, 1977). These issues have also been reviewed by Lowin (1968) and Dachler and Wilpert (1978). Locke and Schweiger (1979) have presented a model that attempts to elucidate the links between participative decision making, employees' reactions, and organizational outcomes.

A look at the environmental context quickly reveals the parochial nature of much psychological research. Thus, organizations will find themselves constrained by technology, the product market, interest groups such as shareholders, consumers, and trade unions, and the overall political climate.

The influence of politics can be seen from the following examples. The U.K. Confederation of British Industry has welcomed shop floor participation: the trade unions either disfavor participation or seek board-level representation (i.e., indirect participation). The Bullock report (1977) sought a balancing system, $2x+y$, which has been shelved. Shutt (1975) has shown how the variants of participation reflected various countries' histories and policies. Thus, the Germans have developed a well-organized system that balances different interest groups but that can be traced to their company law of the last century. The Swedes, confronted by the difficulties of persuading workers to do unappealing work in a well-established welfare state, developed autonomous working groups. In Yugoslavia, self-management was introduced partly to enable Tito to resist Stalin. From Spain comes the Mondragon story (Royal Arsenal Co-operative Society, 1979), reflecting a strong Basque thrust for independence under Franco. The U.K. has a history of participative practices going back to the early 19th century; its developments have been piecemeal, and any nationwide scheme would probably be resisted strongly. That one of its most successful types of cooperatives, namely the building society movement, has become a bureaucratic and financial stronghold is itself interesting.

Speculation with regard to the attraction to individuals of participation would suggest that different reasons for participation might attract those dominated by various motives. Those high on measures of need for achievement (NAch type) would be expected to accept participation if it brought results; those high in need for affiliation (NAff type) to seek cooperative work relationships, and the person high in dominance to use participation to gain a position. That there is no reason for a manager to adopt one style of leadership has been supported by a multinational research study (Heller & Wilpert, 1981).

ORGANIZATIONAL DESIGN AND DEVELOPMENT

The idea that work should fit both technical and social requirements let to the pioneering of the sociotechnical systems concept (Trist & Bamforth, 1951), and Cherns (1976) has suggested how sociotechnical systems principles might be applied. With systems thinking becoming extablished in the 1960s (Randell, 1966; Schein, 1965), psychologists turned to ways of contributing to changing practices in organizations. Clearly, in organizational development (OD), practitioners are confronting some of the most awkward organizational problems. Various approaches such as managerial grids, sensitivity training, process consultation, action research, and surveys with feedback to key personnel are all used. For a review of OD procedures, see Bass and Barrett (1981, Chapter 14). An account of a failure of OD is provided by Blackler (1978).

The impetus behind organizational development programs is the belief that organizations are so complex that simple solutions to problems are inappropriate because they ignore interaction effects and overlook the need for change. OD programs are intended to be strategic not tactical and confront people's known propensity to resist change. As such, these programs are moving away from the traditional FMJ/FJM approach in U.K. occupational psychology, and they also challenge decision-making schemes as they are concerned with major innovation programs, including attitude change ones.

BARGAINING: CONFLICT AND POWER

The large literature on bargaining simulations (e.g., Rubin & Brown, 1975) can only suggest some important negotiating influences. In practice, many industrial relations negotiations are undertaken by experienced representatives attuned to a range of pressures. Historical factors, interunion rivalries, preserving face, the need to work together once a dispute is over, not to mention people's livelihoods are just some of the forces emphasizing the need for field studies such as Walton and McKersie's valuable early work (Walton & McKersie, 1965). It also follows that research studies, such as Morley and Stephenson's (1977), which used students to react to transcripts of disputes, are questionable.

The place of conflict has itself unsettled psychologists because many would hope for cooperative solutions. More recently some, such as Thomas (1976), have maintained that conflict is inevitable and sometimes constructive. He then attempted an analysis in terms of process and structure. Nicholson and Kelly (1980) suggested five themes for strikes: protest, warfare, stratagem, group process, and organizational change. Despite odd exceptions (see Strauss, 1979), psychologists did not venture into industrial relations until the late 1960s. To the few researchers in the 1970s it soon became clear that psychologists' methods were inappropriate and their understanding naive (Strauss, 1979, pp. 372–374).

An adequate industrial relations (IR) methodology will require ways of analyzing and of following participants' and constituents' discussions "offstage." It is also the case that psychologists must accept that negotiators are representing people with interests and that attempts to ease conflict by employing group training or OD approaches that do not take account of this will fail (Strauss, 1979, pp. 383–384). For theory development, it would seem more constructive to undertake research into disputes and negotiation than to try to force disputants' behavior to conform to ideas culled from areas in social psychology (Brotherton & Stephenson, 1975). Although too early to regard as anything other than suggestive, Robbins (1979) has provided a decision analysis framework for conflict management.

Establishing a decision analysis of industrial negotiating will demand an understanding of the nature of power. Generally, this topic has been little researched by occupational psychologists, and a reading of Stogdill's survey (1974, Chapters 25–27) will show the marked influence of social psychological studies with those of an occupational flavor being concerned with issues such as job enlargement and leadership sharing and participation. Although, with such topics, researchers cannot avoid mentioning power, many readers, probably gain the impression that power is not a desirable research area, although Ng (1980) provided a useful starting point for occupational psychologists. Perhaps, though, the last word should remain with the man who can be described as the first political scientist, Machiavelli (1981), for the practitioner will not only find *The Prince* intriguing but knows it has inspired managerial (Jay, 1967) and psychological offspring (Christie & Geis, 1970).

CONCLUSION

This necessarily sketchy overview of ccupational psychology should nonetheless have raised several challenges for decision-making theorists. As both an academic and a practitioner, I would consider at least the following themes and considerations as worth exploring.

1. Occupational psychologists have been involved for decades in decision making. As a result of their experience, technically, they have learned to distrust universal theories; to seek improvements not solutions; to eschew "one-best-way" approaches, and to acknowledge individual differences. Also, it has become clear that contexts must be understood and different but appropriate methods of analysis used. It is perhaps more faith than research that supports the argument that well-formulated aims and carefully developed criteria can lead to significant benefits.

2. Administratively, occupational psychologists know that organizations at best will only tolerate them; that people are not employed to be psychologists' subjects; that information in organizations is scant, inaccurate, and late; and that controlling and monitoring organizations' performances is done by people of different backgrounds and values.

3. Politically, the psychologist has to be aware of many pressures within organizations and that technically appealing approaches may be rejected because they upset balances of power, generate discomfort, or entail risk. The history of the last 20 years has shown clearly an increasing emphasis on employees' rights to influence decisions and attention through such approaches as OD to the need to look at ways to effect change. There can thus be detected a shift away from mechanistic decision-making approaches toward matters of political concern and the problems of implementing decisions.

REFERENCES

Alderfer, C. P., & McCord, C. G. (1970). Personal and situational factors in the recruitment interview. *Journal of Applied Psychology, 56,* 377–385.

Annett, J., Duncan, D. K., Stammers, R. B., & Gray, M. J. (1971). *Task analysis. Department of Employment Training Information Paper No. 6.* London: Her Majesty's Stationery Office.

Anstey, E., Fletcher, C., & Walker, J. (1976). *Staff appraisal and development.* London: Allen & Unwin.

Barnes, R. M. (1963). *Motion and time study* (5th Ed.). New York: Wiley.

Bass, B. M., & Barrett, G. V. (1981). *People work and organizations: An introduction to industrial and organizational psychology* (2nd Ed.). Boston: Allyn & Bacon.

Blackler, F. H. M. (1978). *Job redesign and management control.* Farnborough, Hants: Saxon House.

Blum, M. L., & Naylor, J. C. (1968). *Industrial psychology: Theoretical and social foundations.* New York: Harper & Row.

Brotherton, C. J., & Stephenson, G. M. (1975). Psychology in the study of industrial relations. *Industrial Relations Journal 3,* 42–50.

Brown, J. A. C. (1963). *The social psychology of industry.* Harmondsworth: Penguin Books.

Bullock Report. (1977). *Report of the Committee of Inquiry on Industrial Democracy.* Chairman Lord Bullock, Cmnd 6706. London: Her Majesty's Stationery Office.

Byham, W. C., & Spitzer, M. E. (1971). *The law and personnel testing.* New York: American Management Association.

Cherns, A. (1976). The principles of sociotechnical design. *Human Relations, 29,* 783–792.

Christie, R. & Geis, F. L. (1970). *Studies in Machiavellianism.* New York and London: Academic Press.

Cronbach, L. J., & Gleser, G. C. (1965). *Psychological tests and personnel decisions.* Urbana: University of Illinois Press.

Crossman, E. R. F. W. (1964). Information processes in human skill. *British Medical Bulletin, 10,* 32–37.

Dachler, H. P., & Wilpert, B. (1978). Conceptual dimensions and boundaries of participation in organizations: A critical evaluation. *Administrative Science Quarterly, 23,* 1–39.

Fiedler, F. E. (1967). *A theory of leadership effectiveness.* New York: McGraw-Hill.

Fiedler, F. E., Chemmers, M. M., & Mahar, L. (1976). *Improving leadership effectiveness: The leader match concept.* New York and London: Wiley.

Field, R. H. G. (1982). A test of the Vroom-Yetton normative model of leadership. *Journal of Applied Psychology, 67,* 523–532.

Flanagan, J. C. (1949). Critical requirements: A new approach to employee evaluation. *Personnel Psychology, 2,* 93–102.

Ghiselli, E. E. (1966). *The validity of occupational aptitude tests.* New York: Wiley.

Gibb, C. A. (1954). Leadership. In G. Lindsey (Ed.), *Handbook of social psychology* (Vol. 2). Reading, MA: Addison-Wesley.

Guest, D., & Fatchett, D. (1974). *Worker participation: Individual control and performance.* London: Institute of Personnel Management.

Heller, F. A., & Wilpert, F. (1981). *Competence and power in managerial decision-making: A study of senior levels of organization in eight countries.* Chichester: Wiley, 1981.

Herzberg, F. Mausner, F., & Snyderman, B. B. (1959). *The motivation to work.* New York: Wiley.

Holdsworth, R. F. (1971). Mathematical models and selection decisions. *Occupational Psychology, 45,* 99–109.

Humble, J. (1965). *Improving management performance.* London: British Institute of Management.

ITRU. (1977). *Using the CRAMP system to design a training programme: A study at London Transport* (ITRU Research Paper TR8) Cambridge: Industrial Training Research Unit.

Janis, I. L., & Mann, L. (1977). *Decision-making: a psychological analysis of conflict.* New York: Free Press.

Jaques, E. (1970). *Equitable payment: A general theory of work, differential payment and individual progress.* London: Heinemann Educational.

Jay, A. (1967). *Management and Machiavelli.* London: Hodder & Stoughton.

Keenan, A. (1977). Some relationships between the interviewers' personal feelings about candidates and their general evaluation of them. *Journal of Occupational Psychology, 50,* 175–183.

Khandwalla, P. W. (1977). *The design of organizations.* New York: Harcourt Brace Jovanovich.

Korman, A. K. (1966). Consideration, initiation of structure, and organizational criteria—A review. *Personnel Psychology, 19,* 349–361.

Lewis, B. N., Horabin, J. S., & Gane, C. P. (1967). *Flow-charts, logical trees and algorithms for rules and regulations* (Centre for Administrative Studies CAS Occasional Paper No. 2). London: Her Majesty's Stationery Office.

Lewis, C. (1980). Investigating the employment interview: A consideration of counselling skills. *Journal of Occupational Psychology, 53,* 111–116.

Livy, B. (1975). *Job evaluation: A critical review.* London: Allen & Unwin.

Livy, B., & Vant, J. (1979). Formula for selecting roughnecks and roustabouts. *Personnel Management, 11,* 11–25.

Locke, E. A., & Schweiger, D. M. (1979). Participation in decision-making: One more look. In B. M. Staw (Ed.), *Research in organizational behavior.* Greenwich, CT: JAI Press.

Lowin, A. (1968). Participative decision-making: A model, literature critique, and prescriptions for research. *Organizational Behavior and Human Performance, 3,* 68–106.

Lupton, T. (Ed.). (1972). *Payment systems: Selected readings.* Harmondsworth: Penguin Books.

Lupton, T., & Gowler, D. (1969). *Selecting a wage payment system.* London: Kogan Page.

Machiavelli, N. (1981). *The Prince* (G. Ball, Trans.). Harmondsworth: Penguin Books.

Marriott, R. (1968). *Incentive payment systems: A review of research and opinion.* London: Staples.

Mayfield, E. C. (1964). The selection interview—A re-evaluation of published research. *Personnel Psychology, 17,* 239–260.

McCormick, E. J. (1979). *Job analysis: Methods and applications.* New York: Amacom.

McCormick, E. J., & Ilgen D. (1980). *Industrial Psychology* (7th Ed.). Englewood Cliffs, NJ: Prentice-Hall.

McKersie, R. B., & Hunter, L. C. (1973). *Pay, productivity and collective bargaining.* London: Macmillan.

Meehl, P. E. (1954). *Clinical vs. statistical prediction.* Minneapolis: University of Minnesota Press.

Morley, I. E., & Stephenson, G. M. (1977). *The social psychology of bargaining.* London: Allen & Unwin.

Munsterberg, H. (1913). *Psychology and industrial efficiency.* Boston: Houghton Mifflin.

Nealey, S. M. (1964). Determining worker preferences among employee benefit programs. *Journal of Applied Psychology, 48,* 7–12.

Ng, S. K. (1980). *The social psychology of power.* London: Academic Press.

Nicholson, N., & Kelly, J. (1980). The psychology of strikes. *Journal of Occupational Behavior, 1,* 275–284.

Odiorne, G. S. (1970). *Training by objectives: An economic approach to management training.* New York: Macmillan.

Opsahl, R. L., & Dunnette, M. D. (1966). The role of financial compensation in industrial motivation. *Psychological Bulletin, 66,* 94–118.

Paterson, T. T. (1972). *Job evaluation (Vol. 1): A new method.* London: Business Books.

Plumbley, P. R. (1976). *Recruitment and selection.* London: Institute of Personnel Management.

Porter, L. W., & Lawler, E. E., III. (1968). *Managerial attitudes and performance.* Homewood, IL: Dorsey Press.

Pym, D. (1973). The politics and ritual of appraisals. *Occupational Psychology, 47,* 231–235.

Randell, G. A. (1966). A systems approach to industrial behavior. *Occupational Psychology, 40,* 115–127.

Randell, G. A., Packard, P. M. A., Shaw, R. L., & Slater, A. J. (1972). *Staff appraisal.* London: Institute of Personnel Management.

Reeb, M. (1969). Structured interviews for predicting military adjustment. *Occupational Psychology, 43,* 193–199.

Robbins, S. P. (1979). *Organizational behavior concepts and controversies.* Englewood Cliffs, NJ, and London: Prentice-Hall.

Rodger, A. (1951). *The seven point plan.* London: National Institute of Industrial Psychology.

Rodger, A. (1955). The effective use of manpower. *Advancement of Science, 12,* 237–249.

Rodger, A., Thompson, A. W., Brolly, M. H., Vernon, P. E., & O'Neil, W. M. (1965). The criterion problem in selection and guidance I, II, III, IV and V. *Occupational Psychology, 39,* 77–101.

Royal Arsenal Co-operative Society. (1979). *Mondragon: The Basque co-operatives.* London: RACS.

Rubin, J. Z., & Brown, B. R. (1975). *The social psychology of bargaining and negotiation.* New York and London: Academic Press.

Schein, E. H. (1965). *Organizational psychology.* Englewood Cliffs, NJ: Prentice-Hall.

Schmidt, F. L., & Hunter, J. E. (1977). Development of a general solution to the problem of validity generalization. *Journal of Applied Psychology, 62,* 529–540.

Schmitt, N. (1976). Social and situational determinants of interview decisions: Implications for the employment interview. *Personnel Psychology, 29,* 79–101.

Seymour, W. D. (1966). *Industrial skills.* London: Pitman.

Shutt, H. (Ed.). (1975). *Worker participation in West Germany, Sweden, Yugoslavia and the United Kingdom* (QER Special Report No. 20). London: Economist Intelligence Unit.

Sneath, F. A., Thakur, M., & Medjuck, F. (1976). *Testing people at work.* London: Institute of Personnel Management.

Stogdill, R. M. (1974). *Handbook of leadership: A survey of theory and research.* New York: Free Press.

Strauss, G. (1979). Can social psychology contribute to industrial relations? In G. M. Stephenson & C. J. Brotherton (Eds.), *Industrial relations: A social psychological approach.* Chichester: Wiley.

Taylor, F. W. (1947). *Principles of scientific management.* New York: Harper & Row. (Original work published 1911)

Taylor, H. C., & Russell, J. T. (1939). The relationship of validity coefficients to the practical effectiveness of tests in selection: Discussion and tables. *Journal of Applied Psychology, 23,* 565–578.

Thomas, K. (1976). Conflict and conflict management. In M. D. Dunnette (Ed.), *Handbook of industrial and organizational psychology.* Chicago: Rand-McNally.

Tiffin, J., & McCormick, E. J. (1965). *Industrial psychology* (5th Ed.). Englewood Cliffs, NJ: Prentice-Hall.

Trist, E. L., & Bamforth, K. W. (1951). Some social and psychological consequences of the long-wall method of coal getting. *Human Relations, 4,* 1–38.

Ulrich, L., & Trumbo, D. (1965). The selection interview since 1949. *Psychological Bulletin, 63,* 100–116.

Vroom, V. H., & Jago, A. (1978). On the validity of the Vroom-Yetton Model. *Journal of Applied Psychology, 63,* 151–162.

Vroom, V. H., & Yetton, P. W. (1973). *Leadership and decision-making.* Pittsburgh: University of Pittsburgh Press.

Wagner, R. (1949). The employment interview: A critical review. *Personnel Psychology, 2,* 17–46.

Wall, T. D., & Lischeron, J. A. (1977). *Worker participation: A critique of the literature and some fresh evidence.* London: McGraw-Hill.

Walton, R., & McKersie, R. B. (1965). *A behavioral theory of labor negotiations.* New York: McGraw-Hill.

Webster, E. C. (1964). *Decision-making in the employment interview.* Montreal: Eagle.

Wernimont, P. F., & Fitzpatrick, S. (1972). The meaning of money. *Journal of Applied Psychology, 56,* 218–226.

Whitmore, D. A. (1976). *Work study and related management services.* London: Heinemann.

Wright, O. R. (1969). Summary of research on the selection interview since 1964. *Personnel Psychology, 22,* 391–413.

PART IV

IMPROVING DECISIONS
The Role of Decision Aids

CHAPTER 11

Design of Decision-Aiding Systems

Ayleen D. Wisudha

In this chapter, I will concentrate on describing the role of computerized decision-aiding systems within a decision analytic process, proposing guidelines for designing decision aids, and outlining decision-aiding procedures that may be enhanced by the use of automated systems. I will not attempt to provide a comprehensive review of decision-aiding systems. However, a number will be mentioned for the purpose of illustrating specific functions within such systems. Furthermore, the chapter assumes familiarity with concepts in decision theory and the underlying methods of decision analysis. For background references, readers new to this area are referred to Raiffa (1968), Schlaifer (1969), Brown, Kahr, and Peterson (1974), and Keeney and Raiffa (1976).

INTRODUCTION

This chapter takes the viewpoint that an aided decision-making process involves the interaction between decision makers, decision analysts, and computerized decision-aiding systems. These systems are based on the theoretical principles of decision theory and their implementation through decision analysis.

First of all, let us look at what a decision analysis entails. Decision analysis is a technology that aims to use decision-theoretic concepts as a basis for developing methods of assisting the process of assessing a choice problem. The underlying procedures involve (1) extracting information from the problem owner and (perhaps) various stakeholders; and (2) aiding the individual or the group

Ayleen D. Wisudha • Decision Analysis Unit, London School of Economics and Political Science, London WC2 2AE, England.

of individuals in examining and structuring the information so as to define the alternatives and the criteria on which they are to be evaluated and to identify various possible courses of action and the resulting consequences. A number of techniques are employed to assist in the assessment of (1) the relative values of the various possible consequences on the given criteria; (2) the degree of importance of the criteria; and (3) the uncertainties associated with the various courses of action. These inputs are then integrated using formal and appropriate decision analytic algorithms to derive a preference ordering over choice alternatives. An important overall consideration is that of maintaining coherence, both in the structure of the decision problem and in the judgmental assessments defined therein.

Throughout the decision-making process, the decision maker may wish to amend existing relationships or judgments, to revise the contributing elements, or to request further assistance after a temporary retreat to clarify existing information or to seek further external information. Overall, decision analysis must aim to aid the decision maker in clarifying relationships between components and to see how the elicited information progressively contributes to a holistic understanding and assessment of the decision problem. Whatever action is taken at any stage of the decision-making operation, decision analysis should be responsive to the needs of the decision maker while remaining loyal to theoretical constraints.

So, how can an automated decision-aiding system function within the framework of decision analysis? Where in the decision analytic process will it make a significant contribution? What should it be capable of doing? The principal focus of this chapter will be to answer these questions.

A TAXONOMY OF DECISION AIDS

Because decision analysis typically requires quantitative judgments from decision makers, any automated decision-aiding system will need to carry out routine computations. That is one of the elementary functions of a decision aid. However, the range of possibilities is far greater. In specific formats, decision-aiding systems will vary in detail and complexity.

I will now categorize decision-aiding systems, defined by the type of function they play in a decision-making process. Although general rules permit the formation of distinct categories, in practice, real decision-aiding systems are likely to contain significant functional overlap.

Type 1—Bootstrapping Aids

Bootstrapping aids serve to display and automate rules, implementing normatively specified principles previously generated through consultation with experts. Here, the structure within which the problem is assessed and the process of the decision-making operations are predefined. An early demonstration of this bootstrapping process was reported by Yntema and Torgerson (1961). It is based on the idea that if an automated aid can be generated that captures the judgmental principles of an expert, then its performance will be better than, or as good as, the expert's unaided assessment. Moreover, the process will be protected against the influence of deviant variables, such as the effects of stress and boredom, as they are not systematically coded within the boundaries of the model.

Bootstrapping methods are based on linear statistical models. Such methods prove useful when predictive judgments have to be made on a repetitive basis. Camerer (1981), in conducting a survey of bootstrapping methods, concluded that "bootstrapping will improve judgments slightly under almost any realistic task condition" (p. 411). A bootstrapping system will work providing there is a monotonic relationship between the predictor variables within the system and the external criteria (Dawes & Corrigan, 1974), providing the variables within the system constitute a good paramorphic representation of the expert judge (Hoffman, 1960), and finally, providing the model remains valid. As soon as further variables become relevant, the use of the model will be suboptimal, or even incorrect. Though the model may not accurately map the cognitive processes involved, its output is considered to be satisfactory if it maximizes the expert knowledge strategy it is meant to replicate. Studies that show that bootstrapping procedures produce a higher correlation between the outcome of the model and the expressed criterion than that between the expert's unaided judgment and the expressed criterion have been reported, among others, by Bowman (1963) in the context of managerial decision making; by Goldberg (1970) in the judgmental assessments produced by clinical psychologists; by Dawes (1971) in the evaluation of graduate applicants; and by Ebert and Kruse (1978) in the estimation of future returns of stock.

Another type of decision aid that involves the use of a predefined model, in this case, for the prediction of unique events, are those based on probabilistic information-processing (PIP) models (cf. Edwards, Phillips, Hays, & Goodman, 1968). A PIP system encodes information about the state of the decision problem environment in such a way that an exhaustive set of possible consequences can be generated. The resulting structure is usually represented in the form of a matrix table. Numerical assessment derived from judges form inputs to likelihood ratios that link factual data with hypotheses about the environment. The principles and procedures involved are known beforehand, and the decision aid functions as an automated guide, prompting the user to indicate specific incidences within the predefined structure and finally aggregating the relevant information using the rules of Bayes's theorem. For a summary of various applications of this approach, see Fischer, Edwards, and Kelly (1978).

Type 2—Recomposition Aids

One of the roles of a decision analyst is to assist decision makers in representing their problems within the confines of a decision theoretic structure. Once the problem structure has been defined, recomposition aids can be used to aggregate the contents of the structure. The nature of these types of aids requires users to be proficient in decision analytical methods so they can provide the system with a valid structure. Thus, the use of such systems will be restricted to decision analysts or stakeholders who are familiar with decision analytical technology. With considerable success, these aids take over the task of performing laborious and often repetitive computational operations, leaving the analyst free to perform the more demanding function of monitoring the decision-making process and providing structural guidance when difficulties are encountered. Examples can be seen in systems such as HIVAL, which uses a hierarchical multiattribute utility decomposition method to analyze problems that are characterized in terms of their values on a large number of attributes or criteria; TREE and OPCOM,[1] which can be used to examine alternative courses of action, incorporating a mixture of intermediate decisions and uncertain events.

Apart from dealing with computational operations to provide rapid feedback, an automated recomposition aid can incorporate other facilities. For instance, it can accommodate structural changes during a decision-making session, or perform exploratory sensitivity analysis to determine whether or not a difference in opinion would result in a significant change in the final outcome. Moreover, computer technology offers enhanced facilities, such as the use of color and graphical methods, for clear and rapid displays of feedback material. The use of data storage and retrieval methods gives the user the opportunity to return to the system and work on an existing problem structure to add information and perform further analyses.

So far, I have distinguished bootstrapping aids from recomposition aids. Bootstrapping aids (Type 1) can be described as those that aim to replace the decision maker by automating the entire sequence of the decision-making operation and assisting the user in inserting content to a predefined decision-making procedure. On the other hand, recomposition aids (Type 2) are those that serve to aid the decision analyst and the decision maker in the integration and further examination of the contents specified within any problem structure once it has been defined within the realm of a formalized decision analytical model.

---

[1]HIVAL and TREE were designed and developed by Decision and Designs Inc., McLean, Virginia, U.S.A.; OPCOM was designed and developed by the Decision Analysis Unit, London School of Economics and Political Science, London, England.

Because of the limitations of unaided human information-processing capacity (Fitts & Posner, 1967; Newell & Simon, 1972; Simon, 1978), decision makers can certainly gain some advantage from the use of a decision aid to optimize the use of their knowledge and experience about the problem at hand. The typology outlined so far covers decision-aiding operations that are carried out after a formal problem structure has been attained. Hence, the design of computer software that functions to serve the operations involved is relatively clear, as these operations deal with the manipulation of content within a structure that is, at least initially, predefined. Fundamentally, the operations rely on the implementation of good programming techniques defined by (1) the constraints of decision theoretic algorithms; (2) the design of the user–system interface; and (3) the availability of computer technology. However, the preceding discussion has not yet touched on decision aids that are designed to be operational *before* the decision problem has been clearly formalized. It is the topic of these *problem-structuring aids* that I will now address.

Type 3—Problem-Structuring Aids

The process of formalizing the structure of a problem concerns an important stage of decision making. Systems that purport to assist the operations involved must be capable of stimulating the expression of elements of the problem, expecially in cases where the decision maker is unclear about the problem structure. Problem-structuring aids give a decision maker the opportunity to build a representation of the problem, stage by stage, by assisting in the integration of the component parts of the problem and the clarification of relationships between them. The use of such systems may also lead to the discovery of gaps in the problem structure requiring the decision maker to clarify the missing links.

There are various existing approaches to decision aiding through problem structuring. Most problem-structuring aids include editing facilities and iterative modules that allow the decision maker to insert new information into the problem structure as it emerges or as the need for it is realized. Contrasting examples of such aids can be seen in QVAL (Weiss, 1980), a decision aid that used the direct approach of prompting the user for a list of choice options and attributes in order to build a problem structure rapidly; OPINT (Selvidge, 1976), which uses a graphical method that permits a user to swiftly explore the act–event structure of a simple decision problem. MAUD4 (Humphreys & Wisudha, 1983) uses a series of preconstructed displays that prompt the decision maker to decompose the decision problem in stages. Information entered by the decision maker is used to prompt for further elements of the decision problem resulting in the construction of a problem structure through an iterative process. Another example is GODDESS (Pearl, Leal, & Saleh, 1980), which aids the decision maker in generating a problem structure by using the person's ultimate objectives as a starting point.

Extensive field use of existing decision-aiding systems has led to numerous recommendations for further development. Some comments express suggestions for modifications to displays or rewording of instructions; others involve more serious considerations. For example, Pitz, Sachs, and Heerboth (1980) demonstrated that additional choice options can be generated by displaying the elicited objectives singularly and prompting for possible choice options that may be useful to achieve the particular objective in question; Bronner and de Hoog (1983) suggested that a decision maker's preference values on a set of selected attributes can be mapped onto a data base through a "pattern-matching" process such that a list of alternatives can be generated that matches as closely as possible the preferences expressed. In the latter case, a decision maker's preference values may easily be validated against a data base that contains, for example, information on short-term benefits, long-term prospects, financial gains, and so on. However, it is important to note that a decision aid that concentrates on a fully automated mapping operation cannot rely solely on a factual data base. It will necessarily require the use of a data base that also captures the decision maker's belief system. Moreover, the information must be structured in a format compatible with other subprocesses that together make up a decision-aiding system. As a result, it calls for design concepts that are far more complex than those currently implemented.

PROBLEM REPRESENTATION BASED ON THE NATURE OF THE STRUCTURE

The representation of decision problems can be defined in terms of three types of structures, which bear some correspondence to the types of decision-aiding systems just outlined.

Built-In Structure

The types of decision problem representations that fall under this category are those with structures that are defined within a constant framework. A closer look suggests that such representations can be separated into two categories.

Problem Representations with Fixed Structures

Here, the formal problem structure is predefined for a particular type of application. It is used repetitively to analyze different sets of contents. This method requires a simple interface within the decision-making process that monitors information that is entered in the correct format and deals with erroneous entries. Although assessments using the decision aid may be carried out by the decision analyst, given the constant framework and familiarity with the procedural operations involved, it is more likely that the analyst will step back and hand the system over to the decision maker. The analyst may enter the foreground again to assist in reformalizing the model should the existing structure become invalid.

Partially structured problem representation

These types of problem representations require decision aids that are capable of extracting further information to complete the formalization of the problem structure. Such aids may include the facility to select an appropriate model for the current problem through mapping the problem structure onto a built-in data base consisting of a taxonomy of predefined structures in order to find a match. Such a proposal was suggested by Weiss (1980) in the form of an automated decision aid called GENTREE. It promotes the progression from a partial structure, through a mapping process, into a complete fixed structure, as previously described. Realistically, a suitable analytic model that deals with the problem structure in its final format is usually determined through consultation with the analyst.

Assumed Structure

Problems falling into this category are typically those that require the decision maker with the help of an analyst to generate a structure to a high degree of development such that the material required for the evaluation of the problem is, as it were, ready in a form appropriate for entry into a chosen decision analytic model. In this case, the role of an automated decision aid is to operate on the given structure, manipulating the specified material and combining it using algorithms that obey decision theoretic recomposition rules. Phillips (1982) records a case study that demonstrates the process of modeling a decision problem, based on a requisite representation of the problem. He points out that difficulties are usually encountered in any attempt to construct an optimal model of the decision process due to conflicts in opinion and proposes requisite modeling as the compromising solution. The concept of *requisite modeling* is based on the rule that everything required to solve a problem must be included in the model, or that material that does not fit in the basic model must at least be incorporated in simulation operations to determine the effects. This highlights the essential role of a decision analyst who is required to stimulate the dynamic and iterative development of a model that captures the heart of the problem at hand such that a complete analysis can be performed.

Elicited Structure

We now enter into a discussion of decision-making processes where the set of available alternatives is known but where poor structure dominates the scene and where the analyst may be unavailable for consultation. Here, decision aids play a far more important and complex role, especially when the decision maker is uncertain about the ways in which to construe a subjective preference structure (Humphreys, 1983; Jungermann, 1980). In such situations, the major task lies in the elicitation of not only the contents but of the problem structure itself. It requires an active cooperation between the decision maker and the decision-aiding system in order to determine a structure that gives an accurate representation of the decision problem. The decision-aiding process depends on input from the decision maker. At the same time, the decision maker will rely very heavily on the structural guidance of the decision aid. It is no longer an ergonomic question of how to get efficient interaction with a decision aid carrying out a predefined process, nor is it merely an elicitation question of how to make an isomorphic representation of information in the decision maker's mind. Formulation of the problem structure requires decision aids that are capable of eliciting information in the most optimal way, while remaining sufficiently flexible to represent and identify the structure in an appropriate context. Humphreys and Berkeley (Chapter 12) give an example of a decision aid (MAUD4) operating in this way in interaction with a decision maker facing a career choice problem.

PRINCIPAL CONSIDERATIONS IN SYSTEM DESIGN

The development and elicitation of a problem structure results from the interaction between the decision maker and the decision analytic system. Decision-aiding operations may be carried out by a decision analyst alone, though commonly, a computerized decison-aiding system is also made available. Ideally, the decision-aiding system should aid the decision maker in generating a range of possible options, constructing an attribute structure that can be employed to evaluate options, defining realistic courses of possible consequences, and so on. Moreover, it should also encourage the decision maker to go beyond the immediate information available, providing assistance in the exploration of an internal knowledge system to extract information that may be of added relevance to the decision problem. For example, the system could provide facilities that encourage the decision maker to clarify attributes, elicit a better definition of objectives, reorder preference structure, and so on. In other words, the process may result in a shift in the decision maker's way of thinking about options, attributes, and ideas about these elements in relation to objectives. Consequently, the pattern of the problem structure does not hold a static position in the decision-making process. The generation of a problem structure is an activity that involves the movement of the developing structure within the decision-making system. Its location at any one point will depend on the nature of the problem and the current stage of the decision-making process. The decision-aiding system should play a significant role in situations where confusion, inconsistency, or incomplete information are detected.

In this section, we will examine the prinicipal elements that contribute to the design of a decision-aiding system.

Model Selection

Decision models are usually selected from among those developed within the framework of conventional decision theory. A decision-aiding system will usually involve expected utility (EU) analysis and/or its extension to multiattribute utility (MAU) models (cf. Edwards & Newman, 1982; Keeney & Raiffa, 1976). However, although an EU or MAU model will normally form the core of a decision analysis, various submodels exist to provide aids to various subprocesses (for example, the technique of credence decomposition; see Brown, 1971; influence diagram methods; see Howard & Matheson, 1980).

The choice of a model within which the decision problem is to be structured and represented is usually made by the decision analyst. In a realistic setting, it will often be difficult to generate an optimal model that satisfies all those who have a stake in the decision to be made. In such cases, the decision analyst should ensure that all important issues are considered. This requires a comprehensive study of the effects of contributing elements on the basic model (Phillips, 1982, 1983).

In the direction of developing a system that contains the fundaments of types of decision problems, we can gain some insight from discussions on problem taxonomies. Suggested guidelines are given, among others, by Johnson and Huber (1977) and Kneppreth, Hoessel, Gustafson, and Johnson (1978). Von Winterfeld (1980) goes one step further. In suggesting ways in which a taxonomy of decision problem prototypes can be made operational, he incorporated two important issues, first, that specific models should be built for specific problem types, and second, that the models must be based on substantive rather than formal characteristics.

Although a preselected model gives a decision aid the means for controlling the process of structuring a decision problem in such a way that the problem can then be represented by rules in decision analytic terms, it has been noted that its use may well hinder or complicate the process for the decision maker in providing content to the model (Bronner & de Hoog, 1983; Wooler & Lewis, 1982). Prescreening methods may be used to determine whether or not the elicited decision problem actually lies within the proposed environment and that any conflict in the selection of a set of choice alternatives is in fact a valid one. It is also important to determine the correct problem environment and to ensure that the decision maker is not merely using the system as an excuse to avoid confrontation with a more major emotional problem (Humphreys & Wooler, 1981; Pitz, 1983).

Use of External Data Base

When the nature of a problem is not fully known to the decision maker, there is an abundance of ill-defined elements that are potentially eligible for incorporation into the problem structure. In projecting an external representation of information from a decision maker's internal knowledge system, facilities are required for storing the information and the linkages between elements. A decision-aiding system interacting with the decision maker in performing this task will usually offer one of two options. It may have an empty data base that slowly gains substance as the system gathers pieces of information and records their position in the problem structure. Alternatively, the system may start with a limited set of components in the data base. This second approach is demonstrated in a system called SELSTRA (Wooler & Lewis, 1982) that allows an intermediary expert to prepare an initial attribute hierarchy structure containing general attribute components. This provides a starting point from which the user can break the structure down into more concrete elements. As the intermediary is free to determine the contents of the initial structure, it is possible to design various core structures for different problem areas; moreover, it is also possible to design specific structures for individual users.

Beyond the use of computer storage mechanisms to record incoming information from the user, other possibilities include the provision of an information data base that provides some of the ingredients for a knowledge-base system. For example, in a careers context, information on current job availability and salary scales can be held in a data base giving a user access to up-to-date information. Additionally, a list of salient dimensions that may be of use to a decision maker can also be made available to enhance creative problem representation in a realistic setting. The task of operationalizing the system would involve linking procedures not dissimilar to those in programming operations involving the compilation and linking of modules of computer programs and data bases. Example of such data bases can be drawn from systems currently available; for example, in the field of careers guidance (see Chapman, Katz, Norris, & Pears, 1977; Watts & Ballantine, 1981); medicine (see Winston, 1977); and organizational support systems (see Keen & Scott-Morton, 1978).

In the context of decision analysis, as yet, not many decision aids have comprehensive knowledge systems built into them. Those that do usually revolve around the use of precanned information designed for specific applications. An example can be seen in CARE, a computer-aided risk evaluation system designed by the Decision Analysis Unit. This system was used to automate a risk model for use by insurance underwriters as described by Phillips and Wisniewski (1983). Precanned systems may also be incorporated as a result of tailoring a general purpose decision-aiding system for a specific task. For example IMAS, a general "influence modelling and assessment system," also developed at the Decision Analysis Unit, can be used to store information on cause–consequence relationships in specific applications. It starts by modeling the knowledge of linkages between indicators, causes, and consequences possessed by experienced people in a particular field. Subsequently, the information forms the basis of an associative structure data base. Embrey and Humphreys (1983) demonstrate an application in the form of interactive diagnostic operations in managing "abnormal situations" in nuclear power plant stations, with the aim of bringing such a situation to a safe stable state.

To recap, it may be useful to look briefly at a formal elaboration of the issue of knowledge base in a decision-aiding system. Using the formalization of the first four levels of analysis outlined by Humphreys and Berkeley (Chapter 12), built-in structures reflect the first level of decision making. The data base generated contains factual information, and also to some degree, judgmental data entered by an expert. The structure of such a data base will be fixed, and the operations will center around the manipulation of information within the predefined structure. The second type of knowledge structure is relevant to the types of recomposition aids. Again, the format of the structure is predetermined. The knowledge-base system incorporates an information data base as well as decision analytic rules that can be employed to explore areas of conflict or to simulate outcomes, given a different emphasis of importance on parts of the problem structure. At this level, the distinction between computer programs and data becomes rather fuzzy. For example, subroutine modules can be utilized as data, and once a novel and realistic type of relationship is established, the outcome can be treated as a rule that can be called upon when the need arises. Therefore, although operations at this level involve the use of a predefined problem structure, the procedures employed should enable the decision maker to examine new relationships that are potentially important. The third type of structure incorporates a very different type of knowledge base to aid the decision maker in externalizing a representation of the problem. Thus, as the contents of the problem structure are unspecified at the outset, and as it is usually not clear in the decision maker's mind what constitutes the content of the structure, heuristic structuring methods are required. Beyond this level lies the task of eliciting the problem structure itself. At the third level, although the structure of the decision problem faced by an individual is initially unformalized, the person is restricted to elaborate under a *given* decision analytic model. At the fourth level, we are more concerned with the lack of procedural knowledge and with the task of identifying a problem-structuring language. It is a new area, involving systems that are capable of generating a problem-structuring language that can cater to the needs of individuals or groups of decision makers. The data thus gathered will be organized into a series of propositions, rather than a sequential list of information.

User–System Interface

The challenge of developing an interactive decision-aiding system lies not so much in the design of algorithmic modules that form the basis of the system but more in the creation of a good interface between the user and the decision analytic system. Computer technology must be challenged to its limits, while at the same time unnecessary complications must be avoided so as not to ignore the specifications for a "user-oriented" system. Moreover, the design of the system should also keep abreast with enhanced computer techniques and novel approaches in computer technology that could be put into use to make the system more oriented toward the user's needs. For instance, graphics and color can be used to display information in the form of pictures, reducing the need for lengthy passages and to emphasize different levels of information on a visual display screen; split-screen displays allow the possibility of displaying more than one operation at a time; a light pen or a joystick can be used to ease the passage of information from the user to the system. A recent implementation can be seen in The Friendly Decision Aid designed by Decisions and Designs Incorporated, which allows the user to pass instructions to the system through the use of a touch-sensitive screen. More recently, a mechanism termed *the mouse* (a remote device that can be programmed to point to positions on the screen) also opens new possibilities in a revolutionary approach to interactive communication between the user and the computer system. Once the method of voice recognition has been perfected and made widely accessible, we can also expect a demand for computer systems to incorporate this technology. Furthermore, coupled with the use of a dictionary data base, the use of this technique may eventually lead to the redundancy of the use of keyboards.

MONITORING THE DECISION MAKER

A decision-aiding system must ensure a smooth operation in the process of interacting with a user. In doing so, it should assume the position of an invisible supervisor, allowing the user to proceed uninterruptedly through a decision-making process until such a time when it is required to come forward to display discrepancies in the contents of the information entered by the user.

Decision Aids as a Statistical Monitor

While interacting with an automated decision-aiding system, a decision maker may be confronted with conflicts in the perception of possible actions and the corresponding consequences (Humphreys & McFadden, 1980; Sjoberg, 1980). Within the capacity of an automated system, the decision-aiding system should be sensitive to relational difficulties experienced by the user. In carrying out the role of a statistical monitor, a decision-aiding system can detect possible areas of incoherence within the defined problem structure through the presence of conflicting or, in other cases, nonindependent mathematical relationships among the elements of the decision problem. However, the process of taking the issue further into a psychological interpretation is beyond the capabilities of strictly mathematical algorithms. Ideally, it demands the use of cross-reference procedures that look into several types of data bases, comprising the knowledge/belief system of the person(s) involved (for example, preference for a particular aspect of a job) as well as an information data base (for example, salary scales). Minimally, at least, it should be able to call on procedures that inform the user of possible discrepancies, and if the user verifies that the incident is realistic, the system should then follow the issue up by giving the user the option of proceeding along one of a number of possible routes.

An example of such a facility is demonstrated in MAUD4 (Humphreys & Wisudha, 1983), which incorporates a procedure that checks for valuewise independence between attribute dimensions defined within the problem structure. In doing so, the system uses rules based on the weak conditional utility independence (WCUI) rule outlined by Raiffa (1969), which states that, given that values on all other attribute dimensions remain constant, preferences for values on any attribute dimension should be independent from the values that have been kept constant. MAUD4 informs the user of the issue, and a confirmation of a violation of the rules usually leads to a revision of the problem structure that aims at eliminating or minimizing the effects by the deletion of the attributes that fail to meet the specification and the addition of a further attribute to replace the ones that are lost.

Control in a Decision-Making Process

To ensure that a decision-aiding system does not intrude unexpectedly during a session, it is important that the design of such a system pays attention to the issue of control at the various stages of an interactive session. Though a user (the decision maker) may initially want to experiment to gain familiarity with the system, the opportunity to treat the system as a playground during a difficult stage of the process must be minimized. The system should ensure that the user attends to the problem and provide assistance to resolve the conflicts. A failure to do so may result in the withdrawal of the decision maker's active participation in the decision-making process. If the flow of the decision-aiding process breaks down, the user may be encouraged to move away from the responsibilities of a problem owner. The process may then become less productive and unrealistic if the user decides to carry on with the decision-making process as a bystander rather than as a stakeholder.

A decision-aiding system should always have immediate control of the operation in progress, guided by the decision analytic modules built into the system. It must monitor when and in what form the user may bring in amendments to the structure in order to police coherence of the decision problem representation. At the same time, it must never seem to be oppressive, subjecting the decision maker to unrealistic limits or unnecessary elaborations. For instance, the system may make use of covert monitoring but should only bring intermediary results to the attention of the user if monitoring suggests a conflict in problem representation. At the same time, it is desirable to give the user a degree of control over what is happening, such that the user believes that the system is there as a tool, assisting in the elicitation and asssessment of the real problem rather than imposing/prescribing an unrealistic structure. This encourages a user to work on the problem, while allowing the system to maintain the position of projecting the control imposed by the decision analytic model. This type of facility is most evident in a decision-aiding system that is geared to be "user friendly" and is proven to be especially valuable and effective when used by decision makers untrained in formal decision-making techniques (Humphreys & McFadden, 1980; Humphreys & Wooler, 1981).

The construction of a formal problem structure involves the passage of information between the decision maker and the decision-aiding system. In the process of externalizing a representation of a knowledge structure, the decision maker makes use of material in semantic memory, a cognitive information-processing system that incorporates models of the environment as well as goal structures. Alternative structural formats have been proposed, among others, by Bobrow and Norman (1975), Minsky (1975), Schank (1975), Abelson (1976), and Anderson (1976). On the other hand, in the process of encouraging the elaboration of a problem structure while maintaining coherence in the structure, a decision-aiding system should be able to generate feedback for the purpose of extending the domain of the problem structure and/or clarifying the existing problem representation. In itself, decision theory does not provide any model of semantic memory or of the environment. The interface required, therefore, is one between a system that comprises an information base (semantic memory) that is not formally modeled and a system, the decision theoretic system, that *is* formally modeled (Berkeley & Humphreys, 1982). In such situations, it is not useful to specify procedures on a normative basis as these can only address content on the formally modeled side of the interface. It would seem more appropriate to employ heuristic methods to guide structuring activities that inevitably involve transactions across this interface. The choice of the heuristic procedures employed to aid problem structuring must be governed by the criterion that the structure subsequently generated must be valid and internally consistent. It is by no means a simple task. One way is to employ the production system method (Winston, 1977) to generate a heuristic-based system from which patterns of behavior processes can be generated (Newell, 1973). A production system consists of a set of rules that are made up of conditions that must be met upon which a relevant action, or set of actions, will be carried out. As an example, Humphreys, Wooler, and Phillips (1980) outlined a simple production system that controls the ordering and reordering of the decomposed preference structure within the MAUD4 system. Control is passed on to this subsystem within MAUD4 whenever a decision maker wishes to expand or revise the preference structure currently under consideration, or when MAUD4 detects the need to deal with consistency or valuewise independence.

It is also important to reduce the aspect of intimidation. Together with the notion of giving the user the feeling of ultimate control, decision-aiding systems should be designed such that frames of information are presented in a form understandable to the user, for example, by using as much as possible words or phrases defined by the person. Moreover, the system must ensure that the user is not bombarded with irrelevant information (at any one point) such that the user does not become confused or distracted from the current process. In this instance, the system should be able to suppress information that is currently not relevant and should allow flexible movement within the system whenever it is theoretically possible, for example, by allowing the user to look back on previous processes, frequently giving the user the option of making changes or adding more information, and so on.

IMPLEMENTATIONS OF DECISION SUPPORT TECHNOLOGY

With the advance of computer technology and an increased realization of the ways in which computers can be used to aid the process of problem solving, an abundance of work has been carried out in the area of decision support engineering in an attempt to incorporate computer technology into specific decision-aiding processes. Together with a deeper understanding of the inherent structure of information processing in organizations and the development of knowledge-based systems and language systems based on artificial intelligence concepts, the available technology has been used to formalize and translate ideas into generic frameworks. The effect of this recent technology on the design of systems to support human decision making is clearly marked in the development of support systems in organizational structures. This resulted in the birth of *decision support systems* (DSS) as a term to describe systems that are used to *support*, rather than replace, decision-making operations. The concept of DSS began to appear in the context of information processing and problem solving in organizational structures. McCosh and Scott-Morton (1978) and Bonczek, Holsapple, and Whinston (1981) provide background references in this area. As a support system, DSS is used to complement earlier organizational tools (e.g., electronic data-processing systems, management information systems) that do not accommodate the knowledge of individual expert decision makers. Therefore, although increasing the efficiency of information-processing operations, DSS more importantly aims to improve the *effectiveness* of decision makers by incorporating their expert judgments.

In decision support literature, one tends to find references to the relationship between *structured* and *unstructured* problems. They are described as opposite poles along a single dimension, where *semi-structured* problems occupy the middle space of the continuum (see, for example, Bonczek *et al.*, 1981). Research in decision support engineering looks at ways in which the boundary can be shifted, such that more problems in the semistructured area can be moved toward the structured area (Keen & Scott Morton, 1978). This is usually achieved through a diagnostic process of identifying the types of tasks involved and exploring ways of obtaining an appropriate model through systems design and analysis. The aim is to assist a decision maker by taking over operations located within the more structured or semistructured parts of a larger, only partly formalized problem domain (Lee, 1983). This leads to the design and implementation of decision support systems to aid in the manipulation of information within the identified task structure. As the problem structure has been defined previously, the decision maker can indulge in the manipulation of information without having to go through the process of identifying the key elements of the problem. There is a large number of decision support systems available for aiding decision making in organizations. Keen and Scott-Morton (1978) provide an overview of types of decision support systems, illustrating the range of available systems. Case studies can also be found in Alter (1980); furthermore, examples of specific development can be seen, among others, in McLean and Riesing (1980), Fox (1983), and Takkenberg (1983). A classification scheme aimed at clarifying the relevant issues in most systems used in organizations was proposed by Alter (1980). He summarizes some of the important characteristics of computerized systems within each category and suggests that this may be useful to help users as well as system developers to communicate their experience and to establish the type of assistance a DSS should provide.

Support systems for medical use can also be cited. Such systems incorporate externally fixed criteria and values, usually stored in the system's data base, ready for manipulation. A well-developed example can be seen in MYCIN (Shortliffe, 1976), a problem-solving system that aids in the diagnosis and treatment of bacterial infections. It prompts the physician for detailed information regarding the patient's symptoms and general condition, which are then integrated with information about the history of the patient and laboratory results. Further questions are generated by the system based on the ongoing analysis of previous questions. Conclusions are based on mapping procedures that compare the specific information gathered with a list of conditional relationships in the form of production rules that are stored in an information data base. MYCIN can also give justification to the conclusion it generates by explaining the rules and assumptions it used to arrive at the conclusion. Discrepancies between conclusions drawn by the system and those predicted by the physician are resolved in a step-by-step procuedure that looks into more complex relationships involving the logic of and/or structures. Another example is DENDRAL, which generates chemical structures from formulas and mass spectograms (Buchanan, Sutherland, & Feigenbaum, 1969). The process produces a list of all possible structures, and a mass spectogram is predicted for each structure generated. The spectogram that gives the best match to the actual experimental spectogram is then considered as the correct structure. A more general purpose diagnostic system is INTERNIST-1 (Pople, 1982),which holds information on a large number of internal diseases. The system allows the physician to work on selective sets of assumptions and provides various possible conclusions based on the hypotheses the physician wishes to test.

As such, it is clear that the systems described in this section implement techniques that allow a user to manipulate and extract information within a predefined boundary. In examining such systems, techniques that aim to assist users in examining the elements of a decision problem and structuring their expertise such as to optimize decision-making processes are evidently absent. In this instance, decision analysis presents itself as the missing link, changing the current specifications of decision support systems.

SUMMARY

The preceding sections have dealt with various issues about decision-aiding systems. The immediate attraction of using automated decision-aiding systems lies in the speed with which they perform built-in functions. However, the success or failure of such systems in terms of overall value is essentially a property unique to each individual system. Much relies on the design of the user–system interface and on the integration of the necessary technology into the required modules. It is important that an appropriate division of labor is maintained (Pitz, 1983). The design of a decision-aiding system should be sensitive to the needs and responsibilities of a decision maker and provide assistance such that the decision maker can meet those responsibilities most effectively.

There is also the issue of how to model the expertise of the decision analyst and to see how far the skills can be implemented within an automated aid. The problem arises of interpreting the decision analyst's wishes and studying the possibilities of designing and incorporating standard procedures into a computer program format.

Decision-aiding experts should be concerned about the use of decision aids for incorrect purposes. It is important that the system does not provide the wrong type of aid. There is also a large concern regarding the applicability of a system designed in a closed environment. Some systems may be designed through modeling the problem representation process of an expert in the field or a decision analyst. As a consequence, the use of such systems in real settings reduces the decision-making process to a training operation geared at producing an imitation of the behavior of the model designer, rather than a process that is sensitive to the decision maker's own problem representation.

Problem structuring is an important issue that has to do with the prechoice stage. The design of traditional data base management systems is predicated on the view that information gathering is the main activity to be supported at the prechoice stage. However, a serious consideration of *how* the information is to be used demands that the data gathered must be stored and represented in the form of a realistic problem structure, such that the history of events can be recorded and relationships between elements can be displayed to clarify the structure. This process still remains the most difficult and controversial area in the design and construction of an interactive decision-aiding system. Numerous studies have been dedicated to this area, with emphasis on different aspects of possible solutions (cf. Jungermann, 1980; Payne, Braunstein, & Carroll, 1978; Pitz, 1983; von Winterfeldt, 1980). In a global attempt to challenge the problem, Humphreys & Berkeley (Chapter 12) examine various types of uncertainties, looking at how they are handled and how they relate to the characteristics of problem representation at various levels of abstraction.

Essentially, problem structuring requires the identification of choice alternatives and possible consequences and the elicitation of an attribute structure, which will be the basis on which the identified alternatives will be evaluated. Five conditions must be satisfied by a decision-aiding system designed as a problem-structuring tool:

1. It should be able to initiate the elicitation from the decision maker of salient information such that an appropriate structure of the problem can be formed. The developing structure must be compatible with a decision theoretic model, that is, one that gives the decision maker a framework that provides the possibility of optimal action.

2. It should be able to place incoming information correctly within the framework of the structure, such that it can communicate the basis for the chosen action to the decision maker and to others involved in the acceptance or justification of that action.

3. The system must enable subsequent reevaluation of the structure in the light of further inputs and/or subsequent deletion of redundant material.

4. The system must encourage creativity in generating new options, recognizing additional objectives and abstracting the characterics of further possible outcomes.

5. Finally, it should meet the criterion that will permit the use of decision theoretic algorithms in computing preferences among possible courses of action.

Most decision aids tend to impose a formal structuring method, that is, the decision maker is faced with a prespecified model of the framework within which the representation of the problem is to be developed. For example, some systems assume an additive multiattribute utility model incorporating the direct decomposition of utilities of alternatives into ratings on attributes; others assume a hierarchical utility decomposition. Once the user begins to interact with the system, most systems rely on the user's intuitive judgment to provide the details of the structural organization of the problem. Structuring the problem involves identification of linkages between elements in the problem domain, of types of relationships between the elements, and of the operators in use. Currently, there are restrictions on what may be identified within the process of constructing a representation of the decision problem. That is the price we pay for the benefit of the use of an automated system. However, a multidisciplinary effort together with the advance of new technology may well lead to a relaxation of the imposed limitations.

ACKNOWLEDGMENTS

I would like to thank Larry Phillips, Patrick Humphreys, and Stuart Wooler for the discussions that have contributed to clarifying my ideas in the course of preparing this chapter.

REFERENCES

Abelson, R. P. (1976). Script processing in attitude formation and decision making. In J. S. Caroll & J. W. Payne (Eds.), *Cognition and social behavior.* Hillsdale, NJ: Erlbaum.

Alter, S. L. (1980). *Decision support systems: Current practice and continuing challenges.* Reading, MA: Addison-Wesley.

Anderson, J. R. (1976). *Language, memory and thought.* Hillsdale, NJ: Erlbaum.

Berkeley, D., & Humphreys, P. C. (1982). Structuring decision problems and the "bias heuristic." *Acta Psychologica, 50,* 201–252.

Bobrow, D. G., & Norman, D. A. (1975). Some principles of memory schemata. In D. G. Bobrow & A. M. Collins (Eds.), *Representation and understanding.* New York: Academic Press.

Bonczek, R. H., Holsapple, C. W., & Whinston, A. B. (1981). *Foundations of decision support systems.* New York: Academic Press.

Bowman, E. H. (1963). Consistency and optimality in managerial decision making. *Management Science, 9,* 310–321.

Bronner, F., & de Hoog, R. (1983, August-September). *The intertwining of information search and decision aiding.* Paper presented at the 9th Research Conference on Subjective Probability, Utility and Decision Making, Groningen.

Brown, R. V. (1971). *Research and the credibility of estimates.* Ontario: Irwin.

Brown, R. V., Kahr, A. S., & Peterson, C. R. (1974). *Decision analysis for the manager.* New York: Holt, Rinehart & Winston.

Buchanan, B., Sutherland, G., & Feigenbaum, E. A. (1969). Heuristic DENDRAL: A program for generating explanatory hypotheses in organic chemistry. *Machine Intelligence 4.* New York: Elsevier.

Camerer, C. (1981). General conditions for the success of bootstrapping models. *Organizational Behavior and Human Performance, 27,* 411–422.

Chapman, W., Katz, M. R., Norris, L., & Pears, L. (1977). *SIGI: Field test and evaluation of a computer-based system of interactive guidance and information.* Princeton, NJ: Educational Testing Service.

Dawes, R. M. (1971). A case study of graduate admissions: Application of three principles of human decision making. *American Psychologist, 26,* 180–188.

Dawes, R. M., & Corrigan, B. (1974). Linear models in decision making. *Psychological Bulletin, 81,* 95–106.

Ebert, R. J., & Kruse, T. E. (1978). Bootstrapping the security analyst. *Journal of Applied Psychology, 63,* 110–119.

Edwards, W., & Newman, J. R. (1982). *Multiattribute evaluation.* Beverly Hills: Sage.

Edwards, W., Phillips, L. D., Hays, W. L., & Goodman, B. C. (1968). Probabilistic information processing systems: Design and evaluation. *IEEE Transactions on Systems Science and Cybernetics,* Vol. SSC-4, *3,* 248–265.

Embrey, D., & Humphreys, P. C. (1983, December). *Support for decision making and problem solving in abnormal conditions in nuclear power plants.* Paper submitted for presentation at the Symposium on Expert Systems and Decision Support, British Psychological Society Conference, London.

Fischer, G. W., Edwards, W., & Kelly, C. W. (1978). *Decision theoretic aids for inference, evaluation, and decision making: A review of research and experience* (Technical Report 78-1-30). McLean, VA: Decision and Designs, Inc.

Fitts, P. M., & Posner, M. I. (1967). *Human performance.* Belmont, CA: Brooks/Cole.

Fox, M. S. (1983). The intelligent management system: An overview. In H. G. Sol (Ed.), *Processes and tools for decision support.* Amsterdam: North Holland.

Goldberg, L. D. (1970). Man versus model of man: A rationale, plus some evidence for a method for improving on clinical inferences. *Psychological Bulletin, 73,* 422–432.

Hoffman, P. J. (1960). The paramorphic representation of clinical judgment. *Psychological Bulletin, 57,* 116–131.

Howard, R. A., & Matheson, J. G. (1980). *Influence diagrams.* Menlo Park, CA: SRI International.

Humphreys, P. C. (1983). Decision aids: Aiding decisions. In L. Sjoberg, T. Tyszka, & J. A. Wise (Eds.), *Decision analyses and decision processes.* Lund: Doxa.

Humphreys, P. C., & McFadden, W. (1980). Experiences with MAUD: Aiding decision structuring versus bootstrapping the decision maker. *Acta Psychologica 45,* 51–69.

Humphreys, P. C. & Wisudha, A. (1983). *MAUD—An interactive computer program for the structuring, decomposition and recomposition of preferences between multiattributed alternatives* (Technical Report 83-5). London: Decision Analysis Unit, London School of Economics and Political Science.

Humphreys, P. C., & Wooler, S. (1981). *Development of MAUD4* (Technical Report 81-4). London: Decision Analysis Unit, London School of Economics and Political Science.

Humphreys, P. C., Wooler, S., & Phillips, L. D. (1980). *Structuring decisions: The role of structuring heuristics* (Technical report 80-1). London: Decision Analysis Unit, London School of Economics and Political Science.

Johnson, E. M., & Huber, G. P. (1977). The technology of utility assessment. *IEEE Transactions on Systems, Man, and Cybernetics, SMC-7,* 311-325.

Jungermann, H. (1980). Speculations about decision theoretic aids for personal decision making. *Acta Psychologica 55,* 7-34.

Keen, P. G. W., & Scott-Morton, M. S. (1978). *Decision support systems: An organizational perspective.* Reading, MA: Addison-Wesley.

Keeney, R. L., & Raiffa, H. (1976). *Decisions with multiple objectives: Preferences and value tradeoffs.* New York: Wiley.

Kneppreth, N. P., Hoessel, W., Gustafson, D. H., & Johnson, E. M. (1978). *A strategy for selecting a worth assessment technique* (Technical paper 280). Alexandria, VA: U.S. Army Research Institute for the Behavioral and Social Sciences.

Lee, R. M. (1983). *Data and language in organizations: Epistemological aspects of management support systems* (Working paper WP-83-46). Laxenburg, Austria: International Institute of Applied Systems Analysis.

McCosh, A. M., & Scott-Morton, M. S. (1978). *Management decision support systems.* London: Macmillan.

McLean, E. R., & Riesing, T. F. (1980). Installing a decision support system: Implications for research. In G. Fick & R. H. Sprague (Eds.), *Decision support systems: Issues and challenges,* Oxford: Pergamon Press.

Minsky, M. A. (1975). A framework for representing knowledge. In P. Winston (Ed.), *The psychology of computer vision.* New York: McGraw-Hill.

Newell, A. (1973). Production systems: Models of control structures. In W. G. Chase (Ed.), *Visual information processing.* New York: Academic Press.

Newell, A., & Simon, H. A. (1972). *Human problem solving.* Englewood Cliffs, NJ: Prentice-Hall.

Payne, J. W., Braunstein, M. L., & Carroll, J. S. (1978). Exploring predecisional behavior: An alternative approach to decision research. *Organizational Behavior and Human Performance, 22,* 17-44.

Pearl, J., Leal, A., & Saleh, J. (1980). *GODDESS: A goal directed decision structuring system.* (UCLA-ENG-CSL-8034). Los Angeles: School of Engineering and Applied Sciences, University of California.

Phillips, L.D. (1982). Requisite decision modelling: A case study. *Journal of the Operational Research Society, 33*(4), 303-311.

Phillips, L. D. (1983, August-September). *A theory of requisite decision modelling.* Paper presented at the 9th Research Conference on Subjective Probability, Utility and Decision Making, Groningen.

Phillips, L. D., & Wisniewski, T. K. (1983). Bayesian models for computer-aided underwriting. *The Statistician, 32,* 252-263.

Pitz, G. F. (1983). The human engineering of decision aids. In P. C. Humphreys, O. Svenson, & A. Vari (Eds.), *Analyzing and aiding decision processes.* Amsterdam: North Holland.

Pitz, G. F., Sachs, N.J., & Heerboth, J. (1980). Procedures for eliciting choices in the analysis of individual decisions. *Organizational Behavior and Human Performance, 26,* 396-408.

Pople, H. (1982). INTERNIST-1. In P. Szolovits (Ed.), *Artificial intelligence in medicine.* Boulder, CO: Westview.

Raiffa, H. (1968). *Decision analysis.* Reading, MA: Addison-Wesley.

Raiffa, H. (1969). *Preferences for multiattributed alternatives.* (Memorandum RM-5868-DOT/RC). Santa Monica: The Rand Corporation.

Schank, R. C. (1975). The structure of episodes in memory. In D. G. Bobrow & A. M. Collins (Eds.), *Representation and understanding.* New York: Academic Press.

Schlaifer, R. (1969). *Analysis of decisions under uncertainty.* New York: McGraw-Hill.

Selvidge, J. (1976). *Rapid screening of decision options* (Technical Report 76-12). McLean, VA: Decision and Designs, Inc.

Shortliffe, E. H. (1976). *Computer-based medical consultation: MYCIN.* New York: Elsevier.

Simon, H. A. (1978). Information-processing theory of human problem solving. In W. K. Estes (Ed.), *Handbook of learning and cognitive processes* (Vol. 5): *Human information processing.* Hillsdale, NJ: Erlbaum.

Sjoberg, L. (1980). Volitional problems in a difficult decision. *Acta Psychologica, 45,* 123-132.

Takkenberg, C. A. T. (1983). CAP: A decision support system for the planning of production levels. In H.. G. Sol (Ed.), *Processes and tools for decision support.* Amsterdam: North Holland.

von Winterfeld, D. (1980). Structuring decision problems for decision analysis. *Acta Psychologica, 45,* 71-93.

Watts, A. G., & Ballantine, M. (1981). Computers in careers guidance: An overview. *Careers Journal, 1,* 25-35.

Weiss, J. J. (1980). *QVAL and GENTREE: Two approaches to problem structuring in decision aids* (Technical Report 80-3-97). McLean, VA: Decision and Designs, Inc.

Winston, P. H. (1977). *Artificial intelligence.* Reading, MA: Addison-Wesley.

Wooler, S., & Lewis, B. (1982). Computer-assisted careers counselling: A new approach. *British Journal of Guidance & Counselling, 10,* 124-136.

Yntema, D. B., & Torgerson, W. S. (1961). Man–computer cooperation in decisions requiring common sense. *IRE Transactions of Human Factors in Electronics, 2,* 20-26.

CHAPTER 12

Handling Uncertainty

Levels of Analysis of Decision Problems

Patrick Humphreys and Dina Berkeley

INTRODUCTION

Decision problems encountered in everyday life are invested with uncertainty; if this were not the case, they would not have been conceptualized as problems in the first place.

Even in decision-making tasks presented to subjects in laboratory experiments, uncertainty enters as a major determinant of subjects' behavior and choice. Here, we are not referring only to the uncertainty that the presented task itself may include in its requirements (e.g., if the subject is asked to estimate the likelihood of an uncertain event), but also to the uncertainty related to the purpose of the exercise, the subject's ability to control its outcome, and the implications that the solution he or she will offer to the problem will have on the experimenters' estimation of the subject's qualities. Bruner, Goodnow, and Austin (1956) discuss these uncertainties and outline some "hedgehog solutions" whereby subjects tend to play safe and thus reduce the uncertainty by following "safe" routes. However, although Bruner and his colleagues raised important questions as to the stability of subjects' reactions to experimental tasks, their ideas are often ignored within the experimental decision research literature. As a consequence, questions of motivation lurking behind subjects' *preferred* uncertainty-reducing strategies are not raised. A major consequence is that results of exper-

Patrick Humphreys • Decision Analysis Unit, London School of Economics and Political Science, London WC2 2AE, England. Dina Berkeley • Social Psychology Department, London School of Economics and Political Science, London WC2 2AE, England.

iments are usually reported as having been arrived at through uncertainty-free procedures.

However, our major concern here lies outside the laboratory, focusing on decision making in real life decision problems and how decision makers conceptualize them and handle their inherent uncertainty.

From an evolutionary standpoint, humans can be seen as seeking to reduce uncertainty (Einhorn & Hogarth, 1981; Toda, 1980, 1983). Uncertainty as such creates stress that, being undesirable and dysfunctional, will necessitate its own conditions of resolution (Janis & Mann, 1977). Trial and error and the use of feedback constitute attempts to reduce uncertainty by acting on the world. Another coping mechanism is that of treating uncertain parts of the decision problem as certain, determined by the agency one feels one has in acting upon the world.

Discussing uncertainty as an inherent characteristic of decision problems might encourage one to think of uncertainty as *one* entity capable of being given an overall value that will define how *much* uncertainty is involved in any given decision problem. Such a conceptualization of the role that uncertainty plays in decision problems places stress on its *compound effects* (i.e., as a general agent creating difficulties in problem-solving activities) and ignores its role as a facilitator of innovation and person-specific solutions (a highly predictable and certain world would leave no space for creation, self-expression, change, or even motivation to act within it). To understand uncertainty in this role necessitates that one concentrates on the points where uncertainty enters into the process of conceptualizing a decision problem, thus enabling discussions of how it is handled by the decision maker at each point. This also allows one to examine the consequences of *assuming* that uncertainty at any one of these points does not exist.

TYPES OF UNCERTAINTY

In a previous paper exploring this understanding of the role of uncertainty, we described seven different types as follows (Berkeley & Humphreys, 1982, pp. 206–207).

> (i) Uncertainty about the probabilities of outcomes of subsequent events, *conditional* on what has preceded them in the act–event sequence between immediate acts and consequences.
>
> (ii) Uncertainty about the probabilities of subsequent events, *conditional* on the occurence of other events extraneous to the sequences in (i).
>
> (iii) Uncertainty about how to incorporate prior information (e.g. results of prior sampling, base rate in a reference population) in determining the probability of a subsequent event.
>
> (iv) Uncertainty about how to conceptualize the worth of consequences: assessing a

consequence's utility requires the generation of a single number describing its wholistic (and entire) "moral value." When more than one criterion of worth is involved, uncertainty can arise about how to combine these criteria.

(v) Procedural Uncertainty, which Hogarth *et al.* (1980) describe as "Uncertainty concerning means to handle or process the decision," e.g., specifying relevant uncertainties, what information to seek, and where, how to invent alternatives and assess consequences, etc.

(vi) Uncertainty about how the decision maker (or the persons he or she is deciding for) himself or herself will feel, and wish to act having arrived at a subsequent act (choice point) *after* intervening events have unfolded "for real."

(vii) Uncertainty about the extent one possesses *agency* for inducing changes in the probabilities of subsequent events (conditional on acts yet to be taken, as in [i], above) through being able to alter relations between states of the world (Savage, 1954).

We also argued that decision theory can take into account explicitly only the first four types of uncertainties. Decision theory in its conventional form (Brown, Kahr, & Peterson, 1974; Keeney & Raiffa, 1976; Raiffa, 1968) provides four different structural variants within which the decision maker's operations can be policed. These are shown in Figure 1 and discussed in detail in Berkeley and Humphreys (1982).

The "core" structure within the province of decision theory represents courses of action open to the decision maker in terms of probabilities of outcomes of subsequent events, conditional on what has preceded them in the act–event sequence. Interfaced with this system are three "buffer" systems that extend the province of decision theory (Lindley, 1971) so that it can handle (1) the way the probabilities of subsequent events in the act–event sequence depend upon other extraneous events; (2) the incorporation of prior beliefs about the likelihood of subsequent events with current information about these events; and (3) assessment of overall worth of the consequences where assessments on several criteria of worth have to be combined.

All these systems *assume* that decision problems arrive on the scene ready structured. The act–event system requires as its inputs assessments of probabilities of prespecified subsequent events and predefined consequences. The three buffer systems were developed in response to the difficulties decision analysts experienced when seeking these inputs. Influence diagram technology (Howard & Matheson, 1980; Selvidge, 1976) was developed to handle situations where an assessor, asked for the probability of an event, would say that the value to be given depended on probabilities within a network of other events. Probabilistic information-processing systems (Edwards, Phillips, Hays, & Goodman, 1968) were developed in the case where prior information about the probabilities of events had to be taken into account. Multiattribute utility theory was developed to handle situations where the decision maker wished to assess the worth of consequences on a number of different attributes rather than on a single criterion like "monetary worth" (Keeney & Raiffa, 1976).

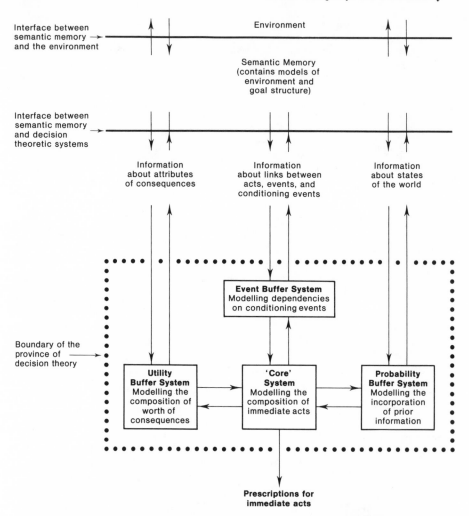

Figure 1. Interfaces between decision-theoretic systems and semantic memory. (In cases where a particular buffer system is not employed, the relevant inputs to and outputs from the core system are interfaced directly with semantic memory. From "Structuring Decision Problems and the 'Bias Heuristic' " by D. Berkeley and P. C. Humphreys, 1982, *Acta Psychologica, 50,* p. 213. Copyright 1982 by Elsevier (North Holland). Reprinted by permission.

Within these four systems, the first four types of uncertainty (Types i to iv as described previously) can be taken explicitly into account within the province of decision theory. However, in facing any ill-structured problem, the decision maker can experience much *procedural* uncertainty (Type v) concerning how to go about *generating the structure* within which the decision problem will be processed. None of the developments with the province of decision theory (Figure 1) comprise techniques handling this type of uncertainty because each decision theoretic technique is predicated on the assumption that the structure within which the decision problem is to be represented has been specified *a priori*. When this is not the case, questions arise that are located outside the province of decision theory: Should the problem be handled by selecting the appropriate structural variant from those offered by decision theory and then generating a problem representation within the variant (and what rules could guide this selection)? Will several different structural variants be involved in the overall problem representation (and how are these variants to be linked together)?

In the few cases where decision aids have been found to be useful by decision makers facing ill-structured problems, this has generally been due to the help they provided in the decision maker's attempts to *develop the structure* within which a composition rule could be applied through, for example, resolution of goal confusion (Humphreys & McFadden, 1980) or consciousness raising about the nature of the "small world" within which the problem was to be located (Jungermann, 1980). The basis for these types of decision aiding cannot be identified within the systems shown in Figure 1 because they are fundamentally concerned with operations located at a higher level than anything shown there. In fact, the results of these operations define the *constraints* that are placed on the systems shown in Figure 1 whenever they are used in handling a specific decision problem.

Examining ways in which the last three of the seven types of uncertainties can be resolved requires moving outside the traditional province of decision theory. The simplest solution is to label them *metadecision theoretic*, to be handled somehow within the realm of the psychology of decision making, rather than within decision theory itself. Here, though, we attempt to offer a different solution, providing an account of levels of abstraction in representing decision problems, which has its roots in both decision theory and the approach to cognitive development through genetic epistemology described by Piaget (1971, 1972, 1977). Within this account we will try to illustrate how all seven types of uncertainty may variously be handled.

HANDLING UNCERTAINTY

Nonroutine decision problems, whether personal or organizational, tackled by an individual or by a group, are located within the social world from which they draw their definitions and where the implementation of any solution will have its consequences. This social world has its impact on the way decision problems are represented (1) in providing available "small worlds" within which the problem may be located; (2) in providing the language that will be used by the decision maker to describe the problem; (3) in suggesting possible ways for structuring the problem; (4) in providing the terrain within which alternative conditions can be explored; and (5) in setting up the conditions of reality within which one's preferences can be stated.

We cannot assume here that different decision makers will generate or accept equivalent representations of any particular problem just because they share the same social world. The history of previous rounds in the decision-making process (Kunreuther, 1983) and the roles and goals of the various parties to the decision (Vari & Vecsenyi, 1984) also play their part in determining the result of the structure-generation process employed by the decision maker. The whole enterprise of decision theory is based on model construction and exploration within a structure that is assumed to be predefined. We shall argue that, in any situation where procedural uncertainty arises, the way in which a decision maker will generate the representation of the structure of his or her problem, and thus define its structure, is of crucial importance.

We shall describe how decision problems can be concepturalized on at least five qualitatively different levels of abstraction, all of which must be taken into account in handling the seven types of uncertainty we listed earlier. We will show how only the first three of these five levels are considered within the province of decision theory but will question whether it is desirable to formalize decision-making operations above the third level. Absence of formalization does not, however, justify the assumption that any uncertainties handled at the higher levels have been resolved *a priori* and so can be treated as fixed or irrelevant within a decision-theoretic perspective.

The levels of abstraction that we will describe are related to those proposed by Jaques (1982) in conceptualizing intellectual task performance within organizational contexts, and they represent an extension of Piaget's account of stages in cognitive development. Fundamental to both theories is the requirement that an individual's ability to understand and apply the operations described at each level develops from a considerable amount of experience and constructive feedback stemming from his or her own problem-structuring operations at the level below. Our account will start at the level reached by most people by adolescence ("concrete operational") and progress through levels reached later in life. Although many people never reach the stage where they gain the confidence to apply structuring operations for themselves at the higher levels of abstraction, this does not mean that these levels of abstraction can simply be ignored in describing the way these people represent their decision problem. Instead, it is important in these cases to study how the form of any particular decision problem representation is fixed at this level through received wisdom (traditionally, historically, or normatively determined). The decision maker will often not be aware of the nature of this "received wisdom" and how it sets constraints on his or her problem-solving activities at lower levels, as it is often simply seen as the "natural" way to approach the problem (Barthes, 1973) without awareness of alternative possibilities.

LEVELS OF ABSTRACTION IN
REPRESENTING DECISION PROBLEMS

Two points should be made at the outset about the formal characteristics of this multilevel problem representation scheme. The first is that the elements modeled at each level are *operations* performed by the decision maker in developing a problem representation, rather than the substantive content of the representation thus developed (cf. Jaques, Gibson, & Isaac, 1978). This distinguishes the enterprise from set-theoretic formal abstraction schemes developed from Whitehead and Russell's (1910) theory of logical types, but it is in line with Piaget's (1971) account of genetic epistemology.

The second point concerns the relations between the levels. In a "two-level" decision-making scheme, what is represented as *form* at the first level can be manipulated as *content* at the second level. But this relation may be continued through further levels of abstraction, that is, what is represented as form at the second level can be manipulated as content at the third level, and so on. This implies, of course, that the content manipulated at each level is qualitatively different, as are the progressively more powerful operators that become available to a person who can understand the principles underlying their employment within the calculus formalized at each progressive level of abstraction.

This brings us to the psychological characteristics of the system. It is no use describing a multilevel scheme comprising operations that decision makers are unable or unwilling to carry out in their actual practice when structuring decision problems. Thus, it is necessary to understand that progressive levels of abstraction must build on the process of cognitive development within decision makers. Our account will start at the level of cognitive development that Piaget calls *concrete operational* (the entry level for any theory of cognitive decision making). In order to move to the second level (equivalent to Piaget's formal operational level), a person must be fullly conversant with the operations used at the first level, so that the pattern of principles underlying these operations (the form at Level 1) can itself be used as an operator at the next level. Lack of experience of, or appropriate feedback from, problem-structuring operations at one level effectively prohibits a decision maker's progress to the next level. This, as we will see, places limits on the applicability of higher level problem representations in practical situations where the decision maker is unable to operate cognitively at the specified level.

Secondly, it is necessary to understand decision making involving a problem representation at any particular level as explicitly supported at all lower levels. If support is absent or developed in an inappropriate way, then the system becomes incoherent, and the decision analysis cannot be completed. In personal decision making, the decision maker is usually responsible for finding this support from material in his or her memory, completing the decision problem representation at every level in order to formulate a policy that is in accord with his or her motivation. In organizational decision making, the decision maker as problem owner (Checkland, 1981; Vari & Vecsenyi, 1984) is still responsible for seeking this support in formulating his or her policy but may delegate the development and exploration of lower levels of the problem representation to experts in specific areas, or proposers of solutions to parts of the problem or an automated "decision support system" (Bonczek, Holsapple, & Whinston, 1981; Humphreys, Larichev, Vari, & Vecsenyi, 1983; McCosh & Scott-Morton, 1978).

It is also necessary to understand that at any level the operations prescribed within a system aiding decision making must match the information-processing capabilities and the language used by the decision maker in exercising these capabilities. This is the basis proposed by Larichev (1984) for the psychological validation of decision methods and is an essential requirement within Phillips's (1984) account of requisite decision modeling.

These general points apply to the nature of problem representations across all levels. We turn now to the characteristics of problem representations at each specific level.

Level 1: Concrete Operational—Making "Best Assessments"

Piaget (1972) described the key principles that have to be understood in controlling operations at this level as those involved in *seriation* ($A < B$; $B < C$, etc.) and the interconnected postulates of *transitivity* and *conservation*. It is also the understanding of precisely these principles that allows one to adhere to what Edwards, Lindman, and Phillips (1965, pp. 272–275) described as the four relatively uncontroversial principles of rationality commonly cited in decision-theoretic accounts of coherent efficient decision making, namely decidability, transitivity, dominance, and the sure thing principle. Hence, achievement of the concrete operational level is a *prerequisite* for being able to handle decision problems in a coherent way (cf. Brown & Lindley, 1982).

The operations actualized at this level are limited, however, to providing assessments of quantities to be represented as content at a defined node in a problem structure that has been fixed *a priori*. This may involve handling uncertainties of Types i, ii, and iii in the case that the node is an event node, where the problem is seen as providing the answer to questions like "What is your best assessment of the probability that the event at this particular node will occur?" If the node represents a consequence that has to be evaluated, then resolution of Type iv uncertainty will be required, answering questions like "What is your best assessment of your relative preference for this outcome compared with the others under consideration?"

Efforts to improve the quality of decision making located exclusively at this level have centered around attempts to ensure that decision makers are "well calibrated" (Lichtenstein, Fischhoff, & Phillips, 1982) through correcting numerical biases in the assessor's intuitive probability assessments. However, Zimmer (1983) has suggested that some of the reported "miscalibration" of probability assessors may well be due to the numerical language that is imposed on them in the experimental task. Using techniques for encoding verbal assessments of probability developed for fuzzy set theory, he was able to show that subjects gave "well-calibrated" answers in task situations where numerical assessments appeared conservatively biased. The solution suggested was to develop assessment techniques involving the use of verbal rather than numerical language because "human subjects are more effective in reasoning with verbal expressions than with numerical expressions, even if the tasks performed rely on frequency information" (Zimmer, 1983, p. 180).

Level 2: Formal Operational—Sensitivity Analysis

Moving up to Level 2 involves understanding the principles underlying what Piaget (1972) called *formal operational thought*. Piaget describes the fundamental characteristic of cognitive abilities at this level as the "capacity to deal with hypotheses instead of simply objects," hypotheses that are expressed as *propositions* rather than facts.

The key formal operations at Level 2 comprise the *INRC group*: operationalizing principles relating to inversion, negation, reciprocity and correlation. Although each of these types of operations may be involved in a decision maker's attempt to provide "best assessments" in Level 1 problem solving, it is at Level 2 that these properties *as a group* are first understood and exploited in exploring aspects of a (prestructured) representation of a decision problem.

In text books on decision analysis (e.g., Brown, Kahr, & Peterson, 1974), this type of exploration of aspects of a problem is generally referred to as "sensitivity analysis": exploring "what if?" questions about changing values at nodes in the structure (e.g., the probability of an event in an act–event sequence) to see what effects are propagated throughout the structure. Hence, at Level 2 the content manipulated within the structure is not "facts" but hypotheses (opinions, views, etc.). It is explicitly recognized that probabilities can vary in reflecting the range of specific participants' interests and preferences in group decision making.

As at Level 1, this may involve handling uncertainties of any of Types i, ii, iii, or iv, but here the task is no longer seen as providing "best assessments" of *fixed* values at each node. Instead, the decision problem representation can be explored through *varying* the value assessed at any chosen node within the structure and investigating the impact of doing this at other points of interest within the current representation. The structure within which this exploration is made, however, is still fixed *a priori*, and only one value is changed at a time (just as an explorer reaches only one point at a time on his or her itinerary). The rest of the structure provides the frame at each point in the exploration.

Level 3: Developing Structure within a Single Structural Variant

Fundamental activities in structuring and restructuring decision problems involves processing a decision problem at Level 3 and above. At Level 3, we move beyond Piaget's account of INRC operations dictating the form of the current problem representation. They now become content manipulated within operations aimed at developing the structure of the problem under the constraint that the variant of structure used to represent the problem remains the same.

The meaning of *variant* here refers to a structure appropriate for handling a particular type of uncertainty from the last four types described by Berkeley and Humphreys (1982). Hence, each box in Figure 1 identifies decision-making systems comprising techniques for generating problem structures of *one* particular kind (act–event linkage, multiattribute utility decomposition, and so on). Restructuring activities that are superordinate to reordering within a single structural variant are handled at Level 4 and above in ways we will outline later.

Humphreys and Berkeley (1983) give an example of personal decision making dominated by problem structuring at Level 3. In this case, the decision maker, faced with a career choice problem, worked with an interactive decision-aiding system called MAUD4 (Humphreys & Wisudha, 1982). MAUD4 possesses decision problem-structuring capabilities at Level 3 in handling a decision maker's uncertainty about how to conceptualize the worth of consequences. At this level, MAUD4 works in interaction with the user, developing and reordering the structure of his or her problem. However, this structure is always expressed in terms of a set of attributes on which part worths (Kneppreth, Gustafson, Leifer, & Johnson, 1974) of the set of options currently under consideration may be represented. The constraints under which MAUD4 operates is that this is the structural variant that is requisite for handling the current decision problem (Phillips, 1982, in press). The Level 3 problem processing system within MAUD4 consists of operations organized in a simple linear processing system (cf. Humphreys, Wooler, & Phillips, 1980). This system contains just 15 ordered production rules implementing procedures handling deletion of part of the current preference structure, change of content within the preference structure, restructuring consequent of the failure of a coherence check of the current structure initiated by MAUD4, and so on. The Level 3 system could be kept simple because each of the "actions" implemented within MAUD4 by a Level 3 production rule is carried out by a particular software module operating in interaction with the decision maker in performing operations located at Levels 1 and 2.

In the example Humphreys and Berkeley (1983) described, because the decision maker was facing a situation where the options under consideration were already well defined, the constraint that the structure employed was an acceptable requisite. The decision maker had to accept one of the four jobs that had been offered to him: a job in community television, a job as a free-lance journalist in the United States, running an arts center in his home town in Wales, or becoming a television critic for a weekly magazine. The problem facing the decision maker was to identify the attributes that really mattered in choosing between these offers.

MAUD4 worked with the decision maker in identifying possible attributes described in the decision maker's own language. The decision maker started out by distingushing between jobs, according to whether they were *natural* or *required much effort* and whether they were *close to family* or *estranged from family*. Through interacting with MAUD4, he found that these two attribute scales meant much the same to him, and so the problem was restructured through replacing both these attribute dimensions with a scale running from *true vocation* to *determination and despair*.

The next attribute distinguished between jobs according to whether they involved *feeling at home* or *feeling alone*, but this was then found to have much the same meaning as the scale running from true vocation to determination and despair. Hence, these two attribute scales were both replaced by the decision maker with a scale running from *culturally fulfilled* to *culturally isolated*.

Moving in a different direction, the decision maker then characterized the jobs according to whether they were *adventurous* or represented *independent maturity* and whether they involved *challenging difficulties* or *escape from relations*. Once again the decision maker found that he had characterized his preferences much the same way on these two attributes; he decided that this was because they had similar meanings to him, and so employed them with a scale characterizing the core of this meaning: *feeling alive* to *feeling depressed*.

At this point the decision maker, while interacting with MAUD4, had introduced eight attributes into his decision problem representation. But as a result of Level 3 restructuring operations, the attributes he had kept were only two: one characterizing intellectual aspects of the jobs (how culturally fulfilling they might be) and one describing his expectations of the emotional states that would be concomitant with working at each job.

To complete his decision problem representation, the decision maker then introduced one more attribute, scaling his preferences between jobs on a scale from *creative* to *boring*. This meant that only three criteria were retained in the final structure, within which trade-offs between jobs on attributes were investigated.

You can see from the decision maker's preference ratings shown in Figure 2 how the choice between the three of the jobs (excluding "critic") depended critically on the way trade-offs were made between the three attributes retained in the final problem representation. The results of how the decision maker worked out these trade-offs in interaction with MAUD4 are summarized by the importance weights shown in Figure 2, which serve to identify "community TV" as the preferred option. When questioned about this result, the decision maker said that he was not entirely happy about it, but at least he now knew what his problem was: characterizing the regret associated with loss (in fantasy) of the opportunities offered by the rejected jobs. One week later, after some thought, the decision maker accepted the offer of a job in community television.

In general, field tests with various versions of MAUD (Bronner & de Hoog, 1983; Humphreys & McFadden, 1980) have indicated that the key to MAUD's success was its ability to aid the decision maker's attempts to work at Level 3

Figure 2. Extract from the summary produced by MAUD4 of an interactive session with a person facing a job decision problem.

in *clarifying* the nature of the attribute structure that could be an appropriate basis for choice, given his or her current goals. However, MAUD4 can fail to provide aid if the decision maker is unable or unwilling to work at Level 3 in conceptualizing the decision problem. It can also fail if the decision maker does not like the constraint imposed by MAUD4 that the decision problem representation be in terms of a multiattribute utility structure. The latter case indicates that procedural uncertainty about what variant of structure to use has been appropriately handled. Handling this type of uncertainty necessitates operations located at Level 4 in the way we will describe later. At Level 3 only the *results* of these operations are evident—where they set the constraints that define the structural variant within which the problem is represented.

Level 4: Problem-Structuring Languages

Decision problem-structuring activities at Level 4 involve the articulation of principles that enable the manipulation of complete Level 3 problem-structuring systems as content. There is, however, no formal language within decision theory that articulates Level 4 principles, as they are superordinate to the forms addressed by that theory (i.e., those shown in the boxes in Figure 1). Hence, in working at Level 4 a decision maker has *either* to articulate these principles within his or her own natural language *or* to learn a new language for generating systems linking Level 3 (sub)problem representations into a structure comprising the whole range of aspects of the problem under consideration. In practice, the language employed by the decision maker serves as a generative problem-structuring calculus at this level (Humphreys & Berkeley, 1983).

Figure 3 shows the results of the use of a problem-structuring language of this type by the manager of the marine claims department of a large insurance company, working in interaction with a decision analyst (details are given in Humphreys, Wooler, & Phillips, 1980, Section 6). This aim was to generate a problem representation that could provide for decision making concerning the expected size of a marine claim, following notification at any time in the future of an incident involving any one of a number of large ships insured with the company. This is called a "hull claim."

In this case, the Level 4 decision problem processing system was not automated: it originated and remained in the mind of the decision maker who used his own "natural" language in developing the problem representation shown in Figure 3. His goal was to be able to assess a single complex consequence (eventual size of settlement) whatever the circumstances. From the way he discussed this consequence, it was evident that it could be "rewritten" in terms of the net size of any claim, inflated by the appropriate "image factor," "relationship factor," and "handling factor." These factors are terms that have meaning in the

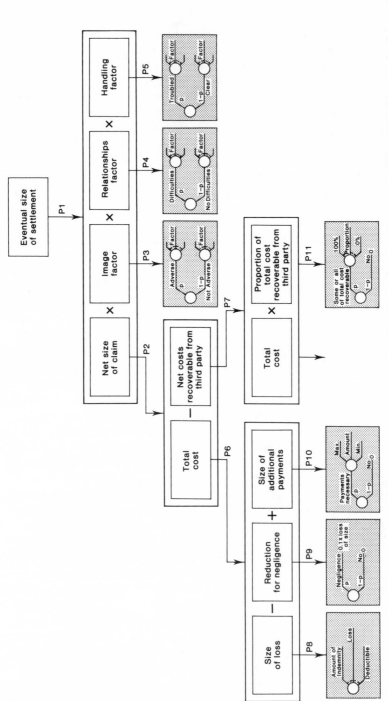

Figure 3. A Level 4 problem representation: The "hull claims" model. From "Problem Structuring Calculi and Levels of Knowledge Representation in Decision Making" by P. C. Humphreys and D. Berkeley, in *Decision Making under Uncertainty*, edited by R. W. Scholz, p. 143. Copyright 1983 by Elsevier (North Holland). Reprinted by permission.

special language used by insurance assessors in communicating to one another. They do not exist *within* decision theoretic terminology because they are names that index Level 3 decision-theoretic problem representations and handle how to take into account the uncertainty about (1) whether the way the claim is settled will adversely affect the company's image; (2) whether it will lead to difficulties in relationships with other clients; and (3) whether the process of handling the claim will be troubled or clear.

A decision analyst worked with the decision maker in developing the structure of the problem at Level 4. However, the aid that the analyst could provide at this level was *not* in teaching the decision maker how to use his language as a problem-structuring calculus. In fact the opposite was the case: The decision analyst had to *learn* the language that the decision maker was using as his intuitive calculus. However, the analyst did not then just learn the decision maker's language. He was able to use the rewriting rules (Chomsky, 1957; Fillmore, 1968) that he could identify in the decision maker's use of his language as elements in a production system that could model the problem structure that the decision maker was implicitly generating. (See Bonczek, *et al.*, 1981, and Lee, 1983, Chapter 10 for discussion of the use of production systems as generative grammars.)

Formalizing the Level 4 structure in this way enabled the decision analyst to check its transitivity, coherence, and stability as it was being generated, through discussions with the decision maker. Larichev (1984) describes how checks like these form the basis for the validation of the decision maker's method. Figure 3 shows the final result of this process. The decision maker's rewriting of "eventual size of settlement" is expressed as production P1. The "image factor," "relationship factor," and "handling factor" are taken into account through productions P3, P4, and P5, respectively. Each of these three productions' right-hand side is a terminal node in the Level 4 system: a Level 3 problem-structuring module.

Unlike P3, P4, and P5, the right-hand side of P2 is not a terminal node in the Level 4 system. When the decision maker was asked about the net size of the claim, he said it was a function of the "total cost" minus the "net costs recoverable from a third party," each of which he wished to express in his own natural language, rather than as decision-theoretic modules. ("Total cost" is the "size of the loss" minus any "reduction that can be obtained from negligence" plus "any additional payments that have to be made to other parties.") Hence, the right-hand sides of P6 and P7 are also nonterminal nodes, as at these nodes the decision maker wished to continue structuring the problem at Level 4.

The decision analyst was able to use decision tree structuring methods to develop the problem representation within each of the Level 3 modules shown in Figure 3. Note that at this lower level, it was the analyst rather than the decision maker who provided the problem-structuring language. Working in an organizational context, the decision maker was primarily interested that his subordinates in the appropriate company departments should *understand the principles* according to which the Level 3 decision tree structures were generated. The subordinates would need to articulate these structures in any instance and report the results to the Level 4 decision maker.

Conversely, the results of the Level 4 analysis carried out by the decision maker appeared, during their implementation in practice, as *constraints* to his subordinates. Working at Level 3, they each had the task of handling a sub-problem represented within a particular variant of structure—an event tree. Each subordinate could seek the help of a decision analyst in developing the structure of the tree and in exploring it at Level 2. He or she could also call upon experts, assigning them the Level 1 task of the probabilities of events modeled within their trees. In this way, support was provided for the marine claims manager's Level 4 decision-making activities at all lower levels, in both conceptual and organizational terms.

Level 5: Scenarios Exploring Small Worlds

Level 4 problem representations often appear to decision makers to be "complete" descriptions of the structure of the decision-making problem they are facing. Yet these Level 4 descriptions are themselves situated within what Savage (1954) described as the *small world* encompassing the decision maker's problem-structuring activities and the knowledge representations that he or she believes to be relevant to these activities. Toda (1976; see also Humphreys, 1982) has discussed the nature of these small worlds and how their boundaries are closed according to the goals of the decision maker. This "boundary setting" for a decision problem changes with changes in motivation, as does the nature of the structures the decision maker will consider requisite in handling any decision problem.

However, methods for representing decision problem structures at Level 5 are as yet relatively undeveloped. A major difficulty is that any description of the small world in which the decision maker situates himself or herself and his or her problem is *beyond* his or her language. This is because the language itself is generated through the decision maker's imagination in exploring the nature of his or her problem along chains of signification within this small world (Lacan, 1977). There is no possibility of the decision maker's using his or her own language to describe his or her small worlds "from the outside."

Procedural uncertainty is not an issue at this level. Rather than involving some guiding procedure, the decision maker simply experiences (in fantasy) movement of events, images and ideas along chains of signification as scenarios unfold. The direction of exploration may be motivated by the decision maker's desire in searching for the existence of possible consequences that express aspects that he or she currently experiences as lacking, while seeking to avoid those that may offer only anxiety or regret (Sjoberg, 1980; Toda, 1980, 1983). The *results* of what is encountered in this search form the material basis for the content manipulated in problem structuring at lower levels where uncertainty about the appropriate procedure may then arise.

However, it is at Level 5 that the last two types of uncertainties identified by Berkeley and Humphreys (1982) come to the fore, as they arise during the *reality testing* of the fantasies that constitute the scenarios explored there. A decision maker must project an idea of himself or herself through the scenarios in order to determine how he or she will feel and wish to act at any choice point encountered. If the fantasy is to guide an effective decision-making process rather than just generate dreams, then there must be a good correspondence between the desire identified as a property of "self" at those points and the feelings that would actually be experienced should that point unfold "for real." Berkeley and Humphreys's (1982) Type vi uncertainty refers to uncertainty about how to ensure this correspondence.

Type vii uncertainty also addresses a correspondence between aspects of fantasies generated at Level 5, and potential reality, but it concerns one's agency over external states of the world rather than over internal feelings. Conventional decision theoretic accounts of "states of the world" assume that no such uncertainty should exist: the theory prescribes that the decision maker has complete agency over his or her own acts, but none over events (including the acts of others). Lacan (1977) describes how the operations involved in exploration of signifying chains are those of "primary process thought"—the type of thought that in structural psychoanalytic theory forms the basis for the construction of dreams (Freud, 1923/1953; Mannoni, 1971). The fundamental characteristic of dream construction is agency over states of the world: these are structured *in the service* of the decision maker's desire.

Resolution of Type vii uncertainty may not simply involve a prescription to curb this aspect of one's desire as "wishful thinking" (McGuire, 1968; Sjoberg, 1980) and follow the tenets of decision theory. For example, Vari and Vecsenyi (1983) describe how senior decision makers in a Hungarian state agency discarded computed subjective expected utilities of alternative research and development projects as a basis for choosing between them, and instead formed their choice on the basis of the *maximum feasible utility* of each of the projects. The maximum feasible utility of a project was that utility that the decision maker considered would characterize the consequence of implementing that project if all potential hitches and pitfalls could be smoothed out of the implementation.

The analysts acting as consultants to these decision makers pointed out the possible lack of correspondence between realization of maximum feasible utility (which seemed to characterize the decision makers' Level 5 scenarios) and the reality that was likely to ensue. To the analysts this seemed like a clear case of wishful thinking. The decision makers saw the issue differently. They did not revise their basis for choice but instead alerted all the organizations involved to the fact that "great attention should be paid to the implementation of the project, and the use of the results in practice" (Vari & Vecsenyi, 1983, p.193). This alternative way of trying to resolve Type vii uncertainty may have some uses in situations where decision makers have real agency over acts of others in the social world of implementation of decisions.

Studying or aiding decision makers' activities at Level 5 requires the use of internal exploratory techniques rather than external, formalizing techniques. Some progress has been made in methods for developing "exploratory" scenarios (Ducot & Lubben, 1980). A technique called GERT (Graphic Evaluation and Review Technique; Moore & Clayton, 1976) has been proposed by Kunreuther (1983) for displaying the results of these explorations. However, Jungermann (1983b) has pointed out that many questions regarding the generation of options and linkages within scenarios are still quite unresolved, although research is planned that could remedy this situation (Jungermann & von Winterfeldt, 1981). The results could be very important in improving our understanding of ways of aiding decision making in situations where more than one party is involved in the decision and where the various parties have quite different motivations. Von Winterfeldt and Rios (1980), Humphreys (1982), and Lathrop and Linnerooth (1983), among others, have described how parties with conflicting motivations will develop quite different scenarios. Vari and Vecsenyi (1984) describe how this in turn leads to preferences for quite different decision-making methods at Levels 2, 3, and 4 among parties with different roles and motivations in a decision-making situation.

Higher Levels of Abstraction

Above Level 5 we move outside the scope of *individual* decision-making activities, as at Level 6 the "small worlds" that define form at Level 5 are themselves placed as content within structures generated at higher levels. Decision making at these higher levels of abstraction must of necessity be *social*. This is because each of the small worlds that is manipulated as content at these levels marks for the individual located within it the boundary of the ways in which he or she can conceptualize scenarios of future personal experiences.

Decision making at levels higher than Level 5 is concerned with choosing between courses of action that, when supported at all lower levels, will lead to the generation and reordering of the cultural structures within which individuals find and exercise their identities. Few decision makers occupy roles with the scope and levels of organizational support that permit them to handle decision-making tasks effectively at these levels of abstraction.

IMPLICATIONS OF THE MULTILEVEL SCHEME
FOR SUPPORTING ORGANIZATIONAL DECISION MAKING

Table 1 shows the correspondence between the levels of abstraction involved in conceptualizing decision problems described here and Jaques's (1976, 1982) levels of abstraction of the demand characteristics of the tasks carried out by decision makers located at the various levels within the hierarchy of a bureaucratic organization.

According to Jaques, the qualitative differences between the levels of organizational roles shown in the first column can be understood in terms of progressive levels of abstraction in the symbolic construction of actions that may be carried out by executives at each level. Moreover, these levels are not viewed as a specific product of organizational forms; rather, bureaucratic levels are parasitic on levels of abstraction of (idealized) tasks within organizations.

The second column in Table 1 gives the typical time span in the problem representation that is requisite for a task carried out by an executive at each level. The time span indicates how far away the decision horizon (Toda, 1976) is usually set for tasks for which the decision maker is held responsible within the organizational context.

The third column in Table 1 summarizes the description of the demand characteristics of the tasks facing personnel with responsibility at a given level in an organization (for a detailed account of these demand characteristics, see Jaques, 1982, pp. 80-85). Jaques was primarily concerned with bureaucratic organizations comprising idealized hierarchies of work stata, and in any actual organizational context we may find personnel at particular organizational levels also responsible for carrying out tasks at lower levels (rather than delegating them to subordinates). Executives may be able to take initiatives at more than one level in organizations where the role structure permits this (for example, as "consultants" or "problem fixers"). However, the precision of the equivalence between organizational roles and task characteristics is not our major concern here. Instead, we were particularly interested in comparing Jaques's description of the *qualitative* differences between the demand characteristics of tasks at each level of abstraction in a bureaucracy (Column 3 of Table 1) with our account of the necessary capabilities for systems able to support problem-structuring operations located at the parallel level of abstraction. This is summarized in the fourth column of Table 1.

The existence of a close correspondence between the entries in Columns 3 and 4 at each level suggests that a decision support system that operates on problem representations at Levels 1 and 2 only (the usual case) will be able to supply adequate support for decision-making activities typically carried out by front-line managerial personnel, that is, the personnel located at Level 2 in the or-

Table 1. Comparison of Demand Characteristics of Tasks Facing Personnel Having Responsibilities at a Given Organizational Level with Structuring Capabilities Required in Representing Decision Problems at That Level[a]

Level number	Organizational level in employment hierarchy	Time span inherent in problem representation at given level[b]	Demand characteristics of tasks facing personnel with responsibility at given level[b]	Structuring capabilities required in representing decision problems at given level (decision support at given level must also include capabilities of all lower levels)	Number of existing DSS incorporating support formalized at given level
	Sociocultural decision making: goal-closed small worlds structured within cultures (in theory, up to level 10)				
7	Chairman/MD of corporate group; head of large government department	20–50 yr	Anticipation of changes in sociological, technological, demographic and political developments; leading corporate strategic development to meet them	Isomorphic with Level 2, except can conduct sensitivity analysis, simulating changes in Level 5 representations; assessing their impact within cultural structure	None
6	Corporate group/ sector executive	10–20 yr	Coordination of social and theoretical systems; translation of corporate strategic development into business direction	Isomorphic with Level 1, except each node is now a Level 5 problem representation within fixed cultural structure	None
	Individual decision making under uncertainty: uncertainties and preferences structured within goal-closed small worlds				
5	Corporate subsidiary/	5–10 yr	Problem not dealt with in context set wholly from above can modify	Articulation of principles for conditional (goal) closing of an	None

	Role	Time span			
	enterprise managing director		boundaries of business within policy	open systems, and/or reopening of a conditionally closed system (e.g., through scenario generation)	
4	General management, (e.g., development, production *or* sales, within work system)	2–5 yr	Detachment from specific cases, seeing them representative examples of issues calling for development of a system	Selecting/interfacing capability between structural types (requiring use of problem-structuring language)	Very few (prototypes)
3	Department managerial/ principal specialist	1–2 yr	Control of trend of tasks and problems arising; extrapolation from trend to ways of formulating problems	Restructuring capability within single fixed structural types (e.g., attribute generation in multi-attribute model)	A few
2	Front line managerial/ professional	3 mo to 1 yr	*Formal operational*, can anticipate changes in tasks due to any *one* of: object, production resource, pathway, or pathway resource	Manipulation of data on one variable at a time within fixed structure (e.g., sensitivity analysis)	Many
1	Shop and office floor	Less than 3 mo	*Concrete operational* limited to tasks concretely and physically at hand	Estimation of values at nodes within fixed structure (e.g., information retrieval system)	Many

aCharacteristics of Levels 8 to 10 can, in theory, be ascertained by extrapolation from Levels 3 to 5, respectively.
bThis information is summarized from the accounts given by Jaques (1976, 1982).

ganizational hierarchy. However, it will not be able to provide adequate support for important aspects of decision making at higher levels.

Nevertheless, the absence of decision support systems that have been designed to have capabilities above Level 3 may not simply represent a failure by DSS designers to meet the demands of high-level decision makers. In our opinion, it is not actually advisable to attempt to formalize Level 5 scenario-generation techniques and Level 4 problem-structuring languages into automated decision support systems. At Level 5, decision makers' scenarios need to be *explored* rather than fitted into formal structures. At Level 4, it is better to develop techniques for the psychological validation of the decision maker's *own* problem-structuring language than to try to invent a universal problem-structuring language that will have to be taught from scratch to high-level decision makers.

IMPLICATIONS OF THE MULTILEVEL SCHEME
FOR THE STUDY OF INTUITIVE DECISION MAKING

Laboratory studies on intuitive (unaided) desision making usually involve a comparison between subjects' responses in a decision-making task and the output of a normative model that is applied to data within a "veridical" representation of the decision problem and hopefully conveyed to subjects through task instructions (Berkeley & Humphreys, 1982; Tversky & Kahneman, 1981).

There are two implications of our analysis of the various levels at which decision problems may be represented for such research: (1) comparisons between normative and intuitive outputs must be made at one, and only one, predefined level of abstraction at a time; and (2) for a comparison between experimenters and subjects to be made at any particular level, there must be a common understanding about how the structure of the problem representation is to be fixed at all higher levels.

Elsewhere, we have described how this means that in making these types of comparisons we should start at the highest level at which there is a possibility of the existence of differences and then work down, level by level, interpreting the differences in output comparisons at the highest level at which they occur (Humphreys & Berkeley, 1983). Here, we wish to conclude by examining the distinction between the *articulated differences* that may be identified between decision makers' problem representations at levels where these problem representations have been generated through operations whose principles were understood by the decision makers, and the *unarticulated differences* that result when problem representations stem from normative, institutional, or historical constraints on decision makers who are unable or unwilling to articulate the basis for the structuring operations that they might carry out at that level (cf. Linnerooth, in press).

Because progressively fewer individuals have the capacity (Jaques, 1976, 1982) to articulate operations as we move up through the levels of abstraction, it follows that differences at Level 5 are very often *unarticulated,* whereas differences at the lowest levels are usually *articulated.* This assumption is implicitly built into most research on decision making within the "conversational paradigm" (Kahneman & Tversky, 1982), where it is assumed that the presented instructions are sufficient to set all the constraints at Level 3 and above in the *same* way for *all* decision makers.

Implicit in this assumption is that (1) subjects do not articulate scenarios for themselves at Level 5 nor develop their own problem-structuring language at Level 4; and (2) that *no* unarticulated differences exist between subjects at these levels, as such differences would lead to variety in the way the constraints were set across subjects. At Level 3, although it is not presumed that subjects use exactly the *same* problem representation as presumed by the normative model, it is assumed that the intuitive representation may be mapped into the normative one in a way that is invariant under transformation (Berkeley & Humphreys, 1982). At the lowest two levels, differences are usually explicitly analyzed as a basis for identifying the "heuristics" (*ad hoc* patterns of operations) that subjects may be using in representing their decision problems at these levels (Tversky & Kahneman, 1974). Different authors take opposing views on whether these differences should be considered to be articulated or not (Hogarth, 1981; Jungermann, 1983a; Phillips, 1983).

In our opinion, there are too many untested assumptions within this paradigm. At each of the five levels of problem representation we have tried to indicate routes to the explicit study of both articulated and unarticulated differences between subjects (and between stakeholders or interest groups in the case of social decision making). We would like to suggest that there might be much to discover through exploring these routes and much to be lost through assuming that nothing of consequence would be revealed.

ACKNOWLEDGMENTS

The theory described in this chapter has been developed with the aid of many discussions inside and outside the Decision Analysis Unit. In particular, we would like to thank Elliott Jaques, Helmut Jungermann, Oleg Larichev, Eric Nappelbaum, Larry Phillips, Stuart Wooler, and Gerard de Zeeuw for contributions that influenced the ideas expressed here, although the responsibility for the way these were incorporated into this chapter lies with the authors.

REFERENCES

Barthes, R. (1973). *Mythologies*. St. Albans: Paladin.

Berkeley, D., & Humphreys, P. C. (1982). Structuring decision problems and the "bias heuristic." *Acta Psychologica, 50*, 201–252.

Bonczek, R. H., Holsapple, C. W., & Whinston, A. B. (1981). *Foundations of decision support systems*. New York: Academic Press.

Bronner, F., & de Hoog, R. (1983). Non-expert use of a computerized decision aid. In P. C. Humphreys, O. Svenson, & A. Vari (Eds.), *Analysing and aiding decision processes*. Amsterdam: North Holland.

Brown, R. V., & Lindley, D. V. (1982). Improving judgement by reconciling incoherence. *Theory and Decision, 14*, 113–132.

Brown, R. V., Kahr, A. S., & Peterson, C. R. (1974). *Decision analysis for the manager*. New York: Holt, Rinehart & Winston.

Bruner, J. S., Goodnow, J. J., & Austin, G. A. (1956). *A study of thinking*. New York: Wiley.

Checkland, P. (1981). *Systems thinking, systems practice*. Chichester: Wiley.

Chomsky, N. (1957). *Syntactic structures*. The Hague: Mouton.

Ducot, C., & Lubben, G. J. (1980). A typology for scenarios. *Futures, 12*, 51–57.

Edwards, W., Lindman, H., & Phillips, L. D. (1965). Emerging technologies for making decisions. In T. M. Newcomb (Ed.), *New directions in psychology* (II). New York: Holt, Rinehart & Winston.

Edwards, W., Phillips, L. D., Hays, W. L., & Goodman, B. C. (1968). Probabilistic information processing systems: Design and evaluation. *IEEE Transactions on Systems, Science and Cybernetics*, SSC-4, 248–265.

Einhorn, H. J., & Hogarth, R. M. (1981). Behavioral decision theory: Processes of judgment and choice. *Annual Review of Psychology, 32*, 53–88.

Fillmore, C. J. (1968). The case for case. In E. Bach & R. T. Harms (Eds.), *Universals in linguistic theory*. New York: Holt, Rinehart & Winston.

Freud, S. (1953). The interpretation of dreams. In J. Strachey (Ed. and Trans.), *Standard edition of the complete psychological works of Sigmund Freud* (Vols. IV & V). London: Hogarth Press. (Original work published 1923)

Hogarth, R. M. (1981). Beyond discrete biases: Functional and dysfunctional aspects of judgmental heuristics. *Psychological Bulletin, 90*, 197–217.

Hogarth, R. M., Michaud, C., & Mery, J. L. (1980). Decision behavior in urban development: A methodological approach and substantive considerations. *Acta Psychologica, 45*, 95–117.

Howard, R. A., & Matheson, J. G. (1980). *Influence diagrams*. Menlo Park, CA: SRI International.

Humphreys, P. C. (1982). Value structures underlying risk assessments. In H. Kunreuther (Ed.), *Risk: A seminar series* (C P-82-52). Laxenburg, Austria: International Institute of Applied Systems Analysis.

Humphreys, P. C., & Berkeley, D. (1983). Problem structuring calculi and levels of knowledge representation in decision making. In R. W. Scholz (Ed.), *Decision making under uncertainty*. Amsterdam: North Holland.

Humphreys, P. C., & McFadden, W. (1980). Experiences with MAUD: Aiding decision structuring versus bootstrapping the decision-maker. *Acta Psychologica, 45*, 51–69.

Humphreys, P. C., & Wisudha, A. (1982). *MAUD4* (Decision Analysis Unit Technical Report 82-5). London: London School of Economics and Political Science.

Humphreys, P. C., Wooler, S., & Phillips, L. D. (1980). *Structuring decisions: The role of structuring heuristics* (Decision Analysis Unit, Technical report 80-1). London: London School of Economics and Political Science.

Humphreys, P. C., Larichev, O. I., Vari, A., & Vecsenyi, J. (1983). Comparative analysis of use of decision support systems in R & D decisions. In H. G. Sol (Ed.), *Processes and tools for decision support.* Amsterdam: North-Holland.

Janis, I. L., & Mann, L. (1977). *Decision making* New York: Free Press.

Jaques, E. (1976). *A general theory of bureaucracy.* London: Heinemann.

Jaques, E. (1982). *Free enterprise, fair employment.* London: Heinemann.

Jaques, E., Gibson, R. O., & Isaac, D. J. (1978). *Levels of abstraction in logic and human action.* London: Heinemann.

Jungermann, H. (1980). Speculations about decision theoretic aids for personal decision making. *Acta Psychologica, 55,* 7–34.

Jungermann, H. (1983a). The two rationality camps. In R. W. Scholz (Ed.), *Decision making under uncertainty.* Amsterdam: North Holland.

Jungermann, H. (1983b). Psychological aspects of scenarios. Paper presented at NATO Advanced Study Institute (ASI), *Technology assessment, environmental impact of assessment and Risk analysis: Contributions from the Psychological and Decision Sciences,* Les Arcs, France.

Jungermann, H., & von Winterfeldt, D. (1981). Cognitive aspects and analytical methods of risk identification: The construction of scenarios. *Workshop on Analysis, Evaluation and Acceptability of Hazardous Technologies and their Evaluation.* Berlin: Science Center.

Kahneman, D., & Tversky, A. (1982). On the study of statistical intuition. *Cognition, 11,* 123–141.

Keeney, R. L., & Raiffa, H. (1976). *Decisions with multiple objectives: Preferences and value tradeoffs.* New York: Wiley.

Kneppreth, N. P., Gustafson, D. H., Leifer, R. P., & Johnson, E. M. (1974). *Techniques for the assessment of worth* (Technical paper 254, AD784629). Arlington, VA: Army Research Institute for the Behavioral and Social Sciences.

Kunreuther, H. (1983). A multi-attribute multi-party model of choice: Descriptive and prescriptive considerations. In P. C. Humphreys, O. Svenson, & A. Vari (Eds.), *Analysing and aiding decision processes.* Amsterdam: North Holland.

Lacan, J. (1977). The agency of the letter in the unconscious. In J. Lacan, *Ecrits.* London: Tavistock.

Lathrop, J., & Linnerooth, J. (1983). The role of risk assessment in a political decision process. In P. C. Humphreys, O. Svenson, & A. Vari (Eds.), *Analysing and aiding decision processes.* Amsterdam: North Holland.

Larichev, O. I. (1984). Psychological validation of decision models. *Journal of Applied Systems, Analysis, 11,* 37–46.

Lee, R. M. (1983). *Data and language in organisations: Epistemological aspects of management support systems* (Working paper WP-83-46). Laxenburg, Austria: International Institute of Applied Systems Analysis.

Lichtenstein, S. C., Fischhoff, B., & Phillips, L. D. (1982). Calibration of probabilities: The state of the art to 1980. In D. Kahneman, P. Slovic, & A. Tversky (Eds.), *Judgment under uncertainty: Heuristics and biases.* New York: Cambridge University Press.

Lindley, D. V. (1971). *Making decisions.* Chichester: Wiley.

Linnerooth, J. (in press). The political processing of uncertainty. *Acta Psychologica.*

Mannoni, O. (1971). *Freud: The theory of the unconscious.* New York: Pantheon.

McCosh, A. M., & Scott-Morton, M. S. (1978). *Management decision support systems.* London: Macmillan.

McGuire, W. J. (1968). Theory of the structure of human thought. In R. P. Abelson, E. Aronson, W. J. McGuire, T. M. Newcomb, M. J. Rosenberg, & P. H. Tannenbaum (Eds.), *Theories of cognitive consistency: A source book.* Chicago: Rand-McNally.

Moore, L., & Clayton, E. (1976). *GERT modelling and simulation.* New York: Petrocelli.

Phillips, L. D. (1982). Requisite decision modelling: A case study. *Journal of Operational Research Society, 33,* 303–311.

Phillips, L. D. (1983). A theoretical perspective on heuristics and biases in probabilistic thinking. In P. C. Humphreys, O. Svenson, & A. Vari (Eds.), *Analysing and aiding decision processes.* Amsterdam: North Holland.

Phillips, L. D. (1984). A theory of requisite decision modelling. *Acta Psychologica, 55,* 29–48.

Piaget, J. (1971). *Structuralism.* London: Routledge & Kegan Paul.

Piaget, J. (1972). *The principles of genetic epistemology.* London: Routledge & Kegan Paul.

Piaget, J. (1977). *The development of thought: Equilibration of cognitive structures.* Oxford: Basil Blackwell.

Raiffa, H. (1968). *Decision analysis.* Reading, MA: Addison-Wesley.

Savage, L. J. (1954). *The foundations of statistics.* New York: Wiley.

Selvidge, J. (1969). *Rapid screening of decision options* (Technical Report 76-12). McLean, VA: Decisions and Designs, Inc.

Sjoberg, L. (1980). Volitional problems in carrying through a difficult decision. *Acta Psychologica, 45,* 123–132.

Toda, M. (1976). The decision process: A perspective. *International Journal of General Systems, 3,* 79–88.

Toda, M. (1980). Emotion and decision making. *Acta Psychologica, 45,* 133–155.

Toda, M. (1983). What happens at the moment of decision? Metadecisions, emotions and volitions. In L. Sjoberg, T. Tyszka, & J. A. Wise (Eds.), *Human decision making.* Lund: Doxa.

Tversky, A., & Kahneman, D. (1974). Judgment under uncertainty: Heuristics and biases. *Science, 185,* 1124–1131.

Tversky, A., & Kahneman, D. (1981). The framing of decisions and the psychology of choice. *Science, 211,* 453–458.

Vari, A., & Vecsenyi, J. (1983). Decision analysis of industrial R & D problems: Pitfalls and lessons. In P. C. Humphreys, O. Svenson, & A. Vari (Eds.), *Analysing and aiding decision processes.* Amsterdam: North Holland.

Vari, A., & Vecsenyi, J. (1984). Selecting decision support methods in organizations. *Journal of Applied Systems Analysis, 11,* 23-36.

von Winterfeldt, D. & Rios, M. (1980). Conflicts about nuclear safety: A decision theoretic approach. In M. H. Fontana & D. R. Patterson, (Eds.), *Proceedings of the ANS/ENS Topical Meeting on Thermal Reactor Safety.* Springfield, VA: NTIS.

Whitehead, A. N., & Russell, B. (1910). *Principia mathematica.* Cambridge: Cambridge University Press.

Zimmer, A. (1983). Verbal versus numerical processing of subjective probabilities. In R. W. Scholz (Ed.), *Decision making under uncertainty.* Amsterdam: North Holland.

CHAPTER 13

Decisions in Design
Analyzing and Aiding the Art of Synthesis

James A. Wise

A poem is a machine for making choices.
—John Ciardi

Most of us spend our lives both using and occupying the products of other people's imaginations. The worlds we inhabit are built environments—designed entities that shelter and succor us, provide us with warmth, illumination, private space, and a host of supports and props that delineate our different work and social roles.

Nothing that we encounter there, which affects us knowingly or subliminally, is the result of chance alone. Everything is *designed*, in a process of one or more persons' considerations and decisions. The end result may reflect ignorance of anthropometric or cultural requirements. It may be the product of a uniquely individual aesthetic or of a restricted social perspective. But it is not an accident. If the components of our environments have come about by design, then they have come about by human choice.

DESIGN DECISIONS AND DESIGN METHODS

Design decision making is often called *the art of synthesis* by its practitioners. Indeed, the notion of *synthesis* enfolds and punctuates any act of design, no matter how it may be conceived (see Jones, 1970). Synthesis is a process by which var-

James A. Wise • Department of Architecture, College of Architecture and Urban Planning, University of Washington, Seattle, Washington 98195.

ious requirements, material properties, and value perspectives are configured into an integral whole. The result is a physical form that may become a building, kitchen product, or someone's backyard. But through design the final physical form becomes a manifest result of the process that created it. If that process is made more systematic, rational, analytic, or guided, will a better design be the result?

This question is at the base of a significant area of work known as *design methods*. Design methods began as a formal discipline in the middle 1960s when many design professionals and educators realized that traditional methods of teaching design in schools of architecture, industrial design, and engineering were inadequate for the complexity of the problems that the designs were supposed to solve. The seeds for this had actually been sown during World War II, when military problems were effectively addressed by operations research and early systems analysis procedures. In the subsequent large-scale European rebuilding of both the environment and the social order, architects and planners asked if their efforts could not also be aided by systematic methods.

The social upheavals that occurred in the United States during the middle and late 1960s gave further impetus to the idea that good design was to help solve problems rather than just be esthetically expressive. The question then became how problem solving was to be introduced in the design process.

To fully appreciate the significant departure this attitude took from historic design education, one need only look at the *école des beaux arts*, the previous traditional European design school. In this regimen, originating in Paris but emulated most everywhere else, the emphasis was on releasing the students' individual abilities to generate forms. There were no building *programs* that specified requirements for occupancy. In fact, students were deliberately kept away from most sources of pragmatic information about site and behavioral use patterns, on the grounds that this interfered with the natural creative process.

With the advent of design methods, however, there was a complete reversal of the beaux arts tradition, from the wholesale avoidance of information seeking in design, to its active, rational, and systematic integration in the design process. Indeed, Gregory (1966) wrote with the conviction that there was a design method equal in significance to the scientific method.

> Design science is concerned with the study, investigation and accumulation of knowledge about the design process and its constituent operations. It aims to collect, organize and improve those aspects of thought...which are likely to be of value to practical designers. (pp. 35–36)

He essentially reaffirmed this attitude a decade later (Gregory, 1977) at the Warsaw Conference on Design Methods. But in the interim, significant evolutionary events had occurred in the field.

First, the original major proponents of systematic design methods, (as described by Rittel, 1972) had by then withdrawn from such work, saying that the whole endeavor had been a terrible mistake. Christopher Alexander, for example, whose *Notes on the Synthesis of Form* (1964) had inspired the field, now wrote that design methods "prevent you from being in the right state of mind to do the design" (Alexander, 1971, p. 4).

J. Christopher Jones, another methodologist, whose book *Design Methods: Seeds of Human Futures* (1970) became a seminal text, now thought that

> the design process is one of devising and experiencing a process of rapid learning about something that does not yet exist by exploring the interdependencies of problem and solution, the new and the old.... To invent something new...is to change not only one's surroundings but to change oneself and the way one perceives. (p. 31)

Succinctly, what had happened to the foremost proponents of the field was the acceptance that the act of design was an intensely subjective process and that "objectifying" it through formal methodology did not guarantee better designs nor better designers.

Even Broadbent (1979), one of the field's most able apologists, recognized that design methodology's achievements are not to be measured in terms of "buildings built, cities designed, and so on" (p. 41).

Thus, so-called first generation design methods came to be replaced (in popularity) during the 1970s with "second generation" methods that emphasized participatory process in design. In these, various charette, group interaction, and modeling techniques were meant to erase the distinction between expert and client. The purpose of a method was no longer as a means of analysis by an expert but as an *aid* to a communication among equals in a shared design process.

Unfortunately, the product of a design process is neither legally, financially, nor technically everyone's responsibility. Clients may know what they want a design to do for them, but they rarely have substantive ideas about *how* the design is to fulfill their intentions for it. The expert designer is still necessary and still confronts the same problem complexity that induced design methods in the first place.

This has prompted the current trend toward yet a "third generation" of methods that Broadbent (1979) perceptively calls "the conjectures and refutations approach" (p. 44).

This approach is analogous to Karl Popper's (1963) views on the methodology of science. Designers, like scientists, begin with personal conjectures about the phenomena they seek to influence. It is their duty to submit these to a thorough sequence of tests that allows refutations to shape the subsequent form of the proposition—or the building. Because many of these tests can originate within clients or other involved groups, this approach is meant to preserve the sense of participation as well as ensuring the systematic development needed by the designer.

Third generation methods are partially enabled by high-technology interfaces. These can provide access to extensive rational data bases, the ability to confer in "real time" from different locations, and even "expert systems" guidance to help a designer through difficult technical considerations. In this third generation view, design becomes neither the province of a formal model nor a social plebiscite. It is a high-technology-assisted endeavor that relies on different analytical models and dialogues throughout the design process.

DECISION MAKING IN THE DESIGN PROCESS

From a decision-theoretic perspective, though, it is apparent that no single decision-making model is either inclusive or appropriate for the entire design process—no matter how systematically it is conceived. Rather, different decision-making processes arise, recede, or are recycled at subsequent stages in the delivery of a design end product. Any and all of these stages may be analyzed or aided by the techniques, models, or experimental results of modern decision theory. But formally and informally, design is a sequential process with many iterations and contingencies that shape the final result.

Contractually, a design process goes through a series of formally recognizable steps that are similar throughout industrialized nations.

- First, a general outline of requirements is prepared.
- Second, there is a general appraisal to ensure functional, technical, and financial feasibility.

Both of these may be subsumed under a process called *programming,* which is essentially a problem-seeking and problem definition phase. There are several popular (and competing) views about how this should proceed (see Pena, 1977; Sims, 1978; Wade, 1977).

- Third, schematic designs are proposed and developed to various levels of specificity.
- Fourth, one of these is chosen for design development.
- Fifth, the design is accepted, and working drawings are prepared to permit construction or manufacture. (Much detail design may also be deferred to this stage.)

Conceptually, this sequence demands from the designer a microcosm of all those capabilities of judgment, estimation, problem structuring, value assignment, and choice that describe human life as a whole. So, throughout this mélange of activities, there are ample opportunities for refinements along the route whereby a design idea becomes a designed form.

It is this particular mental transduction—that of goals, requirements, constraints, and preferences to physical form—that most concerns investigators. How is it accomplished? What sorts of information aid the designer, and in which format is it easiest to assimilate? Many studies have been done that either retrospectively or *in situ* examine this aspect of the design process. The results are intriguing but still incomplete.

Eastman (1968), in one of the earlier experimental studies of design activity, found that, surprisingly enough, physical aspects of proposed designs generated the perceived constraints. He had expected the constraints to generate the partial forms (what he called *design units*).

A decade later, Darke (1979) confirmed this apparent peculiarity in an interview study of seven architects, where she found that designers began with a proposed solution or conjecture, and then tested it against requirements that it suggested. There were no cases where requirements were analyzed in detail *first*. Instead, the initial "form" proposals seemed to be based on subjective values rather than explicit logical considerations.

In another interview and archival study of six English architectural firms, Wareh & Murta (1979) again found that principal ideas of the built form were conceived first, then checked against major constraints and utilized to refine an understanding of the constraints. The initial form proposal did not change substantially during design development. This seems to echo Lawson's (1971) earlier laboratory results that showed architectural students worked within a narrower range of solutions than is necessary. But this seemed to be a function of how they construed the design "problem." In this study, he made the distinction between *open* and *closed-ended* problem solving. The closed-ended problem is constrained, and the goal is specifically defined. The open-ended problem is ill defined or "wicked" (Rittel, 1969), and its formulation is not entirely separate from its solution.

In retrospect, it seems that this is the pivotal point about which so much controversy over design methods and design decision making turns.

There is a conceptual difference between design as an architect (or designer) thinks of it and design as an engineer thinks of it. As Lawson (1971, p. 88) states:

> Engineers are asked to satisfy physical performance specifications, and, working in a closed-ended way, they set out to design a bridge, a road, or a ventilation system. By contrast, a stage designer is only asked to produce atmosphere and *how he achieves it is entirely up to him* [emphasis added].

It seems that an architect first *closes* a problem by hypothesizing a spatial form. Then, she or he searches it for constraints to match against an intuitive understanding of the problem. But the problem has been mentally encoded in terms of the form itself, not in terms of what the form must do to "work." To designers, problems are not encoded and "closed" in terms of a set of distinct performance parameters or constraints as engineering problems are.

It is little wonder that design methods or decision-making aids have had little intuitive appeal to architects.

First, these techniques usually start with a closed problem as a given. In most of decision theory, for example, the alternative hypotheses, or action alternatives, are already identified. It is only then that the methodology "turns on" and moves toward selection as solution.

For an architect, a form is not analogous to a *solution*. It is analogous to a hypothesis. Design methods and decision aids that rely on "putting off" a generated form, in effect leave the architect in conceptual limbo. These techniques work inductively, the way a scientist proceeds when she or he develops a "data-driven" theory. But the architect wants to work deductively *after* proposing a built form as a sort of theory. Specifying probabilities, utilities, and parameter constraints for design ahead of time do very little (if anything) to help a designer generate a form. But, such specifications, if expressed operationally, do provide an explicit series of tests for a proposed form, once it is made.

There is no mystery why all the work in first generation design methods and design decision making did not result in any "new and significant types" of buildings. These efforts simply missed the form generation part of the design process that is so primary to design activity. They were mislabeled and misconstrued as parts of an inductive accumulation of *data* that should have eventually generated a form. But this is not the way that designers mentally work.

Second, most design methods and decision-making procedures work on a basis of alternative comparisons (Wise, 1977). The simplest decision is binary choice, and it assumes that there are two equally well-defined actions or hypotheses with regard to states of the world. But the designer does not work with a closed set of alternative forms that is analogous to a set of alternative choices. Instead, there is one form (or part thereof) that is successively manipulated as it is successively tested. The testing process is a process of resolution, of sequential focusing, that manifests a form "solution." To a scientist, it would be as if one were successively trying to resolve a good research hypothesis, *not* as if one were successively trying to decide among hypotheses.

So, from this point of view, there is little to be gained by placing an optimal decision process on top of a well-developed design proposal. The archietect/designer already knows how the design works in terms of the tests it has passed in its development. To make *another* design proposal in order to have a choice is antithetical to the whole effort. For once the problem is closed in terms of form proposal, that proposal sequentially evolves to the *best solution*.

If a scientist operated like a designer, she or he would evolve an insightful research hypothesis, and then use the experiment as a demonstration of its validity rather than as a test of it.

In the analogy between design method and scientific method, previous investigators have too often connected the wrong parts. A form solution is like a hypothesis, not like an experimental outcome. An experiment decides between alternative hypotheses, but a design emerges as a singular hypothesis for the situation.

Similarly, the entire process of decision analysis, with its emphasis on selection among alternatives, does not parallel the process of design synthesis, with its evolution of a unique product.

However, in closing an open-ended design problem, or in deriving a scientific hypothesis, it is questionable whether different processes may be at work. At least major theorists label these in subtly different ways.

For example, C. S. Peirce (as collected by Goudge, 1969), in his influential work on the philosophy of science, identifies two processes of reasoning that can add to the store of knowledge. One of these is *induction*, the other, *abduction*. The process of induction is familiar to anyone introduced to probability theory. Abduction, however, remains much more mysterious and (apparently) underutilized. Yet, according to Peirce, it is "the only kind of reasoning that supplies new ideas, the only kind which is, in this sense, synthetic"(p. 198).

Logically, abduction is a process of syllogistic reasoning where one premise is certain, the other uncertain, that together generate an uncertain conclusion—a hypothesis. Peirce sees this as the basis of scientific theorizing. By comparison, one of the most comprehensive design theories, developed by Wade (1977), proposes a very similar sounding process for closing ill-defined design problems to create a form hypothesis. In Wade's (1977) approach, an ill-defined design problem needs to be understood in three terms: the initial state, the goal (or desired) state, and the transformation process that connects the two. For the problem to be ready for solution, two of these three terms must be known. In preparation for this, "the problem statement is placed in a form where *adduction* can take place (Wade, 1977, p. 306). He describes adduction as the "derivation of a third term in a problem statement that is in logical relationship with the two already known terms." However, the *Random House Dictionary of the English Language* (Stein, 1981) defines adduction as "to cite as pertinent or relevant, to bring forward in support of"(p. 321).

So it seems that Wade (1977) is making his "adduction" fill the role of Peirce's "abduction." Despite the confusing terminology, it is an intriguing idea that the psychological process that generates a form hypothesis may be the same as that one that generates a symbolic hypothesis. In this case, the creative intuition of the designer is not substantively different from the creative intuition of the scientist.

It is the tools of the trade, the domains of application, and the professionally defined procedures that create the illusion of incompatible psychological descriptions. This equivalency was also explicitly proposed by Westcott (1968) on the basis of a general look at human intuition. It was also explicitly opposed by Steadman (1979), who argued that the nature and purpose of the two enterprises are fundamentally distinct. Design is concerned with making unique material objects to answer to specific purposes; while science is concerned with making statements about the characteristic behavior of general classes of objects of phenomena under given conditions, and defining the limits on these classes and this behavior. (p. 54)

Again, it seems that one is driven to different conclusions about method (that has a significant impact on possible decision-making aids) if one accepts either an internal "process view" or an external "performance view" of the activities that constitute inquiry in both design and science.

AIDING DESIGN DECISION MAKING

Besides the development of formal design methodologies and empirical inquiry into the design process, there have also been significant attempts to create explicit design decision aids. Some of these have been borrowed wholesale from contemporary decision theory, whereas others are the result of an independent, parallel development. Still others reflect designers' rich capability for visual thinking, and they offer a complementary view of decision making to that usually found in social science. This interplay of models from decision theory and design methodology has been extensively reviewed by Wise (1977; reprinted 1981). This section incorporates some of that literature, particularly when a model has shown subsequent maturation. However, the emphasis here is on design decision aids recently developed for that explicit purpose and on other innovative techniques that hold similar promise.

The fundamental distinction to be made between types of design decision aids is whether the technique operates within a closed or open problem formulation. In the first case, an aid either assists problem closure by being a structuring tool, or it can assist the iterative process of inference and evaluation once the problem is closed by some other means. In the second case, the aid can provide a systematic way of operating within the open problem formulation, deliberately using the ambiguity to create multiple perspectives on the situation. In practice, such multiple overlapping descriptions of the same phenomenon often seem to spontaneously generate their own creative solution.

Another way the aid can operate on an open problem is to iteratively derive partial solutions that become more satisfactory as their "misfits" are realized. The design stops when no further inadequacies can be found, even though this point meets no demonstrable optimality criterion. Again, most architects seem to intuitively operate this way, giving rise—at least from a decision-theoretic viewpoint—to the phenomenon of *decision delay* noted by Brill (1983).

The important distinction emphasized here is that design decision aids may have the same general goal—a final design—and yet look very different, depending upon how their originator defined the context of decision making.

Extrapolations from Contemporary Decision Theory

The single most ubiquitous application of a decision aid in design is the use of a linear evaluation model. This is any model of the general form:

$$U = \sum u_i(X_{ij})$$

where U is the total worth of an alternative, and u_i the partial utility or worth of an alternative as measured on a single dimension or attribute. This model says simply that a complex design may be decomposed in such a fashion so as to find the worths of its parts, which are then additively recombined to find the worth of the whole. The decomposition can be done either dimensionally or hierarchically, and there are examples of both throughout the design literature (see Grant, 1974).

The earliest appearance of a generalized approach in aggregating partial utilities to measure building performance seems due to Rittel and Musso (1967). They offered a model that allows a choice of linear, lexicographical, or exponential scoring rules!

Later, Archer's (1971) methodology for "technological innovation" became a detailed, independent re-creation of multiattribute utility theory (MAUT). It is nicely applied to the design of a suitcase by Smith and Archer (1973).

Heimsath (1977) has constructed what appears to be the framework of a hierarchical utility scheme that, like most other efforts, suffers from structural and measurement-theoretic ambiguities. In fact, when proposing evaluation models for design, there seems generally to have been a rather blissful ignorance about the measurement-theoretic properties of scales and their underlying axioms that actually allow one to meaningfully attach numbers to things. Wise (1978) offered an in-depth criticism of Grant's (1976) "alpha-beta model for decision making with multiple objective" on just such grounds. Grant's (1978) response was to call such arguments "idle theoretical speculations" and to maintain that his model is "esthetically and functionally superior to MAUT." The reader is invited to make his or her own comparisons between the two. A very readable review of decision analysis that includes MAUT theory and applications is provided by Keeney (1982).

In lieu of the problems encountered in environmental evaluation, I feel that the most difficult problem in applying *any* general disaggregated evaluation model lies in how the total design is decomposed or carved up to produce parts that have any right to valuewise independence. The best designs *are* the best designs because their partial physical and functional descriptions are richly interdependent. The obvious decompositional strategies (e.g., by rooms or areas in a building plan) totally ignore the relationships that carry most of the "added value" (after Archer, 1971) in a design. An example of a MAUT-type hierarchical decomposition to evaluate proposed improvements to park design is provided by

Beach and Barnes (1983). They decomposed parks along the different kinds of activities the different parks supported rather than along strict descriptions according to physical scale or amenity.

Perhaps the most significant recent contribution to the evaluation of design performance has been Saaty's (1980) "analytic hierarchy process" (AHP). Firmly grounded in measurement theory, this approach derives a scale of relative priorities at different levels of a problem by computing the eigenvector of a pairwise comparison matrix. The matrix is composed of ratios of preferences, cost, judged contributions of effectiveness, satisfaction, or whatever. But each entry in the matrix tells how much more one entity at that hierarchical level either contributes or is worth compared to another entity at the same level. By multiplying priorities *up* branches of the hierarchy, one can derive a measure of how each system, subsystem, or component attribute contributes to the worth of the total system performance. This looks superficially similar to Sayeki's (1972) procedures for handling hierarchical utilities, but it is built on a totally different basis than is utility theory and is more akin to extracting the first principal component in factor analysis. The priorities are also given a ratio rather than an interval scale.

Lera (1981) has performed an interesting study that used AHP to investigate designer's values and the evaluation of their designs. The AHP was used to derive priorities for subjective-valued attributes that architects used to create school designs. Neither their attributes nor their priorities changed after each had developed a sketch plan. Architects evidently had a "fixed view of priorities, and knew the major trade-off" (Lera, 1981, p. 135). Among the six architects, there were demonstrable differences in value attributes and their prioritization that accounted for major differences in the plan proposals. For each architect, there was also a close correspondence between their wholistic prioritization of all six designs and a merit index that combined partial prioritizations of each attribute in a particular school plan with its relative importance for the success of the school.

From these results, AHP might seem to be an ideal tool for aiding the evaluation processes of architectural juries or for making a systematic appraisal of a building design as it is developed. However, where other methods are available for quantifying judgments, such as weights in additive utility models, AHP may not be the appropriate choice.

Schoemaker and Waid (1982) have experimentally compared five such approaches and found that AHP performed poorly in predicting subjects' binary preferences, which may reflect a general judgmental ambiguity regarding assignments of relative importance.

Wise and Alden (1976) have argued earlier for and presented a MAUT approach to architectural jury awards. Saaty and Erdener (1979) have provided an example of the AHP in prioritizing building performance.

As mentioned earlier, designers tend to be strong visual thinkers, and this predisposition often leads them to construct geometric analogs of the evaluation models that decision theorists use. Laseau (1975) has published one of these, but variants on this theme may be found in almost any larger architectural firm that exercises a "quality assurance" program for its work. Superficially, the scheme looks like a pictorial MAUT model, but there are some important operational differences.

First, somewhere between four to seven dimensions are selected to characterize the performance of a design. These might be constructs like *flexibility, use of space, aesthetic appeal, complexity of construction*, and so forth. Then, these dimensions are represented as the equal-spaced axes of a coordinate system (see Figure 1).

Each axis is then numbered in equal increments, say from 1 to 5, depending on the degree of discrimination desired in the evaluation. The larger number indicates greater worth for a design on a dimension.

Following this setup, the evaluator then rates a design on each dimension by placing a point at the number value that best represents the design's achievement in that dimension's terms. These points are then connected to create a polygon (Figure 2).

With competing design proposals, the *areas* of the polygons are then visually compared, and the proposal with the larger area is selected. From the way this evaluation method is presented and used in practice, it is obviously meant as a graphic analog to the algebraic method that MAUT provides. But are the two isomorphic?

First, graphic dimensions may be defined to be valuewise independent as in MAUT (although I have never seen any graphic evaluation aid contain instructions on this point.

Second, the graphic dimensions *could be* differentially weighted, as with MAUT, if the integer hash marks on different dimensions were placed at differing intervals apart from each other. This would have the same effect as a positive multiplier on a dimension.

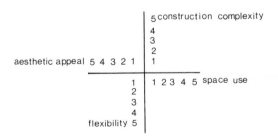

Figure 1. A framework for graphic evaluation.

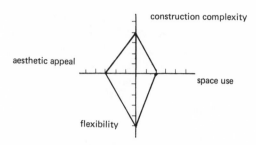

Figure 2. An evaluation polygon for a design proposal.

So, superficially at least, the analogy is borne out. However, it is in the aggregation rule that this correspondence breaks down. Imagine a design proposal evaluated in terms of four equally weighted dimensions and that it has equal values (say 5) on each dimension. Then the diagonal of the square is 10, and the area is 50. If the dimensional values are uniformly decreased by integers, the area (and aggregate value) diminishes to 32, 18, and 8. In this scheme, equal differences on dimensional evaluations do not result in equal differences in the aggregate evaluation. This is the result of using the *area* of the polygon, which introduces a square transformation. Practically, this means that if one has two very good design proposals, they will look, in terms of this model, to be quite different in their respective total worths. Poor proposals, on the other hand, will look very similar. Of course, this is exactly what one does not want to happen, particularly if a choice among proposals implies allocation of future development funds.

There is also another, more subtle distinction that separates such a graphic model from its algebraic counterpart. This can be expressed in terms of the invariance characteristics of the model. For example, a MAUT model with its linear aggregation rule allows one to add up the partial evaluations *in whatever order one pleases*. It makes no difference *how* the dimensions are ordered in the summing process. But such dimensional-labeling invariance is not preserved with a model like Laseau's (1975). Depending on how one labels the original axes, the resulting polygon may have substantially variable areas, as the following sketches show.

With the same dimensional values, these polygons give wildly different impressions of the overall worth of a proposal. But an evaluation method should not be sensitive to such a clearly irrelevant action.

The notion of examining design decision aids by looking at the implied model invariances also helps resolve an older argument in the design methods literature, over whether graphical overlay techniques are really MAUT-type models with unspecified weightings.

Alexander (1966) rejected numerical methods like MAUT on the basis that

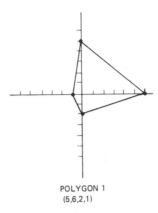

POLYGON 1
(5,6,2,1)

Figure 3. An evaluation polygon with numerical values.

these are limited to maximizing a one-dimensional numerical variable (such as expected utility) that he felt was insufficient to capture the diversity within a designed system. Instead, he proposed *relational methods* that seek to identify and interact "forces" with no restriction on their variety. If one can represent the physical expression every force is seeking and then combine these, one might be able to successfully generate a physical form. Thus, the relational method becomes more synthetic than it is analytical. It works by successively interacting graphic analogs of forces until a stable (satisfactory?) one emerges.

Alexander and Mannheim (1962) have used this procedure to address a highway route selection problem. Here they represented 26 forces such as comfort and safety, user costs, noise, air pollution, drainage patterns, obsolescence, eyesores, weather effects, and the like on clear overlays that were placed on a

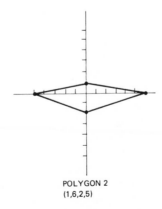

POLYGON 2
(1,6,2,5)

Figure 4. The same evaluation polygon as Figure 3, with a flip of two adjacent axes.

regional map where the highway was to be. The overlays were "grayed" where the map locations would be favorable in terms of each particular force. Then subsets of the overlays were successively "fused" where their grays overlapped—meaning that the respective forces were "seeking" the same form expression. Finally, a sinuous curving dark line could be placed on the regional map, which represented the highway route that had emerged from the interacting forces.

In the intervening years, graphical overlay techniques of this type have become quite popular in landscape planning (see McHarg, 1969). Grant (1974), however, has criticized this methodology for actually being an unspecified numerical weighting scheme but with accidentally varying importance weights. In other words, the so-called relational method is nothing more than a graphic analog of a numeric method like MAUT, albeit with ambiguous values.

Again, looking at the two models in terms of their invariance features shows that this is not the case. Partial utilities may be aggregated in any order with MAUT, but the fusion process described by Alexander and Mannheim (1962) quite clearly demands a specific order if an intelligible result is to be obtained. This relational method is very sensitive to differences in combinations of the overlays that are to be fused on an intermediate basis.

Interestingly enough, although graphic overlays are proposed as a method that does not restrict variety, it would seem that a design problem must be at least tightly closed in order to use them. In retrospect, such graphical methods seem limited to those cases where one can specify ahead of time *what* the final form is to be. For example, I am unaware of any successful application of graphical overlays to a three-dimensional form, such as a building or product design, whereas a highway can always *a priori* be specified as a curving, unbroken line on a map. Still, the notion that with aids one can systematically and progressively work toward a design that resolves a set of qualitatively different criteria is an intriguing goal to pursue. Some tentative ideas toward this end are presented in the last section of this chapter.

In constructing design decision aids, then, methodologists have used decision-theoretic models, attempted graphic analogs of them, and even devised schemes that deliberately avoid such explicit formulation. Most all of these involve comparative evaluations of one sort or another, even though this seems to be one of the less frequently occurring opportunities in design activity. Designers would rather successively develop a single scheme than contiguously develop two or more to a point of comparative evaluation.

Though designers do much more than evaluation activity, curiously, there have been few or no attempts at all to borrow other judgment or inference aids from decision theory. For example, Wise (1983) has argued for the use of Bayesian statistics as an aid to preliminary site planning. In his example, possible tenants' preferences for sizes of units in a proposed condominium development were used to revise the project developer's prior distribution of unit mix. Clearly, where architectural judgments require estimations of preferred size, number of bedrooms, or other design parameters, a Bayesian information-processing aid would be helpful. Particularly if there were competing opinions, the analyst could then work from the "priors" of the different parties and demonstrate how their respective positions ought to converge in the light of new information.

Additionally, the taint of subjectivism that has so perniciously and extensively hampered acceptance of Bayesian statistics in empirical science should prove to be an asset in design applications. Design professionals often seem to prefer subjective estimates to numbers derived from other sources because they feel that each design problem is unique and requires the input of personal, professional experience.

Another potential source of design decision aids that is even more suitable from a theoretic view is possibility theory (Yager, 1979), which is based on Zadeh's (1978) fuzzy sets. Certainly, the sort of measure information available to design efforts is often only ordinal at best, which can make the calculation of probabilities either spurious or irrelevant.

Possibility theory only requires ordinal information, in contrast to the cardinal information needed to construct a probability distribution, so the implication is that one ought to be able to use possibility theory under much more ambiguous circumstances.

Possibility theory may be used to make possibilistic evaluations among alternatives and to aid decisions that are well structured in terms of available options. None of the manipulations require arithmetic operation, and the possibilistic criterion is analogous to maximizing expected utility.

I feel that, although theoretically possibility theory more closely simulates situations of design decision making, it practically confers little or no advantage over the more demanding procedures of decision analysis. This is because, in design, decisions are attached to real world expenditures of money, and it is very easy for an architect or client to compute differences in costs. Will a certain design change that brings an increase in privacy around units be worth the extra $2.38/\text{ft}^2$? Will expanding the available views from interior spaces be worth the extra construction and maintenance costs? To answer questions like these, the designer must either act *as if* she or he has cardinal information, even if none is currently available, or proceed to find such information.

Decision analysis (including Bayesian statistics) is valuable in these situations because it only requires that subjective worth (utility) or degree of belief (probability) meet the cardinality requirements, regardless of the ambiguity in the real world. If one can act consistently at a higher level of metric structure in a situation that will eventually demand an accounting at that level or above, then, as a decision maker, one should do so, despite local ambiguity.

Another technique that seems promising as a source of design decision aids is one that is based on the notion of *proximity metrics*. A proximity metric defines a measure of the distance of a possible solution from an *a priori* defined ideal. It is relevant to design because designers often have general predilections about ideal forms and solution stereotypes (Hawkes, 1976). In this sense, a design decision process becomes a way of progressively leading one incrementally closer to a preestablished, ideal, formal goal.

Roy (1978) discusses three metrics that provide a means of ranking potential or alternative design solutions. These are in Minkowski, entropy, and quadratic forms.

The Minkowski metric is most common. Its general form is

$$D = \left[\sum_{i=1}^{n} |z_i - z_i^0|^r \right]^{1/r}$$

where z_i^0 is the ideal. When $r=2$, this becomes the familiar metric of Euclidean space. Continuing this analogy, the further away a solution point would be from an ideal point in the Euclidean space, the less successful the solution. Quadratic metrics are similarly analogous but with a biasing on each of the spatial dimensions.

The conventional form of an entropy measure is

$$S = - \sum_{i=1}^{n} p_i \ln p_i$$

where S is a measure of uncertainty associated with a distribution of probabilities, p_i. To determine the proximity of any solution to an ideal, the entropy metric is defined as

$$S = 1.0 + (\ln n)^{-1} \sum_{i=1}^{n} q_i \ln q_i$$

Here, q_i is a measure of the relative performance of an alternative on each objective, as a proportion of the performance exhibited by the ideal solution on that objective. This proximity metric gives S a range from $0 \rightarrow 1$, and is zero when every $q_i = 1/n$ and 1.0 when one $q_i = 1.0$, with the remainder zero.

These metrics behave very differently with respect to their ranking of successive, or alternative solutions. The entropy metric has a zero slope near the ideal, and so offers little discrimination as one approaches this point. It also ranks all extreme solutions equally, no matter how close one may be in an Euclidean sense. The Minkowski and quadratic forms are discontinuous at the ideal point, and provide a fine discrimination among closely competing solutions. None of the metrics, however, allow for trade-offs to be made among objectives.

It seems that proximity metrics would be most useful in computer-assisted design work, where the designer could make rapid changes and then immediately see how these affected overall progress toward a design goal. When a design has many performance objectives, it may not be possible to keep all of these in one's mind as design parameters are varied. Roy (1980) has provided just such an example in terms of an engine design problem.

Comparing proximity metrics to an aggregate utility measure shows them to be more a way of *satisficing* than *optimizing* a solution. A design ideal is first defined that will *satisfy* a designer's set of values or preferences, but this ideal is in no way constrained to be optimal. If the designer's goal is to be concerned more with the distribution of utility than its sum, proximity metrics also provide a direct measure—although so do partial utilities in MAUT. Proximity metrics have an obvious geometric interpretation, which should appeal to visual thinkers. Unfortunately, beyond two objectives (dimensions), this analogy does not lend itself to paper-and-pencil jottings. In truly complex design decision problems, the greatest shortcoming of proximity metrics seems to lie in their inability to expeditiously handle trade-offs.

Most design development is a process of giving up performance of one sort to acquire more of another. The idea of a common measure of worth (utility) remains the preeminent means of operationalizing this process. Still, especially for *in situ*, parallel evaluations of computer-assisted designs, proximity metrics offer significant potential as a decision-making aid.

As mentioned earlier, traditional decision theory has usually had very little to say about the process of generating alternatives, as opposed to the process of comparing them. This has been somewhat abetted recently by major studies that examined the hypothesis generation and structuring stages of decision making. The work of Gettys, Manning, Mehle, and Fisher (1980) is most extensive.

Gettys *et al.* (1980) have described 14 experiments on generating hypotheses (functionally equal to design alternatives). They found that hypothesis retrieval from memory is not complete in terms of considering all possibilities. Hypotheses that were generated represented about one-eighth or less of those available. These hypotheses were first checked for logical consistency with data and often were reassessed for plausibility as more data arrived. Misfits, or disconfirming data, generated additional hypotheses more often than confirming data. Subjects also seemed to be "blind to certain classes of hypotheses" (p. 26) when interpretations of the data bias them strongly toward one cognitive schema. This is a well-substantiated phenomenon in the cognitive literature (see Tversky & Kahneman, 1981) and has analogs in other studies of predecisional search (Klayman, 1982).

Gettys *et al.* (1980) conclude that an artificial memory aid may well be the single most important source of additional hypotheses. Prosaically, physicians' references and mechanics' maintenance manuals fulfill this same role. So do the more recent expert systems (Duda & Shortliffe, 1983), although these also provide structural, inferential, and evaluative assists.

The conclusion of Gettys *et al.* (1980) echoes that of Alexander (1982) who investigated how policies were designed. Again, he found that "heuristic search is probably the most common aid to design decision making and policy analysis today" (p. 287). He also feels that superior heuristic search strategies may be indispensable ingredients of creativity.

But designers and policymakers are *unlike* doctors and mechanics in that they want their solutions (designs and policies) to be not only practical but innovative. A creative design does not only work; it is also original. So a reference handbook would be of different value to a designer and physician. The designer would want to use it to generate a solution but then alter this substantially so that at least it does not look like a textbook case.

In this sense, then, another effective aid to heuristic search for designers would be a technique that systematically forces the generation of different solution hypotheses by exhaustively recombining diagnostic aspects of the problem. The most famous of these is the "morphological box" developed by the astronomer Fritz Zwicky (1969) and enthusiastically proposed for designers by Grant (1977), who provides an extensive example and bibliography.

The morphological box is a systematic way of exploring all the possible combinations of design parameters, or factors of a problem. It requires the user to specify the factors and then lay them out so that all possible combinations are generated. The general morphology of all possible elements across all factors forms a lattice structure, which may then be sequentially explored and ordered on different indices.

Thus, the Zwicky Box generates by a process of unlikely combinations. In this way, it is a modern counterpart of the concentric, movable rings used by the 13th-century Spanish mystic, Ramon Lull, to discover all the knowledge of the universe.

Contemporary goals for this method are set somewhat lower. The "morphological box" does produce a thorough, unbiased search. This search, however, is based on the factors and elements within the box. If the designer has used unaided memory to establish these, the box will certainly be an impoverished one. In this sense, it is no better than the human knowledge base it taps. Also, depending on the constituents of the box, it may, for designers, put the intuitive cart before its horse.

Remember that designers treat forms as hypotheses, and so forms come first. If one constructs a morphological box with performance attributes, then after all this work a designer must still start over to find a form that meets its requirements. If conversely, forms are immediately placed into the box (such as different roof or plan strategies), then the designer has little basis for restricting the possible morphologies in terms of what they are supposed to do. There is also no rationale (beyond intuition) for the initial selection of elements to construct the box.

So, to use a morphological box, the design problem must be "closed," and the designer must have a satisfactory degree of knowledge and skill to at least know, on each factor level, what the possibilities are. Once in place, the combinations have a way of rapidly overwhelming the user if some reduction tactics are not followed. Five factors with two elements in each gives $5^2 = 25$ morphologies. If this is raised to five elements in each, there are now 5^5 or 3,125 combinations to explore. This is creativity without selectivity, completeness minus finesse. But as a heuristic search, it has useful applications and fills much the same sort of role as a decision tree, only without the tree's ability to incorporate constraints.

Another graphical hypothesis aid that is more concerned with structure than generation is the *influence diagram*. This concept was developed by Howard and Matheson (1980) as a conceptual and communication tool that helps bridge between qualitative and quantitative experience. It uses nodes and arrows to describe formal relations in a problem structure, and in this sense it bears a close similarity to graph theory. In fact an influence diagram is a directed graph that has no loops. It represents both decision nodes and chance nodes, connected by arrows depicting either informational influences or conditioning influences. The former indicate variables known by a decision maker; the latter, variables on which chance is conditioned.

An influence diagram may be turned into a decision tree if there is a complete ordering of decision nodes and if each decision node and its direct predecessors directly influence all successive decisions nodes.

If designers used decision trees in their analyses, then influence diagrams would be a useful tool to help impose this powerful sort of structure. Designers do use their own sort of visual analog, called *bubble diagrams*, which also try to group parts of the design problem into nodes and show their interconnections. But the rules for the manipulation of bubble diagrams are nowhere near as explicit as those for influence diagrams, and the transform from a bubble diagram to a plan is correspondingly less clear than for an influence diagram to a tree.

By working within a loose visualization without well-defined rules, the designer is at a disadvantage when it becomes necessary to proceed to the next, more structured stage of analysis. Decision theorists have started to learn the value of visual representations as an assist to predecisional structuring. Designers have yet to learn the value of applying operational rules to the visualizations that they perform so naturally. It seems that good decision making, design or otherwise, is abetted in its early stages by both visual and symbolic means. A designer/decision maker must not only "see" a problem to represent it but also operate on that visual representation with explicit logical principles in order to derive its full implications for the work to come.

Methodologies for "Open" Problems in Design

A design problem is open if it has no definitive formulation, no stopping rule, and no absolute, unique solution (Bazjanac, 1974). Because decision theory begins with a list of alternative actions and works to maximize expected utility, the choice problem is already closed and misses the essence of the designer's predicament.

Outside decision theory, there have been attempts to wrestle with the ambiguity of open problems as they occur in the design of buildings, policies, and computer software. Each of these application areas confronts the characteristics described previously, and each of them has derived an appropriate response. Collectively, they begin to describe what a generic methodology to open problems might resemble.

In architecture, Alexander (1977) has made the boldest statement with his *A Pattern Language*, which is a sourcebook of both theory and practice on "right" design.

The pattern language consists of 253 form relationships that are meant to express essential rules for solving spatial problems. Each pattern is in the form of an if-then statement. Example:

> If: The front door of any dwelling. Then: Walls inside the main door so placed that a person standing on the doorstep, with the door open, cannot see into any room, especially the living room or kitchen, nor to any passage connecting rooms. (Alexander & Poyner, 1973, p. 321).

In the text, the authors go on to express the set of privacy norms and social expectations that underlie this strong spatial pattern recommendation. The text (Alexander, 1977) extends these patterns to a wide variety of generic building circumstances, so that designers, when confronted with the relationships, may adapt the pattern to their own preferences. The idea is that the patterns provide the structuring necessary to "close" a design problem.

Pattern language has been criticized (Protzen, 1978), mostly for overstepping its intentions. Many patterns make quite explicit form recommendations, such as *vaulted ceiling* or *window seats* when a designer actually would have a variety of means to satisfy the underlying relations in other ways. The pattern language closes a design problem by decomposing it into smaller sets of relations that proscribe a clear spatial pattern. Then the patterns are embedded at different levels of scale to synthesize the design.

Pattern language is thus like the inferential rules, evidence, and expert opinions that construct an expert system. It is a nonautomated version of what cognitive scientists are providing through software engineering.

To me, pattern language's major defect is that it cannot decide whether to be a form or a performance manual. If "form follows function," then an explicit description of performance requirements for frequently encountered spatial arrangements would be plainly valuable. But by following the designer's practice of making built form itself a hypothesis, the pattern language becomes overly restrictive. The fault seems to lie in a basic difference over what the invariant elements of a design pattern are to be. Pattern language sees these as the spatial forms themselves. They may be more rightly viewed as a performance invariance—that is, what different spatial forms would be always expected *to do*.

The proposed software designer's analog to architect's patterns is a tool called *computational theorizing*, which was introduced by Partridge (1981). Computational theorizing is an iterative process of interacting with models in the form of computer programs. The idea is to attack a wicked problem by proposing partial formulations and to let the computer both keep track and transform these through informed guessing. The programmer and computer, together, work through successive reformulations that iteratively derive an adequate solution—apparently on the basis of being unable to find further misfits. The process is fundamentally nonsequential and relies greatly on "top-down" design, where the wicked part of the wicked problem is progressively stabilized or boxed in.

Computational theorizing is thus a high-tech version of thrashing things out, where the software designer has available a set of heuristic programs and subroutines (like the architect's patterns) that may be called up as needed. As with patterns, it works by taking preestablished ordering elements and progressively elaborating and expanding upon these to impose structure as a whole. There is no guarantee of optimality, except in constrained areas of the total problem.

Once in place, a policy may be seen as a "decision avoidance" tool because it avoids distinctions among the cases it encounters. However, the policy had to be designed in the first place. Policy designers, like those of buildings or computer programs, have also developed their own responses to open or wicked problems. One of the most successful of these is the *scenario planning* procedure developed by Pierre Wack (Lorenz, 1980) at Shell Oil.

Scenario planning works on the assumption that single-line forecasts are intellectual swindles. It deliberately provokes the planning group to present managers with sharply contrasting scenarios of the future. Taken together, these constitute a picture of what *could* happen rather than a guess of what *will* happen. Managerial plans and policies are subsequently made so as to be resilient to the range of scenario possibilities, or at least formulated so as to be rapidly modified if necessary.

A similar scheme of deliberately structuring an ambiguous situation through the widest possible set of different perspectives has been called *the multiple perspective concept* by Linstone (1981). In this application, a planning or assessment analyst develops three complementary perspective inquiries on a problem. These are called the *organizational* perspective, the *technological* perspective, and the *personal* perspective. Each of these responds to a different set of values and ways of encoding the world.

The technological perspective is highly formalistic, quantitative in nature, and reductionist in its use of models. The organizational perspective aims to understand a problem in the sense that professional experience or a procedural manual does. There are established practices to be followed, no matter what, and analytical tools are eschewed as untrustworthy. The personal perspective is guided by appeal to intuition, aesthetics, charisma, and self-interest. It reflects the irrational, the instinctual, and the emotional aspects that constitute feelings about situations.

Linstone (1981) argues that all three of these belong in the processes of human affairs—from the design of policies and technology assessments to new products. Together, they allow an understanding of design consequences that is sensed as much as it is formulated. If "the heart has its reasons that the reason does not know," then the answer is to include both in one's attempts to confront and respond to the world. The organizational, technological, and personal perspectives are meant to capture the peculiarities in the breadth of human concerns and world views that so often frustrate attempts to design or plan from an objective point of view.

Rochat (1981) has recently analyzed barriers to the application of decision aids in the public sector. The difficulties he describes clearly arise from conflicts between the organizational, technological, and personal perspectives. Because each of these perspectives acts to "close" a problem in its own unique way, then just as with scenario planning, it would seem to be only prudent to include the different perspectives in a design process. From this technologist's viewpoint, it is only unfortunate that there seems to be no systematic way to ensure such attitudinal diversity in a single person nor maintain it in a working group. Multiple perspectives, like multiple scenarios, need to be embedded in an ecology that respects their worth.

CONCLUSIONS

The results of this survey and review of design decision processes reinforce those of earlier laboratory and field studies. Design is a complex, iterative procedure that takes place in many professional contexts, with tools that are analogically similar. The designer may begin with some vaguely realized ideal and then subdivide the overall problem into nested hierarchies of parts. This stimulates a succession of synthesis and search cycles that incrementally narrows and focuses the design. *Analysis* and *synthesis*, as emphasized by Akin (1979), are present in all of these phases, so that some parts of the design solution crystallize early and emerge well before others. Thus, as Mintzberg, Raisinghani, and Theoret (1976) have so aptly described it, "The designers grope along, building their solution brick by brick without really knowing what it will look like until it is completed" (p. 256). The design process is an "emergent decision process" (Beach & Wise, 1980) that bears little resemblance to the textbook problems of the decision analyst.

But within the design process, there are cycles of evaluation and inference that could well benefit from decision-theoretic tools. The visual analogs of the designer are inappropriate to the task, erecting only a formal facade before what are otherwise intuitive, wholistic,and often haphazard judgments. That decision-theoretic tools have not been used seems due both to the affinity for visual thinking in the designer and the focus on choices among alternatives in the decision theorist. Nothing that is truly designed is decomposable through the strict algorithmic sequence of a decision tree. Parts may be so described, but the design as a whole often owes as much to metaphor as it does to mathematics. Excesses in either of these, or in the political context of design, are what produce the all too frequent nefarious result. In successful design, the organizational, technological, and personal perspectives are complementarily present.

Today, on the threshold of both decision analysis and design practice, stands the formidable challenge of building "decision support systems" (Alter, 1980; Sage & Lagomasino, 1982). These attempt to incorporate all of the data bases, inferential rules, and information-processing heuristics into a coherent whole that supports and enfolds human decision makers rather than replacing or automating them.

This is a next, natural, evolutionary step for methodolgies that have painstakingly found their own individual bounds. For the designer, who already has computer-assisted drafting, these systems may well become the vehicle that brings decision theory into design in the form that it is needed most—at the service rather than the replacement of the designers themselves. A visual design consultant system of this sort has already been constructed (Roach, Pillman, Reilly, & Savarese, 1982) as a first step. Other substantive aspects of design performance are even more amenable to such a technological assist.

This chapter started with a quote from the poet John Ciardi; one that no doubt seemed somewhat enigmatic to most decision theorists—"A poem is a machine for making choices."

The history of attempts to model or aid decision processes in design reveal the distinction behind this observation. Poems are verbal, sequentially experienced designs. Poems, like designs, are built via a much simpler system of generating factors that perform in surprising and gratifying ways.

Most attempts to improve design decisions have acted as if one were to improve poems by recourse to a rhyming dictionary. They have missed the essential point that decision making in design is an evocative, emergent process wherein a "choice point" hardly ever occurs in an isolated fashion. When decision models can help make design decisions in the way that poems help make choices, this difference will have been resolved in a manner that befits both endeavors.

REFERENCES

Akins, O. (1979). Exploration of the design process. *Design Methods and Theories, 13,* 115–119.
Alexander, C. (1964). *Notes on the synthesis of form.* Cambridge, MA: Harvard University Press.

Alexander, C. (1966). From a set of forces to a form. In G. Kepes (Ed.), *The man-made object.* New York: George Braziller.

Alexander, C. (1971, March). The state of the art in design methodology. *DMG Newsletter,* 3–7.

Alexander, C. (1977). *A pattern language: Towns, buildings, construction.* New York: Oxford University Press.

Alexander, E. R. (1982). Design in the decision-making process. *Policy Sciences, 14,* 279–292.

Alexander, C., & Mannheim, M. (1962). *The use of diagrams in highway route location* (Research Report R-62-3, Civil Engineering Systems Laboratory). Cambridge M.I.T. Press.

Alexander, C., & Poyner, B. (1973). The atoms of environmental structure. In G. T. Moore (Ed.), *Emerging methods in design and planning.* Cambridge.

Alter, S. (1980). *Decision support systems.* Reading, MA: Addison-Wesley.

Archer, L. B. (1971). *Technological innovation: A methodology.* Surrey: Interlink.

Bazjanac, V. (1974). Architectural design theory: Models of the design process. In W. R. Spillers (Ed.), *Basic questions of design theory.* Amsterdam: North Holland.

Beach, L. R., & Barnes, V. (1983). Approximate measurement in a multiattribute utility context. *Organizational Behavior and Human Performance, 32,* 417–424.

Beach, L. R., & Wise, J. A. (1980). Decision emergence: A Lewinian perspective. *Acta Psychologica, 45,* 343–356.

Brill, M. (1983). Everyman as designer. *Industrial Design Magazine, 30*(1), 18–19.

Broadbent, G. (1979). The development of design methods—A review. *Design Methods and Theories, 13*(1), 41–45.

Darke, J. (1979). The primary generator and the design process. *Design Studies, 1,* 36–44.

Duda, R. O., & Shortliffe, E. H. (1983). Expert systems research. *Science, 220,* 261–268.

Eastman, E. (1968). *Explorations in the cognitive processes in design.* Pittsburgh: Carnegie-Mellon University.

Gettys, C. F., Manning, C., Mehle, T., & Fisher, S. (1980). *Hypothesis generation: A final report of three years of research* (TR 15-10-80, University of Oklahoma). Norman, OK: Decision Processes Laboratory.

Goudge, T. A. (1969). *The thoughts of C. S. Peirce.* New York: Dover.

Grant, D. P. (1974). The problem of weighting. *DMG/DRS Journal, 8,* 136–141.

Grant, D. P. (1976). How to use an alpha-beta model for decision making with multiple objectives. *Design Methods and Theories, 10,* 200–211.

Grant, D. P. (1977). How to construct a morphological box. *Design Methods and Theories, 11,* 129–158.

Grant, D. P. (1978). Response to James A. Wise's critical reply to the "alpha-beta" model for decision making. *Design Methods and Theories, 12,* 44–45.

Gregory, S. A. (1966). *The design method.* London: Butterworth.

Gregory, S. A. (1977). Towards design science: Review of twenty years. In W. Gasparksi (Ed.), *Naukao Projektowania.* Warsaw: Polish National Academy of Sciences Press.

Hawkes, D. (1976). Types, norms, and habit in environmental design. In L. March (Ed.), *The architecture of form.* Cambridge: Cambridge University Press.

Heimsath, C. (1977). *Behavioral architecture.* New York: McGraw-Hill.

Howard, R. A., & Matheson, J. E. (1980). *Influence diagrams.* Menlo Park, CA: SRI International.

Jones, J. C. (1970). *Design methods: Seeds of human futures.* London: Wiley.

Jones, J. C. (1979). Designing designing. *Design Studies, 1,* 31–35.

Keeney, R. (1982). *Decision analysis: State of the field* (Technical Report No. 82-2). San Francisco: Woodward Clyde Consultants.

Klayman, J. (1982). Analysis of predecisional information search patterns. In P. C. Humphreys, O. Svenson, & A. Vari (Eds.), *Analysing and aiding decision processes.* Amsterdam: North Holland.

Laseau, P. (1975). *Graphic problem solving*. Boston: Cahners Books International.

Lawson, B. (1971, September). Open and closed ended problem solving in design. In B. Honikman (Ed.), *Proceedings of the Architectural Psychology Conference at Kingston Polytechnic*. London: Kingston Polytechnic and RIBA Publications.

Lera, S. G. (1981). Architectural designers' values and the evaluations of their designs. *Design Studies, 2*, 131–137.

Linstone, H. (1981). *The multiple perspective concept*. Portland, OR: Futures Research Institute.

Lorenz, C. (1980, May). Shell strikes a refined way of exploring the future. *Financial Times*, p. 13.

McHarg, I. (1969). *Design with nature*. New York: Natural History Press.

Mintzberg, H., Raisinghani, D., & Theoret, A. (1976). The structure of unstructured decision processes. *Administrative Science Quarterly, 21*, 246–275.

Partridge, D. (1981). "Computational theorizing" as a tool for resolving wicked problems. *IEEE Transactions on Systems, Man and Cybernetics, 11*, 318–321.

Pena, W. M. (1977). *Problem seeking*. Glenview, IL: Cahners Book International.

Popper, K. (1963). *Conjectures and refutations*. London: Routledge & Kegan Paul.

Protzen, J. P. (1978). The poverty of the pattern language. *Design Methods and Theories, 12*, 191–194.

Rittel, H. (1969, February). *Reflections on the scientific and political significance of decision theory* (Working paper #115). Berkeley: University of California Press.

Rittel, H. (1972, January). Interview with D. Grant and J. Protzen. In *Design Methods Group: Fifth Anniversary Report* (DMG Occasional paper, #1).

Rittel, H., & Musso, A. (1967). *Measuring the performance of buildings*. Unpublished manuscript. St. Louis: Washington University.

Roach, J., Pittman, J. A., Reilly, S., & Savarese, J. (1982). A visual design consultant. *Proceedings of the 1982 IEEE International Conference on Cybernetics and Society* (pp. 189–193). Piscataway, NJ: IEEE Service Center.

Rochat, J. C. (1981). Some remarks on the application of decision aids in the public sector. *European Journal of Operational Research, 7*, 191–195.

Roy, G. G. (1978). *Proximity metrics for multiobjective decision problems*. (Tech. Rep.) Nedlands, Western Australia: University of Western Australia, School of Architecture.

Roy, G. G. (1980). A man–machine approach to multicriteria decision making. *International Journal of Man-Machine Studies, 12*, 203–215.

Saaty, T. L. (1980). *The analytical hierarchy process*. New York: McGraw-Hill.

Saaty, T. L., & Erdener, E. (1979). A new approach to performance measurement: The analytic hierarchy process. *Design Methods and Theories, 13*, 64–72.

Sage, A. P., & Lagomasino, A. (1982). Knowledge representation and interpretation in decision support systems. *Proceddings of the 1982 IEEE International Conference on Cybernetics and Society* (pp. 658–662). Piscataway, NJ: IEEE Service Center.

Sayeki, Y. (1972). Allocation of importance, an axiom system. *Journal of Mathematical Psychology, 9*, 55–65.

Schoemaker, P., & Waid, C. (1982). An experimental comparison of different approaches to determining the weights in additive utility models. *Management Science, 28*, 182–196.

Sims, W. (1978). Programming environments for human use: A look at some emerging approaches to generating user oriented design requirements. In W. E. Rogers & W. H. Ittleson (Eds.), *Proceedings of EDRA 9*. Washington DC: EDRA.

Smith, G. & Archer, L. B. (1973). *A methodology for consumer design* (Tech. Rep.). Columbus, OH: Ohio State University, Department of Systems and Industrial Engineering.

Steadman, P. (1979). The history and science of the artificial. *Design Studies, 1*, 49–58.

Stein, J. (Ed.). (1981). *The Random House dictionary of the English language*. New York: Random House.

Tversky, H., & Kahneman, D. (1981). The framing of decisions and the psychology of choice. *Science, 211,* 453–458.

Wade, J. (1977). *Architecture, problems and purposes.* New York: Wiley.

Wareh, M., & Murta, K. (1979). Design procedures for buildings of quality. *Design Methods and Theories, 13,* 122–124.

Westcott, J. (1968). *Toward a contemporary psychology of intuition.* New York: Holt, Rinehart & Winston.

Wise, J. A. (1977). Decision theory and design methodology. In W. Gasparski, D. Miller, & A. Strazaleckiego (Eds.), *Zagadniena psychologii projektowania.* Warsaw: Polish National Academy of Sciences Press. (Reprinted in *Design Methods and Theories,* 1981, *15,* 91–103)

Wise, J. A. (1978). A critical reply to Donald Grant's "alpha-beta" model for decision making with multiple objectives. *Design Methods and Theories, 12,* 40–43.

Wise, J. A. (1983). *Bayesian statistics in design research* (Technical Report 4-83). Seattle: University of Washington.

Wise, J. A., & Alden, R. (1976). Decision theory applied to environmental design: Multiattribute utility theory for architectural evaluation. IN P. Sudfeld & J. A. Russell (Eds.), *The behavioral basis of design* (Vol. 2). Stroudsburg, PA: Dowden, Hutchinson & Ross.

Yager, R. (1979). Possibilistic decision making. *IEEE Transactions on Systems, Man, and Cybernetics, 9,* 388–392.

Zadeh, L. A. (1978). Fuzzy sets as a basis for a theory of possibility. *Fuzzy Sets and Systems, 1,* 3–28.

Zwicky, F. (1969). *Discovery, invention, research through the morphological approach.* New York: Macmillan.

PART V

JUDGMENTAL FORECASTING

CHAPTER 14

Prediction, Diagnosis, and Causal Thinking in Forecasting

Hillel J. Einhorn and Robin M. Hogarth

Imagine that you lived several thousand years ago and belonged to a tribe of methodologically sophisticated cave dwellers. Your methodological sophistication is such that you have available to you all present-day means of the methodological arsenal—details of the principles of deductive logic, probability theory, access to computational equipment, and the like. However, your level of substantive knowledge lags several thousand years behind your methodological sophistication. In particular, you have little knowledge about physics, chemistry, or biology. In recent years, your tribe has noted an alarming decrease in its birth rate. Furthermore, the tribe's statistician estimates that unless the trend is shortly reversed, extinction is a real possibility. The tribe's chief has accordingly launched an urgent project to determine the cause of birth. You are a member of the project team and have been assured that all means, including various forms of experimentation with human subjects, will be permitted to resolve this crucial problem.

The preceding story illustrates the following points:

1. The ultimate goal of forecasting is to provide guidance for taking action. Therefore, forecasting is intimately tied to decision making and should be evaluated within this context. For example, although the tribe's statistician may use a time series model of past birth rates to predict the downward trend, this is of

This chapter originally appeared in the *Journal of Forecasting*, 1982, *1*, 23–36. Copyright 1982 by John Wiley & Sons, Ltd. Reprinted with permission.

Hillel J. Einhorn and Robin M. Hogarth • Center for Decision Research, Graduate School of Business, University of Chicago, 1101 East 58 Street, Chicago, Illinois 60637. Support for this work was provided by a contract from the Engineering Psychology Program, Office of Naval Research.

limited usefulness to the tribe's leaders. Indeed, one might find small consolation in the fact that the date of the tribe's extinction can be precisely predicted. Clearly, the need to take appropriate action to change the process is of paramount concern.

2. Although much attention in the forecasting literature is devoted to forecast accuracy (see Hogarth & Makridakis, 1981, for a review), this focus may be misplaced. In particular, when viewed within the broader context of how forecasts affect actions, and how both affect outcomes, the criterion of forecast accuracy is problematic. In order to illustrate this, consider the following three situations and the relevance of forecast accuracy in each: (a) A weather forecaster predicts that a hurricane will come ashore at a certain time and place, and actions contingent on the forecast are taken (e.g., boarding up property, evacuation). Because these actions do not affect the hurricane itself, the relevance of forecast accuracy as a criterion is obvious and its evaluation relatively simple. However, even in those cases where one cannot typically exert control over the process (as when large physical systems are involved), actions can sometimes be taken to affect the process; consider, for example, "seeding" hurricanes (Howard, Matheson, & North, 1972); (b) Economic forecasters predict a recession next year and the government reacts by taking action to stimulate the economy. Clearly, action is taken to intervene in the process, and the resulting outcomes are a joint function of the factors on which the prediction is based and the action taken. Under these circumstances, the meaning of forecast accuracy is ambiguous; in fact, one can imagine that forecast accuracy is *not* desirable. For example, the more effective the action is in changing the process, the less accurate the initial forecast will be; (c) People in a small town hear a rumor that the banks are about to fail. They think that if this forecast is accurate, they had better withdraw their money as fast as possible. Accordingly, they go to the banks to close their accounts (those sceptical of the forecast see many people withdrawing money, and either take this as a sign that the rumor is true or foresee the consequences of waiting too long, thus joining the crowd in either case). By the end of the day the banks have failed, thereby confirming the rumor. This case differs from (b) in that the actions taken lead to confirmation of the predictions (demonstrating the so-called self-fulfilling prophecy effect). The perniciousness of these cases is that awareness of the effect of actions on outcomes is low and can lead to overconfidence in forecasts that are of low or even zero accuracy (see Einhorn, 1980; Einhorn & Hogarth, 1978).

3. In order to understand the relations between predictions, actions, and outcomes, one needs a causal model of the process. Such a model must be developed through the use of what we call *diagnostic* or *backward inference*. That is, past observations, events, and data are used as evidence to infer the process(es) that produced them. Such inferences are called diagnostic because they involve going from visible effects such as symptoms, signs, and the like, to their prior

causes. For example, one might consider a particularly large decline in last month's sales as symptomatic of a more fundamental malady (such as an incompetent sales force). We consider diagnostic inference to be based on causal thinking, although in doing diagnosis one has to mentally reverse the time order in which events were thought to have occurred (hence the term *backward inference*). On the other hand, predictions involve forward inference; that is, one goes forward in time from present causes to future effects. However, it is important to recognize the dependence of forward inference/prediction on backward inference/diagnosis. In particular, it seems likely that success in predicting the future depends to a considerable degree on making sense of the past. Therefore, people are continually engaged in shifting between forward and backward inference in both making and evaluating forecasts. Indeed, this can be eloquently summarized by Kierkegaard's observation that "life can only be understood backwards; but it must be lived forwards."

A second important aspect of diagnostic inference concerns the process by which hypotheses are formed and relevant variables found. For example, why are certain variables chosen as "relevant" to the phenomenon in question, whereas others are considered irrelevant or of lesser importance? This issue goes to the heart of all prediction problems although it has not received the attention it deserves. For example, consider the clinical versus statistical prediction controversy in psychology, which has raged off and on for over 25 years (Dawes, 1979; Meehl, 1954; Sawyer, 1966). One succinct conclusion of this literature (and one that we subscribe to) has been made by Dawes and Corrigan; namely, "the whole trick is to decide what variables to look at and then to know how to add" (1974, p. 105). Assuming that we can add, *how* do we decide what variables to look at? On this crucial point we have little guidance other than some ill-defined notions of experience, intuition, gut feeling, hunch, and so forth. From our perspective, one must have some hypothesis or theory for selecting relevant from irrelevant variables. Indeed, relevance can only be understood in relation to some model (usually implicit) of what generates the variable to be predicted. For example, imagine being asked to predict the result of mixing two chemicals with known atomic structures. Without some knowledge of chemistry and physics, picking relevant from irrelevant variables is meaningless. Therefore, prediction depends on backward inference that involves both the forming of hypotheses to interpret the past and the choosing of relevant from irrelevant variables in that interpretation.

We now turn to consider the details of the diagnostic process with particular emphasis on how people seek relevant variables and test for causal significance. These issues are examined in the following way: (1) we discuss the role of similarity and differences in directing attention to variables; (2) we posit the existence of probabilistic signs used for inferring causal relations and call these *cues to causality*; (3) we identify the following cues and discuss their roles in causal thinking: temporal order, constant conjunction, contiguity in time and space, number of alternative explanations, similarity, predictive validity, and robustness; (4) the role of the cues in inferring causality is emphasized by discussing the nature of spurious correlation and the existence of causal relations in the absence of correlation; and (5) we conclude by considering implications for forecasting.

THE DIAGNOSTIC PROCESS

We conceive of diagnosis as consisting of three interrelated phases: (1) finding relevant variables; (2) linking variables into causal chains; and (3) testing the causal significance of the links in those chains. In this paper we limit ourselves to how two, or at most, three variables become linked in a causal manner. We begin by first discussing the general issues of what directs attention to variables and what is meant by *causal relevance*.

Much psychological research indicates that processes of perception and judgment are sensitive to differences or deviations from present states, adaptation levels, and reference points (e.g., Helson 1964; Kahneman & Tversky, 1979). Therefore, we propose that in searching for a cause of some effect, which is itself a deviation from the normal or average, attention is directed toward prior deviations or abnormal states of comparable length and strength. For example, our cave dwellers probably asked themselves what unusual event (or events) preceded the decline in births. Moreover, if the effect of interest is large (i.e., is of substantial duration and/or strength), we expect that the suspected cause(s) are judged to be of comparable size. These conjectures follow from what Kahneman and Tversky call the *representativeness* heuristic (1972), which in this case implies that similar causes have similar effects. Indeed, Mill noted that this is a deeply rooted belief that "not only reigned supreme in the ancient world, but still possesses almost undisputed dominion over many of the most cultivated minds" (cited in Nisbett & Ross, 1980 p. 115). Mill thought that such a belief was erroneous, and many cases exist in which similarity has been misleading (see e.g., Shapiro, 1960; Shweder, 1977). On the other hand, it is difficult to imagine how one could search for variables without using some notion of similarity. Of particular importance is the nonliteral use of similarity through analogy and metaphor (e.g., Ortony, 1979). Indeed, analogies and metaphors provide models of phenomena and thus direct attention to specific aspects and variables. Moreover, their use engages one's prior knowledge so that the explanation for a new or poorly understood phenomenon can be integrated with what is already known or believed. For example, in trying to understand how the brain works, one could consider it as a computer, a muscle, or a sponge. Note how the metaphors direct attention to different, but known, variables and processes. Thus, a computer model suggests informational input, retrieval, and computational processes; a muscle model suggests that processes are strengthened and weakened with amount of use, that thinking can be a strain (cf. Shugan, 1980), and so on; a sponge model suggests a more passive "soaking up of information," and the like. As should be clear, the choice of a particular metaphor is crucial because it directs attention to a limited set of variables, thereby excluding others. However, this is precisely the function it should serve (we consider this further in the Implications section).

Although analogies and metaphors help direct attention to variables, not all variables considered are seen as *causally* relevant. Therefore, it is important to delineate how this occurs. In order to do so, we discuss the concept of a *causal field* and a causal variable as a difference-in-that-field (Mackie, 1974). The following example illustrates both concepts: Imagine a worker in a chemical plant who contracts cancer and sues the company for causing his disease. His lawyer argues that the cancer rate of workers in this factory is nine times the national average for workers in comparable industries. Note that the "field" in this argument is industries of a certain type, and the causal argument rests on *a difference (higher cancer rates) in this field*. However, the defense lawyer asks: "Would the worker have gotten cancer if he didn't work in the chemical plant?" In order to answer this, he then shows that there is a history of cancer in the worker's family (none of whom worked in chemical factories); the worker has smoked cigarettes for 20 years prior to getting cancer; and so on. The important point to note is that the field has now shifted to people who have certain family histories and habits; and in this field, cancer is not unusual and thus not a difference in the field. Hence, this particular case of cancer is not causally related to working in chemical factories. Of course, one could strengthen the prosecution case if the field were again changed—e.g., showing that the particular chemical plant had nine times the cancer rate of other chemical plants making the same products. The reason that this information strengthens the prosecution's case is that by narrowing the field to chemical plants making the same products, the possibility of alternative explanations is reduced, thereby making the difference in the narrowed field more causally relevant.

Although people are sensitive to differences-in-a-field, there are many differences to which one could attend. Therefore, what mechanisms guide the allocation of attention to those variables of greatest causal significance? An important consideration in this regard concerns the factors that distinguish between differences that are causal versus those that are called *conditions*. For example, imagine a house fire in which a gasoline can was found. Although the flammable material is a difference in the field (because most people do not have gasoline cans in their homes), it is not likely to be seen as the cause of the fire. Indeed, one is more likely to consider the throwing of a lighted match or cigarette near the can as the cause. As Mackie (1974) points out, there are no general rules for distinguishing causes from conditions, although the following are useful: (i) events are more causal than standing conditions (sparks rather than flammable material cause fires); (ii) events that are intrusive are more causal than those that generally occur; (iii) something abnormal or wrong is more causal than what is normal and right (e.g., the accident was caused by the person veering to the left—not by the other person who drove straight ahead). It is important to stress that there are exceptions to all three rules; e.g., poverty, which is a standing condition, may be seen as the cause of social unrest. Therefore, each of these rules only provides probabilistic evidence for distinguishing causes from conditions.

The mechanism by which causal links are formed and tested is now considered by introducing the concept of *cues to causality*. We consider the term *cues* as having a specific meaning that corresponds with its use in Brunswik's psychology (1952; see also Campbell, 1966; Hammond, 1955). Specifically: (1) the relation between each cue and causality is probabilistic. That is, each cue is only a fallible sign of a causal relation. (2) People learn to use multiple cues in making inferences in order to mitigate the potential errors arising from the use of single cues. (3) The use of multiple cues is facilitated by the intercorrelation (redundancy) between cues in the environment. Such intercorrelation reduces the negative effects of omitting cues and aids in directing attention to the presence of other cues. (4) Although multiple cues reduce uncertainty in inference, they do not entirely eliminate it. This is as true for backward as it is for forward inference.

In order to provide a conceptual framework for discussing the cues, imagine that one has a causal candidate in mind (X) for explaining some effect, Y. The causal strength of X will depend on its being a difference-in-the-field, which can be assessed by considering it relative to Y *and* $\bar{Y}$; that is, does X discriminate between the occurrence or absence of Y? For example, in trying to determine why some people got sick after eating in a particular restaurant (Y), we immediately want to know if those who didn't get sick ($\bar{Y}$), ate the same food (X). If the number of cases of $X \cap \bar{Y}$ and $X \cap Y$ is comparable, the strength of the connection is clearly diminished. However, this is not the only difference that can be considered. One could further ask whether Y is a difference-in-the-field of X versus $\bar{X}$; that is, the field is reversed so that what is figure becomes ground, and vice versa. In this case we wish to compare the number of people who got sick *without* eating the suspected food ($\bar{X}$), to those who did not get sick ($\bar{Y} \cap \bar{X}$). These differences, as well as those previously discussed, can be summarized in a standard 2×2 table, as shown in Table 1. The frequencies in each of the four cells can be thought of as individual components that are combined in various ways to judge the relation between X and Y. The cues to causality come into play by directing attention to different parts of the 2×2 table. We now consider the cues.

1. The cue of *temporal order* has two related functions: (a) because causes

Table 1.   Contingency Table between X and Y

	Y	$\bar{Y}$
X	Cell $a=$ $f(X \cap Y)$	Cell $b=$ $f(X \cap \bar{Y})$
$\bar{X}$	Cell $c=$ $f(\bar{X} \cap Y)$	Cell $d=$ $f(\bar{X} \cap \bar{Y})$

Note. f stands for frequency.

are assumed to precede effects, the search for relevant causal variables focuses on only those events that preceded the effect and thereby reduces the number of variables to be considered; (b) in terms of Table 1, temporal order is used to label the axes of the 2×2 table as being either X (independent variable) or Y (dependent variable).

2. The cue of *constant conjunction* is defined as the degree to which two variables occur together, holding contiguity in time and space constant. For example, consider a specific case of classical conditioning where a bell is repeatedly paired with food such that an animal learns to salivate at the sound of the bell. However, when the bell is not always followed by food, the relation is more difficult to learn. Note that temporal order is also involved in this example; in fact, attempts at "backward conditioning" (giving food and then the bell) have generally been unsuccessful (however, see Spetch, Wilkie, & Pinel, 1981). In terms of Table 1, we consider that constant conjunction directs attention to the joint frequency of X and Y (cell a).

3. We treat the cues of *contiguity in time and space* together although they are conceptually distinct. The reason for considering them together is that they both influence the relevance of constant conjunction as a causal cue and thus concern cell a in Table 1; that is, contiguity is viewed as a cue to causality via its effects on constant conjunction. This occurs in two ways: (a) together with similarity, attending to differences-in-a-field, and temporal order, contiguity in time and space aids in focusing attention on what variables occurred close in time to, and in the vicinity of, some effect Y. Indeed, Siegler has shown that for young children (5-6 years old), temporal contiguity is a very strong cue for inferring causality (Siegler, 1976; Siegler & Liebert, 1974). Moreover, these studies show that older children are less dependent on contiguity alone, being able to make use of multiple cues. Nevertheless, in the absence of high contiguity, variables that are causally related may not be noticed as important, as in the low temporal contiguity between pregnancy and intercourse. Additionally, the importance of contiguity cues can be seen by noting that certain causal distinctions are made when contiguity conflicts with other cues to causality. For example, consider the distinction between a *precipitating* and underlying cause. The former is generally some action or event that is high in temporal and spatial contiguity but low

in similarity of length or strength with the effect. Thus, the precipitating cause of World War I was an assassination in Sarajevo but the underlying cause(s) were economic upheaval, German nationalism, and so on. (b) Once variables have been identified, we hypothesize that constant conjunction is weighted by the degree of temporal and spatial contiguity between the variables. Therefore, although two variables may have a high joint frequency of occurrence, we would expect their judged causal strength to be lowered as temporal and spatial contiguity were decreased. Similarly, we expect that increased contiguity in time and space will strengthen the causal relevance of variables (including those with low joint frequency).

4. The *number of alternative explanations,* or competing variables as causes of Y, is an important negative cue to causality (i.e., the greater the number, the less the causal relevance of some X for Y). As stressed by Campbell and colleagues (Campbell, 1975; Campbell & Stanley, 1963; Cook & Campbell, 1979), causal strength should be evaluated by the ruling out of alternative explanations. Indeed, Mackie (1974) states that the primitive notion of a cause involves asking oneself the question: "Would Y have occurred if X had not?" The greater the number of alternative explanations underlying a "yes" answer, the lower the causal relevance of X for Y. Note that the posing and answering of the preceding question (which is called a *counterfactual conditional*) may either involve doing a real experiment or what is called a *thought* experiment. In the former, one compares the effect of X on Y with that of $\bar{X}$ on Y (the control group condition). In this way, the counterfactual question is easily answered. Moreover, note that a control group allows one to infer that X is the only difference in the field that can affect Y (because the control group *is* the field). However, even in real or quasi-experiments, alternative explanations can exist if other cues to causality are ambiguous. For example, Campbell (1969) points out that: (a) the gradual introduction of some experimental change makes the determination of its causal impact more difficult than a sharp introduction, as for example when a remedial program is phased in over a long time period rather than implemented all at once; (b) unless replication of the $X \cap Y$ relation is accomplished by the introduction of X over multiple time periods or over different units within the same time period, evidence of constant conjunction is weak; (c) the determination of causal relations when effects are not contiguous in time and space with the manipulated variables is problematic. For example, variables that have "lagged" effects or cumulative effects over time are difficult to isolate.

When real or quasi-experiments are not possible, one can nevertheless engage in the following thought experiment in order to answer the question, "Would Y have occurred if X hadn't?": Imagine the world before X, go forward to where X would occur, and then delete it from the scenario. Now run the scenario forward from that point to see if Y happens or not. Clearly, in such thought experiments the construction of "possible worlds" and imaginary scenarios is crucial for judging causal significance. In fact, according to Mackie (1974),

> The key item is a picture of what *would* have happened if things had been otherwise, and this is borrowed from some experience where things *were* otherwise. It is a contrast case rather than the repetition of like instances that contributes most to our primitive concept of causation. (p. 57)

The use of alternative explanations as a cue to causality has important implications for making inferences in general and for interpreting experiments in particular. As recognized by Hume, "not only in philosophy, but even in common life, we may attain the knowledge of a particular cause merely by one experiment, and after a careful removal of all foreign and superfluous circumstances" (as quoted in Mackie, 1974, p. 25). As a case in point, consider the following one-shot case study with a single datum: the occurrence of a huge explosion near Los Alamos, New Mexico, in July 1945 that no one doubted to be the effect of detonating an atomic bomb. Clearly, inferring causality in this poorly designed experiment was not difficult, whereas assessing causality in the most meticulously designed experiments in social science is often problematic at best. When one considers why the causal inference is so strong in the bomb example, ask yourself the following question: "Would an explosion of such magnitude have occurred if an atomic bomb had not gone off?" Although it is possible to think of alternative explanations for the explosion, they are so unlikely as to be virtually nonexistent. Moreover, note how the other cues to causality point to a causal relation (temporal order, contiguity in time and space, similarity of the "unusualness" of effects and cause, and so on). Therefore, even in one-shot case studies with no control group, causality can be inferred (see Campbell, 1975, for an illuminating discussion of this issue).

The use of counterfactual questions for assessing alternative explanations can be conceptualized by referring back to Table 1. Note that in backward or diagnostic inference, the question "Would Y have occurred if X hadn't?" focuses attention on cell c, which contains the $Y \cap \bar{X}$ instances. In forward inference, on the other hand, one can ask the question "Would not-Y occur if X had?" In this case, attention is focused on cell b, containing the $\bar{Y} \cap X$ cases. In either situation, one moves from considering only cell a in Table 1 to other components of the X, Y relation.

5. As noted earlier, *similarity* plays a crucial role in the finding of relevant variables. Furthermore, analogy and metaphor can be used to understand new phenomena by linking them to one's prior knowledge. However, one can ask how good a certain analogy might be, as for example, between the human brain and the computer. Whereas both possess many common features, they also contain distinctive aspects. Tversky (1977) has proposed a theory of how such common and distinctive aspects are combined to form similarity judgments. Specif-

ically, he posits that the judgment of similarity between two objects is a weighted linear function of the features they have in common less the distinctive features of each. The parameters of this function reflect differential attention paid to common and distinctive components. Tversky's formulation parallels the judgment of causal strength in the following way. Consider Table 1 and note that the frequencies in cells a and d can be seen as representing the constant conjunction of the variables (analogous to common features), whereas the frequencies in cells b and c can be seen as instances that disconfirm constant conjunction or affirm alternative explanations (analogous to the distinctive features of two objects). If one considers how attention can be shifted to these different aspects by such factors as whether the task involves forward or backward inference, or what other cues to causality are present (temporal order, contiguity), then judged causal strength can be seen as a weighted linear function of confirming and disconfirming evidence (for experimental results, see Schustack & Sternberg, 1981).

6. The degree to which one variable can predict another, denoted as *predictive validity*, is an important cue to causality. Predictive validity is commonly measured by the correlation coefficient, and it is noteworthy that this involves all four cells of Table 1. That is, the correlation between X and Y, denoted by r_{xy}, is given by the formula, $r_{xy} = (ad - bc)/[(a+b)(c+d)(a+c)(b+d)]^{1/2}$. Other things being equal, the greater the predictive validity of some variable, the greater its causal relevance. However, when other causal cues are involved, things are *not* equal. This makes the use of statistical correlation as a causal cue more uncertain than is generally realized. We discuss this in some detail by considering the meaning of *spurious correlation*. Thereafter, we consider what we call *causalation*, which results when variables that *are* causally related show low or no statistical correlation.

On the Psychology of Spurious Correlation

Every student who has taken an introductory statistics course containing a section on correlation is told: correlation does not imply causation. Unfortunately, the factors that do imply causation are rarely if ever discussed, and students are left without further guidance. To make matters worse, several days later the same students are warned against *spurious correlation*, that is, the correlation between two variables due to the common causal influence of some third factor. Because the concept of spurious correlation suggests that some correlations are more (or less) causally related than others, it is natural to ask how one can tell the difference (cf. Simon, 1954). However, one is disappointed to learn that there are no simple rules for doing this and that one must exercise one's judgment in this matter. This is not to say that such judgments will always be difficult to make or that they will vary according to the person doing the judging. For example, consider the correlation between the number of pigs and the amount of pig iron

(Ehrenberg, 1975). Such a correlation does seem spurious when the common causal factor, economic activity is considered. On the other hand, consider the correlation between amount of rain and number of auto traffic accidents in a city, over the course of a year. Such a correlation does not seem spurious. What is the difference between these two cases?

If we make use of the cues to causality, the spuriousness of the correlation between pigs and pig iron becomes apparent. First, consider the cues that do point to a causal relation; namely constant conjunction, contiguity in time, and predictive validity. However, the cues that point away from a causal relation are temporal order (which cannot be used to specify which variable is cause or effect); low contiguity in space (it being unlikely that farms and factories are in close physical proximity); many alternative explanations for either variable (for example, the answer to the question "Would pig production have gone up if the production of pig iron hadn't?" has many yes answers); the similarity of the variables is only with respect to their names, all else being quite dissimilar; the robustness of predictive validity seems low when, for example, one considers the lack of relation in nonindustrialized countries. Taken together, the negative evidence regarding a causal relation seems much stronger than the positive evidence. Indeed, the judgment that the relation is spurious is made easily and quickly.

Now consider the second case: the temporal order of rain and accidents is clear; constant conjunction, contiguity in time and space, and predictive validity are all high; similarity, via the use of prior knowledge about the effects of slippery roads, is high; robustness is also high because predictive validity holds in many cities over widely dispersed geographical locations. The only negative cue is the number of alternative explanations because the answer to the question "Would accidents have increased if it hadn't rained?" might be yes. However, even in this case, there may be few competing alternatives. Therefore, taken together, the cues strongly point to a causal relation, and a judgment that the correlation is nonspurious seems warranted.

The generalization that can be made from the preceding is the following: the judged strength between variables is a joint function of their correlation *and* the causal cues that are implicit in the labeling of the variables. This statement has several important implications: (1) the labeling of variables should have a major effect on their judged relational strength, holding statistical correlation constant. Evidence for this comes from a study by Jennings, Amabile, and Ross (1982). They found that when people viewed scatterplots of variables labeled X and Y, the statistical correlation had to be quite high for people to see a relationship. However, when the variables were given labels that engaged prior knowledge (making use of the cues to causality), the statistical correlation needed to see a relationship was much lower. (2) The effects of labeling have also been studied in probability learning tasks and confirm the importance of cues to causality in learning the relations between variables. For example, Adelman (1981) found that subjects in a multiple-cue probability task learned quite well when variable labels were congruent with statistical predictiveness, but not otherwise. Camerer (1981) showed that subjects were able to learn a disordinal interaction only when the variables were labeled in accord with prior beliefs (this involved factors that were thought to affect the price of wheat futures in a commodity market). When the same task was given as an abstract problem with variables labeled as X_1, X_2 and Y, no learning occurred. (3) When statistical correlation and cues to causality conflict, spurious correlation is not the only outcome; for example, a low or zero statistical correlation could mask a true causal relation. In order to illustrate this, let us return to our cave dwellers, who have hit upon the hypothesis that sexual intercourse is related to pregnancy. Accordingly, they designed and carried out the following experiment: One hundred females were allocated at random to an intercourse condition, and 100 to a nonintercourse condition. As indicated in Table 2, 25 females became pregnant, and 175 did not. Given our present world knowledge we can state that the 5 people in the no-intercourse/yes-pregnancy cell represent *measurement error*, that is, faulty memory in reporting, lying, and so on. Is intercourse important for pregnancy? The statistical correlation is small ($r = .34$) and our cave dwellers, in their methodological sophistication, might well question whether the hypothesis is worth pursuing. Indeed, if the sample size were smaller, the correlation might not even be statistically "significant". Moreover, even with a significant correlation, $r^2 = 0.12$, which is hardly a compelling percentage of the Y variance accounted for by X.

The important implication of the preceding hypothetical experiment is the following: although correlation *does not* necessarily imply causation, *causation does not necessarily imply correlation*. We have somewhat facetiously labeled examples of the latter as *causalations*, giving them equal standing with the better known and opposite concept of spurious correlation. The importance of causalation is that it demonstrates that sole reliance on statistical measures for understanding and interpreting data is insufficient (see also Simon, 1954). This

Table 2.   Data Matrix for Hypothetical Intercourse–Pregnancy Experiment

		Pregnancy		
		Yes	No	
Intercourse	Yes	20	80	100
	No	5	95	100
		25	175	200

conclusion is not surprising to those who have always maintained that judgment is a part of the evaluation of evidence. However, the delineation of the cues to causality gives one some hint as to the components of such judgments.

7. We have used the conceptual device of Table 1 to show how the various cues to causality direct attention to different aspects of causal strength. However, the cue of *robustness* goes beyond a single 2×2 table and explicitly raises the question as to whether, and to what degree, the predictive validity between X and Y varies as a function of other variables (see Toda, 1977). For example, imagine that there is a positive correlation between smoking (X and $\overline{X}$) and lung cancer (Y and $\overline{Y}$). Now consider that the correlation is computed separately for men and women with the following result: the correlation is positive for men but negative for women (that is, women who *do not* smoke are more likely than smokers to get lung cancer). Note that by subdividing the original sample into subgroups, one now considers several 2×2 tables and asks whether the overall correlation holds in each. If it does not, the relation is not robust, and the causal relevance of X for Y is decreased. In the preceding example, one is likely to be suspicious of any causal relation if the sign of the correlation changes in one of the subgroups. On the other hand, if predictive validity is robust, it points more strongly to a causal relation.

IMPLICATIONS

We now consider three implications of the preceding analysis for forecasting: (1) the selection of variables and the building of forecasting models; (2) the evaluation of forecast accuracy; and (3) learning to improve forecasting ability.

1. We have emphasized the role of similarities and differences as well as the cues to causality in directing attention to variables in the diagnostic process. However, a significant feature of causal/diagnostic thinking is the remarkable speed and fluency that people seem to have for generating explanations and accommodating discrepant facts into expanded hypotheses (Fischhoff, 1975; Slovic & Fischhoff, 1977; Tversky & Kahneman, 1980). A useful analogy of this process is provided by multiple regression analysis. In deriving a model (backward inference) one seeks the combination of variables and parameters that maximizes some measure of fit, for example, R^2. Furthermore, by increasing variables, R^2 approaches 1. However, and often to the user's surprise, the measure of fit typically "shrinks" on prediction. Thus, the power of post hoc explanations is unfortunately matched by the paucity of predictive validity.

Because diagnostic thinking is so fluent, one must guard against the way cues to causality quickly restrict our interpretation of the past. Of particular significance in this regard is the use of metaphors in guiding attention and providing models of complex phenomena. Because metaphors, like other cues to causality, are of imperfect validity, errors can be made by relying on single images. "The map," as the general semanticists remind us, "is not the territory," and thus we specifically recommend the *method of multiple metaphors* as a way of guarding against the premature adoption of a single model. That is, instead of focusing on a single metaphor, experiment with several. For example, consider how one might view forecasting. In this chapter we have adopted a medical metaphor by focusing on the diagnostic process and the effects of treatments (actions) on outcomes. However, consider a ballistics metaphor in which forecasting is likened to aiming and shooting at a target (see Hogarth, 1981). Such a metaphor leads to consideration of quite different variables and issues. Therefore, although no single model is correct, each directs attention to different factors, thereby providing a more complete picture of the phenomenon.

Whereas the cues to causality play an important role in structuring and stabilizing our perceptions of reality, such stability may be purchased at the cost of novelty and originality. That is, the cues direct attention to what is obvious, thereby reducing innovation and creativity. This suggests that one way to facilitate creative thinking might be to go specifically against the cues. For example, when dealing with a complex outcome, one might search for a dissimilar and simple causal candidate rather than a similar and complex one.

2. As emphasized at the beginning of this chapter, the evaluation of forecast accuracy is problematic without a causal understanding of the factors that influence outcomes. In particular, we stressed the fact that forecasts are made to aid decision making, and this makes outcomes a function of actions as well as predictions. The difficulties of evaluating forecast accuracy under these conditions can be conceptualized by considering two factors: (a) to what extent are people aware that their actions can affect outcomes?; and (b) to what extent do their actions *actually* affect outcomes? If, for the sake of simplicity, we only consider two levels of each factor (that is, aware–not aware and, actions affect outcomes–do not affect outcomes), Table 3 presents a convenient way to summarize the various possibilities.

Cells 1, 2, and 4 were discussed earlier in our examples of economic forecasting, rumors of bank failure, and hurricane prediction, respectively. We simply note that in the first two cases (cells 1 and 2), the evaluation of forecast accuracy should be conditioned on the action taken. That is, let Y be some outcome, X a forecast, and A an action based on the forecast; one is then interested in $p(Y|X,A)$ rather than $p(Y|X)$. As we have noted elsewhere (Einhorn & Hogarth, 1978), when actions affect outcomes, forecasts and outcomes are not conditionally independent of action; that is, $p(Y|X,A) \neq p(Y|X)$.

The situation represented in cell 3 deserves special attention because it involves taking action to affect outcomes when such actions are useless. When action involves physical manipulation or direct intervention, Langer (1975) has shown that people are prey to an "illusion of control," that is, actions are seen to af-

Table 3.   Categorization of Forecasting Situations by
Awareness and Efficacy of Actions

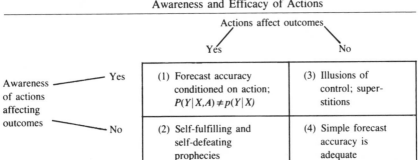

Actions affect outcomes	Yes	No
Awareness of actions affecting outcomes — Yes	(1) Forecast accuracy conditioned on action; $P(Y\mid X,A) \neq p(Y\mid X)$	(3) Illusions of control; super-stitions
Awareness of actions affecting outcomes — No	(2) Self-fulfilling and self-defeating prophecies	(4) Simple forecast accuracy is adequate

fect outcomes that are generated by random processes (cf. Lopes, 1982). For example, people tend to believe that the lottery tickets they personally select have a greater chance of winning than those selected for them by lottery administrators. Similarly, the cognitive activities of planning and forecasting in organizations can lead to illusions of control and overconfidence by restricting attention to those consequences one can imagine while diverting attention from those not considered (Hogarth & Makridakis, 1981). Moreover, it should be noted that illusions of control are conceptually identical to certain types of superstitious behavior. Indeed, the joint presence of randomness and the cues to causality (especially temporal order, constant conjunction, and high contiguity in time and space) inevitably lead to some superstitious behavior (Skinner, 1966). Thus, one can consider superstition as the cost one pays to gain causal knowledge. The issue remains, of course, as to whether the cost outweighs the associated benefits (cf. Killeen, 1978).

3. Given the difficulties of evaluating forecast accuracy, what can be done to improve forecasting ability? We consider two related approaches: experimentation to untangle the forecast-action-outcome sequence, and systematizing thought experiments.

Opportunities for experimentation are often overlooked. For example, consider personnel selection or advertising. In both cases one could carry out full or partial experiments by randomly selecting employees or stopping advertising completely. Although such experiments are typically infeasible, partial experiments could provide much useful information. For example, one could randomly admit a small percentage of candidates, and advertising could be stopped in selected time periods or areas (see Cook & Campbell, 1979, for relevant experimental designs).

To systematize thought experiments, we suggest the following procedure. Imagine that sales have increased and you wish to determine the causal significance of a prior advertising campaign. A real experiment would involve using a control group to test whether no campaign would have led to the same level of sales. Using the symbols of Table 1, the control group outcome would focus on the $\bar{X} \cap Y$ cell (i.e., c). Moreover, in the absence of a real experiment this datum would be supplied by the answer to the counterfactual question "Would Y have occurred if X hadn't?" However, answering only this question would be a weak form of inference. We also suggest that people ask themselves questions that illuminate the $X \cap \bar{Y}$ and $\bar{X} \cap \bar{Y}$ cells. The former involves imagining whether no sales increase ($\bar{Y}$) would have followed the advertising campaign (X); the latter asks whether no campaign ($\bar{X}$) would have been followed by no increase in sales ($\bar{Y}$). Systematically posing these different counterfactual questions can increase the power of thought experiments by generating information analogous to that available from real experiments.

CONCLUSION

Forecasting depends on the use of data and the exercise of judgment. Indeed, a colleague has succinctly summarized the theme of this chapter by saying that one cannot understand statistics without psychology (see also Hogarth, 1975). Although agreeing, we also note that the meaning and effects of uncertainty are central to the psychology of thinking and thus call for statistical expertise. In this chapter we have emphasized the probabilistic nature of cues to causality and the uncertainties associated with backward and forward inference. Moreover, we have stressed the need to understand how judgment affects the generation and testing of formal statistical models. We believe that the development and use of statistical techniques will benefit from understanding judgmental processes. Without such understanding, which depends crucially on causal thinking, simply forecasting the future will not ensure the future of forecasting.

REFERENCES

Adelman, L. (1981). The influence of formal, substantive, and contextual task properties on the relative effectiveness of different forms of feedback in multiple-cue probability learning tasks, *Organizational Behavior and Human Performance, 27*, 423–442.

Brunswik, E. (1952). *The conceptual framework of psychology*, Chicago: University of Chicago Press.

Camerer, C. F. (1981). *The validity and utility of expert judgment*. Unpublished Ph.D. dissertation, University of Chicago.

Campbell, D. T. (1966). Pattern matching as an essential in distal knowing. In K. R. Hammond (Ed.), *The psychology of Egon Brunswik*. New York: Holt Rinehart & Winston.

Campbell, D. T. (1969). Reforms as experiments. *American Psychologist, 24*, 409–429.

Campbell, D. T. (1975). Degrees of freedom and the case study. *Comparative Political Studies, 8*, 178–193.

Campbell, D. T., & Stanley, J. C. (1963). *Experimental and quasi-experimental designs for research*. Chicago: Rand-McNally, 1963.

Cook, T. D., & Campbell, D. T. (1979). *Quasi-experimentation: Design and analysis for field settings.* Chicago: Rand-McNally.

Dawes, R. M. (1979). The robust beauty of improper linear models in decision making. *American Psychologist, 34,* 571–582.

Dawes, R. M., & Corrigan, B. (1974). Linear models in decision making. *Psychological Bulletin, 81,* 95–106.

Ehrenberg, A. S. C. (1975). *Data reduction: Analyzing and interpreting statistical data.* New York: Wiley.

Einhorn, H. J. (1980). Learning from experience and suboptimal rules in decision making. In T. S. Wallsten (Ed.), *Cognitive processes in choice and decision behavior.* Hillsdale, NJ: Erlbaum.

Einhorn, H. J., & Hogarth, R. M. (1978). Confidence in judgment: Persistence of the illusion of validity. *Psychological Review, 85,* 395–416.

Fischhoff, B. (1975). Hindsight ≠ foresight: The effect of outcome knowledge on judgment under uncertainty. *Journal of Experimental Psychology: Human Perception and Performance, 1,* 288–299.

Hammond, K. R. (1955). Probabilistic functionalism and the clinical method. *Psychological Review, 62,* 255–262.

Helson, H. (1964). *Adaptation-level theory.* New York: Harper.

Hogarth, R. M. (1975). Cognitive processes and the assessment of subjective probability distributions. *Journal of the American Statistical Association, 70,* 271–289.

Hogarth, R. M. (1981). Beyond discrete biases: Functional and dysfunctional aspects of judgmental heuristics. *Psychological Bulletin, 90,* 197–217.

Hogarth, R. M., & Makridakis, S. (1981). Forecasting and planning: An evaluation. *Management Science, 27,* 115–138.

Howard, R. A., Matheson, J. E., & North, D. W. (1972). The decision to seed hurricanes. *Science, 176,* 1191–1202.

Jennings, D., Amabile, T. M., & Ross, L. (1982). Informal covariation assessment: Data-based vs. theory-based judgments. In D. Kahneman, P. Slovic, & A. Tversky (Eds.), *Judgment under uncertainty: Heuristics and biases,* New York: Cambridge University Press.

Kahneman, D., & Tversky, A. (1972). Subjective probability: A judgment of representativeness. *Cognitive Psychology, 3,* 430–454.

Kahneman, D., & Tversky, A. (1979). Prospect theory: An analysis of decision under risk. *Econometrica, 47,* 263–291.

Killeen, P. T. (1978). Superstition: A matter of bias, not detectability. *Science, 199,* 88–90.

Langer, E. J. (1975). The illusion of control. *Journal of Personality and Social Psychology, 32,* 311–328.

Lopes, L. L. (1982). Doing the impossible: A note on induction and the experience of randomness. *Journal of Experimental Psychology: Human Learning and Memory, 8,* 626–636.

Mackie, J. L. (1974). *The cement of the universe: A study of causation.* Oxford: Clarendon Press.

Meehl, P. E. (1954). *Clinical versus statistical prediction: A theoretical analysis and review of the literature.* Minneapolis: University of Minnesota Press.

Nisbett, R. E., & Ross, L. D. (1980). *Human inference: Strategies and shortcomings of social judgment.* Englewood Cliffs: Prentice-Hall.

Ortony, A. (1979). Beyond literal similarity. *Psychological Review, 86,* 161–180.

Sawyer, J. (1966). Measurement *and* prediction, clinical *and* statistical. *Psychological Bulletin, 66,* 178–200.

Schustack, M. W., & Sternberg, R. J. (1981). Evaluation of evidence in causal inference. *Journal of Experimental Psychology: General, 110,* 101–120.

Shapiro, A. K. (1960). A contribution to the history of the placebo effect. *Behavioral Science, 5,* 109–135.

Shugan, S. M. (1980). The cost of thinking. *Journal of Consumer Research, 7,* 99–111.

Shweder, R. A. (1977). Likeness and likelihood in everyday thought: Magical thinking in judgments about personality. *Current Anthropology, 18,* 637–658.

Siegler, R. S. (1976). The effects of simple necessity and sufficiency relationships on children's causal inferences. *Child Development, 47,* 1058–1063.

Siegler, R. S., & Liebert, R. M. (1974). Effects of contiguity, regularity, and age on children's causal inferences. *Developmental Psychology, 10,* 574–579.

Simon, H. A. (1954). Spurious correlation: A causal interpretation. *Journal of the American Statistical Association, 49,* 467–479.

Skinner, B. F. (1966). The phylogeny and ontogeny of behavior. *Science, 153,* 1205–1213.

Slovic, P., & Fischhoff, B. (1977). On the psychology of experimental surprises. *Journal of Experimental Psychology: Human Perception and Performance, 3,* 544–551.

Spetch, M. L., Wilkie, D. M., & Pinel, J. P. J. (1981). Backward conditioning: A reevaluation of the empirical evidence. *Psychological Bulletin, 89,* 163–175.

Toda, M. (1977).Causality, conditional probability and control. In A. Aykac, & C. Brumat (Eds.), *New developments in the applications of Bayesian methods.* Amsterdam: North Holland.

Tversky, A. (1977). Features of similarity. *Psychological Review, 84,* 327–352.

Tversky, A., & Kahneman, D. (1980). Causal schemas in judgments under uncertainty. In M. Fishbein (Ed.), *Progress in social psychology (Vol. 1).* Hillsdale, NJ: Erlbaum.

CHAPTER 15

A Comparative Evaluation of Objective and Subjective Weather Forecasts in the United States

Allan H. Murphy and Barbara G. Brown

INTRODUCTION

Weather forecasts today are prepared by both objective and subjective methods. Objective methods generally involve the use of numerical (i.e., physical/dynamical) and/or statistical models. These methods are objective in the sense that, for a particular procedure and set of relevant data, the forecasts produced do not depend on a meteorologist's judgment, although subjectivity *is* involved in the choice of a procedure and a set of data. Subjective methods, on the other hand, are methods in which the formulation of the forecasts is based at least in part on the judgments of one or more meteorologists. According to these definitions, the official forecasts issued to the general public and specific users by the National Weather Service (NWS) in the United States usually are considered to be subjective forecasts.

For more than a decade, the NWS has maintained an extensive operational program in which objective forecasts of a variety of weather variables are routinely provided to its forecasters as guidance (Glahn, 1985). In many cases, these objective forecasts are identical in form and content to the official fore-

This material is reprinted with permission from *Journal of Forecasting*. Copyright 1984 by John Wiley & Sons, Ltd.

Allan H. Murphy and Barbara G. Brown • Department of Atmospheric Sciences, Oregon State University, Corvallis, Oregon 97331. The work reported here was supported in part by the National Science Foundation (Division of Atmospheric Sciences) under grant ATM-8209713.

casts that the forecasters themselves must formulate. The existence of these directly comparable sets of forecasts provides an opportunity to evaluate and compare objective (i.e., model-based) and subjective (i.e., judgment-based) forecasts in a meteorological context, and such an analysis is the primary purpose of this chapter. In addition, some results are presented concerning recent trends in the quality of these two types of weather forecasts.

In the next section, we briefly describe the weather forecasting process in a modern national weather service such as the NWS, with particular reference to the respective roles of numerical/statistical models and human forecasters in this process. This section also contains information concerning some aspects of the current NWS operational forecasting program. Three different types of objective and subjective forecasts are evaluated and compared in the third section, Objective versus Subjective Forecasts; namely, probabilistic forecasts of precipitation occurrence, categorical (i.e., nonprobabilistic) forecasts of maximum and minimum temperatures, and categorical forecasts of cloud amount. Recent trends in the quality of these forecasts are examined in the fourth section. The fifth section, Subjective Weather Forecasting, consists of a discussion of the role of objective forecasts in the formulation of subjective forecasts and of the impacts of the former on the latter. For example, this section addresses questions such as the extent to which the quality of subjective forecasts is determined by the performance of objective guidance forecasts. Similarities and differences between weather forecasting and forecasting in other fields are examined in the sixth section. The final section consists of a brief summary and some concluding remarks.

WEATHER FORECASTING PROCEDURES AND PRACTICES: AN OVERVIEW

Weather forecasting as practiced by the NWS—and by modern weather services in other countries—is a complex, multifaceted process. For the purposes of this discussion, it is sufficient to identify the following stages or components of the process: (a) the collection, assimilation, and analysis of vast quantities of meteorological data provided by a global observing system; (b) the prediction of the behavior and evolution of the large-scale features of the atmosphere using numerical models; (c) the utilization of the output of numerical models, together with observations and other data, to produce objective forecasts of surface weather elements using statistical procedures; and (d) the integration by human forecasters of the output of the numerical and statistical models as well as the (direct) output of the observing system to formulate the official weather forecasts. Each stage of the forecasting process is conducted at regular time intervals, generally two or four times a day. A detailed description of these components of the forecasting process is beyond the scope of this chapter. Instead, we will focus on the roles of objective (statistical) models and human forecasters in this process.

As indicated in the previous paragraph, statistical procedures are used to produce objective forecasts of surface weather elements (e.g., temperature, precipitation, wind speed, cloud amount). The procedure most frequently employed at this stage of the forecasting process is multiple regression analysis. Predictors considered for inclusion in the regression equations generally consist of the output of numerical models as well as observations of relevant variables. The statistical equations can be designed to produce categorical or probabilistic forecasts, by treating the predictand as a continuous variable or as a set of one or more binary variables, respectively. Objective statistical weather forecasts are prepared on an operational basis by the NWS, and these forecasts are routinely provided to NWS forecasters as guidance.

Weather forecasters in the U.S. are charged with the responsibility of preparing the official forecasts disseminated to the general public and specific users. In formulating these forecasts, the forecasters aggregate information from many different sources, including the output of numerical and statistical models as well as observational data. The aggregation process and the process of determining the form and content of the official forecasts (i.e., the words and numbers that constitute such forecasts) are largely conducted in an intuitive or subjective manner. Moreover, the impact of guidance information in general and the objective statistical forecasts in particular on the official forecasts vary greatly from forecaster to forecaster and from occasion to occasion for each forecaster. In some cases a forecaster may "adopt" the guidance forecast as the official forecast without modification, whereas in other cases a forecaster may completely ignore the guidance forecast. In general, the effect of guidance forecasts lies somewhere between these two extremes. Because even the complete adoption of the objective forecast involves a conscious decision on the part of the forecaster, it seems reasonable to consider the official forecasts as subjective forecasts. Further discussion of the role and impact of objective guidance forecasts in the forecasting process will be deferred to in the section Subjective Weather Forecasting.

Objective statistical forecasts for a variety of weather elements have been prepared on an operational basis by the NWS since the early 1970s (Glahn, 1985). Moreover, the number of variables for which such forecasts have been formulated has increased significantly over the intervening period. At present, approximately 180,000 statistical equations are used to produce almost 600,000 objective forecasts each day. These large numbers result from the fact that the objective forecasting system involves, in addition to a substantial number of variables, a large network of stations over the U.S. as well as several lead times and cycle times (the term *cycle times* refers to the times each day that forecasts are prepared; currently, objective forecasts generally are issued twice a day). The objective forecasts for many of the variables are formulated initially in probabilistic terms (Murphy, 1985). In most cases, however, the forecasts provided to the forecasters as guidance contain categorical as well as probabilistic information (the former is derived from the latter). These objective forecasts usually are available to the forecasters 2 to 4 hours prior to the time that they must formulate the official forecasts.

Subjective weather forecasts have been prepared and disseminated to the general public and specific users by the NWS for approximately 100 years. The amount and type of information provided to forecasters—on the basis of which they are expected to formulate the official forecasts—has increased dramatically over this period, especially in the last two decades. Objective guidance information in the form of weather forecasts first became available to NWS forecasters on a regular basis about 1970; prior to that time, guidance forecasts (when available) were prepared subjectively by forecasters located at regional or national centers. The official forecasts currently produced by NWS forecasters generally are expressed in categorical terms, with the exception of the precipitation probability forecasts (see next section).

OBJECTIVE VERSUS SUBJECTIVE FORECASTS

In this section we compare the quality of three types of objective and subjective forecasts: (a) probabilistic forecasts of precipitation occurrence; (b) categorical forecasts of maximum and minimum temperatures; and (c) categorical forecasts of cloud amount. These forecasts have been selected for evaluation here because they represent distinct and important types of weather forecasts. Thus, this section is intended to provide an overview of the current quality of objective and subjective forecasts and of the differences in quality between such forecasts. Each subsection contains a brief description of the forecasts of interest, the methods used to evaluate the forecasts, and some results of such an evaluation.

Probabilistic Forecasts of Precipitation Occurrence

The Forecasts

The NWS forecasts of the probability of occurrence of measurable precipitation (≥ 0.01 inches) usually are referred to as probability of precipitation (POP) forecasts. POP forecasts are point forecasts, in the sense that they relate to the occurrence of at least 0.01 inches of precipitation at a particular location (usually the official rain gauge at which precipitation is measured). The forecasts are issued every 12 hours and are valid for three consecutive 12-hour periods or lead times (e.g., today, tonight, and tomorrow). The set of probabilities used in POP forecasts generally includes the following 13 values: .00, .02, .05, .10, .20, .30, .40, .50, .60, .70, .80, .90, 1.00.

Verification Methods

In evaluating probability forecasts, several attributes (i.e., desirable properties) of the forecasts are of interest. These attributes include reliability, accuracy, and skill. Reliability refers to the degree of correspondence between forecast probabilities and observed relative frequencies. That is, POP forecasts are reliable if the relative frequency of occurrence of measurable precipitation on occasions with a forecast probability p tends to be very close to p. The reliability of POP forecasts can be examined in a reliability diagram in which forecast probability is plotted against observed relative frequency for specific probability values. The diagonal 45° line in such a diagram represents perfect reliability in the sense that the relative frequencies exactly equal the probabilities.

Accuracy relates to the average degree of correspondence between individual forecasts and observations. In the case of POP forecasts, accuracy generally is measured by the average Brier score ($\overline{BS}$) (Brier, 1950), a strictly proper quadratic scoring rule. For a sample of K POP forecasts, $\overline{BS}$ can be defined as follows:

$$\overline{BS} = (2/K) \sum_{k=1}^{K} (r_k - d_k)^2 \qquad (1)$$

where r_k is the POP forecast on the kth occasion and d_k equals 1 if measurable precipitation occurs on the kth occasion and 0 otherwise. The range of $\overline{BS}$ is the closed interval from 0 to 2, with 0 (2) representing the best (worst) possible score. Meteorologists generally report $\overline{BS}^* = (\frac{1}{2})\overline{BS}$ rather than $\overline{BS}$ itself, and we will follow this practice here. The range of $\overline{BS}^*$ is the closed unit interval [0,1]. In effect, $\overline{BS}^*$ is the mean square error of the probabilistic forecasts of precipitation occurrence.

Skill refers to the accuracy of the forecasts of interest relative to the accuracy of forecasts produced by some standard of reference. For POP forecasts, a common standard of reference is a "constant" forecast of the climatological probability of measurable precipitation (i.e., the probability of measurable precipitation based on data from an appropriate historical period). If $\overline{BS}_c$ denotes the average Brier score for such (constant) forecasts, then a skill score (SS) can be defined as follows:

$$SS = [1 - (\overline{BS}/\overline{BS}_c)] \times 100 \qquad (2)$$

SS in (2) represents the percentage improvement in the average Brier score for the forecasts of interest over the average Brier score for the corresponding climatological forecasts (for convenience, we generally will use abbreviated expressions such as "percentage improvement in the Brier score for the forecasts over climatology" in this context).

Some Results

Reliability diagrams for objective (OBJ) and subjective (SUB) POP forecasts issued during the 1-year period 1 October 1980 to 30 September 1981 are presented in Figure 1. These forecasts are the first-period POP forecasts for approximately 85 stations in the conterminous U.S. The sample of forecasts has been divided into cool season (October–March) and warm season (April–September) subsamples because the characteristics of precipitation are different in the two periods.

The reliability curves in Figure 1 indicate that the objective and subjective POP forecasts are quite reliable in both the warm and cool seasons. That is, the curves correspond closely to the diagonal 45° line representing perfect reliability. Moreover, the differences in reliability between the OBJ and SUB forecasts (and/or between the two seasons) are quite small. The insets in these diagrams describe the relative frequency of use of the probability values in each season. These distributions indicate that the extreme probability values (i.e., .00 and 1.00) are used more frequently by the forecasters (i.e., by SUB) than by the OBJ technique and that these extreme probabilities are used more frequently in the cool season than in the warm season by both OBJ and SUB.

Average Brier scores ($\overline{BS}^*$) and skill scores (SS) for these objective and subjective POP forecasts for all three lead times are presented in Table 1. These results indicate that both the OBJ and SUB forecasts possess positive skill (relative to climatological probabilities that are allowed to vary from station to station and from month to month for each station), with levels of skill substantially higher in the cool season than in the warm season. This difference in skill is due largely to seasonal differences in precipitation systems. Precipitation occurrence in the cool season is governed primarily by large-scale weather systems, and these systems are inherently more predictable than the small-scale weather systems that govern precipitation events in the warm season. Moreover, verification statistics derived from a widely spaced network of stations are more representative of skill in forecasting large-scale precipitation than of skill in forecasting small-scale precipitation. In addition, the results in Table 1 indicate that skill generally decreases as lead time increases in both seasons (an exception is the slight increase in skill from the second period to the third period for the SUB forecasts in the cool season).

A "subjective skill score" also is reported in Table 1. This score represents the percentage improvement in the Brier score for the SUB forecasts over the OBJ forecasts. The results presented here indicate that the SUB forecasts are

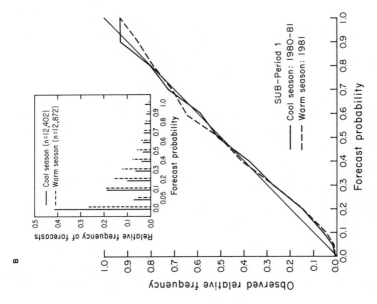

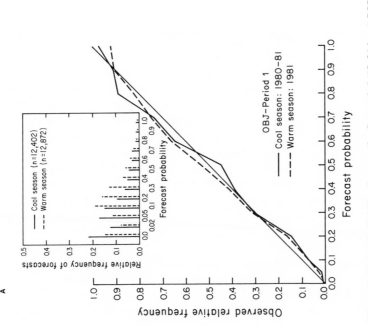

Figure 1. National reliability diagrams for first-period (12–24 hour) POP forecasts in 1980–1981 cool season and 1981 warm season formulated by (A) objective (OBJ) procedures and (B) subjective (SUB) procedures. Insets indicate relative frequency of use of forecast probability values.

Table 1. Average Brier and Skill Scores for Objective and Subjective 0000 GMT POP Forecasts for the Cool and Warm Seasons of 1980–1981. The Skill Score (SS) Is Defined as the Percentage Improvement in Average Brier Score of the Forecasts over Climatology, whereas the Subjective Skill Score Is the Percentage Improvement in Average Brier Score of the Subjective Forecasts over the Objective Forecasts.

A. Cool season (October 1, 1980–March 31, 1981): 85 stations					
	Number	Average Brier score ($\overline{BS}$*)		Subjective	Skill score (SS) (%)	
Lead time (h)	of cases	Objective	Subjective	skill score (%)	Objective	Subjective
12–24	12402	0.0772	0.0733	5.1	46.8	49.5
24–36	12392	0.0912	0.0926	−1.5	34.2	33.4
36–48	12401	0.0959	0.0946	1.4	33.2	34.2

B. Warm season (April 1, 1981–September 30, 1981): 89 stations					
	Number	Average Brier score ($\overline{BS}$*)		Subjective	Skill score (SS) (%)	
Lead time (h)	of cases	Objective	Subjective	skill score (%)	Objective	Subjective
12–24	12872	0.1094	0.1054	3.7	27.7	30.6
24–36	12788	0.1239	0.1225	1.1	21.0	22.0
36–48	12790	0.1281	0.1285	−0.3	16.2	16.2

more skillful than the OBJ forecasts in the cool and warm seasons for the first period. On the other hand, differences in skill between the two types of forecasts are quite small for the second and third period forecasts in both seasons.

Categorical Forecasts of Maximum and Minimum Temperatures

The Forecasts

The maximum and minimum temperature forecasts produced on an operational basis by the NWS are categorical forecasts. That is, they are expressed in the form of specific temperature values (the uncertainty inherent in these forecasts is not specified). Both the objective and subjective temperature forecasts are formulated twice a day for lead times up to 60 hours. However, the former pertain to maximum and minimum temperatures in a 24-hour midnight to midnight period, whereas the latter pertain to maximum and minimum temperatures in 12-hour daytime and nighttime periods, respectively.

Verification Methods

Several familiar measures of performance can be used to verify categorical forecasts of continuous variables such as maximum and minimum temperatures. These measures include the mean error (ME), the mean absolute error (MAE), and the root mean square error (RMSE). The ME is a measure of overall reliability, whereas the MAE and RMSE are measures of accuracy. The MAE, which is the primary measure used to verify the maximum and minimum temperature forecasts in this chapter, can be defined as follows:

$$MAE = (1/K)\sum_{k=1}^{K} |T_k^f - T_k^o| \tag{3}$$

where T_k^f and T_k^o are the forecast and observed temperatures, respectively, on the kth occasion. The observed temperatures are the maximum and minimum temperatures in 24-hour midnight to midnight periods, thereby corresponding more closely to the definition of the objective forecasts than to the definition of the subjective forecasts.

Some Results

Verification scores for the objective and subjective maximum and minimum temperature forecasts formulated during the 1-year period from October 1980 through September 1981 are presented in Table 2. As in the case of the POP forecasts, the results are aggregated over a large number of stations, and they are divided into warm and cool seasons. The accuracy of the forecasts (as measured by the MAE) ranges from less than 3°F for 24-hour maximum temperature forecasts in the warm season to approximately 5°F for 60-hour minimum tempera-

Table 2. Verification Scores for Objective and Subjective 0000 GMT Forecasts of Maximum and Minimum Temperatures for the Cool and Warm Seasons of 1980–1981. The Subjective Skill Score Here Is Defined as the Percentage Improvement in MAE of the Subjective Forecasts over the Objective Forecasts.

A. Cool season (October 1, 1980–March 31, 1981): 85 stations

Forecast type/ lead time (h)	Number of cases	Mean absolute error (°F)		Subjective skill score (%)	Relative frequency of absolute errors $\geq 10°F$ (%)	
		Objective	Subjective		Objective	Subjective
Maximum/24	12876	3.3	3.3	0.0	3.6	3.6
Maximum/48	12861	4.4	4.4	0.0	9.0	9.3
Minimum/36	12865	4.0	4.1	−2.5	6.5	7.5
Minimum/60	12875	4.8	5.0	−4.2	11.8	12.9

B. Warm season (April 1, 1981–September 30, 1981): 88 stations

Forecast type/ lead time (h)	Number of cases	Mean absolute error (°F)		Subjective skill score (%)	Relative frequency of absolute errors $\geq 10°F$ (%)	
		Objective	Subjective		Objective	Subjective
Maximum/24	13492	2.9	2.8	3.4	2.5	2.6
Maximum/48	13404	3.6	3.6	0.0	5.5	5.6
Minimum/36	13399	3.0	3.0	0.0	1.9	2.8
Minimum/60	13393	3.5	3.6	−2.9	4.2	5.0

ture forecasts in the cool season. Generally, the warm season forecasts are more accurate than the cool season forecasts (for corresponding lead times), due largely to the fact that the variability of temperature is less in the warm season than in the cool season. The accuracy of the forecasts decreases as lead time increases in both seasons (with regard to the latter, it is necessary to distinguish between maximum and minimum temperature forecasts).

The subjective skill scores in Table 2 indicate the improvement (in percentage terms) of the MAE for the subjective forecasts over the objective forecasts. These results suggest that the subjective forecasts are more accurate than the objective forecasts for the 24-hour maximum temperatures in the warm season, but that the opposite is true for 36-hour minimum temperatures in the cool season and for the 60-hour minimum temperatures in both seasons. For the other combinations of forecast type (maximum/minimum) and season, the subjective skill scores are equal to zero. In comparing the objective and subjective forecasts, the lack of correspondence betwen the definition of the latter and the definition of the observations should be kept in mind. Specifically, special care must be exercised in drawing conclusions regarding the relative merits of the two types of temperature forecasts in situations in which the OBJ forecasts are more accurate than the SUB forecasts.

Another dimension of the performance of the objective and subjective temperature forecasts relates to the number of large errors in the forecasts. This dimension is described in Table 2 in terms of the relative frequency (in percentage terms) of errors equal to or greater than 10°F. These results indicate that, as in the case of the mean absolute errors, the number of large errors is greater in the cool season than in the warm season. With regard to differences between the objective and subjective forecasts on this dimension, the relative frequency of large errors for the objective forecasts generally is less than that for the subjective forecasts. Moreover, the differences between these relative frequencies tend to be larger for the minimum temperature forecasts than for the maximum temperature forecasts.

Categorical Forecasts of Cloud Amount

The Forecasts

The objective cloud amount forecasts produced by the NWS on an operational basis are expressed initially in probabilistic terms. Specifically, these forecasts indicate the likelihood of occurrence of four categories of cloud amount (see Table 3 for definitions of these categories). The objective probabilistic forecasts are transformed into categorical forecasts by employing a procedure that—over a developmental sample of forecasts and observations—yields approximately the same number of forecasts and observations for each category. Subjective cloud amount forecasts formulated by NWS forecasters are expressed initially in terms of words or phrases such as "partly cloudy" and "mostly cloudy." For the purposes of verification and comparison with the objective forecasts, these subjective forecasts are translated into categorical forecasts of the cloud amount categories described in Table 3. The objective and subjective cloud amount forecasts are issued twice a day for three lead times (18 hours, 30 hours, and 42 hours).

Verification Methods

The measure of accuracy used to verify these objective and subjective forecasts is the percent correct (PC)—that is, the number of correct forecasts of the cloud amount categories, expressed as a percentage of the total number of forecasts. The number of correct forecasts is the sum of the diagonal elements in a 4×4 contingency table containing the joint distribution of forecast and observed cloud amount categories. The skill of the forecasts is determined by computing the Heidke skill score (HSS), where HSS can be defined as follows:

$$HSS = (PC - PC_c)/(100 - PC_c) \qquad (4)$$

in which PC is the percent correct for the forecasts of interest and PC_c is the percent correct for "chance forecasts" derived from the marginal totals in the contingency table. As in the cases of the precipitation and temperature forecasts, a subjective skill score is used to measure the improvement in the accuracy measure (in this case, PC) for the subjective forecasts over the objective forecasts.

Some Results

Verification scores for the objective and subjective cloud amount forecasts are presented in Table 4. The values of PC indicate that the overall accuracy of the forecasts is approximately the same for the warm and cool seasons and that, as expected, accuracy generally decreases as lead time increases. Excep-

Table 3. NWS Categories of Cloud Amount

Cloud amount category	Opaque sky cover (tenths)
1	0–1
2	2–5
3	6–9
4	10

Table 4.   Verification Scores for Objective and Subjective 0000 GMT Forecasts of Cloud Amount for the Cool and Warm Seasons of 1980–1981. The Subjective Skill Score Here Is Defined as the Percentage Improvement in Percent Correct of the Subjective Forecasts over the Objective Forecasts.

		A. Cool season (October 1, 1980–March 31, 1981): 90 stations				
	Number	Percent correct (PC)		Subjective	Heidke skill score (HSS)	
Lead time (h)	of cases	Objective	Subjective	skill score (%)	Objective	Subjective
18	14497	52.4	50.4	−3.8	0.345	0.343
30	14144	57.1	46.8	−18.0	0.345	0.285
42	14068	46.2	39.6	−14.3	0.260	0.209

		B. Warm season (April 1, 1981–September 30, 1981): 95 stations				
	Number	Percent correct (PC)		Subjective	Heidke skill score (HSS)	
Lead time (h)	of cases	Objective	Subjective	skill score (%)	Objective	Subjective
18	16143	50.9	49.3	−3.1	0.338	0.314
30	15782	52.9	43.9	−17.0	0.314	0.245
42	16142	47.2	41.7	−11.7	0.286	0.206

tions to the latter statement can be noted for the 30-hour objective forecasts in both the warm and cool seasons. The values of *HSS* reveal that the two types of forecasts possess positive skill (relative to chance) for all lead times in both seasons and that skill generally decreases as lead time increases.

With regard to differences in accuracy between the objective and subjective cloud amount forecasts, the results in Table 4 reveal that the objective forecasts are more accurate than the subjective forecasts for all lead times in both seasons. The differences in accuracy are relatively small for the 18-hour forecasts, but they are quite large for the longer lead times. In evaluating these results, it should be recalled that the subjective forecasts of cloud amount considered here are prepared only for verification purposes, and this fact raises some serious questions concerning the validity of any comparison of the two types of forecasts. Specifically, it seems reasonable to believe that the subjective forecasts would increase in accuracy if they were formulated in terms of the categories defined in Table 3 and subsequently included—in this form—in public weather forecasts. This practice would provide forecasters with the same motivation in the case of cloud amount forecasts that already exists in the cases of precipitation probability and temperature forecasts.

RECENT TRENDS IN FORECAST QUALITY

In this section we describe some recent trends in the quality of objective and subjective weather forecasts. The examination of these trends will provide an indication of changes in the levels of performance of objective and subjective forecasts in both absolute and relative terms. As in the previous section, three types of forecasts are considered: (a) precipitation probability forecasts; (b) maximum and minimum temperature forecasts; and (c) cloud amount forecasts.

Probabilistic Forecasts of Precipitation Occurrence

Trends in the skill score (SS) for objective and subjective POP forecasts over the period April 1972 through September 1981 are shown in Figure 2. Separate diagrams are presented for the cool and warm seasons, and curves are included for the first period (12 to 24 hours) and the third period (36 to 48 hours). (Curves for the second period generally fall between the first and third period curves, and the differences between the objective and subjective forecasts usually are similar for the second and third periods. Thus, the curves for the second period were omitted to simplify the diagrams.) Two types of objective forecasts were formulated during this period, and they are denoted here by OBJ-1 and OBJ-2. The OBJ-2 POP forecasts first became available in April 1977. To simplify the diagrams, the skill scores for the OBJ-1 forecasts are only shown up to the time that these forecasts either were replaced or were outperformed by the OBJ-2 forecasts.

Overall, both the objective and subjective forecasts show moderately strong trends toward higher skill scores in the cool season (see Figure 2A). For example, the skill of 36- to 48-hour forecasts has increased from approximately 18% to almost 35% over the 10-year period. In the warm season, however, increases in skill are relatively modest, especially for the 12- to 24-hour forecasts (see Figure 2B). Meteorologists generally attribute the relatively larger increases in skill in the cool season than in the warm season to improvements in numerical models—the latter currently are more successful in forecasting precipitation in the cool season than in the warm season. Moreover, the level of skill of the cool season forecasts is markedly higher than that of the warm season forecasts (for corresponding lead times) and, as expected, the skill of the first-period forecasts is considerably higher than the skill of the third-period forecasts in both seasons.

With regard to a comparison of the skill of the objective and subjective forecasts and of the trends in skill of the two types of forecasts, the curves in Figure 2 reveal several interesting features. First, the subjective forecasts clearly are more skillful than the objective forecasts for the first period in both seasons. However, the differences in skill between the two types of forecasts for this lead time appear to have decreased over the 10-year period. For the third period, the differences in skill between the objective and subjective forecasts are relatively small in both the cool and warm seasons. It also is evident from a comparison of the curves for the objective and subjective forecasts (for all combinations of season and lead time) that these curves generally tend to rise and fall together.

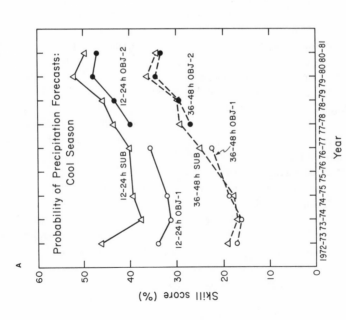

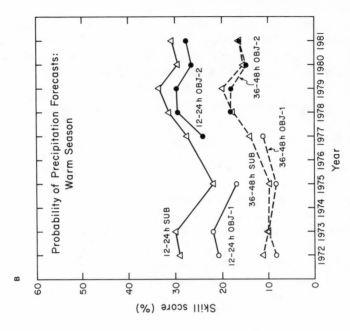

Figure 2. National trends in skill score for first-period (12–24 hour) and third-period (36–48 hour) objective (OBJ) and subjective (SUB) POP forecasts for (A) cool seasons from 1972–1981 and (B) warm seasons from 1972–1981.

That is, increases (and decreases) in the skill of the two types of forecasts usually occur at the same time. Finally, the increase in skill of the objective forecasts exceeds that of the subjective forecasts for the first period, and the third-period forecasts—both objective and subjective—realize somewhat larger increases in skill than the first-period forecasts over the 10-year period.

When comparing national skill scores (or other measures of performance) for objective and subjective forecasts, it should be kept in mind that these scores generally vary from region to region. Trends in skill of the 12- to 24-hour objective and subjective POP forecasts in the cool season during the period 1977–1981 for the four NWS regions in the conterminous U.S. are shown in Figure 3 (the figure also contains the national trends in skill over this period). The subjective forecasts are noticeably more skillful than the objective forecasts in the Western and Southern Regions, whereas differences in skill between the two types of forecasts are quite small in the other regions. Differences in performance between objective and subjective forecasts undoubtedly are due in part to the forecasters' ability to take local effects into account in a more realistic manner than is currently possible using objective methods, and these local effects are particularly important in the mountainous terrain of the Western Region. In addition, in the mid-1970s the management of the NWS Western Region initiated a program in which forecasters were encouraged to make judicious use of the objective forecasts in formulating the official forecasts, but were advised not to rely solely on this one source of guidance information (Snellman, 1977).

Categorical Forecasts of Maximum and Minimum Temperatures

Trends in mean absolute error (MAE) of the maximum and minimum temperature forecasts over the April 1971–September 1981 period are displayed in Figures 4 and 5, respectively. Separate diagrams are presented for the cool and warm seasons. Three objective forecasting systems were used over the 10-year period, with the "changeovers" here occurring in September 1973 and in April 1978.

The cool season forecasts show larger reductions in mean absolute error than the warm season forecasts over the period as a whole. One explanation for this difference is similar to that offered for the difference between improvements in cool and warm season POP forecasts in the preceding subsection. In addition, the fact that the variability in cool season temperatures exceeds that in warm season temperatures provides a greater opportunity for improvements in forecasts of the former than in forecasts of the latter. Nevertheless, even the warm season forecasts exhibit at least modest trends toward lower MAE values. It is of interest to note that the warm season forecasts are more accurate (i.e., smaller MAE) than the cool season forecasts for both maximum and minimum temper-

12-24 PROBABILITY OF PRECIPITATION FORECASTS: COOL SEASON

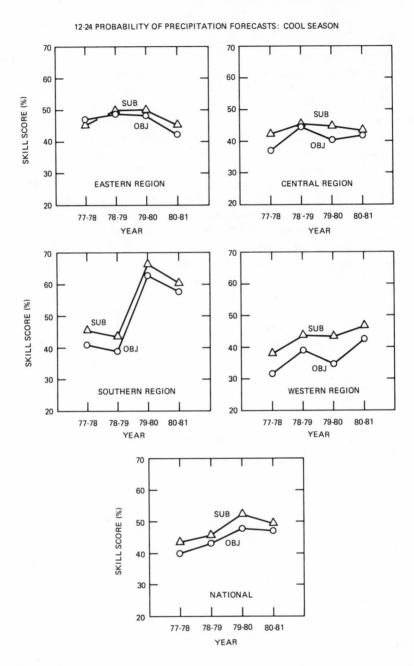

Figure 3. Regional and national trends in skill score for first-period (12–24 hour) objective (OBJ) and subjective (SUB) POP forecasts for cool seasons from 1977–1981.   .

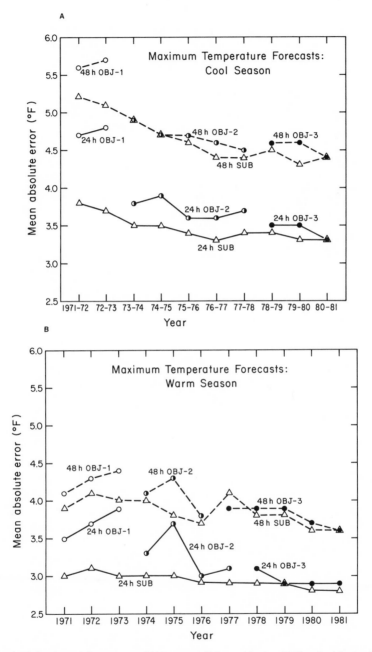

Figure 4. National trends in accuracy of 24-hour and 48-hour objective (OBJ) and subjective (SUB) maximum temperature forecasts for (A) cool seasons from 1971–1981 and (B) warm seasons from 1971–1981.

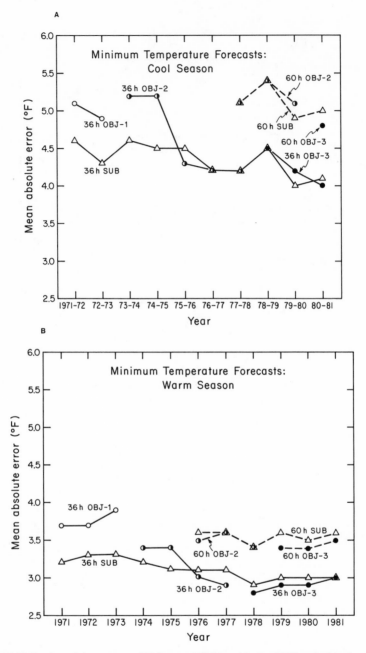

Figure 5. National trends in accuracy of 36-hour and 60-hour objective (OBJ) and subjective (SUB) minimum temperature forecasts for (A) cool seasons from 1971–1981 and (B) warm seasons from 1971–1981.

atures. As expected, accuracy generally decreases as lead time increases for both types of temperature forecasts.

With regard to a comparison of the objective and subjective forecasts, the results for temperature forecasts are similar in several respects to the results for POP forecasts. For example, the subjective forecasts clearly are more accurate than the objective forecasts at the beginning of the 10-year period (note that the 60-hour minimum temperature forecasts have been produced only for the latter half of the 10-year period), but the difference in accuracy between these two types of forecasts currently is quite small for all combinations of season and lead time. Thus, the objective forecasts have exhibited a stronger trend toward increasing accuracy than the subjective forecasts. It also appears that the accuracies of the objective and subjective temperature forecasts generally rise and fall together, although this tendency is much less pronounced here than in the case of the POP forecasts.

Categorical Forecasts of Cloud Amount

Trends in the Heidke skill score (HSS) for the forecasts of cloud amount category over an 8-year period from 1974 to 1981 are presented in Figure 6. As in the cases of the POP forecasts and temperature forecasts, separate diagrams are included for the cool and warm seasons. The changeover in objective forecasting systems from OBJ-1 to OBJ-2 occurred in October 1976 for the 18-hour forecasts and in October 1977 for the 42-hour forecasts (the curves for the 30-hour forecasts were omitted to simplify the diagrams).

The curves for the cool season in Figure 6A reveal only modest trends toward higher skill scores for both the objective and subjective forecasts—however, the increases in HSS over the 8-year period are somewhat greater for the objective forecasts than for the subjective forecasts. In the warm season (Figure 6B), the objective forecasts exhibit moderately strong trends toward higher skill scores, whereas the subjective forecasts exhibit little if any increase in HSS over the period from 1975 to 1981. The curves in Figure 6 also reveal that skill scores in the cool season are higher than skill scores in the warm season (for corresponding lead times) and that, as expected, skill decreases as lead time increases in both seasons.

A comparison of the skill—and trends in the skill—of the objective and subjective cloud amount forecasts indicates that the former are now more skillful than the latter for all combinations of season and lead time (see Figure 6). The differences in quality between the objective and subjective forecasts are larger for the 42-hour lead time than for the 18-hour lead time. However, in evaluating these differences, the previous discussion regarding the validity of any comparison of the two types of cloud amount forecasts should be kept in mind. Finally, as noted earlier in the cases of the precipitation probability and maximum/minimum temperature forecasts, a tendency exists for the curves

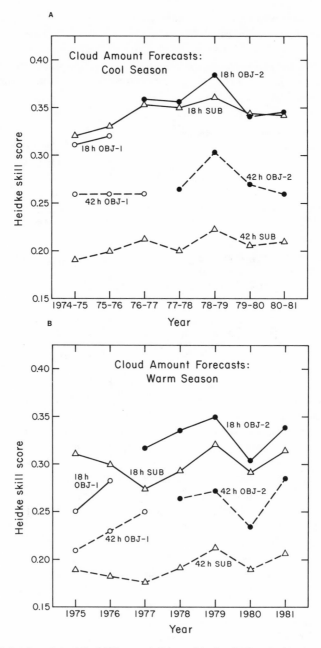

Figure 6. National trends in skill of 18-hour and 42-hour objective (OBJ) and subjective (SUB) cloud amount forecasts for (A) cool seasons from 1974–1981 and (B) warm seasons from 1975–1981.

describing the changes in skill of the objective and subjective cloud amount forecasts to rise and fall at the same time.

SUBJECTIVE WEATHER FORECASTING: ROLE AND IMPACT OF OBJECTIVE FORECASTS

In comparing the current quality—and recent trends in the performance—of objective and subjective weather forecasts, it has been assumed implicitly that these two types of forecasts are prepared independently of each other. (N.B.: Of course, the objective and subjective forecasts themselves are *not* independent of each other in a statistical sense. In fact, two sets of forecasts, each of which exhibits a relatively high degree of accuracy, necessarily must be positively correlated.) However, as already noted, the objective forecasts generally are available to the forecasters when they prepare the subjective forecasts. As a result, it is logical to ask a number of questions concerning the relationship between the two types of forecasts. For example, what role do the objective guidance forecasts play in the formulation of the subjective forecasts? What impact do these objective forecasts have on the subjective forecasting process and on the forecasts produced by this process? To what extent is the quality of the subjective forecasts determined by the performance of the objective forecasts? As we shall discover, it is difficult to provide definitive answers to these and other related questions. Nevertheless, a discussion of the range of possible answers to such questions should provide a useful background against which to judge the results presented in the two preceding sections. Moreover, it seems reasonable to conduct this discussion within a somewhat broader context than simply that of the relationship between objective and subjective forecasts; the appropriate context would appear to be the subjective weather forecasting process itself.

How are subjective weather forecasts actually formulated? It is difficult to describe this process with any degree of specificity or generality because the process is conducted largely in an intuitive manner and because it varies from forecaster to forecaster and even from occasion to occasion for each forecaster. Furthermore, the subjective weather forecasting process has been studied in only a few situations. For example, Murphy and Winkler (1971, 1974b) asked forecasters to indicate the relative importance of different sources of information and the order in which they examined these information sources, in the context of precipitation probability forecasting. In addition, a few meteorologists have attempted to use procedures such as decision trees and expert systems (or algorithms) to provide forecasters with a logical framework within which to formulate forecasts in specific situations (e.g., Belville & Johnson, 1982; Gaffney & Racer, 1983; Simpson, 1971). Moreover, Allen (1982) recently has investigated the aggregation of information by weather forecasters and the existence of various cognitive biases in their judgments. Although these studies have yielded some information concerning the subjective weather forecasting process in certain contexts, they have provided only limited insight into the general nature and structure of this process.

As indicated in the section Weather Forecasting Procedures and Practices, forecasters can consult a large number of sources of information in the preparation of the official subjective forecasts. These sources range from analyses and prognoses of the large-scale features of the atmospheric circulation (e.g., long waves, jet streams, highs, lows, fronts) to the latest data from satellite, radar, and conventional observing systems. Thus, the objective guidance forecasts provided by statistical forecasting procedures represent only one of many sources of potentially relevant information. However, because the objective forecasts themselves combine information from several different sources, because these forecasts generally are expressed in a form identical or very similar to that required for the subjective forecasts, and because the guidance forecasts generally are of relatively high quality, they obviously "command" the forecaster's attention, especially in the process of formulating the corresponding subjective forecasts.

Although the difficulties inherent in describing the subjective weather forecasting process should now be evident, it may be useful to consider briefly two "forms" that this process can take—forms that illustrate the range of roles that may be played by the objective guidance forecasts. In one form, a forecaster first examines the sources of information—especially the output of the numerical models—with the goal of obtaining a general picture of the current behavior and evolution of the large-scale features of the atomosphere. Then, the forecaster employs this picture (or understanding) together with other relevant information, including the objective statistical forecast, to arrive via an intuitive assimilation process at his or her official subjective forecast. Meteorologists generally consider this form of the subjective forecasting process to be the preferred procedure.

Alternatively, the forecaster can begin the forecasting process by adopting the objective guidance forecast as his or her initial subjective forecast. Then, he or she modifies this forecast in light of the current content of other information sources. The process of modification is accomplished in an intuitive manner, and the effort expended by the forecaster in this process is limited in practice only by factors such as cognitive skill and time constraints. Nevertheless, this form of the forecasting process tends to place heavy weight on the objective guidance forecast and may lead to forecasting practices that improperly discount the content of other information sources. In fact, forecasts formulated in this manner might be expected to suffer from cognitive biases such as "anchoring" (e.g., see Tversky & Kahneman, 1974).

What is the impact (in a qualitative or quantitative sense) of the objective forecasts on the subjective forecasting process and on the official forecasts themselves? We are aware of only one study that specifically attempted to investigate this issue. This study consisted of an experiment in which experienced forecasters in two NWS offices subjectively assessed precipitation probabilities both before and after consulting the corresponding objective POP forecasts (Murphy & Winkler, 1974a). Moreover, the forecasters were instructed to examine all of the other information sources prior to making their initial forecast (thus, the objective POP forecast was the last item of information examined in the forecasting process). The results of this experiment indicated that the quality of the objective and subjective POP forecasts was comparable; more importantly, in the context of this discussion, the latter were 20% "closer" to the former on the average after the objective forecasts had been consulted than before they had been examined. Thus, the guidance forecasts appear to have had only a modest impact on the official subjective forecasts. However, the results of a single study of these impacts certainly are not conclusive, in part because of the severe constraints imposed on the experimental forecasting process. In summary, little evidence currently exists on which to reach any conclusions concerning the impact of objective forecasts on the subjective forecasting process. Nevertheless, we will briefly describe the major positions presently taken on this issue by members of the meteorological community.

One group of meteorologists believes that the current level of skill of the official subjective forecasts is due in large measure to the performance of the corresponding objective guidance forecasts and that the latter largely account for any improvement in the former in recent years (e.g., Charba & Klein, 1980). This point of view appears to be supported by the tendency for increases (decreases) in the level of skill of the objective forecasts to accompany increases (decreases) in the level of skill of subjective forecasts (e.g., see Figures 2 to 6). However, similar trends in *aggregate* skill scores for the two types of forecasts are not sufficient in themselves to prove that changes in performance of subjective forecasts are due to changes in performance of objective forecasts. For example, it is also possible that these concurrent changes in levels of skill are due to another factor, such as variations in the relative frequency of occurrence of the relevant events.

Another group of meteorologists, although not necessarily advocating the elimination of the objective guidance forecasts, argues that such forecasts may adversely affect the subjective forecasting process (e.g., see Golden, Chappell, Little, Murphy, Burton, & Pearl, 1978; Snellman, 1977). Specifically, these individuals believe that the availability of such forecasts enhances any tendency on the part of the forecasters to make less than full use of their knowledge and diagnostic abilities and makes it extremely difficult for forecasters to assign proper weight to potentially relevant information from other sources. Moreover, NWS management practices related to ex post "rewards" (or "penalties") associated with departures of the official subjective forecasts from the objective guidance forecasts tend to reinforce certain undesirable habits (vis-à-vis the forecasting process) developed by some forecasters. However, the evidence currently available is not sufficient to draw any firm conclusions regarding the practical significance of these (or other) possible adverse effects of objective forecasts.

The lack of studies of the subjective weather forecasting process may be surprising to some readers, especially to those individuals familiar with the substantial efforts to analyze and model judgmental (i.e., subjective) forecasting procedures in other contexts (e.g., Kahneman, Slovic, & Tversky, 1982). However, the operational setting in which weather forecasting traditionally is practiced presents some serious obstacles to the design and conduct of controlled experiments. These obstacles include the difficulties associated with limiting the information sources available to forecasters and the time constraints imposed on forecasters by operational schedules and deadlines (as well as by a myriad of duties and responsibilities). Although such obstacles are not insurmountable, the nearly complete absence of controlled experiments of any type in an operational context attests to the difficulties associated with conducting these experiments in the field of meteorology. Moreover, a more fundamental difficulty may arise in conjunction with conducting experiments of this type, a difficulty that is analogous in some respects to Heisenberg's *uncertainty principle*. This difficulty relates to the fact that any attempt to observe or "measure" the subjective forecasting process in an operational context almost inevitably leads to modifications of the process. These considerations may help to explain in part the lack of studies of the impact of objective guidance forecasts on subjective weather forecasts.

Of course, it is possible to conduct weather forecasting experiments in a controlled laboratory setting, assuming that experienced weather forecasters are available to participate in these studies. However, some problems also arise in connection with such experiments, including the need to prepare realistic sets of materials for the forecasters' use in making experimental forecasts (assuming historical data are used to create forecasting situations) and the difficulties associated with properly simulating operational weather forecasting situations in the laboratory. Nevertheless, a few isolated pilot studies of the subjective weather forecasting process have been conducted in this context (e.g., see Allen, 1982; Winkler & Murphy, 1973). To date, such studies have provided only limited insight into the forecasting process and little information concerning the impact of guidance forecasts on subjective weather forecasts. If forecasters are expected to provide users with accurate and timely weather forecasts consistent with the current state of the art, then it would appear to be of paramount importance to investigate the subjective forecasting process in detail and to study the impacts of various inputs (e.g., the objective forecasts) on this process.

WEATHER FORECASTING AND FORECASTING
IN OTHER FIELDS: SIMILARITIES AND DIFFERENCES

It seems appropriate in this context to briefly examine the similarities and differences between weather forecasting and forecasting in other fields. By examining these similarities and differences, we believe that forecasters in other fields will gain a deeper understanding of the characteristics of weather forecasting and a better appreciation of any lessons that can be learned from the forecasting experience in meteorology. To facilitate this discussion, some important characteristics of weather forecasting are identified in Table 5. It should be noted that the characteristics listed in this table pertain to several different components or aspects of the weather forecasting system (or process). In this section, we briefly describe these characteristics and discuss the extent to which (to our knowledge) they are or are not shared by forecasting systems in others fields.

Weather forecasting possesses a strong physical/dynamical foundation in the fundamental laws of fluid mechanics and thermodynamics (C1). These laws—expressed in the form of a set of nonlinear differential equations—constitute a framework for the formulation of the numerical models that are used to forecast the behavior and evolution of the atmosphere. Although such models are by no means perfect, they currently provide quite accurate predictions of the large-scale atmospheric circulation as well as a sound scientific basis for the subsequent preparation—either objectively or subjectively—of weather forecasts. Although fields such as economics certainly possess some laws that describe the behavior of economic systems, these laws do not appear to provide the same degree of predictability as the fundamental physical/dynamical laws in meteorology.

On a more pragmatic level, although no two weather situations are ever exactly identical, similarities do exist between meteorological situations on different occasions (C2). These similarities frequently are useful from a forecasting perspective and, for example, have provided the basis for an objective procedure generally referred to as *analogue forecasting* (e.g., see Kruizinga & Murphy, 1983). Moreover, such similarities often are used by forecasters to guide their subjective weather forecasting process. In many other fields, reasonably similar situations occur only infrequently, and thus modelers and forecasters in such fields cannot depend on this approach to provide reliable information.

The existence of objective analyses and forecasts of the large-scale features of the atmosphere means that forecasters (modelers) have available a very large amount of potentially useful information on which to base their forecasts (their objective *weather* forecasting models) (C3). In fact, the problem that faces such individuals, in many cases, is one of information overload rather than one of information scarcity. Thus, modelers/forecasters in meteorology must concern themselves with ways of aggregating and assimilating this information in an ef-

Table 5.   Some Characteristics of Weather Forecasting
(See Text for Additional Details)

WEATHER FORECASTING
Some Characteristics

(C1)	Existence of physical/dynamical basis
(C2)	Similarities among forecasting situations
(C3)	Availability of general analyses and forecasts
(C4)	Experience in developing and implementing operational objective forecasting procedures
(C5)	Availability of objective guidance forecasts for many variables
(C6)	Experience in making many forecasts for specific variables and locations
(C7)	Availability of rapid, formal and/or informal, outcome feedback
(C8)	Experience in quantifying uncertainty in forecasts
(C9)	Outcomes not influenced by forecasts
(C10)	Forecasts provided to wide spectrum of actual and potential users

ficient and effective manner. This situation is quite different than that faced by forecasters/modelers in many other fields in which equivalent general guidance information is limited in amount and/or marginal in quality.

Meteorologists have had considerable experience in developing and implementing operational objective weather forecasting procedures (C4). The current objective weather forecasting system in the U.S. provides a good example of this work (similar systems also exist in other countries, although they generally are more modest in size and of more recent vintage). Such systems usually are preceded and accompanied by substantial efforts in the areas of model refinement and testing. Moreover, the forecasts produced by these operational systems are subject to routine and detailed evaluation. Statisticians, economists, and others also have devoted considerable attention to the development of objective forecasting procedures. However, experience with the implementation and evaluation of *operational* forecasting systems in these other fields is not as extensive as it is in meteorology.

As noted previously, weather forecasters frequently have available, as guidance, objective forecasts that are identical in form to the official forecasts that the forecasters themselves must formulate (C5). Although the impacts of such forecasts may not always be beneficial (see preceding section), their availability provides a relatively high and stable threshold of quality under the subjective forecasting process. Such a threshold may be especially important in the case of inexperienced forecasters. To the best of our knowledge, objective guidance forecasts of this type generally are not available to forecasters in other fields.

Weather forecasters make forecasts for the same variables and locations several times each day (C6). Moreover, because the lead times of these forecasts generally are relatively short (i.e., a few hours to a few days) and observed weather conditions are reported on a regular basis, informal and /or formal feedback regarding outcomes is routinely available to the forecasters (C7). Thus, they gain forecasting experience concerning these variables and locations under a wide variety of meteorological conditions in a relatively short time (i.e., a few months to a year or two). Moreover, assignment as a full-fledged forecaster usually is preceded by a period of on-the-job training in which novice forecasters work with experienced forecasters and make "practice" forecasts. We do not believe that these generally beneficial aspects of subjective weather forecasting are all shared by the forecasting processes in other fields.

All forecasts are inherently uncertain, and meteorologists have had considerable experience in quantifying the uncertainty in weather forecasts (C8). For example, objective and subjective probability forecasts for selected weather variables have been formulated on an operational basis in several countries for many years. Although modelers and forecasters in other fields have long recognized the need to quantify the uncertainty in their forecasts, it is only quite recently that they have made efforts to formulate probability forecasts even on an experimental basis. To the authors' knowledge, operational probability forecasting currently is practiced only in meteorology.

The formulation and dissemination of forecasts in meteorology have no known effect on the subsequent weather conditions (C9). That is, the observed weather conditions (i.e., outcomes) are not influenced by the forecasts, and this characteristic *is* shared by forecasting in many other fields. However, in some fields (e.g., economics) in which human behavior can influence subsequent events, reactions to forecasts can lead to modifications of outcomes. Obviously, such effects further complicate the forecasting process, especially in the area of forecast evaluation.

Weather forecasts are disseminated routinely to the general public and to specific users (C10). The presence of these actual and/or potential users provides meteorologists with a strong motivation for conducting the forecasting process in an efficient and effective manner and for providing accurate and timely forecasts consistent with the current state of the art. Moreover, feedback from users of weather forecasts frequently contains information regarding possible improvements in the forecasting process or in the forecasts themselves. In many other fields, forecasting undoubtedly also benefits from the fact that the relevant forecasts are used by various individuals to make important decisions. Whenever forecasting is conducted in the absence of such users, it will be lacking in this fundamental aspect of motivation.

The foregoing discussion indicates that weather forecasting possesses many desirable characteristics—the characteristics are desirable in the sense that they generally contribute to success in forecasting. Some of these characteristics are shared by forecasting in other fields, but few if any fields share all of the characteristics. This fact may help to explain, in part, the *relatively* high level of success achieved in weather forecasting. Such a statement should not be interpreted to mean either that forecasting in other fields is not successful (or skillful) or that weather forecasting is almost perfect and cannot be improved. The results presented in the third and fourth sections of this chapter provide ample evidence that weather forecasting is far from perfect and that substantial opportunity for improvement still exists.

In considering any possible lessons or implications of the weather forecasting experience for forecasting in other fields, it is important to distinguish between two categories of characteristics of forecasting systems, namely characteristics that can be controlled and characteristics that cannot be controlled (in this context, the term "controlled" relates to a forecasting system's ability to *acquire* the characteristics of interest). Of the characteristics listed in Table 5, C3, C5, and C7 (in some cases) appear to fall into the first category, whereas C1, C2, C7 (in other cases), and C9 appear to fall into the second category. Thus, individuals developing forecasting systems in other fields may want to investigate the possibility of providing forecasters with general objective guidance information (C3) and/or specific objective guidance forecasts for the relevant variables (C5), and they may want to consider implementing procedures that routinely provide forecasters and modelers with formal feedback concerning the performance of their forecasts (C7).

SUMMARY AND CONCLUSION

Objective and subjective forecasts of precipitation occurrence, maximum and minimum temperatures, and cloud amount have been evaluated and compared. Both types of probability of precipitation (POP) forecasts were found to be reliable and skillful. The objective and subjective categorical temperature forecasts generally were quite accurate, with the accuracy of warm season forecasts exceeding the accuracy of cool season forecasts. Evaluation of the two types of categorical forecasts of cloud amount also yielded positive skill scores. Comparison of objective and subjective POP and temperature forecasts revealed that the subjective forecasts generally were more skillful (or accurate) than the objective forecasts for the shorter lead times, whereas the two types of precipitation and temperature forecasts were of approximately equal skill (accuracy) for longer lead times. The objective cloud amount forecasts were more skillful than the subjective cloud amount forecasts for all lead times.

Examination of trends in performance indicated that all three types of forecasts increased in skill (or accuracy) over the period from 1971 to 1982. Improvements over this period generally were greater for the longer range forecasts than for the shorter range forecasts and for the cool season than for the warm season. Moreover, the objective forecasts generally exhibited greater improvement than the subjective forecasts over the 10-year period.

We believe that these results are representative of the current state of the art of weather forecasting in the U.S. National Weather Service and other modern national meteorological services, at least for those weather elements traditionally considered in public forecasts. Nevertheless, some readers may want to obtain further details concerning the quality of these forecasts or to investigate the performance of objective and/or subjective forecasts of other weather elements (e.g., wind speed and direction, ceiling height, precipitation type and amount, severe thunderstorms and tornadoes). The following list of references will provide these readers with some sources of relevant information: Carter, Glahn, and Cooley (1982), Charba and Klein (1980), Glahn (1985), Murphy (1985), Polger (1983), and Zurndorfer, Bocchieri, Carter, Dallavalle, Gilhousen, Hebenstreit, and Vercelli (1979).

The role of the objective forecasts in the subjective forecasting process—and the impact of the objective forecasts on the subjective forecasts—are issues of considerable interest and importance in meteorology, and these issues were discussed in some detail. Although this discussion revealed that very little concrete evidence currently is available concerning the actual role and impact of such forecasts, it provided some indication of the range of *possible* roles and impacts of such forecasts. Some difficulties inherent in conducting studies of the subjective forecasting process in general—and of the impact of the objective forecasts in particular—were also described, and these difficulties were offered as a partial explanation for the lack of studies (and evidence) concerning the issues of interest here.

If the weather forecaster continues to play the roles of assimilator of information from many sources and of producer of the official forecasts, then it seems inevitable (at least to the authors) that studies of the subjective forecasting process will become increasingly important in the future. Thus, meteorologists must overcome the obstacles—and any resistance on the part of the meteorological community—to the design and conduct of such studies. An important subset of these studies would include investigations of the impact of objective guidance forecasts on the subjective forecasting process and its output—the official subjective forecasts. Such studies offer considerable promise as a means of making more effective use of the available sources of information (including the guidance forecasts) and of producing more accurate and skillful weather forecasts. Meteorologists can draw in part on recent work and experience in fields such as artificial intelligence, psychology, systems analysis, and statistics to guide their efforts in exploring and developing this new area of applied research.

Some characteristics of weather forecasting were described in the previous section, and they were used to illustrate similarities and differences between weather forecasting and forecasting in other fields. The fact that weather forecasting possesses such characteristics generally is believed to contribute to its relatively high level of success. Some of these characteristics can be controlled—for example, the preparation of objective guidance forecasts and the provision of feedback regarding performance—and forecasters in other fields may want to investigate the more extensive use of such information in their own fields in the future.

In conclusion, it is appropriate to consider the issue of objective vis-à-vis subjective forecasts in the context of the forecasting system as a whole. In this context, the forecasting process generally involves the use of both objective and subjective inputs and requires the continuous updating of the system's state of knowledge. The experience in weather forecasting, as revealed by the comparison of objective and subjective forecasts, indicates that the information contained in these inputs frequently is not assimilated in an effective manner. Thus, the basic issue is the way in which the process of assimilating such inputs should be accomplished to provide the most accurate and timely forecasts. One possibility is to use an objective model to aggregate both objective and subjective inputs. Alternatively, forecasters could assimilate the objective and subjective information, and weather forecasting as currently practiced corresponds most closely to this approach. Other possibilities involving the combined use of objective and subjective assimilation procedures also exist. In any case, both objective and subjective inputs provide potentially valuable information for forecasting in most fields, and the development of procedures to combine or assimilate these inputs appears to be an important and fertile area of research.

ACKNOWLEDGMENTS

We would like to express our appreciation to G.M. Carter of the Techniques Development Laboratory, U.S. National Weather Service, for his assistance in obtaining the verification data on which the sections Objective versus Subjective Forecasts and Recent Trends in Forecast Quality are based. The authors also would like to thank H. R. Glahn, L. W. Snellman, and R. L. Winkler for their comments on earlier versions of the chapter.

REFERENCES

Allen, G. (1982). Probability judgment in weather forecasting. *Preprints of the 9th Conference on Weather Forecasting and Analysis.* Boston: American Meteorological Society.

Belville, J. D., & Johnson, G. A. (1982). The role of decision trees in weather forecasting. *Preprints of the 9th Conference on Weather Forecasting and Analysis.* Boston: American Meteorological Society.

Brier, G. W. (1950). Verification of forecasts expressed in terms of probability. *Monthly Weather Review, 78,* 1–3.

Carter, G. M., Glahn, H. R., & Cooley, D. S. (1982). Quality and trends in National Weather Service forecasts. *Preprints of the 9th Conference on Weather Forecasting and Analysis.* Boston: American Meteorological Society.

Charba, J. P., & Klein, W. H. (1980). Skill in precipitation forecasting in the National Weather Service. *Bulletin of the American Meteorological Society, 61,* 1546–1555.

Gaffney, J. E., Jr., & Racer, I. R. (1983). A learning interpretive decision algorithm for severe storm forecasting support. *Preprints of the 13th Conference on Severe Local Storms.* Boston: American Meteorological Society.

Glahn, H. R. (1985). Statistical weather forecasting. In A. H. Murphy & R. W. Katz (Eds.), *Probability, statistics, and decision making in the atmospheric sciences.* Boulder, CO: Westview Press.

Golden, J. H., Chappell, C. F., Little, C. G., Murphy, A. H., Burton, E. B., & Pearl, E. W. (1978). What should the NWS be doing to improve short-range weather forecasting?—A panel discussion with audience participation 12 April 1978, Boulder, CO. *Bulletin of the American Meteorological Society, 59,* 1334–1342. (See comments by A. H. Murphy)

Kahneman, D., Slovic, P., & Tversky, A. (1982). *Judgment under uncertainty: Heuristics and biases.* Cambridge: Cambridge University Press.

Kruizinga, S., & Murphy, A. H. (1983). Use of an analogue procedure to formulate objective probabilistic temperature forecasts in The Netherlands. *Monthly Weather Review, 111,* 2244–2254.

Murphy, A. H. (1985). Probabilistic weather forecasting. In A. H. Murphy & R. W. Katz (Eds.), *Probability, statistics, and decision making in the atmospheric sciences.* Boulder, CO: Westview Press.

Murphy, A. H., & Winkler, R. L. (1971). Forecasters and probability forecasts: The responses to a questionnaire. *Bulletin of the American Meteorological Society, 52,* 158–165.

Murphy, A. H., & Winkler, R. L. (1974a). Subjective probability forecasting experiments in meteorology: Some preliminary results. *Bulletin of the American Meteorological Society, 55,* 1206–1216.

Murphy, A. H., & Winkler, R. L. (1974b). Probability forecasts: A survey of National Weather Service forecasters. *Bulletin of the American Meteorological Society, 55,* 1449–1453.

Polger, P. D. (1983). National Weather Service public forecast verification summary April 1978 to March 1982. *NOAA Technical Memorandum NWS FCST 28.* Silver Springs, MD: National Weather Service.

Simpson, R. H. (1971). The decision process in hurricane forecasting. *NOAA Technical Memorandum NWS SR 53.* Fort Worth, TX: National Weather Service.

Snellman, L. W. (1977). Operational forecasting using automated guidance. *Bulletin of the American Meteorological Society, 58,* 1036–1044.

Tversky, A., & Kahneman, D. (1974). Judgment under uncertainty: Heuristics and biases. *Science, 185,* 1124–1131.

Winkler, R. L., & Murphy, A. H. (1973). Information aggregation in probabilistic prediction. *IEEE Transactions on Systems, Man, and Cybernetics, SMC-3,* 154–160.

Zurndorfer, E. A., Bocchieri, J. R., Carter, G. M., Dallavalle, J. P., Gilhousen, D. B., Hebenstreit, K. F., & Vercelli, D. J. (1979). Trends in comparative verification scores for guidance and local aviation/public weather forecasts. *Monthly Weather Review, 107,* 799–811.

PART VI

Decision Theory
Areas of Future Impact

CHAPTER 16

Education and Decision Theory
A Personal View

Jack Dowie

First of all, in the grand tradition—and spirit—of Murphy, Parkinson, and Sod, I want to offer you a law: the "law of disciplinary myopia." It goes like this: Each academic discipline possesses a limited number of key insights into the world and how we can come to know and understand it better. The number is usually greater than one but rarely more than two or three. These key insights are documented, embroidered, stretched, qualified, and paraphrased until they are all but lost to many students, even specialists (perhaps most of all specialists). But *that* is not the law of disciplinary myopia, just an academic manifestation of Parkinson. The law of disciplinary myopia says that in its own operations (organization and teaching), a discipline will ignore, deny, and betray its own key insights.

I offer a few examples, culled from many hours on faculty boards, subcommittees, and working groups. The order is no indication of seriousness or vindictiveness. Additions and amendments are solicited: my diplomatic aim is to be equally offensive to all disciplines if possible.

Economists will typically be found arguing that their students can never have enough economics. If students are permitted to do two noneconomics options out of eight papers in single honors, economists will argue that it is essential that they do seven economics papers; if students are allowed one "wild" option, economists will argue they also need the eighth paper in order to become an adequately qualified professional. The concepts of opportunity cost and diminishing marginal returns have no relevance in Economics with a capital *E*.

Jack Dowie • Faculty of Social Sciences, The Open University, Milton Keynes MK7 6AA, England.

Statisticians will typically be found arguing that the performance of the sample of students who *voluntarily* enroll in their courses, however small in number, is evidence that their broad approach and teaching methods are satisfactory. The law of large numbers does not apply to assessments of the significance of statisticians' efforts.

Psychologists will typically be found ignoring the individual differences in their students, concentrating on mass teaching by standardized tests.

Sociologists will typically be found expressing amazement that students' essays reflect the beliefs and values of the subculture from which they come and not those of the lecturer; they will grade them accordingly.

Political scientists will typically be found remarking that students seem to be obsessed with pursuing abstract rights of representation and consultation—as if the university was some sort of power struggle, which it clearly is not because "we all have their best interests at heart."

And so on.

Physician, heal thyself? Of course. So what is the diagnosis for the *decision theorist* as teacher? From now on I am above all talking to, and criticizing, *myself,* even though it will not always sound that way.

The decision theorist (and I shall use *decision theory* as an umbrella term covering both normative and behavioral perspectives on decision making) typically fails to recognize—to "re-cognize"—the educational process as a set of mutually interacting decision processes, at the microlevel, the teacher's processes on the one hand and the student's on the other. Almost irrespective of the more macro- (institutional) context, I suggest that one of the last things that would enter the head of someone starting out to design and teach a course on normative decision theory would be to set out the main possible options regarding content and pedagogy, identify the possible end states, elicit multiattribute utilities for each of these, assess the probabilities (subjective naturally) of each branch of the tree, and select the option that maximizes expected utility. Or, think to start the course by telling the students why it was impossible or undesirable to do (e.g., because of "game" characteristics of their relationship).

Obversely, one of the last things that would enter the mind of the teacher of a course in decision behavior would be to assume (and act on the assumption) that all actions of the students—appearances at lectures, verbal and nonverbal responses to questions in tutorials, alternatives ticked in a multiple choice test, contents of an essay—are the results of a decision process. Within a *humanistic* framework the implication of such an assumption would be that the significance of any such student action can be judged only in the light of the structure and contents of their decision process. Of course they can be judged (period), but unless we have treated the action as rational from the actor's point of view, *until it is proved otherwise,* we have not made a meaningful judgment. The humanist, as seen by the decision theorist (or at least *this* decision theorist), is one who assumes that a human being is maximizing expected utility until proved guilty. I think (fortunately for human beings) that expected utility theory is untestable in principle (Dowie, 1982), so that the discourse can never be closed or definitive judgment pronounced.

Parenthetically, one point should be emphasized because failing to do so has seriously reduced the chances of the economist's approach being widely accepted: conceptually, maximizing expected utility has nothing to do with maximizing *material self-interest*. *Minimizing* material self-interest may be maximizing expected utility. Mother Teresa has just as much claim to this sort of "rationality" as J. R. Ewing of "Dallas" (or some local real-life approximation that you care to supply). It is still ends–means rationality, I agree, but Mother Teresa should be no less concerned with this just because the welfare of *others* dominates her preferences.

This assumption concerning burden of proof—the essential humanistic assumption—does not rule out, indeed it rules very much "in," the questions of whether the decision is a *good* or *bad* decision, *better* or *worse* decision, *right* or *wrong* decision. To be more precise, whether

1. the uncertainty assessments (probabilities) that have explicitly or implicitly gone into it are accurate or inaccurate, biased or unbiased;
2. the outcome evaluations (utilities) that have explicitly or implicitly gone into it are moral or immoral, aesthetic or unaesthetic; and
3. the integration of uncertainties and values has been properly or improperly carried out.

There are so many scare quotes needed in this statement that it might be simpler if you put them round all of it. (They indicate, of course, the vast scope of the areas to be contested.)

The central humanist assumption, then, *merely* sets the agenda and the burden of proof. All the issues of *whose* probabilities, utilities, and integrating procedures are to be the standard remain. The law tackles this issue in many jurisdictions by postulating the existence of an *ordinary reasonable person,* defining the decision of this person in a particular case as that arrived at by 12 individuals (selected with *some* element of randomness from the community). It then protects the construct by preventing any examination or discussion of how the particular individuals generated it. This either solves the problem or evades it, depending on how one looks at it. The distinguishing feature of education is surely that *however* we look at it, evading is not good enough.

The educational implication is obvious; its implementation is painful to contemplate. Teaching decision theory and processes above all else (though it might be argued that at its widest it subsumes much of the "all else") needs to be unremittingly *reflexive*. It is either personally relevant at almost every moment, or it is nothing. Or rather it comes dangerously close to being a fraud perpetrated

by the teacher on the student; *whether or not* the latter is an all too willing ac-
complice in the depersonalization is not wholly irrelevant, but it cannot in itself
provide a justification.

A course in decision theory should be its own main resource. The typical
response to this suggestion—"sounds very incestuous...it wouldn't interest the
students...washing dirty linen in public...let's just teach the *subject*"—
embraces a variety of objections and each does have *some* validity. But after years
of reflection I am convinced that a root of the objection is *fear* of the implication: that the teacher's personal attitudes (beliefs and values) and actions will be
addressed and opened up for discussion and criticism in front of the students.
And the equally great fear is that in classes and essays the students' personal attitudes (beliefs and values) and actions will be addressed and opened up for discussion and criticism in front of the teacher. The fear is, in other words, that
we will address each other in class as human beings and not as role incumbents
who talk about things in the third person. (The belief that not using "I" makes
things impersonal and objective is still surprisingly widespread. In redrafting this
chapter I feel constant pressure to change from first- to third-person phrasing.)
I confess to being as scared as anyone of indulging publicly in good faith—in
fact it terrifies me—but it does seem difficult to avoid the conclusion that if we
cannot aim at it in *education* there is little hope of that process being much more
than either training or indoctrination. Some, of course, think education ought
to be, basically, training, and for them this will be anathema. Others, of different political suasion, see education as just one aspect of hegemony maintenance,
and for them this will be unbelievably naive. All we can hope to do is to open
up discourse with both about the beliefs and values that underlie such reactions
and interpretations.

RESTRUCTURING THE INSTITUTION

What would the humanist institution of higher learning look like in its decision theoretized form? At the Thomas Bayes Academy, there is only one
faculty, composed of everyone in the institution. Call it "the faculty." Everyone must contribute to its teaching, which is clearly separate from that of the
two subfaculties: the "subfaculty of uncertainties" and the "subfaculty of
values." Staff can specialize to some degree, but the rule would be something
like this: a minimum of x percent of every member's time must be given to *each*
of the faculty, the subfaculty of uncertainties, and the subfaculty of values. The
remaining percentage $(100-3x)$ may be given to any of the three elements in
whole or any part. I would favor an x in the region of 20, but settle for a minimum of 10. A similar rule would apply to students' course profiles.

The decision theorist does not, therefore, want to abolish or merge the "two cultures'' of uncertainty and value; he or she wants to insist on their simultaneous distinctiveness and interdependence. Neither can do without the other. The chimera is perhaps the appropriate metaphor, a chimera being the conjunction of two distinct animals, not a crossbreed in which each loses its identity. *Duality not dualism* is the slogan.

There are just two subfaculties (although plenty of internal specialization within them). There is nothing left when we have allocated everyone involved in studying and teaching uncertainties, values, or both. Let us see why.

The subfaculty of uncertainties has the task of studying the uncertainties (probabilities) of *everyone* for *every event*, not just, as science faculties largely do at the moment, concentrating on the low uncertainties/high probabilities of "those who know most," that is, searching exclusively for *certainties* or what used to be called *the truth* or *the facts*. The uncertainties of the most lowly person in the society about the most supposedly trivial events are as much part of its obligation as those held by the most eminent about the most supposedly significant.

The subfaculty of values has the task of studying the values of *everyone* for *everything*, not just, as arts faculties largely do at the moment, concentrating on the high values/high utilities of "those who know best," that is, searching exclusively for *perfection* or what used to be called *the good* and *the beautiful*. The values of the most uncultured person in the society about the most supposedly valueless things are as much part of its obligation as those of the most sensitive about the most supposedly excellent.

There is no room or necessity for an evasive middle subfaculty that allows those who want to "cream off" the high probability events (most natural scientists) or the high utility events (most arts people) for themselves to get away with it. So as the science and arts faculties are transformed almost beyond recognition, social (or behavioral) science disappears. In one sense it is dismembered and allocated to the subfaculty of its particular concern. In another sense, it becomes a core part of the faculty, the place where all questions that in any way or for any reason bring uncertainties and values together are addressed—including how they are and should be distinguished.

RETHINKING THE CURRICULUM

If such a structural revolution is unlikely ever to come about, what about the curriculum and its teaching, as seen through decision-theoretic spectacles? I want to speculate briefly about this, also, by comparing the education system with the news media. There are, of course, lots of differences between them, but curriculum planners and news programmers have in common the problem of how to allocate a finite amount of resources (space/time) among competing uses (items/subjects). The amount may be flexible within a range, but the range is usually quite narrow (so many pages/class hours).

Let us look first at the news editor. Given the availability and costs of reports, photos, film, and the like, his or her task is to fill the available space with items that vary in coverage with their news value. What is this mystical thing, *news value*? If you ask newspapermen about it, they will refer you to the seats of their pants, or their noses, or their water, or their gut—anything but their minds—saying it is all a matter of *intuitive* judgment. But the decision theorist is predisposed to believe that we will be able to capture the editor's actions in terms of two central dimensions—probability and utility, uncertainty and value.

A little reflection leads me to the following suggestion. The news value of an event, N, approximated by column inches weighted by prominence, will vary inversely with its probability, P, and directly with the absolute value of its utility, U. (U runs from plus infinity to minus infinity, via 0. An event has 0 utility where there is indifference to its occurrence or nonoccurrence.) The function might be linear (e.g., $N=U/P$) or quadratic (e.g., $N=U^2/P$ or U^2/P^2). In all these cases, good news and bad news are equally newsworthy. If good news has to be proportionally more good than bad news is bad in order to generate the same N, we would have respectively $N=kU/P$; kU^2/P; kU^2/P^2 when $U>0$ and as before when $U<0$.

Mapping a function such as $N=U^2/P$ we get a set of news contours, lines of equal news value. I shall christen them *isofleets* (a fleet being taken as the fundamental unit of news value). I will leave you to speculate where different sorts of events will or would be located (e.g., a royal wedding, a presidential death after long illness, a nuclear war, announcement of a miracle cure for cancer). Also I will leave you to speculate on how different editors' and audiences' average Ps and Us will differ; obviously a successful editor is one whose perceptions of the Ps and Us of a substantial section of the community are accurate. (In the *long* run, does the media create the Ps and Us it then services? Probably partly. There is also probably interaction between Ps and Us over time, so that, for example, rarer events come to have higher or lower U simply because of their rarity.)

And the curriculum? What does the function for educational value, E, look like (as perceived by curriculum planners)? It seems in many ways to be *opposite* to that for N. E would seem more likely to vary *directly with* P than inversely—education is more concerned with the more likely than with the less likely. And *if* the E function is asymmetric it will be positive U events that get disproportionate coverage rather than negative U ones—education is more concerned to teach about the more highly valued than about the more lowly or negatively valued. Over time we again have a problem, of course: U may be influenced by P. In the arts, for example, the best is, almost by definition, the rarest—at one tail of the distribution. It is also possible that, over time, P may be influenced by *U*. Indeed, our educational efforts are presumably premised on the hope that we can make more desirable events more common.

But if the news and educational value functions seem to be very different, it is interesting to note that an increasingly frequent explanation (or defense) of the news media's focus on disasters (low probability, high disutility events) is that such events signal our need to learn so that we can take action to reduce their *P* still further. That is, the *news* is assigned an important *educational* function. If so, why is not the educational system doing *its* bit in the negative utility/low probability area? (If we envisage a 2 × 2 table in which the dichotomies are high and low *P* and positive and negative *U*, educational time seems to be taken up almost completely by the three high *P* or high *U* cells.) The broad answer is, as I have already implied, that education has been seen as *teaching the certain and the best* rather than *learning from the uncertain and the normal/worst*. If it is antielitist to say that the *balance* needs shifting, so be it.

All I hope to have achieved so far is to leave the thought that decision theory may provide a new and perhaps more productive framework within which to fight many ancient and long-running battles about the structure and content of education. If there are unresolved questions in your mind—not least about the definition of the events or statements to which the *P*s and *U*s discussed previously relate and how individual's *P*s and *U*s should be aggregated—that is all to the good; my purpose will have been accomplished if your attempts to resolve them encourage looking at the curriculum through new spectacles.

REEXAMINING ASSESSMENT

To get to some flesh and bone. It is in relation to *assessment* that the implications of a decision-theoretic approach in education can be made clearest—and implemented even now to some extent, given the will.

Aggregating Components

To begin with, consider the task of arriving at an overall mark for each student, given their set of marks on individual papers or components. Simon French (and his colleagues) have been developing the case for viewing this problem as one parallel to that of assessing a multiattribute value function:

> Suppose we suggest in a non-pejorative sense that, when an examiner judges one candidate to have performed better than another, he is expressing a preference for the first candidate over the second. If further we suggest that a candidate's marks on the n components correspond to levels on n attributes, then our problem is essentially identical to that of assessing a multi-attribute value function. . . . This parallel between examination assessment and multi-attribute value theory is not just of academic in-

terest, because it enables us to see how we may proceed practically in the prescriptive modelling of examiners' judgements.... First, one would ask examiners about general properties that they should like their judgements to embody. Examples like that [below] would enable them to understand clearly and simply concepts of independence and so decide whether they wish to adopt them in their judgements. Next one would ask the examiners for their judgement of performance for carefully chosen pairs of, perhaps hypothetical, candidates with [different mark] profiles.... The pairs would be carefully chosen so that the examiners' responses quickly determine [the aggregate mark function] exactly.

Candidate	Paper			
	1	2	3	4
A	70	65	60	40
B	40	80	60	40
C	70	65	80	60
D	40	80	80	60

There are a number of points to be made about this procedure. Firstly, the number of judgements which the examiners would be required to make would not be excessive. The procedure would be feasible in the time available. Secondly, the examiners would not be asked to compare pairs of candidates whose mark profiles were different in the majority of the components. Typically, the comparisons would involve profiles that differ in two components only. Thus, the judgements required of the examiners would be ones that they are most able to make consistently. Thirdly, the procedure would be iterative. No judgement of the examiners would be taken as immutable. If their judgements of the relative performance of pairs of candidates were incompatible with the consistency properties that they desire, then they could be informed of this and encouraged to revise their statements. In this way, the examiners may come to appreciate the need to understand their task better. Finally, at no point in the procedure would the examiners be asked direct questions about what the [overall mark] function should be. Throughout the procedure, one would require only that they answer questions of the form: is the overall performance of this candidate better than that candidate's? They would not be asked questions of the form: what are the relative weights of papers 1 and 2? Thus, the procedure would not require the examiners to be at all numerate. Decision analysis has been applied and used by—if they will forgive me—quite innumerate decision-makers, and the translated procedures could be used by quite innumerate examiners. Moreover, the advent of cheap microcomputing power means that the assessment...can be achieved in a quick "user-friendly" manner. (French, 1983, pp. 27-29)

It is clear that French is concerned to protect the assessor as much as possible from contact with the formal structures of decision analysis. This is undoubtedly advisable in general courses at least for the time being, but, if, as I now argue, the assessment process in decision-theoretic courses should become explicitly reflexive, the possibility as well as desirability of this tactic is questionable. The reasons can be best looked at in the context of the perhaps more fundamental task of arriving at a mark for an individual component (essay, dissertation, etc.).

Marking Components

Multiattribute utility theory again provides a normative basis for component assessment. We derive a set of utility-independent attributes using a personal construct (repertory grid) program and weights to aggregate them by a standard gamble method. (Patrick Humphreys's MAUD program will do it all; see Humphreys & McFadden, 1980.) We then mark a piece of work separately on each attribute and combine the separate marks mechanically. It would be good practice, however, also to assign a global/synthetic mark and to explore, through time, the extent to which we can capture our own marking policy on the basis of the decomposed assessments. ("Rubbish!" is not, for the decision theorist, a decomposed assessment.)

Whose attributes and weights would we use? Ours as teachers, of course. *Of course?* I am not so sure that in an *educational* process, as compared with a *training and certification* process, only *our* utilities should count. Agreed, it is not completely analogous to the *medical* situation in that the educational one is *by definition* one where the client should generally admit that he or she does not have fully developed end state preferences. Indeed, clients are involved partly in order to develop them, and they ought to be prepared to concede to the teacher what they should not necessarily cede to the doctor. But the case for taking *some* account of students' preferences seems unarguable, and teachers of decision processes could at least demonstrate the contribution decision analysis can make to conflict resolution by negotiating a teaching and assessment contract—adhering to it if the resulting terms are professionally defensible. Very briefly, each side (teachers, students) would establish its own multiattribute utility function for all attributes potentially at issue; then (in interactionist jargon) "alter-cast" the other side to establish *its* function. A contractual space is thereby established by each side, and this will contain an efficiency frontier of optimal contracts. Negotiations would typically proceed by the offering of suboptimal contracts and then improving the offer at no cost to oneself, when it is rejected. The whole process is repeated dynamically as information about the other side becomes available during negotiation.

If, on every single attribute, the utility functions of the two sides are diametrically opposed, the situation is obviously zero sum—and nothing, not even decision analysis, can help. Education is, however, not the sort of zero-sum situation where the technique has *nothing* to offer. On some issues students and teachers are probably in considerable agreement (e.g., length of essays). On many they will be in far from complete *dis*agreement (e.g., treatment of plagiarism or near plagiarism). So even though there will be some issues where we approach zero sum (e.g., grade assignment), this approach would not be ruled out in principle and certainly not *as a teaching device*. The humanist educational contract would always ideally be one between individual student and teacher. Individual values and beliefs *are,* of course, formed within a social environment, even if they are not completely determined by them. The social context may therefore heighten or lessen conflict between teachers and students considered collectively. But whatever the social context, there will still be some conflict between *individual* teacher and *individual* student; for example there is always the clash between grading *this* essay correctly and encouraging the student to do better next time by a mark (too soft or too harsh) designed to motivate.

Scoring Multiple Choice Items

The other assessment component I want to look at is the multiple-choice test. One of the key attributes we typically wish to assess is the student's knowledge (or at least knowledge relative to other students). The forced-choice multiple-choice test has long been seen as the most "objective" way to do this. The student usually selects one answer from a set of alternatives provided. Over a set of items the score is the percentage of correct answers selected (or some corrected transformation of it).

This procedure contradicts what I see as a central implication of the humanistic approach: that a student in responding to a test question has a right to be able to maximize expected value by being *honest* about his or her knowledge/beliefs. The standard multiple-choice test does not permit honesty because it makes no provision for the expression of uncertainty, or more precisely, of the *degrees* of belief that, for the decision theorist, embody the student's (typically partial) knowledge. Subjective probabilities of 100% are a *special* case: requiring the selection of one alternative forces the student to transform distributed degrees of belief into such a zero-entropy distribution in *every* case. Both teacher and student lose. *We* cannot gain an accurate measure of the students' knowledge on the item, that is, their degree of belief (subjective probability) that the correct alternative (according to us) *is* the correct alternative. And *the students* cannot maximize expected value by being honest, because they cannot be honest; they must claim to know for *certain* even when they know they do not.

The alternative is to allow the students to respond with their degrees of belief about each alternative in an item and score these responses by a strictly proper scoring rule. The latter ensures that the student who wishes to maximize expected value in mark terms can do so by responding with their honest degrees of belief and not some set of distorted ones. Note that we *cannot* simply assign the students a score equivalent to the probability assigned the correct alternative. That is *our* measure of their relative knowledge concerning the item, but if we used that as the *score* we would in effect be going back to the standard deterministic multiple-choice question. Students who wished to maximize expected value could not do so, under this rule, by being honest: to do so they should always *pretend* to be (100%) *certain* that the alternative they thought *most likely* to be correct, was correct—even if the "most likely" was only 51% for a two-alternative item. To see why, consider the case where the students' honest degrees of belief are (.60, .40) and we assign a score equivalent to the correct alternative's probability. In deciding whether to *respond* A (.60, .40) or B (1.00, 0) students will calculate the expected values to be, respectively,

$$A \quad .6(.6) + .4(.4) = .52$$
$$B \quad .6(1.00) + .4(0) = .6$$

Pretending to be certain always pays off under this rule (it can be shown), *ex ante,* of course, which is all that is relevant. So a proper scoring function, such as the log of the probability assigned to the correct alternative, is needed to make honesty the best policy.

The other great advantage of items requiring probabilistic responses (or *probers* as we have christened them at the Open University) is that they permit consideration of the *components* of the knowledge measure—of its partitioning into elements reflecting abilities such as calibration and resolution. Debate currently continues as to the *best* partitioning of proper scores—as to the precise nature of calibration and whether or not there are two different sorts of calibrations (Murphy 1973; Yates, 1982). The important point for us is that these issues, resolved or unresolved, should become part of the decision-theoretic *curriculum,* as assessment becomes an integral part of that curriculum.

But do we not have to ask whether probers are *practical?* As early as 1968 Lord and Novick argued that the "complexity" of a probabilistic system might well involve increased measurement error variance, sufficient to outweigh the reduced ability-related variance it promised. The *reliability* of probabilistic assessment has subsequently been accepted as the key issue by proponents as well as opponents.

> In theory, a probability system has the potential of avoiding the measurement error inherent in a binary system. In theory, probability scoring is perfectly reliable, because it reproduces perfectly what a person knows; thus it reduces the error variance in the observed score to zero. In practice, however, probability scoring may introduce undesirable variability through errors in using the system, misunderstanding of instructions, or failing to realize the consequences of one's response. A probability system is likely to be somewhat difficult to teach to most examinees and could not be taught to some. All of the above practical problems would contribute to error-related variance. Therefore, if the examinee does not understand and correctly utilize the scoring procedure, it is clear that test reliability will be less than perfect. (Poizner, Nicewander, & Gettys, 1978, p. 84)

This worry has not actually been sustained in practice. The most satisfactory of the empirical investigations (Poizner *et al.,* 1978; Pugh & Brunza, 1975; Rippey & Voytovich, 1982, 1983) show significantly *higher* reliability for probabilistic systems than for conventional systems.

But it is important to question the terms of this debate anyway. Because non-probabilistic systems cannot produce *valid* measures of partial knowledge at an item level, the *comparative* reliability of probabilistic systems is irrelevant. It is therefore *not* necessary, contrary to Lord and Novick's assertion, to show that a probabilistic system "adds more relevant ability variation to the system than error variation, and that any such relative increase in information is worth the effort" (1968, p. 314). The only issue is how we can raise the absolute reliability of probabilistic systems—by addressing the sources of unreliability listed previously. This, I would argue, can only be done successfully if those being assessed are fully introduced to the philosophical and methodological bases of the approach (especially payoff considerations) as part of their curriculum. (This is part of the curriculum that must *itself* be assessed, of course: ideally any set of items, regardless of its substantive topic focus, should include some that address the student's understanding of the assessment system.) Seen in this light, the practical difficulties of probabilistic systems actually become *merits* rather than weaknesses, forcing out into the open that fundamental conflict between education and assessment that, resolved covertly in favor of the latter, prostitutes the former.

Outside the Open University, Rippey and Voytovich's use of a probabilistic system for a second-year introductory course in clinical medicine at the University of Connecticut appears to be the only sustained routine application (as distinct from experiment). Using three alternative questions and presenting (truncated logarithmic) scores on a display of equilateral triangles, they give students a 25-item practice test, a 49-item midterm test, and a 97-item final exam. Feedback to the first two tests included a Realism Improvement score and a Knowledge Improvement score, derived by fitting a regression to each student's data (proportion correct at each probability assigned) and rescoring after removing the miscalibration ("unrealism") in the original responses indicated by this regression line. Overconfidence is, as usual, the typical bias found. Because, however, there is considerable "slop" in regressions based on such limited data it is incumbent on those employing probabilistic modes to practice what they preach and not be overconfident about their students' overconfidence. Again, only a deeper, curricular concern with the approach, not merely instructions in the context of assessment, seems to allow this sort of *assessor* uncertainty to be conveyed and discussed.

Rippey and Voytovich actually allow their students to choose either conventional or probabilistic response modes or both. Because students were informed that anyone who scored higher than 1.2 standard deviations below the mean by *either* method would pass, all naturally chose both. The authors do not report the "right-answer-only" score *deducible* from the probabilistic responses, so we cannot tell what "bonus" conventional scoring would yield in their case. (It is approximately 10% on average at the Open University, that is, the proportion correct *inferred* from the probabilistic responses exceeds the mean probability assigned to the correct alternative by that amount.) Incidentally, the introduction of a specific pass mark undermines any proper scoring rule; in this case the necessary uncertainty about what the mark will be, given its ex post parametric definition, may be sufficient to prevent the undermining. In the Open University context, where we have to *transform* the proper scores on the prober exam to bring them into line (parametrically) with other assessment components, I make considerable effort to get students to appreciate *why* they should accept the need to remain as uncertain as possible about what the pass (or class) marks are. I say something like the following:

> Yes, we do do this, but for reasons you [the students] should appreciate I cannot tell you anything about this transformation without undermining the whole basis of the system. If I tell you what the pass score is, you will perhaps try to maximize your chances of achieving that, rather than maximizing your expected value in mark terms. You would do this, for example, if you have a discontinuous utility function and try to maximize expected utility. I would like to allow you to maximize expected utility in principle (*and* to do it by being honest), but that would mean eliciting every student's individual utility function and applying an appropriate [different] scoring function in each case. This, I hope you will see, shows the fundamental incompatibility of assessment for *education*/learning and assessment for *extrinsic certification*. So because you seem to be interested at least partly in the latter I'm afraid the price you have to pay [and I pay in another sense] is being deceived—or kept less than fully informed—at some stage. My commitment is to making that stage as late and as minimal as possible—and having the issue itself as part of the *content* of the course, so that you will be rewarded by understanding the reasons for it. (*How* rewarded will depend on you!)

Probers have been running for 5 years in connection with a course on risk at the Open University now. Student reactions are varied. I quote a few from Dowie and Lefrere, (1984, p. 139) which also contains further details.

> As I see it many of us are torn between a wish to be honest, and a wish to play the system, and a wish to understand course material thoroughly. A simple right/wrong exercise is more useful than something using so much computer time and paper . . . . All I want to know is am I doing well or not. This, the printout never says. All I want is a high mark; I do not find Probers "fun" at all.

> I guess my thinking must have been influenced—at this stage I am not sure how. I suspect that the prober system has much to commend it—unfortunately so far I have not been able to spot the advantages. I continually feel that there has to be a system (like roulette) whereby one can win the prober game. So far I have not been able to find the formulae. Probably I am missing something. Is this a cumbersome way of teaching that one has to consider that there is a probability that one is not always absolutely correct? You're too clever for me.

> Has introduced an element of "discipline" when contemplating possibilities. Find myself amused when listening to those who forecast probabilities with conviction when they must be dealing with uncertainty.

I used to be very black and white in my judgments and initially sprinkled 100's [i.e., 100% on one alternative—complete certainty] liberally only to be proved I didn't know as much as I thought I did. I've now become more "gray" and make fewer snap judgments. I've found the exercise stimulating and regard it as infinitely more worthwhile educationally to be able to express shades of uncertainty.

It has tempered my "risk" factor. Unless I would truly put my "all" on my knowledge, I will now assign a probability of *less* than 100 percent certainty. This has noticeably informed my approach to my job, and came in very useful when giving expert evidence recently at a technical arbitration!

At work I have to predict the outcome (profit/loss) of building contracts. I used to put forward more "safe" minimum figures. Now [thanks to Probers] I can happily increase them, estimating probabilities of their accuracy. (Unfortunately, as no one else has taken U201, I suspect that they are immediately reconverted to "safe" figures.)

When people use the word *certain* I start wondering *how* certain, etc. I calculate my chances in a risky situation now automatically. I probably take more risks but they are "safer" risks.

The most difficult challenge is the inner battle which must be fought in order to score well i.e. that of admitting to yourself that you DON'T know what the answer is. I am better at doing that now.

I think it will be evident that these reactions, however much they indicate the problems with the approach as an *assessment* mode, signify the rich educational resource that it provides. I have never found students more interested or motivated in discussing *anything*. If the interest and motivation sometimes spill over into stronger emotions, including anger, this is easy to accept— intellectually—as the price of role undistancing. It is, of course, much harder to accept in person, but that phrasing tells its own story.

CONCLUSION

In suggesting that as teachers in the decision area we should take some steps toward practicing what we preach—or at least teach—I am not simply trying to open up an appalling can of worms *for its own sake*. I am suggesting that the main justification for studying decision theory and processes is in helping others open up and disentangle their own particular cans of worms (as well as who built the cannery, where and why)—and that it ill behoves us to overlook the implications close to home. It is pedagogically ill advised. And it is ethically dubious.

Decision theory, I believe, will be one of the key principles around which the curriculum of the 21st century is organized. It will provide a central focus of the educational portfolio in which thinking/deciding/judging and "cognitive" activities in general are balanced with ingredients of an "expressive" and "practical'' nature. A portfolio view of the curriculum grows naturally out of the decision analytic approach to choice under uncertainty. But it also symbolically reflects a view of education as the most formal process by which the individual is assisted in the task of constructing his or her life portfolio of activities. Activities designed to bring about personal and social *change* should, of course, be as vital a part of this portfolio as ones designed to ease adaptation to *prevailing* personal and social circumstances.

REFERENCES

Dowie, J. (1982, July). *The catch .22 of utility theory.* Paper presented to Health Economists Study Group, Brunel University.

Dowie, J., & Lefrere, P. (1984). Probabilistic responses to multiple-choice tests. In E. S. Henderson & M. B. Nathenson (Eds.), *Independent learning in higher education.* Englewood Cliffs, NJ: Educational Technology Publications.

French, S. (1983, January). *The weighting of examination components.* (Notes in Decision Theory No. 117). University of Manchester.

Humphreys, P. C., & McFadden, W. (1980). Experiences with MAUD: Aiding decision structuring versus bootstrapping the decision-maker. *Acta Psychologica, 45,* 51–69.

Lord, F. M., & Novick, M. R. (1968). *Statistical theories of mental test scores.* Reading, MA: Addison-Wesley.

Murphy, A. H. (1973). A new vector partition of the probability score. *Journal of Applied Meteorology, 12,* 595–600.

Poizner, S. B., Nicewander, A., & Gettys, C. F. (1978). Alternative response and scoring methods for multiple choice items: An empirical study of probabilistic and ordinal response modes. *Applied Psychological Measurement, 2,* 83–96.

Pugh, R. C., & Brunza, J. J. (1975). Effects of a confidence-weighted scoring system on measures of test reliability and validity. *Educational and Psychological Measurement, 35,* 73–78.

Rippey, R. M., & Voytovich, A. E. (1982). Adjusting confidence tests for realism: The favorable consequences. *Evaluation and the Health Professions, 5,* 71–85.

Rippey, R. M., & Voytovich, A. E. (1983). Linking knowledge, realism and diagnostic reasoning by computer-assisted confidence testing. *Journal of Computer-Based Instruction, 9,* 88–97.

Yates, J. F. (1982). External correspondence: Decompositions of the mean probability score. *Organisational Behaviour and Human Performance, 30,* 132–156.

CHAPTER 17

Choice Decision
and the Anticipation of Events

Lawrence C. Currie

INTRODUCTION: CHOOSING AN APPROACH

There is considerable confusion about the domain of decision making. Sometimes the term is used rather precisely as in the case of probabilistic and stochastic treatments. Other times it can appear in a more parsimonious scenario, as when it is inferred in most areas of psychology. In fact one could be forgiven for suggesting that it could stand as a synonym for psychology. Virtually all of our psychological processes are involved in some sophisticated choice reaction-time task, or a discrimination learning task, solving a problem, detecting a signal, perceiving some object or person, or identifying some unusual (or usual!) personality. We are all very busy processing information, the object of which is to make some judgment, to choose and eventually to decide (or not to decide). Lockhead suggests that perhaps we should study "choice and decision behaviour in cognitive processing, rather than the reverse" (Wallsten, 1980, p. xi).

Should the decision makers be our focus of attention? If we know something about them, their personality, characteristics, what makes them tick—their motivation—we may be able to "guess" their choices, even make an attempt at predicting their decisions.

If we consider humans as "economic man," then some normative model may suffice, particularly if we can come to terms with their utility function.

Maybe a physiological explanation could be sought: particular patterns of neuronal firing may provide an explanation for the decisions we make! We may

Lawrence C. Currie • Department of Psychology, City of London Polytechnic, London E1 7NT, England.

even trace the loci of our decision making; left hemisphere for analytical decision making and, presumably, right hemisphere for nonanalytical decision making (Jones, 1980). Evidence for hemispecialization stems from studies involving psychophysics based on a dependent variable of time.

Another approach is to transfer the focus of attention to the task tackled by the decision maker. Some theorists have suggested that it is too parsimonious to consider invariant cognitive processes used by the individual across differing task environments. These theorists claim that the information processing in the decision maker is highly contingent upon the demands of the task. "The most important empirical results in the period under review have shown the sensitivity of judgment and choice to seemingly minor changes in tasks" (Einhorn & Hogarth, 1981, p. 61).

Certainly it is difficult to accept that the same information processing is involved when one is faced with say (a) a procedural choice between two switches on a control panel, and (b) developing an antiinflation economic program.

Or why not take a systems approach to decision making and consider the decision maker as part of the system. Human factor specialists are quite familiar with this model but tend to be criticized for seeking too mechanistic an explanation, to the point of automating decision making through some symbiotic process not yet achieved by scientists.

Wallsten talks about a schism that "has existed between behavioural decision theorists and the rest of cognitive psychology" (Wallsten, 1980, p. ix). Pitz (1977) suggests that this separation occurred because of the differential evolution: decision theory developed in the joint environment of economics and statistics and cognitive psychology in the philosophical schools of associationism and rationalism.

Normative models of decision making are "mathematically sound, the data collection methods are tractable, and there are prescribed ways to get about in our uncertain world" (Lockhead, 1980, p. 143). Yet our own uncertainties grow about the efficacy of these models to explain human behavior, and particularly human decision-making behavior. Tversky and Kahneman (1974) have developed a number of theoretical lines backed by empirical findings to account for some of the inconsistencies between the decisions individuals actually make and those they ought to make. Such notions, considered under heuristics and biases are (a) the availability (or accessibility of information); (b) the representativeness of events (comparator model); and (c) adjustments and anchoring. Meister (1976) uncovers a number of other empirical findings about decision makers, admittedly considered largely from a static decision-making point of view. He has considered such things as information uncertainty exerting a greater influence on decision making behavior than other factors, for example, the decision maker is more willing to gamble on a difficult (very uncertain) choice than on an easy (very certain) choice; that more information is required for a decision maker to change a decision than to make it originally: that the rate at which information is presented is more important than whether it is presented on request or automatically; and, finally, that there is a level of information availability at which the decision maker's performance is maximized.

In the past, theorists involved with the expectation models (i.e., the EV, EU, and SEU models) defended their stances by providing an experimentation usefulness rationale. In other words, the hypothesis of SEU maximization does not explain what is going on when the decision maker chooses, but it does provide information that enables the experimenter to predict choices made by the decision maker (Edwards, 1955).

Payne (1973), in an interpretive review of the literature on individual decision making under risk, concludes that

> If one's research goal is uncovering the underlying information-processing strategies of the decision maker, an approach based on the explicit risk dimensions would seem more appropriate. (Payne, 1973, p. 452).

All of these doubts and apparent coming to terms with the place of normative models in decision-making research point toward an approach that considers the observer's (decision maker's) perceptions of the task (Lockhead, 1980). More precisely, we could be seeking an understanding of the decision maker's construing of the situation and of their own decision-making processes.

Yet another way to categorize decision making is by considering the time available to make the decision: short-term and long-term decision making may require quite different decision-making processes. Payne's (1982) discussion of intuition and analyses refers to the importance of the relation between time and modes of thought and goes on to comment on prospect theory (Kahneman & Tversky, 1979), particularly the key concept of risky-choice behavior consisting of a two-phase process. I agree with Payne's suggestion that

> a combination of the Hammond (1980) and Kahneman and Tversky (1979) ideas suggests that a complex risky-choice problem will involve a progression from intuitive to analytical cognition [and that] the influence of various task variables will vary systematically over the course of the risky-problem-solving episode. (Payne, 1982, p. 399)

However, I would assert that an explanation of the individual's decision-making processes can be found within a complete theory of personal construing (*The Psychology of Personal Constructs*, Kelly, 1955) and in particular the kind of processing suggested previously is well explained in Kelly's choice corollary and two dimensions of transition: (a) the circumspection, preemption, and control cycle (CPC cycle) and (b) the creativity cycle, which are described later. Incidentally, the CPC cycle incorporates a similar idea to that of Payne's, that is, "the process of intuitive to analytical cognition could be short circuited at any time" (Payne, 1982, p. 399).

A BRIEF DESCRIPTION OF PERSONAL CONSTRUCT THEORY

The following section is a summary of Chapters 2, 3, and 10 from G. A. Kelly's *Psychology of Personal Constructs* (1955) using his expressions and freely adapted to suit our topic.

The Fundamental Postulate and Corollaries

Kelly's *Psychology of Personal Constructs* is underpinned by the philosophical principle of *constructive alternativism* which briefly states that "reality does not directly reveal itself to us but rather it is subject to as many alternative ways of construing as we ourselves invent" (Adams-Weber, 1979, p. 1). Kelly called these patterns *constructs* and went on to suggest that the individual endeavors "to improve his constructs by increasing his repertory by altering them to provide better fits and by subsuming them [the constructs] with superordinate constructs or systems" (Kelly, 1955, p. 9).

Personal construct theory (PCT) is expressed by means of a fundamental postulate that states that—a person's processes are psychologically channelized by the ways in which events are anticipated. The postulate is elaborated through eleven corollaries which are listed below.

- *Construction Corollary*. In order to anticipate events, a person construes or places an interpretation on their replication.
- *Individuality Corollary*. To the extent that construing is an individual process, one person's construction of events will differ from those of others.
- *Range Corollary*. A construct is convenient for the anticipation of a finite range of events only. In construing, things or events that are abstracted by a construct are called *elements,* and these elements must fall within the realm or range of convenience of the particular construction system.
- *Organization Corollary*. It follows from the preceding that some sort of organization will evolve to generate "a construction system embracing ordinal relationships between constructs" (Kelly, 1955, p. 56). These ordinal relationships may be of many levels, with some constructs subsuming others and those, in turn, subsuming still others. When subsuming, a construct is termed *superordinal* and when subsumed, it is termed *subordinal.*
- *Dichotomy Corollary*. In noting the replicative aspects of, say, two events, it stands to reason that another event, by the same token, may not be a replication of the said two events. In choosing some aspect, the person determines what shall be considered either similar or contrasting. In other words, the person notes features in a series of elements that are characteristic of the construct and by the same token are uncharacteristic of other

elements in the series. What is evolving, then, is a structure of constructs of similarity and contrast. It is assumed that the notion of, say, *tall* cannot exist in a vacuum; it exists in contrast to *small* or *not tall*. Kelly's statement of this sitution is so succinct and important for an understanding of the rationale of PCT as to be quoted in full.

A construct which implied similarity without contrast would represent just as much of a chaotic, undifferentiated homogeneity as a construct which implied contrast without similarity would represent a chaotic particularised heterogeneity. The former would leave the person engulfed in a sea with no landmarks to relieve the monotony; the later would confront him with an interminable series of kaleidoscopic changes in which nothing would ever appear familiar. (Kelly, 1955, p. 51)

These similarity and contrast aspects of the elements within the range of convenience of the construct describe the dichotomous nature of the construct: it is an important aspect of the methodology derived from PCT and, "in its minimum context," states that "a construct is a way in which at least two elements are similar and contrast with a third, i.e. there must be at least three elements in the context," (Kelly, 1955, p. 61).

- *Choice Corollary.* We now come to the corollary that has the most relevance to decision making. It is stated formally as "a person chooses for himself that alternative in a dichotomised construct through which he anticipates the greater possibility for extension and definition of his system" (Kelly, 1955, p. 61). I shall delay further discussion on this corollary until the section on the perception of danger as I wish to place it within the context of decision making relevant to dangerous situations.

  Also, apart from defining the remainder of the corollaries (and other theoretical concepts), I shall not elaborate them because either they have less relevance for the topic of this chapter, or, like the choice corollary, they are better discussed in context.
- *Experience Corollary.* A person's construction system varies by successively construing the replications of events.
- *Modulation Corollary.* The variation in a person's construction system is limited by the permeability of the constructs within whose ranges of convenience the variants lie.
- *Fragmentation Corollary.* A person may successively employ a variety of construction subsystems that are inferentially incompatible with each other.
- *Commonality Corollary.* To the extent that one person employs a construction of experience that is similar to that employed by another, the psychological processes are similar to those of the other person.
- *Sociality Corollary.* To the extent that one person construes the construction processes of another, the person may play a role in a social process involving the other person.

The Nature of Constructs

Kelly discussed a triad of notions that have to do with the nature of the control that a construct implicitly exercises over its elements.

A *preemptive construct* is a construct that preempts its elements for membership in its own realm exclusively. An accident is nothing but an accident. All things that are accidents are excluded from the realms of other constructs. The "nothing but" expression epitomizes the preemptive construct.

A *constellatory construct* permits its elements to belong to other realms concurrently but fixes their realm membership. Stereotypes belong to this category: an accident, to be an accident, must also be other specified things. A dogmatic form of thinking is implied in constellatory statements.

Both the preemptive and constellatory categories restrict the elaborative possibilities of construing by preventing reinterpretation or alternative ways of viewing, say, an accident.

A *propositional construct* carries no implications regarding the other-realm membership of its elements. It acknowledges the possibility of other interpretations and elaborations. The "as if" expression is characteristic of such a construct.

Obviously, our thinking is not conveniently pigeonholed into these three categories of construing, and it is more realistic to consider the propositional construct as representing one end of a continuum, with the preemptive and constellatory representing the other end. Also, it is not implied that a person uses, say, propositional constructs exclusively. Such a person would be in a permanent state of confusion, unable to make a definite commitment. It is more likely that a superordinate construct, propositional in nature, that subsumes other constructs treats its subordinates as if they were constellatory.

Dimensions of Transition

Cycles of Construction

In discussing the sequence of construction employed by people in order to meet everyday situations, Kelly draws our attention to a related pair of these sequences. The first is called the *circumspection-preemption-control* (CPC) cycle that has to do with action decisions involving the self, and the other is called the *creativity cycle* that has to do with a person's originality.

The CPC cycle is a sequence of construction involving, in succession, circumspection, preemption and control, and leading to a choice that precipitates the person into a particular situation.

The creativity cycle is one that starts with loosened construction (one that leads to varying predictions but retains its identity) and terminates with tightened and validated construction (one that leads the construer to unvarying predictions) and represents the compatibility between these predictions and the outcomes observed.

Constructs Related to Dislodgement

From what has been said previously, one's construction system is dynamic: it never experiences homeostasis. The successive stages of the person's construction system will be treated as elements. This calls for superordinate construction (i.e., where the successive stages of the changing construction system are being treated as elements). Whether the new constructions will be acceptable in the person's superordinate construction will depend on its permeability (the construct's ability to admit to its range of convenience new elements that are not yet construed within its framework). One's variation is subordinate (a subordinate construct is one that is included as an element in the context of another)

> to certain more permeable constructions. His variation, to the extent that it involves successive use of subordinate constructs which are inferentially incompatible with each other, is not tolerated unless his superordinate constructions are permeable to the new outlooks, are tight enough to make them practically meaningful, and yet are loose enough to permit some reshuffling of elements. (Kelly, 1955, p. 488)

Four terms relevant to transition are defined as follows:

- *Threat.* The awareness of an imminent comprehensive change in a person's core structure (one which governs the person's maintenance processes).
- *Fear.* The awareness of an imminent, incidental change in one's core structures.
- *Anxiety.* The awareness that the events with which one is confronted lie outside the range of convenience of one's construct system.
- *Guilt.* The awareness of dislodgement of the self from one's core role structure. A role is a psychological process based upon the role player's construction of aspects of the construction systems of those with whom he attempts to join in a social enterprise.

CONSTRUING DANGER

The Perception of Danger

To investigate this topic I thought that an attempt to establish the individual's construing of danger may be a reasonable approach. Having been previously impressed by J. J. Gibson's notion of the perception of danger and the problems of safety where he considers the problem on the one hand "a matter of the ecology of danger and natural and artificial signs of danger and, on the other hand, a matter of the psychology of the perceptions and reactions aroused by these signs" (Gibson, 1961, p. 302). I decided to pose the problem in personal construct terms.

The construing of danger must be a rather important feature of a person's anticipation of events, and these events arise out of encounters with the environment. Some of these encounters will inevitably be dangerous, and some will result in mishap, although not necessarily injurious mishap. Many of our dangerous situations result from our attempts to elaborate that which is partly strange. Most of us would agree that the imminent likelihood of a sudden reconstruction of the core of our personalities "constitutes a signficant disturbance." Take the case of a child playing with apparently fearful things; he or she is probably doing it within the overall control of certain subordinate aspects of his or her system and very likely will gradually reorganize his or her core structure to bring it into line with the reality of dangerous things. (This kind of reasoning is not unfamiliar. Students of Hebb, 1949, Hunt, 1960, Berlyne, 1960, Piaget, 1936, and Miller, Gallanter & Pribram, 1960, will recognize the rationale.) Kelly states the "novelty" experience nicely when he says that "we are threatened by hauntingly familiar things and frightened by unexpectedly strange things" (Kelly, 1955, p. 494). Fear, threat, and anxiety, as dimensions of transition, are important influences on the development of a perception of danger.

Before proceeding further, it will be necessary to explain in greater detail some of these relevant notions from PCT. However, I must stress the point that I consider all of PCT to be relevant to the study of decision-making processes, but I shall not belabor the point by discussing all the dimensions of transition and each of the 11 corollaries in terms of the perception of danger. A few examples will give the flavor of what I am driving at.

Dimensions of Transition and Corollaries Relevant to the Perception of Danger

Many of our notions about risk, hazard, and decision making in general may be discussed within the choice corollary. Choice and decision making are inextricably related and are consequent upon the perception of danger in an event involving physical, economic, or otherwise social hazard: all of these things are about uncertainty, and it would appear that we could not tolerate complete and absolute certainty. It is in anticipation of events (and in so doing reducing uncertainty) that the interest for the individual lies.

It would be useful at this point to exploit a coincidence in the literature. Both Janis and Mann (1972) and Kelly (1955) draw on the soliloquy from Hamlet to demonstrate aspects of their views on decision making. Janis and Mann suggest that the passage

> deserves to be quoted in full in a psychological study of decision making because it captures the sequential form, as well as the content, of an internal debate on the most vital of all human decisions. First come thoughts of the desirability of terminating all evils that make life seem unbearable; then comes a sharp realisation that there could be unknown dangers that might constitute the rub; finally the decision maker becomes keenly aware of his painful state of conflict and struggles against wanting to procrastinate. (Janis & Mann, 1972, p. 232)

Contrast this with Kelly's treatment of the same passage.

> We assume, therefore, that whenever a person is confronted with the opportunity for making a choice, he will tend to make that choice in favor of the alternative which seems to provide the best basis for anticipating the ensuing events.
>
> Here is where inner turmoil so frequently manifests itself. Which shall a man choose, security or adventure? Shall he choose that which leads to immediate certainty or shall he choose that which may eventually give him a wider understanding? For the man of constricted outlook whose world begins to crumble, death may appear to provide the only immediate certainty which he can lay hands on. And yet in the words of Shakespeare's Hamlet:
>
>> But that the dread of something after death—The undiscovered country, from whose bourn No traveler returns—puzzles the will; And makes us rather bear those ills we have Than fly to others that we know not of?
>
> Whatever the breadth of his viewpoint, it is our assumption that man makes his choice in such a fashion as to enhance his anticipations. If he constricts his field of vision, he can turn his attention toward the clear definition of his system of constructs. If he is willing to tolerate some day-to-day uncertainties, he may broaden his field of vision and thus hope to extend the predictive range of his system. Whatever the choice may be—for constricted certainty or for broadened understanding—his decision is essentially elaborative; he makes what we shall call hereinafter the elaborative choice. . . .
>
> Internal conflict, as in the case of Hamlet, is often a matter of trying to balance off the secure definiteness of a narrowly encompassed world against the uncertain possibilities of life's adventure. One may anticipate events by trying to become more and more certain about fewer and fewer things or by trying to become vaguely aware of more things on the misty horizon. (Kelly, 1955, pp. 64–65, 67)

With regard to, "and thus the native hue of resolution is sicklied o'er with the pale cast of thought. . .and lose the name of action," Kelly uses it to demonstrate an aspect of the CPC cycle.

> For even though he may succeed in preemptively construing his situation, he may find that his effort to make the final elaborative choice throws him back upon circumspection before the cycle has run its normal course. (Kelly, 1955, p. 517)

Therefore, there is no action. Janis and Mann, on the other hand, use it to illustrate what they call

the very core of what we have been describing as the fundamental value of fear of
the unknown...the unknown dangers of life after death, which give Hamlet pause
of the desirability of going on living, by postponing action until the mood of complete despondency subsides. (Janis & Mann, 1972, p. 233)

In contrast to the Janis and Mann interpretation where they think the soliloquy captures a "sequential form of an internal debate," Kelly construes it as an
example of the operation of the CPC cycle. The pause that Hamlet experiences
is the clue to this interpretation.

Janis and Mann's reference to the postponement of action seems to unwit-
tingly imply the change from preemption to circumspection in the CPC cycle under the influence of threat, anxiety, and possible guilt, as defined by the dimensions of transition. The implications of these transitionary constructs for decision
making are better understood from Kelly's definition of them.

As indicated before, "a person may endeavor to move towards that which
appears to make his construct system more explicit and clear cut" (Kelly, 1955,
p. 67), but in so doing may narrow the field of vision and so curtail the predictive range of the system. One could be perceptive of danger to the point of ob-
session. For instance, consider the difference between the timid and the foolhardy: one moves towards "the secure definiteness of a narrowly encompassed
world [whereas the other remorselessly pursues] the uncertain possibilities of
life's adventure" (Kelly, p. 67). Maintaining a margin of safety seems to involve
balancing these idealized construct systems. All decision making involves risk,
hazard, and danger to some extent, and Kelly's understanding of decision making, that is, that "man makes decisions which critically affect himself and which
affect other objects only subsequently—and then only if he manages to take some
effective action" (Kelly, 1955, p. 65), makes a lot of sense when considering
the development of a perception of danger. In conclusion, let me emphasize
Kelly's statement that his theory of choice is not a commercial one: his is a very
fundamental and profound notion: "Men change things by changing themselves
first" (Kelly, 1970, p. 17). It is this implication that I wish to bring out in this
chapter.

How often have we heard the expression "accidents are caused by inex-
perience"? I submit that such a statement, or, at least, the implied opposite,
safety is dependent on experience, only makes sense if we interpret experience
as explained in the experience corollary, that is, only if the

person's construction system varies as he successively construes the replication of
events. The successive revelation of events invites the person to place new constructions upon them whenever something unexpected happens. Otherwise one's anticipa-
tions would become less and less realistic. (Kelly, 1955, p. 72)

It is experience, in this sense, that hones our perceptions of danger to provide
appropriate safety margins for us.

Permeability of constructs, as defined in the modulation corollary, has obvious relevance for the notion of perception of danger. Consider the person who has fairly impermeable constructs about danger. One might expect him or her to approach safety in a prescriptive fashion. Unfortunately, safety is construed by experts as though the bulk of the population lacked modulation in their construction systems: we are expected to be rule followers so far as safety is concerned. Up to a point, the *dos* and *don'ts* approach serves us well in encounters with very similar dangerous events. However, permeability of safety constructs would be necessary when confronted with novel dangerous events—the constructs must have the capacity to embrace new elements of the event class, in this case the event class of "danger."

If a child terminates (either by volition or due to the intervention of a caretaker) the elaboration of a particular fearful field of experience before working out some new solution to the fears, the termination of play may indicate (or cause, if terminated involuntarily) that "his construct in that area of experience has become impermeable, rigid and even perseverative" (Kelly, 1955, p. 734). Left this way, "his fear may be approaching the status of a phobia." On the other hand, the exploration of danger-seeking and, in some cases, the apparent accompaniment of discomfort-seeking behavior, could be an elaboration of the person's psychological system in an area where existing constructs are permeable enough to permit such elaboration. So that whenever behavior is spontaneous, mishap may be an unavoidable consequence, but the presence of the danger in the event brings with it enriching experience. Considered this way, exploration is the spontaneous activity that involves the constructs and continues to elaborate the system, provided experience does not result in impermeability and truncation of the elaborative process. Parenthetically, the cause of this truncation could be a primitive response to the experience of pain.

I think the implications of the fragmentation corollary for this chapter can be grasped from the following example: an individual may apparently have a subsystem of constructs relating to their occupation, which on the surface (at least to an observer) is not consistent with the subsystem of, say, the individual's driving constructs or the constructs about activities in the home. However, faced with some sort of threat, that is, the possible change of some core construction, the individual may fall back on more primitive but also more permeable constructs. The person may be obviously aggressive in driving, not show aggression on the job, and certainly be a paragon of patience and pacificity in the home, but the occurrence of some danger on the job or in the home may reveal a similar aggression in coping with the danger. It is in trying to cope with apparent inconsistencies in safety behavior that the fragmentation corollary may help.

So far as the commonality and sociality corollaries are concerned, the place of these in safety research are, I think, fairly obvious. For those trying to find common factors or characteristics, say, common to an occupation or differences between occupations with regard to accident occurrence, the reference to these corollaries would be very important. As an example of the commonality corollary, three people may be alerted to the danger of fire by the differential importance each of them places on phenomenally different stimuli. That is, one may be alarmed by the smell of burning, another by the presence of smoke, and yet another by the crackling sound of a fire. In other words, their personal experiences of fire, though different, may lead to a similar perception about the external event—all may conclude that a fire has started.

In the case of the sociality corollary, driving poses a good example of its implications. The mutual safety of drivers, to a large extent, depends on each person's ability to predict the behavior of the other. Each subsumes the others' behavior in construing the situation. To avoid collision, we need to construe at a fairly molar level. This would be quite difficult if it were not for the fact that we make a number of our constructs explicit as "rules of the road." As a social activity this provides the mutual understanding and trust necessary for the successful performance of such an activity. In personal construct terms, this is greatly assisted because to some extent, our construction system subsumes the construction systems of others, and theirs in part subsume ours.

Now let us consider an area of study that I think lends itself to a PCT interpretation, namely game theory.

GAMES AND IMPERFECT RATIONALITY

A Primitive Game

At this stage I wish to use Watkins's (1970) "state of nature" game to provide an example of the CPC cycle in action. Unlike the "prisoner's dilemma" game, the players (in this case the combatants Alex and Bobby) have the advantage of being able to communicate with each other. Both have suffcent weaponry to kill each other and are not in a position to flee from the encounter. They hesitate on the sight of each other, and before combat can commence Alex suggests that rather than engage in mortal combat, they place their fate in the lap of the gods: Bobby, happy to agree with this suggestion, recommends counting and on the count of 10, each of them would throw away their weapons (as far behind them as possible). No sooner has the counting started than the time on their hands is occupied with deep thought about the contract, about whether or not each will throw away the weapon. If both renege on the contract, they will engage in a fight to the finish from which it is unlikely that either will survive, and it is more likely that even the survivor will be severely injured. On the other hand, if one reneges on the other, the fate of the unarmed combatant will be entirely in the hands of the reneger, who is quire likely to kill the "sucker" who fell for the "con"!

Hobbesian psychology suggests that the combatants' motivation will be driven by the "desire to triumph and the fear of being killed"; however, it is suggested that fear will overpower the desire and, given a choice between placing their fate in the hands of the gods and having a 50/50 chance of winning the fight or being killed, Alex and Bobby will both choose the former.

Watkins, using the method devised by von Newmann and Morgerstern (1953) for measuring utility values, constructs a matrix to present the payoff and strategy details of the state of nature game as shown in Table 1.

Watkins eschews the possibility that game theory can avoid the rational decision makers arriving at the A2B2 outcome and being unfortunately rewarded with the equally disadvantaged payoff. He asserts that even with communication the problem remains unaltered, that is, whether each dare keep the covenant. Two other major difficulties confront the game theorists in trying to come up with an optimal solution: first, the State of Nature game is not repeatable; it can only be played once. Secondly, according to the prediction paradox (O'Connor, 1948), even if Alex and Bobby could play the game over and over, a terrible regression would result in their being continually thrown back to the A2B2 outcome, that is, the "equilibrium" outcomes for rational players. Watkins thinks that there is no optimal solution to the state of nature game and that the thinking generated during the count to 10 will be plagued by "oscillating conclusions" (presumably by both Alex and Bobby!).

Now, if the combatants reason step by step in a similar fashion, and thus the way the decisions go depends on the point at which they break off their reasoning, then, if the steps are synchronized "exactly," the conclusions and

Table 1.   Consequence Matrix for State of Nature Game[a]

		Bobby	
		B1	B2
Alex	A1	Alex and Bobby Equally advantaged Both unscathed	Bobby advantaged triumphs over Alex Alex disadvantaged probably dead
	A2	Alex advantaged triumphs over Bobby Bobby disadvantaged probably dead	Alex and Bobby Equally disadvantaged Both injured or dead

[a]Where A1 = discard weapon and A2 = retain weapon, where B1 = discard weapon and B2 = retain weapon. The corresponding consequences are indicated in the four cells. These consequences are based on the payoffs assigned in the Prisoner's Dilemma game: if Alex and Bobby are "rational" according to game theory, they would both lose, whereas if they are "irrational" they would both win.

thus the decisions will be determined by the coincidence of the step with the time limit (e.g., at the count of 10!). What is more feasible is the development of some desynchrony so that the step reached by each combatant at the count of 10 will decide the choice.

One could argue that too much time is allowed to pass, by counting to 10, and that a count of 3 would provide a better chance for the covenant to be honored. On the other hand, a longer period of time might allow alternative negotiating to be tried; for instance, they could endeavor to educate each other on the advantages of working toward an A1B1 outcome. They could have emphasized rewards for keeping the contract, rather than the penalties for breaking it.

And what of the aftermath of an A1B1 outcome? Having discarded the murderous weapons, they may have reflected on the task they had embarked on, which brought them to this point of choice (i.e., foraging) and gone on to conclude a social contract (post-Hobbesian) that would give them the security of mutual defense against other competitors and a more productive approach to their foraging. But then we have strayed far away from game theorizing, and the rules of game theory would not allow such speculation. One must agree with Watkins's conclusion that game theory does "impute a kind of ruthless self disinterestedness," just as Hobbes imputed to human beings in general. However, one could surely impute a push as well as a pull nature to humans in that some notion of reward could be negotiated into the covenant and thus not depend entirely upon the "sword to accompany the words."

PCT Interpretation of the Game

Supposing we had taken a personal construct theoretical approach to the state of nature situation in which Alex and Bobby found themselves. At the very least it could provide an alternative method with which to approach the problem. It is no more a stretch of the imagination to see Hobbesian "man" in PCT terms than it is to see him in game-theoretical terms. Therefore, we start with the fundamental postulate: "A person's [even a Hobbesian person's] processes are psychologically channelised by the ways in which he anticipates events" (Kelly, 1955, p. 46). Both Alex and Bobby presumably were trying to anticipate the events following their encounter. As to their attempt to construe the replication of this event, we are left to speculate. They could have experienced similar encounters in differing degrees of recurrence. We can also be more sympathetic with the notion that each of them differed in their construction of events in general, although in the case of this event, they probably had more in common than they had differences. At least we are led to believe that both of our combatants are pretty sophisticated in their ability to evolve a construction system embracing ordinal relationships between constructs. Alex and Bobby can go beyond this by deriving (or being able to evaluate) numerical indifference. We can presume that both combatants' construction systems are composed of a finite number of dichotomous constructs, and, in this case, within the range of convenience: relating, triumphing, and being killed. The next corollary is crucial for finding an explanation of Alex and Bobby's behaviors: by choosing for themselves "that alternative in a dichotomous construct, through which [each of them may] anticipate the greater possibility for extension and definition of [their construct] systems" (Kelly, 1955, p. 64), they may endeavor to place relative values upon the ends of their dichotomies, for example, fight/flee, kill/be killed, negotiate/not negotiate. However, this does not preclude the use of constructs in a relativistic manner, that is, in terms of the outcomes evolved in the matrix. The choice corollary may provide the ground rules upon which we can make some predictions about the actions of Alex and Bobby once they have construed the issues with which they are faced. From what we have been told, it may seem rational for both of them to avoid a fight. But such a course of action may seem to one or the other of them to limit the definition and extension of his construct system as a whole. Using the choice corollary saves us from the awkward issues raised by hedonism and motivational theory. Similarly, we do not need to seek stimulus–response connections. There is no need to imply that either Alex or Bobby is hell-bent on seeking pleasure or avoiding punishment if they break the covenant, or that they will be rewarded for keeping the covenant. In other words, the commercial implications of many of the decision and choice theories can be avoided.

The important point to remember at this point is that "men change things by changing themselves first and they accomplish their objectives, if at all, only by paying the price of altering themselves" (Kelly, 1955, p. 65). It seems to make more sense to consider humans' choice being governed by their own awareness of the possibilities involved and to see the alternatives as being expressed in the construct and not between the objects separated out by means of the construct.

I have previously indicated the place of the range corollary and hinted at the importance of the experience corollary. It is one of the biggest shortcomings of the Hobbesian model of the "state of nature" that it assumes equal experiences; "Hobbesian men are supposed to be, and to realise that they are equally good at killing each other" (Watkins, 1970, p. 203).

Unless we are suggesting that the experiences of primeval human beings were restricted and similar to the point of ritual, then we must accept that each human's construction system varied as he or she successively construed the replication of events. It is made very clear in the description of the event involving Alex and Bobby that their experiences are different enough to make each uncertain about the other's response.

Although both the modulation and experience corollaries have their place in trying to understand Alex and Bobby's decision processes, it is by means of the choice, the commonality and the sociality corollaries, that we can better study the decision-making processes of our two combatants. If we can establish that both Alex and Bobby employ similar constructions of experience, then we may reasonably assume that their psychological processes are similar.

It is difficult to imagine one person's construing events to the exclusion of other people's construction systems. The sociality corollary suggests that to some extent we construe the construction processes of others and, as such, we play a role in a social process involving other people. Alex and Bobby found themselves in what is a commonplace situation; that is, both were on a collision course, just as drivers, statesmen, generals, and even chicken-run gamesters find themselves, and, for the purpose of avoiding collisions, it is enough that each understands or subsumes only certain specific aspects of each other's construction system.

Listening to the playback of bridge players' construing of their game reveals this mutual subsuming of aspects of the partner's construction processes, and we can assume from Watkins's hypothetical account that at least Alex is capable of construing aspects of Bobby's construction processes (and vice versa).

Finally, so far as the state of nature situation vis-à-vis PCT is concerned, we must involve the CPC cycle and constructs of transition.

When individuals construe circumspectively, they employ a series of propositional constructs and this kind of construing may be identified by their statements. Further, despite the fact that "he may employ these constructs successively or more or less simultaneously.... this does not mean that he sees them as linked into a constellation" (Kelly, 1955, p. 515). At times, the person may employ preemptive constructs, but there is no linear mechanism of progression from circumspection to preemption: there may be several circumspections before the construer moves on to the preemptive stage of the cycle. It is this preemption of issues that characterizes a person of action, and in Alex and Bobby we appear to have two likely candidates for this title.

During the circumspection stage of the CPC cycle one might imagine Alex and Bobby's construing to be along the following lines: If I throw my club away first, on the point of release, Bobby will see it and in keeping the covenant will be reassured to the point of throwing the other club away. On the other hand, in the event that Bobby does not throw it away, what will I do then?

A preemptive stance may be expressed—I will throw away my club if and only if Bobby throws the club away first. There is a third alternative open to both; that is, to be dogmatic in their thinking and express themselves in a constellatory manner—For me to throw away my club, you must comply with certain specified conditions.

As previously indicated, it is very seldom that individuals use only one kind of construct, that is, only propositional or only preemptive, and it is unlikely that propositional constructs represent one end of a continuum and preemptive or constellatory constructs represent the other end.

It is more than likely that Alex and Bobby would proceed through the CPC cycle to the point where they each perceive a more precise control (superordination) by preempting, and in so doing choose the most relevant axis along which to construe their situation and either temporarily or permanently disregard the relevance of all other issues that may be involved. This is a way of explaining the termination of the oscillating conclusions and is analogous to Watkins's further reduction of the decision scheme and simplification that may lead to a decision. Watkins 1970, p. 206 suggests that in normative decision theory

> a decision scheme should consist of—(i) a complete specification of the possible outcomes; (ii) a complete preference map or; (iii) a complete allocation of payoff values to the outcomes; and, where appropriate (iv) a comprehensive apparatus for dealing with risks and uncertainties.

The use of the word *complete* gives a ring of unreality to such a (perfect) scheme. However, actual decision schemes are usually very imperfect; more likely they are built up bit by bit from information as it arrives at the decision maker, and Watkins further suggests that "the arrival of an isolated bit of situational information may have quite disproportional influence" (Watkins, 1970, p. 206). The decision maker may vascillate between factors. Further reduction of the scheme and simplification may lead to a decision.

This is all very reminiscent of the CPC cycle where the decision maker "may seize upon a few features and pick-out a few interesting possibilities in the given problem-situation" (Watkins, 1970, p. 206), which is analogous to the circumspection (seizing upon a few features) and preemption (pick out a few interesting possibilites) and choice/control (may lead to a decision).

PCT Applied to War Games and Driving Games

In trying to establish the influence of communication between the two players of the game it may be necessary for the game theorist to introduce a notion from the "theory of metagames" (Howard, 1971). This extends the concept of strategy to cover the step-by-step responses of the opponents to each other's possible strategy choices. The concept "involves choosing a rule to select a strategy conditional upon the strategy choice of one's opponent which may be thought of as a strategy for selecting a strategy" (Brams, 1976, p. 87).

The main opponents in the Cuban missile crisis, Kennedy and Kruschev, probably did not know that they were involved in a nonzero-sum game like chicken, but no doubt some of their advisers would be well acquainted with game theory. As it turned out, this crisis was not really a noncooperative game. Communication was not only permitted but exploited, and it is asserted that it was through these communications that the two leaders were able to arrive at the cooperative outcome.

> Metagame theory specifies rather precisely, if indirectly, the content of the commu-
> nications and the nature of the bargaining necessary to reach compromise. (Brams,
> 1976, p. 120)

The exchanges of information concerning intentions relating to concessions and threats enabled each side (if not the leaders themselves, then their advisers) to estimate more accurately the probable reactions of the other side to the range of alternative actions that they considered taking.

I venture to suggest that the two sides were communicating at the circum-spection end of their continuums, that is, making propositional statements to each other, and only after many rounds of the CPC cycle did each feel confident enough to choose and, at least in the case of Kruschev, consolidate all the possible perspectives of the crisis in terms of one dichotomous issue and then make his choice between the only two alternatives he allowed himself to perceive, that is, withdraw concessions from U.S. versus maintain stance on missiles and probably experience defeat. The negotiations probably proceeded from expressions of subordinate level of intentions to superordinate implications derived from the propositional construing during the CPC cycle.

On the other hand, Kennedy must have reached a similar point of preemption in his CPC cycle and similarly consolidated the perspectives of the crisis, that is, commence air strike and risk starting nuclear war versus concede tit for tat by promising not to invade Cuba (and redeploy Turkish-based missiles!).

The hypothetical account of the decision processes adopted by the adversaries in the Cuban missile crisis (which fortunately had time on its side) could be applied to subsequent crises such as the present arms race, nuclear war strategies, and many other less momentous negotiations. However, many of the dangers we face do not permit us the luxury of time to indulge in repeated CPC cycles: so many of our day-to-day dangers, at work, at leisure, traveling, or just living at home, require a rapid, once-only cycle of CPC.

It might be suggested that a set of safety rules are necessary to enable the person to respond in a habitual fashion because the sequence of events happens so rapidly as to make an adequate assessment of the alternative actions impossible. Unfortunately, no two dangerous situations are alike, and a habitual response may only exacerbate the imminent hazard. A study by the author (Currie, 1974) showed that subjects in a simulated driving task who had habituated the action of braking as a means of avoiding collision found themselves sitting ducks when this previously appropriate response (braking) was illicited instead of accelerating to clear a narrow single lane before an oncoming vehicle entered the same lane from the opposite direction. Such perspicacity cannot be explained by rule following. Some researchers may explain the action as an audacious piece of risk taking; others may say it arose from previous experience, and, as such, was rehearsed. The latter explanation could be accommodated in PCT by using the CPC cycle and the experience corollary. By successively construing and reconstruing events, the person may begin to see an orderliness that suggests an action as though the experience had occurred before. Thus, the circumspection part of the cycle may be truncated in favor of a preemption that suggests some control over the outcome of the action.

Another study by Prentice (1974) on driver's evasive action is also interpretable through PCT. A game theory approach was used to suggest "good strategies that will avoid an accident or minimize the severity of the resulting crash" (Prentice, 1974, p. 146). Details of a similar incident are shown in Figure 1.

Prentice uses the criteria of minimax loss (Horowitz, 1965) to explain a decision-making process that provides as a "good" decision a strategy that minimizes the loss regardless of what the other driver does. Similar criteria are used on a larger series of strategies suggested by the present author. The "extra" strategies have been added merely to remind the reader of the range and complexity of the actions available to drivers in such an intersection incident. The strategies have been arranged in descending order of potential crash severity, as in the incident cited by Prentice. The resulting (unwieldy) matrix is shown in Table 2.

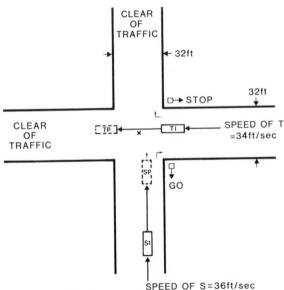

Figure 1. Schematic representation of the driving incident. Diagram shows from initial sighting positions (SI and TI) to projected positions (SP and TP) of cars after 1 sec in time. In the event, both drivers locked their brakes and skidded to a collision. Car dimensions: 15ft long×6ft wide ("average compact").

Table 2. Consequence Matrix for the Driver's Game[a]

Driver Sam		Strategy	Tammy Most severe crash to least severe crash[b]							
			T1 Veer left	T2 Brake	T3 Veer right	T4 No change	T5 Veer rt. then lt.	T6 Accel.	Row Max	Min
Most severe crash	S1	Accelerate	36	34	27	32	28	31	36	
	S2	Veer left	33	35	18	30	26	25	35	
	S3	Veer right	15	14	13	7	11	5	15	*
to	S4	No change	24	29	12	8	23	3	29	
least severe crash	S5	Veer right Then left	16	20	22	6	21	4	22	
	S6	Brake	17	10	9	2	19	1	19	
Column		Max	36	35	27	32	28	31		
		Min			*					

[a]Assumptions: (i) Any braking by Tammy tends to increase danger; any braking by Sam tends to decrease danger. (ii) Any acceleration by Tammy tends to decrease danger; any acceleration by Sam tends to increase danger. (iii) Braking and effective turning, acceleration and effective turning, veering left then right. (All deemed implausible.)

[b]Criteria for ordering (as perceived by author): (i) likelihood of cells strategy occurring (ii) severity of consequences if crash occurs. Rank ordering used rather than arbitrary values because the former provides finer discrimination.

Incidentally, it is worth noting that Prentice's results are highly dependent have evasive actions available to them that could conceivably avoid a crash, they choose to forego these and, instead, choose the action that will assume a low level of crash severity" (Prentice, 1974, p. 146). Two other important features from our point of view are

> Since there is no pre-crash communication between drivers, neither driver is willing to change his strategy due to his uncertainty about the actions of the other driver

and in Prentice's opinion

> the decision made by each driver to brake [turn right in our example] was in fact a good decision. If either is faced with a similar situation in the future, he should make the decision to brake [turn to the right in our example] again. (Prentice, 1974, p.149)

However, the degree of similarity is rarely high on future occasions and, as the preceding results (Currie, 1975) indicate, such a decision could, on a future occasion, aggravate an already dangerous situation.

The conclusion drawn by Prentice is that although Tammy and Sam "both on his own reasoning regarding the outcomes of the strategies (particularly the weightings for the severity of the crashes). A different kind of construing can produce different predictions about the end results and speeds presented in Figure 1 that Tammy would be clear of the intersection before Sam arrived at the intersection (provided Sam's estimate of her distance from Tammy was accurate). So a strategy of "no change" in speed or direction would ensure that Sam's car would never reach Tammy's car. A number of other strategies can now be included and one strategy certainly discouraged: any attempt by Sam to accelerate while turning left can only aggravate the existing dangerous situation. If the strategies open to Tammy and Sam are those given in Table 2, then the saddle point that emerges is one that supports the taking of similar evasive action, namely S3-T3 (both Tammy and Sam veer right). Yet another saddle point results if we remove all strategies involving turning (on the basis that turning is not possible in the space provided at the intersection). This time S6-T6 (Sam brakes and Tammy accelerates) is indicated as the "best" strategy.

The game theory approach to evasive action by drivers seems to suggest (in PCT terms) a preemptive style of responding. Whether it be braking or accelerating, or turning in a predetermined direction, each driver makes a preemptive decision, for example: By braking and only by braking can I minimize my loss." Such a decision rules out any alternative action.

The reason why we arrive at a saddle point that produces preemptive construing is (we assume) because there is no pre-crash communication. Certainly there is no chance of verbal communication but communication of intention is possible. By again referring to the sociality corollary we can assume that each driver's conduct is construed as part of the other driver's construct system. If the drivers were trained by rehearsing similar driving incidents, it might be possible to influence their construing of each other and, by the application of the CPC cycle in this training procedure, develop a skill for dealing with whole classes of driving hazards. Simulations could assist with the development of such a training scheme.

Let us now consider the preceding incident from a PCT point of view. If in the first instance the two drivers construed the situation propositionally, then, considering the sociality corollary, it is possible that the S6-T6 solution or the S6-T4 solution could have been acheived as follows:

Tammy construes: At the distance I am from Sam's car, if I accelerate she may see me gaining speed and she may then brake, allowing me to clear the intersection. I may even get clear of Sam if she brakes and I carry on. If we both act in this way we could avoid a collision.

Sam construes: Tammy has jumped the lights. If I slow by braking, she may see me slowing and accelerate to clear the intersection (even if she hasn't seen me, at the distance I am from her, she could quite easily clear the intersection at her present speed if I slowed down by braking). The CPC cycle would continue with a preemptive "try," possibly with a further circumspection stage, but quickening until control is achieved by both drivers.

Many of the strategies listed in Table 2 could now be possible if the above type of construing could be learned through training.

The CPC cycle could be very quick if experience of similar incidents was gained through simulation. (At a cruder level the "talking-it-out" procedure adopted by police driving instructors is not unlike the CPC cycle construing suggested before.)

To conclude this section, I am suggesting a consistent rationale for an individual's decision processes, whether the decision has long-or short-term consequences: the task does determine the nature of the judgment and choice, not because the individual has a repertoire of decision-making schemes, but more likely because of the frequency of construing at each stage of the CPC cycle and the rate at which the decision maker moves through the cycle, something that, with practice, can become a skill.

A SUITABLE THEORY FOR DESCRIBING AND EXPLAINING DECISION-MAKING PROCESSES

The study we have just discussed illustrates the difficulty we (as scientists) have in matching the more or less rapid progression of the CPC cycle with the apparently leisurely verbalizing commentary on this process. This may be because we have difficulty in perceiving a gestalt that involves preverbal, nonverbal, and verbal constructs. The feedback we receive is made up of all these components.

> A person's behavior may be based upon many interlocking equivalence–difference patterns which are never communicated in symbolic speech. Many of these preverbal or non-verbal governing constructs are embraced in the realm of physiology. That is to say they deal with elements which fall within the ranges of convenience of physiological construction systems." (Kelly, 1955, p. 51)

Kelly's notion of construing has a wide range of convenience, "if we choose to use it that way" (Kelly, 1955, p. 51). As he sees it, the functions of psychological and physiological systems overlap to such an extent as "to make it clear that psychology and physiology ought not to try to draw preemptive boundaries between themselves" (Kelly, 1955, p. 51).

One way of exploring such notions is to contrive an experiment that enables us to observe and measure the overt behavior and record the construing of the subject so that a complete account of the process involved in executing the task may be obtained.

This author (Currie, 1971) designed such an experiment where the subject performed (1) a dangerous task and verbalized their strategies during the task; (2) construed danger similarities in a series of events; and (3) ranked their judgments on (a) chance of mishaps separately from (b) the consequences of these mishaps. Relationships were obtained between the strategies, the first principal component of the subjects' construct system and their performance on the chance/consequence task, such as to provide confidence in the use of the choice corollary (and particularly the CPC cycle) as a means of understanding the decision-making process involved in coping with dangerous situations.

What is required are suitable simulations to provide the replication of events to enable a trainee to have practice with the CPC cycle and the creativity cycle.

In the Multi-Attribute-Utility-Decomposition (MAUD) decision aid (Humphreys Wisudha, 1983), we already have an example of the application of at least one corollary of PCT, that is, the dichotomy corollary. I think that the most important benefit of this decision aid is the insight it brings to the decision maker regarding decision-making processes.

As suggested in the driving incident (Prentice, 1974), simulations of similar hazardous events could provide increasingly rapid replications of such events to permit the trainee to practice the CPC cycle or at least to enable him or her to understand his or her own decision-making process via the CPC cycle.

Studies by Blignaut (1979a, 1979b) lend support to the idea that people can improve their skill in perceiving warnings of danger through training even in the hazardous environment of mining.

Bearing in mind that the statistics of probability are based upon the concept of replicated events (and contrived to measure the predictability of further replications of the events), it is no more the domain of the experimenter in discerning patterns in the data obtained from subjects (decision makers) than it is the domain of the decision makers themselves in discerning a pattern from the information available to them in the task set for them by the experimenter. Both need a number of replications to observe and features on which to base similarities and contrasts to enable abstractions among the replications to be made and thus make predictions (i.e., decide). Both are faced with the problem of representative sampling that can be relied upon to upset prediction. The mathematical expressions developed through normative models of decision making, as we have seen, are at best approximations when applied to real events. The alternative approach suggested here is to take as our baseline the personal construct that "may be regarded as essentially a dichotomous differentiating and integrating unit." From this baseline, "we may proceed to erect either categories or continua, and upon which we are free to project any behavior in our effort to understand our world" (Kelly, 1969, p. 104).

In pointing out that elements and constructs are both sides of the same coin, please forgive the pun when I suggest that decision theorists have missed this important interrelation in their commitment to the statistical notions surrounding the tossing of this coin.

If our processes are psychologically channelized to anticipate events, whether we are experimenter or subject (we are all decision makers!), we appear to find it easier to seek patterns and meaningfulness from the information (rather than by direct probabilistic weightings) through what I have contended before, that is, processes such as the CPC cycle and the creativity cycle, not unlike the notions put forward by Johnson (1972), Campbell (1960), and Hogarth (1980).

There is an unfortunate tendency among psychologists to prematurely separate data from theory in our impatience to establish facts—we should not consider the data as abstractions in our construction systems. The data and theory are intertwined in the processing of experiences and ideas (Levy, 1980). In suggesting an alternative faith based on "interpretability," "plausibility," "generalizability," and "communcability" (Levy, 1980), we may be in a better position to discover the meaning in the patterns (constructs) we endeavor to fit to the events of our world. I think that personal construct theory provides a suitable framework to make these discoveries, particularly as applied to our decision-making processes.

REFERENCES

Adams-Weber, J. R. (1979). *Personal construct theory: Concepts and applications.* New York: Wiley.

Berlyne, D. E. (1960). *Conflict, arousal and curiosity.* New York: McGraw-Hill.

Blignaut, C. J. H. (1979a). The perception of hazard.I. Hazard analysis and the contribution of visual search to hazard perception. *Ergonomics, 22*(9), 991–999.

Blignaut, C. J. H. (1979b). The perception of hazard. II. The contribution of signal detection to hazard perception. *Ergonomics, 22*(11), 1177–1184.

Brams, S. J. (1976). *Paradoxes in politics. An introduction to the non-obvious in political science.* New York: The Free Press.

Campbell, D. T. (1960). Blind variation and selective attention in creative thought as in other knowledge processes. *Psychological Review, 67,* 380–400.

Currie, L. C. (1971). *The perception of danger in a number of occupations in the construction and other industries.* Unpublished manuscript.

Currie, L. C. (1975). Habit as the source of an inappropriate response. *Ergonomics, 18*(4), 435–442.

Edwards, W. (1955). The prediction of decisions among bets. *Journal of Experimental Psychology, 50,* 201–204.

Einhorn, H. J., & Hogarth, R. M. (1981). Behavioral decision theory: Processes of judgment and choice. *Annual Review of Psychology, 32,* 52–88.

Gibson, J. J. (1964). The contribution of experimental psychology to the formulation of the problem of safety. A brief for basic research. In W. Haddon, *et al.* (Eds.) *Accident Research: Methods.* New York: Harper & Row.

Hammond, K. R. (1980). *The integration of research in judgment and decision theory.* Unpublished manuscript, University of Colorado.

Hebb, D. O. (1949). *The organization of behavior.* New York: Wiley.

Hogarth, R. M. (1980). *Judgement and choice: Strategies for decisions.* New York: Wiley.

Horowitz, I. (1965). *Introduction to quantitative business analysis.* New York: McGraw-Hill.

Howard, N. (1971). *Paradoxes of rationality: Theory of metagames and political behaviour.* Cambridge, MA: M.I.T. Press.

Humphreys, P. C., & Wisudha, A. (1983). *MAUD 4—An interactive computer program for the structuring, decomposition, and recomposition of preferences between multi-attributed alternatives* (Technical Report 83-5). London: Decision Analysis Unit, London School of Economics.

Hunt, J. McV. (1960). Experience and the development of motivation: Some reinterpretations. *Child Development, 31,* 489–504.

Janis, I. L., & Mann, L. (1977). *Decision making.* New York: The Free Press.

Johnson, D. M. (1972). *A systematic introduction to the psychology of thinking.* New York: Harper & Row.

Jones, B. (1980). Decision making and hemispherical specialisation. *Acta Psychologica, 44,* 235–243.

Kahneman, D., & Tversky, A. (1979). Prospect theory: An analysis of decisions under risk. *Econometrica, 47,* 263–291.

Kelly, G. A. (1955). *The psychology of personal constructs* (Vol. 1). *A theory of personality* (Vol. 2). New York: W. W. Norton.

Kelly, G. A. (1969). A mathematical approach to psychology. In B. Maher (Ed.), *Clinical psychology and personality: The selected papers of George Kelly.* New York: Wiley.

Kelly, G. A. (1955). *The psychology of personal constructs: Vol. 1, A theory of personality;* Vol. 2, *Clinical diagnosis, and psychotherapy.* New York: W. W. Norton.

Levy, P. (1981). On the relation between method and substance in psychology. *Bulletin of the British Psychological Society, 34,* 265–270.

Lockhead, G. R. (1980). Know, then decide. In T. S. Wallsten (Ed.), *Cognitive processes in choice decision behavior.* Hillsdale, NJ: Erlbaum.

Meister, D. (1976). *Behavior foundation of system development.* New York: Wiley.

Miller, G. A., Gallanter, E., & Pribram, K. H. (1960). *Plans and the structure of behavior.* New York: Holt, Rinehart & Winston.

O'Connor, D. J. (1948). The prediction paradox. *Mind, 57,* 227.

Payne, J. W. (1973). Alternative approaches to decision making under risk: Moments versus risk dimensions. *Psychological Bulletin, 30*(6), 439–455.

Payne, J. W. (1982). Contingent decision behavior. *Psychological Bulletin, 92*(2), 382–401.

Piaget, J. P. (1936). *The origins of intelligence in children* (M. Cook, Trans.). New York: International University Press.

Pitz, G. F. (1977). Decision making and cognition. In H. Jungerman & G. de Zeeuw (Eds.), *Decision making and change in human affairs.* Dordrecht: Reidel.

Prentice, J. W. (1974). The evasive action decision in an intersection accident: A game theory approach. *Journal of Safety Research, 6*(4), 146–149.

Tversky, A., & Kahneman, D. (1974). Judgment under uncertainty: Heuristics and biases. *Science, 185,* 1124–1131.

von Neumann, J., & Morgerstern, O. *Theory of games and economic behavior* (3rd ed.). Princeton: Princeton University Press.

Wallsten, T. S. (Ed.). (1980). *Cognitive processes in choice and decision behavior.* Hillsdale, NJ: Erlbaum.

Watkins, J. (1970). Imperfect rationality. In R. Borger & F. Cioffi (Eds.), *Explanations in the behavioral sciences.* Cambridge: Cambridge University Press.

Wood, G. (1983). *Cognitive psychology: A skills approach.* Monterey, CA: Brooks/Cole.

Index